The Joan Palevsky Imprint in Classical Literature

In honor of beloved Virgil—

"O degli altri poeti onore e lume . . ."

—Dante, *Inferno*

The publisher and the University of California Press Foundation
gratefully acknowledge the generous support of the
Joan Palevsky Imprint in Classical Literature.

Conversion to Islam in the Premodern Age

Conversion to Islam in the Premodern Age

A Sourcebook

Edited by

Nimrod Hurvitz, Christian C. Sahner, Uriel Simonsohn, and Luke Yarbrough

UNIVERSITY OF CALIFORNIA PRESS

University of California Press
Oakland, California

Library of Congress Cataloging-in-Publication Data

Names: Hurvitz, Nimrod, editor. | Sahner, Christian C., editor. | Simonsohn, Uriel I., editor. | Yarbrough, Luke B., editor.
Title: Conversion to Islam in the premodern age : a sourcebook / edited by Nimrod Hurvitz, Christian C. Sahner, Uriel Simonsohn, and Luke Yarbrough.
Description: Oakland, California : University of California Press, [2020] | Includes bibliographical references and index.
Identifiers: LCCN 2020017091 (print) | LCCN 2020017092 (ebook) | ISBN 9780520296725 (hardback) | ISBN 9780520296732 (paperback) | ISBN 9780520969100 (ebook)
Subjects: LCSH: Conversion—Islam—Early works to 1800. | Conversion—Islam—History—Sources.
Classification: LCC BP170.5 .C665 2020 (print) | LCC BP170.5 (ebook) | DDC 297.5/7409—dc23
LC record available at https://lccn.loc.gov/2020017091
LC ebook record available at https://lccn.loc.gov/2020017092

27 26 25 24 23 22 21 20
10 9 8 7 6 5 4 3 2 1

CONTENTS

Acknowledgments *xi*
Timelines *xiii*
Maps *xviii*

General Introduction *1*
The Editors

PART ONE. THE PROPHET AND THE EMPIRES OF THE CALIPHS (CA. SEVENTH–TENTH CENTURIES) *31*
Nimrod Hurvitz and Christian C. Sahner

1. Conversion in the Qurʾān *41*
Abdullah Saeed
2. The Conversion of Khadīja bt. Khuwaylid, *by Muḥammad b. Isḥāq* *46*
Sean W. Anthony
3. On Three Jewish Converts to Islam from the Banū Qurayẓa, *by Ibn Hishām* *51*
Michael Lecker
4. Women Converts and Familial Loyalty in the Time of the Prophet, *by Muḥammad b. Saʿd* *54*
Keren Abbou Hershkovits
5. Reports on Tribal Delegations to the Prophet, *by Muḥammad b. Saʿd* *58*
Ella Landau-Tasseron

6. The Spread of Islam in Arabia: Expressing Conversion in Poetry, *by Selected Early Arabic Poets* 63
Peter Webb

7. Early *Ḥadīth* Touching on Marriage and Conversion, *by Ibn Abī Shayba* 69
Christopher Melchert

8. Practicalities and Motivations of Conversion as Seen through Early *Ḥadīth* and Law, *by ʿAbd al-Razzāq b. Humām al-Ṣanʿānī and Abū Bakr Aḥmad b. Muḥammad al-Khallāl* 74
Yohanan Friedmann

9. Christian Conversions to Islam in the Wake of the Arab Conquest, *by Anastasius of Sinai* 79
Yannis Papadogiannakis

10. Jacob of Edessa's Canonical Responsa about Conversion and Islam, *by Jacob of Edessa* 83
Jack Tannous

11. A Multireligious City in Khurāsān Converts to Islam? *by Shaykh al-Islām Abū Bakr ʿAbd Allāh al-Wāʿiẓ al-Balkhī* 88
Arezou Azad

12. ʿUmar II and the Treatment of the *Mawālī, by Aḥmad b. Yaḥyā b. Jābir al-Balādhurī, Muḥammad b. Jarīr al-Ṭabarī, and Abū Muḥammad ʿAbd Allāh b. ʿAbd al-Ḥakam* 94
Gerald Hawting

13. Mass Conversion of Christians in Northern Mesopotamia, *by Joshua the Stylite of Zuqnīn* 101
Christian C. Sahner

14. Conversion and Martyrdom in ʿAbbasid Damascus, *Anonymous* 105
Johannes Pahlitzsch

15. Three Accounts of Zoroastrian Conversion to Islam, *by Muḥammad b. ʿAbdūs al-Jahshiyārī, ʿAlī b. Yūsuf al-Qifṭī, and Abū al-Faraj al-Iṣfahānī* 109
Michael Cooperson

16. Conversion to Islam among the Armenian Elite, *by Tʿovma Artsruni* 114
Tim Greenwood

17. Conversion and Martyrdom in Córdoba, *by Eulogius of Córdoba* 119
Kenneth Baxter Wolf

18. A Christian Intellectual Declines to Convert to Islam, *by Ḥunayn b. Isḥāq* 123
Barbara Roggema

19. The Religious Commitment of the ʿAbbasid "Slave Soldiers," *by Muḥammad b. Jarīr al-Ṭabarī and Aḥmad b. Yūsuf "Ibn al-Dāya"* 128
Matthew Gordon

20. Zoroastrian Priests Offer Legal Advice about Conversion, *by Ādurfarnbag son of Farroxzād and Ēmēd son of Ašawahišt* 131
Christian C. Sahner

21. A Muslim Poet Consoles a Christian Friend Whose Nephew Has Converted to Islam, *by al-Qāsim b. Yaḥyā al-Maryamī* 136
Luke Yarbrough

PART TWO. THE ISLAMIC COMMONWEALTH (CA. TENTH–THIRTEENTH CENTURIES) 139
Uriel Simonsohn

22. A Christian Convert's Examination of His Former Faith, *by al-Ḥasan b. Ayyūb* 147
Clint Hackenburg

23. A Monk's Conversion to Islam, *by Abū al-Faraj al-Iṣfahānī* 152
David Cook

24. The Conversion of the Volga Bulgars, *by Aḥmad b. Faḍlān b. al-ʿAbbās b. Rāshid b. Ḥammād* 156
Gerald Mako

25. Notarial Forms for the Conversion of Non-Muslims to Islam, *by Ibn al-ʿAṭṭār* 160
Linda G. Jones

26. A Monk Deploring the Assimilation of the Christians to the Hagarenes, *attributed to a monk called Apollo* 167
Arietta Papaconstantinou

27. The Foundation of Shaykh Abū Isḥāq Kāzarūnī's Congregational Mosque, *by Maḥmūd b. ʿUthmān* 172
Neguin Yavari

28. Conversion to Islam under the Fatimid Caliph al-Ḥākim bi-Amr Allāh, *by Michael of Damrū (Mīkhāʾīl al-Damrāwī), Bishop of Tinnīs* 178
Mark Swanson

29. Conversion from Motives of Expediency, *by Sibṭ Ibn al-Jawzī* *184*
D. G. Tor

30. Conversion, Confession, Prayer, and Apostasy, *by Ibn Rushd al-Jadd al-Qurṭubī* *186*
Maribel Fierro

31. The Conversion of the Turks, *by Michael the Syrian* *193*
Maria Conterno

32. The Tribulations of a Converted Man's Daughter, *by Bar Hebraeus* *196*
Maria Conterno

33. A Polemical Treatise by a Twelfth-Century Jewish Convert to Islam, *by Abū Naṣr Samawʾal b. Yaḥyā al-Maghribī* *199*
Gregor Schwarb

34. Anecdotes about Conversion in Twelfth-Century Syria, *by Shams al-Dīn al-Dhahabī, Ibn Rajab, and Ḍiyāʾ al-Dīn al-Maqdisī* *205*
Daniella Talmon-Heller

35. Selections from Two Armenian Martyrologies, *Anonymous* *210*
Sergio La Porta and Zaroui Pogossian

36. A Letter of Maimonides about Conversion and Martyrdom, *Attributed to Moshe ben Maimon (Maimonides)* *215*
Ryan Szpiech

37. Apostasy in Jewish Responsa, *by the Geonim of Babylonia and Abraham Maimonides* *220*
Oded Zinger

38. Several Documents from the Cairo Geniza Concerning Conversion to Islam, *Anonymous* *227*
Moshe Yagur

39. Conversion to Islam in the Period of the Crusades, *by John of Ibelin, Odo of Deuil, Pope Alexander III, and Anonymous* *232*
Uri Shachar

40. Conversion Tales in the Vita of Shaykh ʿAbd Allāh al-Yūnīnī, the Lion of Syria, *by Aḥmad b. Muḥammad b. Aḥmad ʿUthmān* *238*
Daphna Ephrat

PART THREE. SULTANS, CONQUERORS, AND TRAVELERS (CA. THIRTEENTH–SIXTEENTH CENTURIES) 243
Luke Yarbrough

41. The Conversion of Medieval Ghāna as Narrated by a Later Ibāḍī Scholar, *by Abū al-ʿAbbās Aḥmad b. Saʿīd al-Darjīnī* 253
Luke Yarbrough

42. Cheraman Perumal and Islam on the Malabar Coast, *Anonymous* 256
Luke Yarbrough

43. The Conversion Miracles and Life of the Dervish Sarı Saltuq, *by Muḥammad b. ʿAlī b. al-Sarrāj* 263
A. C. S. Peacock

44. The Providential Conversion of the Mongol King of Iran, *by Abū al-Qāsim ʿAbd Allāh b. ʿAlī b. Muḥammad al-Qāshānī and Rashīd al-Dīn Faḍl Allāh Abū al-Khayr* 267
Jonathan Brack

45. The Conversion of ʿAbd al-Sayyid, a Damascene Jew, *by Quṭb al-Dīn Mūsā b. Muḥammad al-Yūnīnī* 272
Yehoshua Frenkel

46. An Account of the Conversion of Egypt's Copts under Duress at the End of the Thirteenth Century, *by Taqī al-Dīn Aḥmad b. ʿAlī al-Maqrīzī* 275
Frédéric Bauden

47. A Syriac Communal Lament over Apostasy, *Anonymous* 280
Thomas A. Carlson

48. Conversion to Islam in South Asia as Transformation of the Heart, *by Ḥażrat Khwāja Niẓām al-Dīn Awliyā and Amīr Ḥasan ʿAlā Sijzī* 286
Raziuddin Aquil

49. A Jurist's Responses to Questions Regarding the Conversion of One Spouse, *by Ibn Qayyim al-Jawziyya* 290
Antonia Bosanquet

50. Anselm Turmeda/ʿAbd Allāh al-Tarjumān: A Former Mallorcan Franciscan in the Service of the Ḥafṣids in North Africa, *by Anselm Turmeda/ʿAbd Allāh al-Tarjumān* 295
Clint Hackenburg

51. Three Stories of Conversion from the Life of Sayyid Aḥmad Bashīrī, a Sufi of Timurid Central Asia, *Anonymous (or Nāṣir b. Qāsim b. Ḥājjī Muḥammad Turkistānī Farghāna'ī)* 300

Devin DeWeese

52. The Conversion of the Kingdom of Pasai, Indonesia, *Anonymous* 306

Alexander Wain

53. A Tract against "Unbelieving Believers" in West Africa, *by Muḥammad b. ʿAbd al-Karīm al-Maghīlī* 313

Ulrich Rebstock

54. Conversions to Islam in a Late Medieval Chronicle from Damascus, *by Shihāb al-Dīn Aḥmad b. Ṭawq and Shams al-Dīn Muḥammad b. Ṭūlūn* 317

Tamer el-Leithy

55. Documentary Records of Conversions among Ottoman Palace Personnel, *by Ottoman Officials and Elite Servants of the Sultan* 323

Sanja Kadrić

56. A Conversion Tale from Java, Indonesia, *Anonymous* 326

Ronit Ricci

57. The Story of Master She Yunshan's Conversion in Changzhou, China, *by Zhao Can* 330

Suofei Liu and Zvi Ben-Dor Benite

Appendix: Sources 337
List of Contributors 349
Index 351

ACKNOWLEDGMENTS

The idea for this reader was born during the conference "Reading into Islamization," which was convened at Ben-Gurion University of the Negev by the Center for the Study of Conversion and Inter-Religious Encounters (an I-Core initiative), January 4–6, 2016. We would like to thank the center's directors, Chaim (Harvey) Hames and Ephraim (Effie) Shoham-Steiner, for their encouragement and financial support. Support for portions of Luke Yarbrough's work on this project was provided by the New York University Abu Dhabi Institute and by Saint Louis University.

We are also grateful to the Barr Ferree Publication Fund of Princeton University, which aided us in funding the production of the book's maps, and we express our gratitude to Shane Kelley for plotting these fine maps. The Metropolitan Museum of Art of New York City is also deserving of thanks for making freely available the image on the cover.

We would also like to extend our appreciation to Hanna Siurua and Marian Rogers for editing the manuscript and saving us from many mistakes.

We would like to thank Eric Schmidt and Austin Lim of the University of California Press for guiding us through the intricacies of this project. We have also benefited from the comments made by the five anonymous readers who reviewed the book proposal and the two anonymous readers who read the full manuscript, and would like to express our gratitude for their remarks. Finally, we are indebted to the nearly five dozen contributors who lent the project their time and expertise.

TIMELINES

	Major Events in Islamic Political History	Accounts Featured in this Book
550 CE	570—Muḥammad's birth	
600 CE		
	610—First revelations of Qurʾān to Muḥammad	1. Conversion in the Qurʾān
		2. The conversion of Khadīja bt. Khuwaylid
	622—*Hijra* from Mecca to Medina	3. On three Jewish converts to Islam from the Banū Qurayẓa
	632—Muḥammad's death	4. Women converts and familial loyalty in the time of the Prophet
	632–634—Wars of apostasy (*ḥurūb al-ridda*)	5. Reports on tribal delegations to the Prophet
	632–661—"Rightly Guided" caliphs	
	636—Battles of Yarmūk and Qādisiyya	
650 CE	656–661—First *fitna*	6. The spread of Islam in Arabia: Expressing conversion in poetry
	657—Battle of Ṣiffīn	
	661–750—Umayyad caliphate	7. Early *ḥadīth* touching on marriage and conversion
		8. Practicalities and motivations of conversion as seen through early *ḥadīth* and law
	680—Battle of Karbalāʾ	
	680–692—Second *fitna*	9. Christian conversions to Islam in the wake of the Arab conquest
		10. Jacob of Edessa's canonical responsa about conversion and Islam
700 CE		11. A multireligious city in Khurāsān converts to Islam?

	705–715—Conquests of al-Andalus, India, and Transoxania	
		12. ʿUmar II and the treatment of the *mawālī*
	732—Battle of Poitiers (France)	
	744–50— Third *fitna* and ʿAbbasid revolution	
750 CE	751—Battle of Talas (Transoxania)	
	762—Establishment of Baghdad	13. Mass conversion of Christians in northern Mesopotamia
		14. Conversion and martyrdom in ʿAbbasid Damascus
800 CE	809–813—ʿAbbasid civil war (fourth *fitna*)	
		15. Three accounts of Zoroastrian conversion to Islam
	839—Conquest of South Italy and part of Sicily by the Aghlabids	
850 CE	850—ʿAbbasid restrictions on non-Muslim subjects	16. Conversion to Islam among the Armenian elite
		17. Conversion and martyrdom in Córdoba
	861—Assassination of ʿAbbasid caliph al-Mutawakkil	18. A Christian intellectual declines to convert to Islam
		19. The religious commitment of the ʿAbbasid "slave soldiers"
		20. Zoroastrian priests offer legal advice about conversion
	875—Aḥmad b. Ṭūlūn consolidates independent power in Egypt	21. A Muslim poet consoles a Christian friend whose nephew has converted to Islam
		24. The conversion of the Volga Bulgars
900 CE	909—Establishment of Fatimid caliphate in North Africa	
	929—Umayyad ruler of al-Andalus, ʿAbd al-Raḥmān III, declares himself caliph of Córdoba	
		22. A Christian convert's examination of his former faith
	945—Buyids take Baghdad	23. A monk's conversion to Islam
		25. Notarial forms for the conversion of non-Muslims to Islam
950 CE		26. A monk deploring the assimilation of the Christians to the Hagarenes
	969—Byzantine reconquest of northern Syria; Fatimid conquest of Egypt	27. The foundation of Shaykh Abū Isḥāq Kāzarūnī's congregational mosque
	996–1021—Reign of Fatimid caliph al-Ḥākim bi-Amr Allāh in Egypt	28. Conversion to Islam under the Fatimid caliph al-Ḥākim bi-Amr Allāh
1000 CE	998–1030—Maḥmūd of Ghazna conquers parts of northern India, leading to mass conversions	
1050 CE		
	1055—Oghuzz Turkic Seljuqs overthrow Buyids	

	1071—Battle of Manzikert: Seljuq Turk victory over Byzantines opens Anatolia to Turkic influx	
	1077—Seljuqs found Sultanate of Rum in Asia Minor	29. Conversion from motives of expediency
		30. Conversion, confession, prayer, and apostasy
	1091—End of Muslim rule in Sicily	
	1096–1099—First Crusade results in Frankish Christian conquest of Jerusalem	
1100 CE		
	1147–1149—Second Crusade	31. The conversion of the Turks
1150 CE		
		32. The tribulations of a converted man's daughter
	1171—End of Fatimid caliphate in Egypt	33. A polemical treatise by a twelfth-century Jewish convert to Islam
	1174–1193—Saladin is Ayyubid Sultan in Egypt and Syria	36. A letter of Maimonides about conversion and martyrdom
	1187—Battle of Ḥaṭṭīn; Saladin recaptures Jerusalem	
		34. Anecdotes about conversion in twelfth-century Syria
	1189–1192—Third Crusade	
	1192—Muslim takeover of Delhi; end of Seljuq rule	
		35. Selections from two Armenian martyrologies
1200 CE	1202–1204—Fourth Crusade	37. Apostasy in Jewish responsa
	1212—Battle of Las Navas de Tolosa: Iberian Christian kings defeat Almohads	
		38. Several documents from the Cairo Geniza concerning conversion to Islam
	1217–1221—Fifth Crusade	
		39. Conversion to Islam in the period of the Crusades
		40. Conversion tales in the vita of Shaykh ʿAbd Allāh al-Yūnīnī, the Lion of Syria
	1248–1254—Sixth Crusade	
1250 CE	1250—Mamluks overthrow Ayyubids in Egypt	41. The conversion of medieval Ghāna as narrated by a later Ibāḍī scholar after
	1258—Mongols sack Baghdad; end of ʿAbbasid line in Iraq	42. Cheraman Perumal and Islam on the Malabar Coast
	1260—Battle of ʿAyn Jālūt: Mamluks defeat Mongols in Syria	
		52. The conversion of the Kingdom of Pasai, Indonesia

		43. The conversion miracles and life of the dervish Sarı Saltuq
		46. An account of the conversion of Egypt's Copts under duress at the end of the thirteenth century
	1295—Conversion of Ilkhanid Ghāzān Khān	44. The providential conversion of the Mongol king of Iran
1300 CE		45. The conversion of ʿAbd al-Sayyid, a Damascene Jew
		47. A Syriac communal lament over apostasy
	1323—Death of Osman I, founder of Ottoman Dynasty	
		48. Conversion to Islam in South Asia as transformation of the heart
		49. A jurist's responses to questions regarding the conversion of one spouse
1350 CE		
		50. Anselm Turmeda/ʿAbd Allāh al-Tarjumān: A former Mallorcan Franciscan in the service of the Ḥafṣids in North Africa
	1398—Timur Lang (Tamerlane) sacks Delhi	
1400 CE	1400—Sultanate of Malacca	51. Three stories of conversion from the life of Sayyid Aḥmad Bashīrī, a Sufi of Timurid Central Asia
1450 CE	1453—Ottomans take Constantinople	
	1468—Sonni Ali, builder of Songhai Empire, conquers Timbuktu	
	1492—Christians capture Granada: end of Muslim rule in Iberian Peninsula	53. A tract against "unbelieving believers" in West Africa
	1498—Portuguese enter Indian Ocean	
1500 CE	1504—Funj Sultanate in Sudan	54. Conversions to Islam in a late medieval chronicle from Damascus
	1511—Portuguese gain control of Malacca	
	1514—Battle of Chaldiran establishes Ottoman-Safavid border zone	
	1516–1517—Ottoman conquest of Syria and Egypt	
	1526—Establishment of Mughal Empire in South Asia	56. A conversion tale from Java, Indonesia
1550 CE		55. Documentary records of conversions among Ottoman palace personnel
	1565—Deccan sultanates overthrow Vijayanagar (South Asia)	
	1570—Ottomans take Cyprus	
	1587–1629—Reign of Safavid Shah ʿAbbās	
1600 CE	1605—Death of Mughal emperor Akbar	

	1644—Manchu (Qing) conquest of China	
1650 CE	1656—Ottoman Köprüllü viziers centralize power	
	1659—Accession of Mughal emperor Awrangzeb	
		57. The story of Master She Yunshan's conversion in Changzhou, China

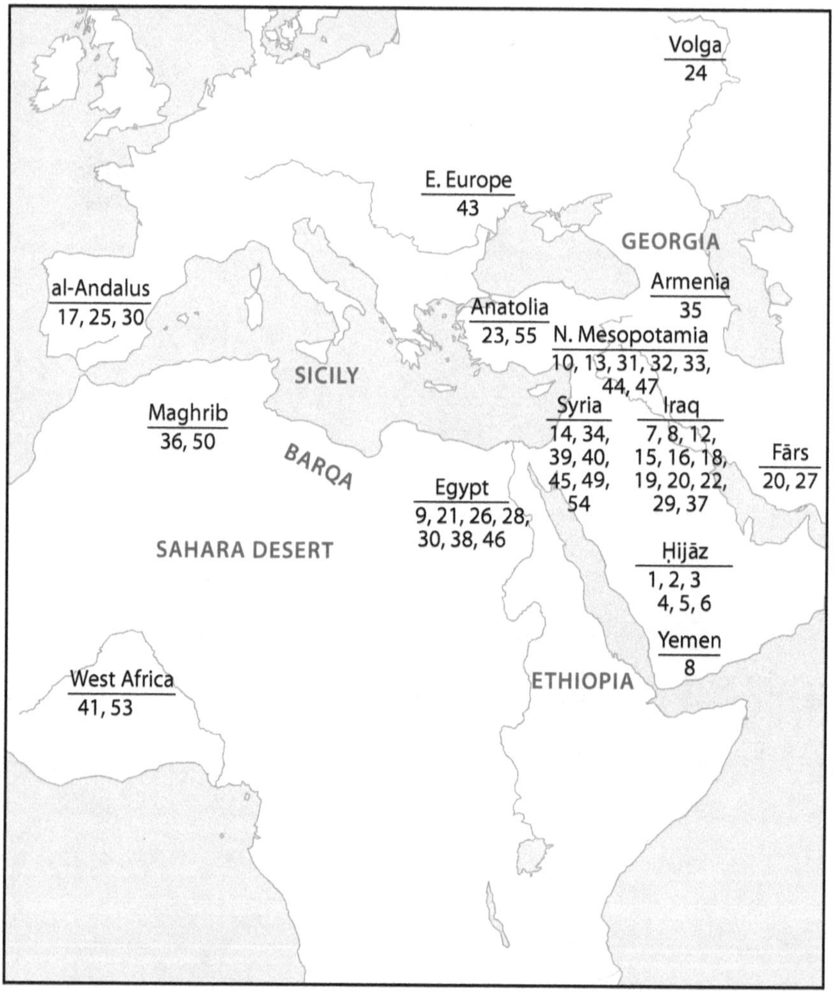

MAP 1. The geographical distribution of the sources in this book, by selection number. Designed by the editors and executed by Shane Kelley.

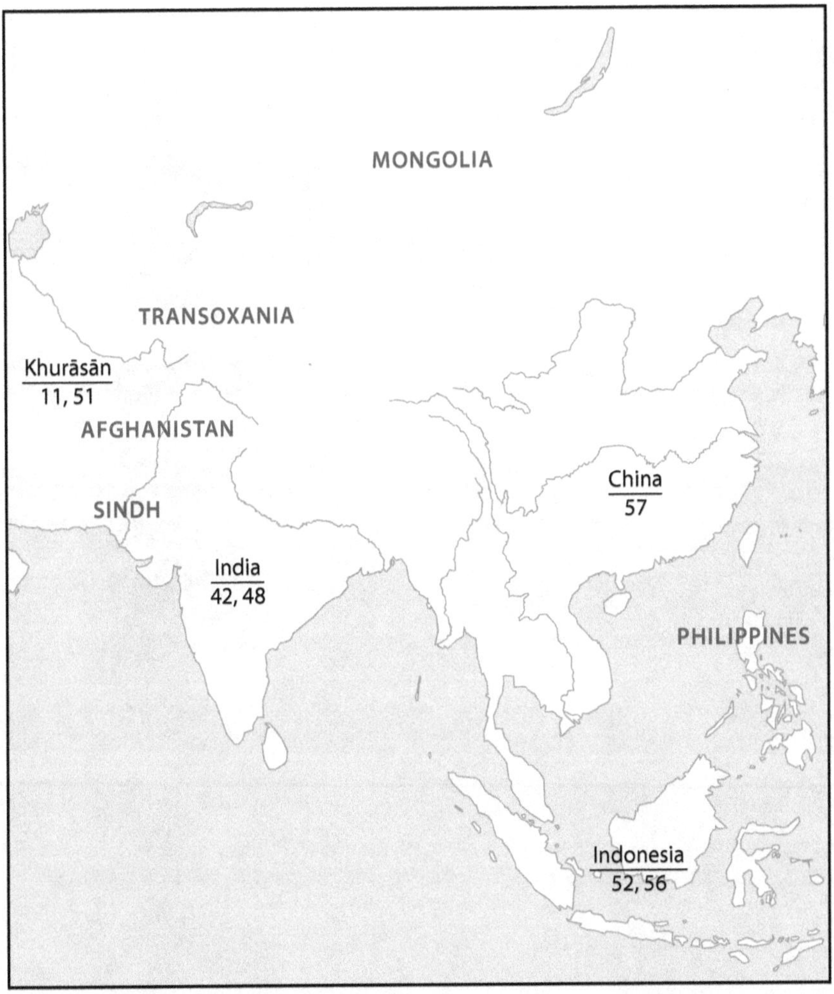
MONGOLIA
TRANSOXANIA
Khurāsān
11, 51
AFGHANISTAN
SINDH
India
42, 48
China
57
PHILIPPINES
Indonesia
52, 56

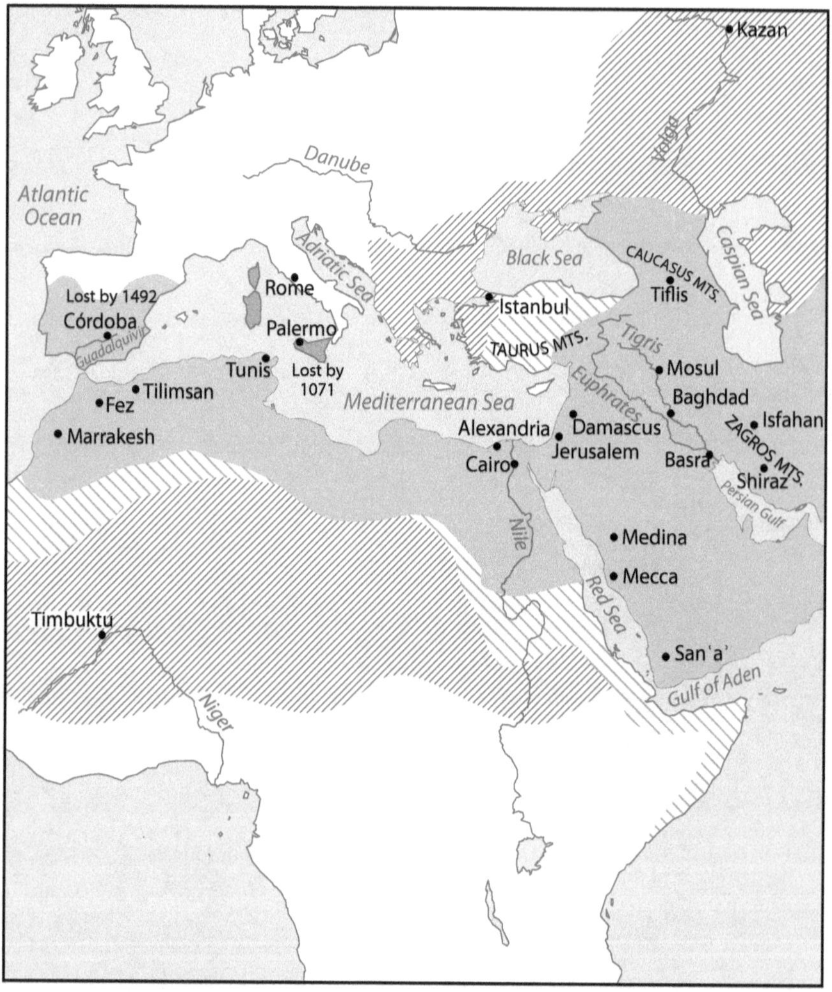

MAP 2. The expansion of Muslim political rule to the sixteenth century CE. Designed by the editors and executed by Shane Kelley.

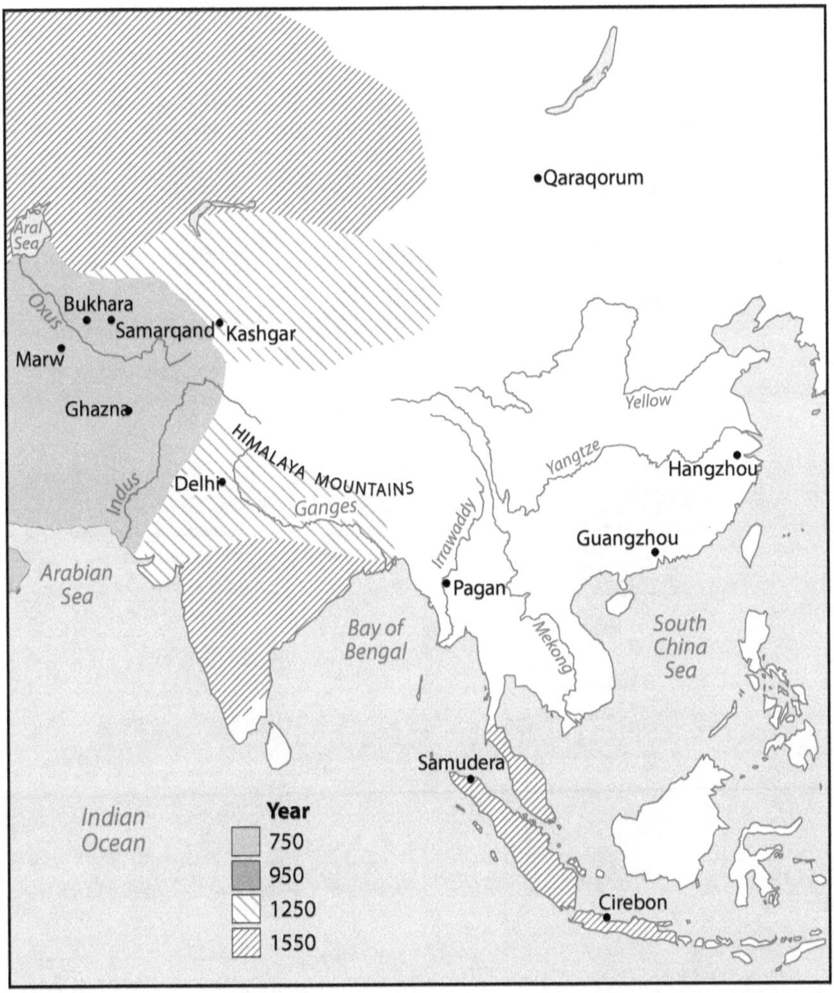
Qaraqorum
Aral Sea
Oxus
Bukhara
Samarqand
Kashgar
Marw
Ghazna
Indus
Delhi
HIMALAYA MOUNTAINS
Ganges
Yellow
Yangtze
Hangzhou
Irrawaddy
Guangzhou
Arabian Sea
Pagan
Bay of Bengal
Mekong
South China Sea
Samudera
Indian Ocean
Year
750
950
1250
1550
Cirebon

General Introduction

The Editors

Conversion constitutes one of the most important themes of premodern Islamic history, or indeed of world history in general. Islam is the only world religion whose name—*al-islām*—denotes not only a faith but also an act: that of submitting to the one true God and thereby becoming a Muslim. More broadly, we could hardly speak of "Islamic societies," "Islamic cultures," or "Islamic civilizations" without the prior decisions of countless individuals and groups across time to convert. Their choices have created a world in which around a quarter of the human population is now Muslim.

Conversion is a phenomenon of great complexity and, depending on one's perspective, a cause for celebration, alarm, bemusement, or curiosity. This book's purpose is to open a window for scholars, students, and general readers onto the historical antecedents that lie beneath these and myriad other modern perspectives on conversion to Islam. It gathers together, for the first time, some of the most vivid and neglected sources on conversion to Islam from the first millennium of Islamic history, in lands stretching from West Africa to China and from the Volga to South Asia, newly translated from languages as varied as Armenian and Malay.

ISLĀM AS CONVERSION ACROSS THE FIRST ISLAMIC MILLENNIUM

To grasp conversion's significance across time, consider the vision of the Islamic world offered by the famous Moroccan writer Ibn Baṭṭūṭa, who traveled across West Africa, the Middle East, Central and South Asia, and the Far East during the fourteenth century.[1] Ibn Baṭṭūṭa was fascinated by the local expressions of Islam he encountered across this vast stretch of the earth. But he was also fascinated by Islam's coherence. As he wandered from his native Tangiers to Timbuktu, Damascus, Tabriz, Samarqand, the Deccan, and Sumatra—places that had had little to do with one another prior to the emergence of Islam—he found a world held together by a common set of beliefs, languages, customs, and political structures that we might call generally "Islamic."

These were societies characterized by reverence for the Qurʾān; the role of Arabic as a language of daily life, religion, and/or high culture; the division of time according to the five daily prayers and the sacred months; the presence of men and women of religion such as *ʿulamāʾ* (religious scholars), *fuqahāʾ* (jurists), and Sufis in their countless orders; the dominance of a patchwork of emirates, sultanates, and slave armies; and unique forms of transregional connectivity, such as the Meccan pilgrimage and scholarly travel (Ar. *al-riḥla fī ṭalab al-ʿilm*). Together, these elements, common to so many of the Muslim communities Ibn Baṭṭūṭa observed in the course of his journeys, created a spiritual and cultural commonwealth of surprising unity in spite of its vast size and internal variety. In many ways, Ibn Baṭṭūṭa was the first chronicler of a global Islamic world.

Now imagine for a moment a fictional Muslim writer of an earlier age, the early eighth century, who, like Ibn Baṭṭūṭa, traversed vast distances in the hopes of meeting Muslims in far-flung corners of the globe.[2] Unlike Ibn Baṭṭūṭa, such a traveler could have journeyed from Córdoba to Alexandria, Jerusalem, Basra, Marw, and Sindh under the flag of a single Islamic empire. But Islamic imperial rule did not mean that the peoples within the borders of this state necessarily espoused Islam. Our traveler would have certainly met Muslims along the way, but they would have been relatively few in number and concentrated in a handful of cities and garrison towns. In the immense spaces in between—the rural areas where the majority of any population lived in premodern times—he would sometimes have found no Muslims at all.

In such places, the inhabitants were still Christians, Zoroastrians, Jews, Manicheans, Buddhists, and adherents of countless other ancient religions that kept on keeping on despite the political ruptures of the conquest. They also spoke a babel of tongues other than Arabic, including Greek, Aramaic, Coptic, Latin, Persian, Berber, Armenian, and Georgian. What is more, they continued to look to the traditions of numerous now-deposed kingdoms, such as those of the Romans, the

1. For an introduction, see David Waines, *The Odyssey of Ibn Battuta: Uncommon Tales of a Medieval Adventurer* (Chicago: University of Chicago Press, 2010).

2. Such a writer is indeed fictional: our earliest accounts of geographical writing (from which travel writing springs) date to the ninth century; see S. Maqbul Ahmad, "Djughrāfiyā," in *Encyclopaedia of Islam*, 2nd ed.

Sasanians, the Visigoths, the Armenians, and the Sogdians, which had been swept away by the conquests. Thus, although he might have encountered faint outlines of the transregional Islamic culture Ibn Baṭṭūṭa observed centuries later, our traveler would not have described a recognizably Islamic world, but rather a fractured, largely non-Muslim cosmos much like the one that had existed in Late Antiquity.

The story of how the world of our eighth-century traveler became the world of Ibn Baṭṭūṭa is, in large part, a story of conversion to Islam and its long-term effects on many societies. This process, the people who experienced or witnessed it, and the sources they produced lie at the heart of the present book. This introduction provides context for the sources by sketching the larger story of premodern conversion to Islam and its major themes, by giving an overview of recent academic debates, and by guiding readers on how to use this book and benefit from its contribution to the growing literature on conversion in Islamic history.[3]

A THUMBNAIL SKETCH OF PREMODERN CONVERSION TO ISLAM AND ITS MAJOR THEMES

A Historical Overview of Premodern Conversion to Islam

The Prophet and the Empires of the Caliphs (600s–900s) Historians debate the extent to which Muḥammad and his companions insisted that the first people to respond to his message abandon their old ways. Much as many early Jewish followers of Jesus regarded him simply as the fulfillment of biblical covenants between God and the Jewish people, many passages in the Qur'ān and early sources by Muslim authors depict the Prophet not as the apostle of a new religion, but as a man through whom God would complete the Jewish and Christian monotheisms that had come before. Modern scholars have speculated that some of the Prophet's earliest followers did not make a clean break with their Jewish and Christian identities.[4] This was not the case, however, for the Arabian polytheists whom the sources portray as being dominant in the Prophet's milieu. The Qur'ān and early

3. For general accounts of premodern conversion to Islam, see (among others) Ira Lapidus, *Islamic Societies to the Nineteenth Century: A Global History* (Cambridge: Cambridge University Press, 2012), 75–78, 198, 284–85, 343–53, 513–16; Richard Bulliet, "Conversion to Islam," in *The New Cambridge History of Islam*, vol. 3, ed. David Morgan and Anthony Reid (Cambridge: Cambridge University Press, 2010), 529–38; David J. Wasserstein, "Conversion and the *Ahl al-Dhimma*," in *The New Cambridge History of Islam*, vol. 4, ed. Robert Irwin (Cambridge: Cambridge University Press, 2010), 184–208; Thomas Carlson, "When Did the Middle East Become Muslim? Trends in the Study of Islam's 'Age of Conversions,'" *History Compass* 16, no. 10 (2018): 1–10.

4. Patricia Crone and Michael Cook, *Hagarism: The Making of the Islamic World* (Cambridge: Cambridge University Press, 1977); Fred M. Donner, *Muhammad and the Believers: At the Origins of Islam* (Cambridge, MA: Belknap Press of Harvard University Press, 2010).

reports about the Prophet's life reflect little sympathy for or tolerance of Arabian polytheism. Conversion—which entailed rejection of the old Arabian gods as well as affirmation of the Prophet's message—was thus imperative for most early members of the Prophet's movement.

This, at least, is how the beginnings of Islam are portrayed in the vast majority of surviving sources. Like all such sources, however, the ones used by historians of Islam must be approached with both sympathy and healthy skepticism. Human events often happen in messier, more complex ways than written sources let on. Care is certainly warranted when studying early conversion to Islam, for which contemporary documents are almost nonexistent. Most of the extant narrative accounts of early conversion were written down decades or centuries later. Modern historians now increasingly believe that joining Muḥammad's movement was less a story of sudden individual conviction or the decisive smashing of idols than one of tribal affiliations, military alliances, and gradual change among a mostly preliterate population.[5] It seems, however, that most of the tribes and towns of the Arabian Peninsula had entered into some form of alliance with that movement by the time of the Prophet's death in 632 CE, or shortly thereafter. Historians generally agree that for Arabians, making such an alliance entailed some affirmation of Muḥammad's message: that the one true God was calling people, through His prophet, to worship Him alone; that a final Judgment Day was imminent; and that a sacred scripture bristling with allusions to salvation history and prescribed details of piety and worship had been revealed in the Arabic language. Only a few tribes, mostly outside Arabia proper, remained Christian for very long while also allying themselves with the Prophet's movement; most broke fairly quickly with their previous communal loyalties. For this reason, the Arabians who carried out the stupendous military conquests of the ensuing decades would mostly have affirmed the basic Muslim profession of faith, the *shahāda:* "There is no god but God; Muḥammad is the Messenger of God."

The Arabian tribesmen soon came to rule over a dizzying array of peoples within the borders of an empire that stretched from the Atlantic Ocean to Central Asia. These groups espoused many different religious teachings in addition to Judaism, Christianity, and Zoroastrianism, the state religion of the Persian Sasanian Empire, which the conquerors quickly overran. Some of their beliefs, such as Manichaeism, are now all but forgotten, while others, such as Buddhism and other religions of Central and South Asia, are often overlooked when thinking about early Islam. In this early period, up to the fall of the Arab Umayyad dynasty in

5. Harry Munt, "What Did Conversion to Islam Mean in Seventh-Century Arabia?," in *Islamisation: Comparative Perspectives from History,* ed. A.C.S. Peacock (Edinburgh: Edinburgh University Press, 2017), 83–101; Jack Tannous, *The Making of the Medieval Middle East: Religion, Society, and Simple Believers* (Princeton, NJ: Princeton University Press, 2018).

132/750, relatively few non-Arabs converted to Islam. The people who did so were usually those who had thrown in their lot with the rulers of the new empire: individuals who joined the conquerors' armies, settled in the quasi-colonial garrison cities they founded, or formally joined Arab tribes by becoming *mawālī* (sing. *mawlā*), or tribal "clients," non-Arabs who entered Islamic society by becoming honorary or affiliate members of Arab kinship networks. Indeed, the non-Arab subjects of the empire, unlike the polytheists of Arabia, by and large experienced little pressure to convert. This was partly because some early Muslims regarded Islam as exclusively for Arabs, and partly because Muslim governors and rulers, or "caliphs," valued the poll tax (*jizya*) that non-Muslims paid. This tax was reportedly lifted from converts by the pious Umayyad caliph ʿUmar b. ʿAbd al-ʿAzīz (r. 99–101/717–20). Non-Muslims who paid the poll tax, remained loyal to the new rulers, and showed public deference to Islam were generally permitted to continue living and worshipping more or less as they had done before the conquests.[6] Muslim jurists referred to them as *dhimmīs*, or peoples possessing a pact of security, a category that included Jews, Christians, and Zoroastrians.

The Umayyad dynasty was toppled in 132/750 by the revolt of the ʿAbbasids, a dynasty that was more closely related to the Prophet. The ʿAbbasids' supporters had criticized the Umayyads for their alleged impiety and ethnic exclusivity. In the ʿAbbasid Empire, the rate of conversion to Islam appears to have picked up, even as the military conquests continued to slow. A steady flow of converts came from Zoroastrianism, which had now long been deprived of state support and splintered among a welter of abortive revivalist movements.[7] Part of the reason for Iran's seemingly rapid conversion, at least in its eastern reaches, lay in the tendency of Arab soldiers to settle among local populations. This pattern contrasted with that in southern Iraq, another area of intensive Arab settlement, where the Muslims sequestered themselves in garrison towns (Ar. *amṣār*). Christianity, too, seems to have experienced considerable attrition to Islam in some regions.[8] It remained vibrant, however, even in the newly founded capital city of Baghdad, where Christians soon took to writing their scholarly works in Arabic, as their coreligionists in the monas-

6. For overviews of the three major non-Muslim communities in this period, see Mark R. Cohen, *Under Crescent and Cross: The Jews in the Middle East* (Princeton, NJ: Princeton University Press, 2008); Sidney H. Griffith, *The Church in the Shadow of the Mosque: Christians and Muslims in the World of Islam* (Princeton, NJ: Princeton University Press, 2008); Jamsheed K. Choksy, *Conflict and Cooperation: Zoroastrian Subalterns and Muslim Elites in Medieval Iran* (New York: Columbia University Press, 1997).

7. Patricia Crone, *The Nativist Prophets of Early Islamic Iran: Rural Revolt and Local Zoroastrianism* (Cambridge: Cambridge University Press, 2012).

8. Christian Sahner, *Christian Martyrs under Islam: Religious Violence and the Making of the Muslim World* (Princeton, NJ: Princeton University Press, 2018).

teries of Palestine had begun doing a few decades earlier.[9] But the conversion of more and more non-Arabs, coupled with the conquerors' adoption of local customs and the spread of the Arabic language, narrowed the cultural gap between Muslims and local peoples across the empire.

This was also a time when larger numbers of signal converts began entering Islam. These were individuals of high social and economic standing—including officials, theologians, jurists, and literati of various sorts—who brought the expertise and cultural capital of their old communities into the new. On occasion, as under the ʿAbbasid caliph al-Mutawakkil in 236/851, they converted as a result of coercive state decrees that required non-Muslims to accept Islam or relinquish influential positions.[10] Such converts served as important vectors for the transmission of ideas and practices into Muslim societies. Through them and within more established Muslim communities, Islam itself was becoming more complex, intellectually formidable, and widely attractive; the text of the Qurʾān, for example, was well established by the middle to late seventh century, and Islamic legal and doctrinal teachings were extensive and highly ramified by the early ʿAbbasid period.[11] The way was thus paved for conversion to gain pace, as Islam acquired more stable, impressive, and widely attractive intellectual and institutional forms than it had possessed in the immediate years after the Prophet's life. Many scholars have argued that demographic majorities in some regions of the empire outside Arabia, particularly in Iran and North Africa, became Muslim during the first century of ʿAbbasid rule. These claims are disputed, however, and there is broad agreement that in other regions, such as Egypt and Syria, Muslims remained a demographic minority for a long time, and that the nature of the Islam espoused by converts in this early era was highly variable and sometimes quite vague (see further discussions in subsequent sections of this introduction).[12] Nevertheless, it is plain that becoming Muslim allowed converts not only to join the imperial elite and escape onerous taxes but also to fill deep psychological needs and forge ties of solidarity and sympathy across the largest empire the world had yet seen.

The Islamic Commonwealth (900s–1200s) By the time the ʿAbbasid Empire began to fall apart in the late ninth century, the regional powers that arose to take

9. See the collected essays in Sidney H. Griffith, *The Beginnings of Christian Theology in Arabic: Muslim-Christian Encounters in the Early Islamic Period* (Aldershot: Ashgate, 2002).

10. Luke Yarbrough, *Friends of the Emir: Non-Muslim State Officials in Premodern Islamic Thought* (Cambridge: Cambridge University Press, 2019), 88–109.

11. A. F. L. Beeston, et al., eds., *Arabic Literature to the End of the Umayyad Period* (Cambridge: Cambridge University Press, 1983).

12. Tannous, *Making of the Medieval Middle East,* 225–505; Thomas Carlson, "Contours of Conversion: The Geography of Islamization in Syria, 600–1500," *Journal of the American Oriental Society* 135, no. 4 (2015): 791–816.

its place were led almost exclusively by Muslims. In other words, Islam had become firmly rooted in the conquered territories through conversion and intermarriage, such that the contraction of imperial control did not entail a recession of Islam, as might have occurred if the Umayyad Empire had disintegrated rather than being supplanted. On the contrary, local leaders and rebel movements saw fit to couch their political claims in Islamic terminology. This development facilitated conversion to local and regional forms of Islam under the potpourri of dynasties that succeeded the ʿAbbasids in the tenth and eleventh centuries and beyond. Most of these dynasties were led or backed by non-Arab Muslim groups: Berber peoples in North Africa, for example, and Iranian ones in Iraq and to its east. In some regions, new caliphates rose to power, such as the Arab Shiʿi Fatimids in North Africa and Egypt (909–1171), who claimed to be divinely guided descendants of the Prophet and whose core supporters were Berbers. Their missionaries fanned out across the Islamic world, winning converts in lands as distant as Yemen and South Asia. In other places, such as Northwest Africa under the Berber Almohad dynasty (1130–1269), non-Arab leaders laid their own claim to the title and religious authority of the caliphs.

Among the transformations of Islam in this era, however, none was more consequential than the conversion of the Turkic-speaking tribesmen on the frontiers of the Central Asian steppes. Turkish professional soldiers—many of them enslaved, converted, and manumitted—had already become indispensable in the armies of the ʿAbbasids, contributing both to the caliphs' defense and to their estrangement from their Muslim subjects. But the conversion of intact Turkish tribes in the tenth and eleventh centuries transformed the politics and the geography of Islamic history.[13] The Turkish Muslim Oghuz tribal confederation, led by the Seljuq clan, conquered Iran and Iraq from the east in the mid-eleventh century. The Seljuqs inflicted a serious defeat on the Byzantine army in 1071, opening Anatolia to further Muslim settlement. The growth of new expressions of Islam facilitated these developments.

Sufism, a term that encompasses a variety of experiential, ascetical devotional practices, was more accessible to many in the lower echelons of society than were the highly learned, abstract, and juristic forms of Islam that had been developed in the early Islamic cities. It flourished in the Seljuq domains.[14] Seljuq rule did not last long, but it promoted a model of symbiosis among foreign military rulers, Muslim jurists, and Sufi holy figures that would be replicated for centuries in the central Islamic world. This model created conditions for further conversion to Islam. It entailed the maintenance of Muslim power, sometimes by dynasties of freshly

13. See Nicholas Morton, "The Saljuq Turks' Conversion to Islam: The Crusading Sources," *Al-Masaq* 27, no. 2 (2015): 109–18, and studies cited there.

14. A. C. S. Peacock, *Early Seljūq History: A New Interpretation* (London: Routledge, 2010), 99–127.

converted slave soldiers, who consistently taxed and marginalized adherents of other religions; charismatic preaching by spiritual masters, increasingly with state support; and the stabilizing presence of Muslim scholars who advised sultans, competed with non-Muslim elites for patronage, and built an intellectual foundation of Islamic scholarship that provided ballast to Islamic societies.[15] Amid the combined pressures and inducements that Islam thus presented, large demographic majorities from Morocco to Afghanistan may have become Muslim by the fourteenth century, even as Muslim rule on the fringes of the Mediterranean was pushed back on its heels by the growing power of European states.[16]

Sultans and Conquerors (1200s–1500s) As the Seljuq model spread within the Islamic world in the twelfth and thirteenth centuries, conquest and conversion were expanding the presence of Islam at and beyond the margins of Muslim political control. In West Africa, for example, Muslim traders and preachers in several regions persuaded local rulers to convert. These rulers thereby facilitated trade with the Mediterranean littoral, their own ability to draw on Muslim political ideology, and their capacity to recruit skilled Muslim scholars into their service, though their own subjects were often slower to profess Islam.[17] In East Africa, Muslim traders had long settled along the coast and intermarried with local elites. Conversion there contributed to the formation of a hybrid Muslim Swahili culture, while military incursions by the rulers of Egypt eventually eroded Christian power inland, in Nubia and Sudan.[18] South Asia, too, was invaded from the north after the tenth century, by ethnically Turkish, culturally Persian Muslim dynasties. There, the ruling elite and certain merchant and lower-caste groups, though never a demographic majority, adopted forms of Islam that were often heavily shaped by

15. Osman Turan, "Les souverains seldjoukides et leurs sujets non-musulmans," *Studia Islamica* 1 (1953): 65–100; Speros Vryonis, "The Experience of Christians under Seljuk and Ottoman Domination, Eleventh to Sixteenth Century," in *Conversion and Continuity: Indigenous Christian Communities in Islamic Lands, Eighth to Eighteenth Centuries*, ed. Michael Gervers and Ramzi Bikhazi (Toronto: Pontifical Institute of Mediaeval Studies, 1990), 185–216.

16. Paul M. Cobb, *The Race for Paradise: An Islamic History of the Crusades* (Oxford: Oxford University Press, 2014).

17. M. El Fasi and I. Hrbek, "Stages in the Development of Islam and its Dissemination in Africa," in *General History of Africa*, vol. 3, *Africa from the Seventh to the Eleventh Century*, ed. M. El Fasi and I. Hrbek (London: Heinemann, 1988), 56–91.

18. For Africa more generally, see Nehemiah Levtzion and Randall L. Pouwels, eds., *The History of Islam in Africa* (Athens: Ohio University Press, 2000); Sean Hanretta and Shobana Shankar, "Islam in African History," in *A Companion to African History*, ed. William H. Worger et al. (Hoboken, NJ: John Wiley and Sons, 2019), 225–46. For specific cases, see Randall L. Pouwels, *Horn and Crescent: Cultural Change and Traditional Islam on the East African Coast, 800–1900* (Cambridge: Cambridge University Press, 2002); Joseph Cuoq, *Islamisation de la Nubie chrétienne, VIIe–XVIe siècle* (Paris: Geuthner, 1986).

Sufism and open to covert synthesis with indigenous traditions.[19] In Southeast Asia, particularly the peninsulas and archipelagoes of what are today Malaysia and Indonesia, Muslim traders and preachers managed to convert local elites beginning in the thirteenth century. As in West Africa, rulers in Southeast Asia found in Islam a means of accessing trade networks and expressing ideologies of competition with neighboring rulers, and there, too, Islam took on distinct local flavors.[20]

Transformative conversion took place not only in lands invaded by Muslim armies but also among non-Muslim peoples who invaded territories long since peopled by Muslims. The Mongols who ruled Central Asia, Iran, and Iraq, which they had devastated by conquest in the mid-thirteenth century, converted amid great fanfare by the century's end.[21] Indeed, Islam spread by Sufis and merchants became the preeminent religion of Central Asia in the late medieval period and even won adherents in China.[22] Only at the margins of Christian Europe—in Iberia and Sicily, for example—did Islam experience serious setbacks. But the Turkish Ottoman Empire, which in the early fourteenth century had consolidated the gains of Turkish raiders and tribesmen in Anatolia, became the preeminent military power in the Mediterranean and eastern Europe by the sixteenth century. Conversion among its numerous subject peoples, particularly in Anatolia but also in the Balkans, eastern Europe, and the Middle East, was integral to its success. A large proportion of the Ottoman ruling elite was recruited more or less involuntarily from among the children of Balkan Christians. These recruits converted to Islam as part of their professional training, and their subsequent patronage in their home territories facilitated further conversion.[23]

19. Richard Eaton, *The Rise of Islam and the Bengal Frontier, 1204–1760* (Berkeley: University of California Press, 1996); Bruce Lawrence, "Islam in India: The Function of Institutional Sufism in the Islamization of Rajasthan, Gujarat, and Kashmir," in *Islam in Local Contexts*, ed. Richard C. Martin (Leiden: Brill, 1982), 27–43.

20. Azyumardi Azra, *Islam in the Indonesian World: An Account of Institutional Formation* (Bandung: Mizan, 2006).

21. Peter Jackson, *The Mongols and the Islamic World: From Conquest to Conversion* (New Haven, CT: Yale University Press, 2017).

22. Devin DeWeese, *Islamization and Native Religion in the Golden Horde: Baba Tükles and Conversion to Islam in Historical and Epic Tradition* (University Park: Pennsylvania State University Press, 1994); Donald Daniel Leslie, *Islam in Traditional China: A Short History to 1800* (Canberra: Canberra College of Advanced Education, 1982); Zvi Ben-Dor Benite, *The Dao of Muhammad: A Cultural History of Muslims in Late Imperial China* (Cambridge, MA: Harvard University Asia Center, 2005).

23. Tijana Krstic, *Contested Conversions to Islam: Narratives of Religious Change in the Early Modern Ottoman Empire* (Stanford, CA: Stanford University Press, 2011); Anton Minkov, *Conversion to Islam in the Balkans: Kisve Bahası Petitions and Ottoman Social Life, 1670–1730* (Leiden: Brill, 2004).

Themes and Trends in Premodern Conversion to Islam

The Spiritual Appeal of Islam Islam held tremendous spiritual appeal for many converts in different places and times.[24] In the early generations after the Prophet's death, when the armies of his followers were still conquering much of the ancient world, conversion was attractive precisely because it offered hope of joining God's "winning team." Indeed, there was no greater proof of the power or truth of the Muslim God than the victories He seemed to bestow on His followers on the battlefield.[25] One also wonders whether the simplicity and austerity of the Muslim God, coupled with the direct access to Him that believers were understood to enjoy, was particularly appealing.[26] This may have been especially true of converts from late antique societies—Christian and otherwise—in which conceptions of the divine were often complex, even bewildering to the average unlettered person. These were also societies in which the universe was thought to be filled with a range of intermediary beings between God and man, whether human agents, such as priests and saints, or supernatural agents, such as angels.[27] By contrast, as a largely nonclerical religion, and one that emphasized the direct connection between God and His creation, Islam could short-circuit the need for intercession (though Islam would develop its own "cult of saints"—both living and dead—in later centuries).[28] This sense of direct connection was supercharged by the radical otherness of the Muslim God, a deity who was at once immediately available to believers and also beyond human experience and understanding in certain ways.

The Qurʾān was also a major pull for prospective converts. Then as now, Muslims regarded their sacred text as the direct speech of God. It is an intensely allusive scripture, and the practice of reciting it in the original language had the effect of reenacting the original moment of revelation.[29] No less appealing for those who

24. Ali Köse, "The Assessment of Various Factors in the Spread of Islam during the Medieval Period," *Islâm Araştirmaları Dergisi* 1 (1997): 65–89, esp. 84–87.

25. A point made by Crone, *Nativist Prophets*, 14.

26. Michael Cook, *Muhammad* (Oxford: Oxford University Press, 1983), 25–30.

27. There is a vast literature about the subject; see Peter Brown, *The Cult of the Saints: Its Rise and Function in Latin Christianity*, 2nd ed. (Chicago: University of Chicago Press, 2012); Robert Bartlett, *Why Can the Dead Do Such Great Things? Saints and Worshippers from the Martyrs to the Reformation* (Princeton, NJ: Princeton University Press, 2013).

28. Chase F. Robinson, "Prophecy and Holy Men in Early Islam," in *The Cult of the Saints in Late Antiquity and the Middle Ages: Essays on the Contribution of Peter Brown*, ed. James Howard-Johnston and Paul Antony Hayward (Oxford: Oxford University Press, 1999), 241–62; Joseph Meri, *The Cult of the Saints among Muslims and Jews in Medieval Syria* (Oxford: Oxford University Press, 2002); John Renard, *Friends of God: Islamic Images of Piety, Commitment, and Servanthood* (Berkeley: University of California Press, 2008).

29. Michael Cook, *The Koran: A Very Short Introduction* (Oxford: Oxford University Press, 2000); Nicolai Sinai, *The Qur'an: A Historical-Critical Introduction* (Edinburgh: Edinburgh University Press, 2017).

contemplated joining Islam was the figure of the Prophet Muḥammad himself. On the one hand, Muslims were adamant that he was a mere man, unlike Jesus Christ, whom Christians regarded as divine. On the other hand, God had created the Prophet as near to perfect as a man could be, making him attuned to the highest ideals and the smallest failures of the human condition. He was thus a model for his followers to emulate, near to them in condition, but just beyond what they could ever aspire to actually be.[30]

On a practical level, Islam must have also been attractive because of its low barrier to entry. Formal conversion entailed the recitation of the *shahāda* ("There is no god but God; Muḥammad is the Messenger of God"), usually but not necessarily in the presence of witnesses.[31] Conversion might entail certain signal changes, such as the adoption of a new name, documentary attestation before a judge, male circumcision, or emigration to a Muslim-majority settlement, but these were accidents, not essences of conversion. By contrast, in many forms of ancient Christianity, converts had to undergo lengthy rites of initiation, such as baptism and chrismation, as well as rigorous catechetical training, before they could formally join the church.[32] The conversion process in Islam eventually acquired detail and formality, but these may not have been present at the beginning.[33]

Not only was the process of conversion to Islam relatively straightforward, but many new Muslims found they did not necessarily have to give up their former practices. This was true in the first centuries among converts of Jewish and Christian backgrounds. Treasured forms of piety—such as fasting, the contemplation of sacred scripture, pilgrimage, belief in a looming judgment, and even devotion to certain biblical figures and saints—could easily survive the shift from the synagogue or the church to the mosque.[34] Finally, on a personal level, conversion to Islam seems to have been appealing thanks to its emphasis on solidarity among Muslims. The notion of a transregional *umma*, or community, that bound together

30. Cook, *Muhammad;* Kecia Ali, *The Lives of Muhammad* (Cambridge, MA: Harvard University Press, 2016); M. J. Kister, "The *Sīrah* Literature," in *The Cambridge History of Arabic Literature: Arabic Literature to the End of the Umayyad Period,* ed. A. F. L. Beeston (Cambridge: Cambridge University Press, 1983), 352–67.

31. On the early history of the *shahāda,* see M. J. Kister, " . . . *Illā bi-ḥaqqihi* . . . : A Study of an Early *Ḥadīth,*" *Jerusalem Studies in Arabic and Islam* 5 (1984): 33–52.

32. For but one example from late antique Syria, see Daniel L. Schwartz, *Paideia and Cult: Christian Initiation in Theodore of Mopsuestia* (Washington, DC: Center for Hellenic Studies/Cambridge, MA: Harvard University Press, 2013).

33. Pedro Chalmeta, "El matrimonio según el Kitab al-Wata'iq de Ibn al-'Attar (s. x): Análisis y observaciones," *Anaquel de Estudios Árabes* 6 (1995): 29–70.

34. Donner, *Muhammad and the Believers,* 56–89; on the specific case of asceticism, see Christian C. Sahner, "'The Monasticism of My Community Is Jihad': A Debate about Asceticism, Sex, and Warfare in Early Islam," *Arabica* 64 (2017): 1–35.

believers of different kinds in distant places promoted a radical sense of equality among Muslims.[35]

This last feature did not necessarily exist at the start of Islamic history amid the rancorous debates over the alleged superiority of Arabs during the Umayyad and ʿAbbasid periods.[36] As we have seen, non-Arab converts often entered the Muslim community as "clients" (*mawālī*) of particular tribes.[37] Such clientage was widespread in the early generations of Islam and guaranteed that Arabs would remain on top. But by the tenth century, as the *umma* became more heterogeneous, the practice of clientage-based conversion became obsolete.[38] Indeed, a sense of egalitarianism became a defining feature of many expressions of Islam and a benefit conferred by conversion.

The Social and Economic Appeal of Islam Second, there were numerous economic and social incentives to convert.[39] In the lifetime of the Prophet and the early caliphs, when the nascent Islamic state was bringing the tribes of Arabia and the Fertile Crescent to heel, it was the threat of violence and the prospect of security that drove large groups of Arabs to join the Muslim community.[40] The flip side of this coercive process was a factor that has already been mentioned—namely, conversion as a way of enjoying the fruits of victory on the battlefield. The coffers of the early Islamic state quickly swelled with the treasures of defeated empires, and conversion guaranteed new Muslims access to this conquest booty.

Even after the conquests were over, the same broad principle held true: conversion offered individuals and groups the chance to enjoy the social and economic life of the imperial upper class. This was especially so during the first centuries, when Muslims constituted an elite ruling over vast numbers of taxpaying, non-Muslim subjects. Seldom in the history of the world has there been a religion like Islam that promised so many material benefits to prospective converts while keeping the barrier to entry so low.[41]

35. On this discourse across the medieval period, see Louise Marlow, *Hierarchy and Egalitarianism in Islamic Thought* (Cambridge: Cambridge University Press, 1997).

36. One manifestation of this debate was the literary movement known as the *shuʿūbiyya,* which advocated for the equality of Arab and non-Arab Muslims; see Sarah Bowen Savant, "Naming Shuʿūbīs," in *Essays in Islamic Philology, History, and Philosophy,* ed. Alireza Korangy et al. (Berlin: De Gruyter, 2016), 166–84, and studies cited there.

37. Patricia Crone, "Mawlā," in *Encyclopaedia of Islam,* 2nd ed.

38. On the decline of *walāʾ* as seen through the representation of clients within the scholarly class over time, see John Nawas, "The Birth of an Elite: *Mawālī* and Arab *ʿUlamāʾ*," *Jerusalem Studies in Arabic and Islam* 31 (2006): 74–91.

39. Köse, "Spread of Islam," 77–80.

40. On tribal conversion in Arabia, see Munt, "What Did Conversion to Islam Mean?"

41. Crone, *Nativist Prophets,* 16.

The desire to maintain or increase one's social status probably lay at the heart of many decisions to convert. We see this motive in the cases of various pre-Islamic elites who converted in the interest of staying on top in the new Islamic cosmos, whether they were Sasanian and Byzantine aristocrats in the seventh century, Sogdian princes in the ninth, Turkish chieftains in the eleventh, or Mongol warlords in the fourteenth. There were also many converts from servile or peasant backgrounds who embraced Islam in the hope of improving their otherwise miserable lots in life. This created a topsy-turvy world in which former members of the lower classes found themselves in positions of authority over former elites, who naturally resented the imbalance of power.

Over time, Muslims developed an elaborate legal system for maintaining a sense of hierarchy and distinction between themselves and their non-Muslim subjects, and many non-Muslims converted in the hope of escaping this structure. The most important of its elements were the special taxes levied on non-Muslims, including the *jizya* (poll tax). Conversion liberated non-Muslims from such burdens, which could have a debilitating effect on individuals and communities.[42] More broadly, these laws effectively transformed non-Muslims into second-class citizens. The laws were cast in various literary forms, including the so-called Pact of ʿUmar, which has been studied extensively by scholars over the years.[43] There is considerable debate over whether the laws were actually enforced, and if so, whether they had a serious effect on non-Muslims in the long term. The consensus is that enforcement was highly variable, but that the laws contributed to the marginalization—and thus eventual conversion—of groups outside the Muslim fold.

Demographic and Regional Trends Third, what can we say about demographic and regional trends in the history of conversion during the Middle Ages? Written sources make clear that conversion followed different patterns, even within the same time period. For example, early biographies of the Prophet portray many individual conversions in Mecca and Medina, in which notable converts embraced Islam as a matter of conviction, often after transformative spiritual experiences. At the same time, the sources also describe many instances of group conversion, in which whole families, tribes, settlements, and cities went over to Islam en masse, often as a result of political, military, or economic pressures. Because the early sources were written and redacted some 150–200 years after the events they describe, it is difficult to peel apart the layers of history and legend in such accounts. Suffice it to say that while there were certainly early converts whose path into

42. The classic study remains Daniel C. Dennett, *Conversion and the Poll Tax in Early Islam* (Cambridge, MA: Harvard University Press, 1950).

43. Most recently, see Milka Levy-Rubin, *Non-Muslims in the Early Islamic Empire: From Surrender to Coexistence* (Cambridge: Cambridge University Press, 2011).

Islam resembled a modern, Protestant model of conversion—personal and life-changing—the majority of converts in the seventh and eighth centuries (and indeed at later points in Islamic history) may have entered Islam through far more collective, contingent, and nondoctrinal processes.[44]

The history of conversion is also a history of sizable regional variation across the greater Islamic world.[45] Although reliable statistics are impossible to obtain for the premodern period, most scholars agree that certain areas of the Middle East crossed the threshold of a Muslim majority relatively early. These include the Arabian Peninsula, southern Iraq, and parts of the Iranian plateau, all of which witnessed mass tribal conversion and/or intensive Arab settlement at an early date. They contrast with areas that converted to Islam late and inconsistently, such as Egypt, greater Syria, and parts of northern Mesopotamia, which retained large pockets of Christians until modern times.[46] Here we must also remember that not everyone who converted to Islam became a Sunni Muslim, at least by the standards of the medieval scholars, largely based in cities, who have left behind the bulk of our written sources. Indeed, there were many areas that entered Islam via "heterodox" or " nonimperial" forms of the religion, such as the coastal mountains of Syria and Lebanon, where Druzes, ʿAlawīs, and Twelver Shiʿis flourish to this day; the highlands of northern Iran along the Caspian Sea, which became home to large Zaydī and Ismāʿīlī communities; and the remote oases and mountain valleys of North Africa, which became havens of Kharijism, the original sectarian movement in Islam.[47] This phenomenon reflects a tendency of many disenfranchised groups in the medieval Middle East—including the *mawālī*—to enter the Muslim community through various opposition movements. In such movements, ethnic, political, and cultural grievances toward the ruling class were expressed by embracing radical interpretations of Islam premised on protest and revolution.

Regional variation owes much to the circumstances of Islam's arrival in a given area. In some places, conversion occurred in the wake of military conquests, as we see in the case of the central lands of the caliphate in the seventh and eighth centuries,

44. Tannous, *Making of the Medieval Middle East.*

45. For a broad treatment of regional trends, see Richard W. Bulliet, *Conversion to Islam in the Medieval Period: An Essay in Quantitative History* (Cambridge, MA: Harvard University Press, 1979). For a treatment of regional variations in relation to the early and medieval Islamic West, see Dominique Valérian et al., eds., *Islamisation et arabisation de l'Occident musulman médiéval (VIIe–XIIe siècle)* (Paris: Publications de la Sorbonne, 2011).

46. On late conversion in Syria, see, for example, Gideon Avni, *The Byzantine-Islamic Transition in Palestine: An Archaeological Approach* (Oxford: Oxford University Press, 2014), 331–37; for Egypt, see, for example, Tamer El-Leithy, "Coptic Culture and Conversion in Medieval Cairo, 1293–1524 A.D." (PhD diss., Princeton University, 2005).

47. For a broad overview of these communities, see Farhad Daftary, "Varieties of Islam," in *The New Cambridge History of Islam*, vol. 4, *Islamic Cultures and Societies to the End of the Eighteenth Century*, ed. Robert Irwin (Cambridge: Cambridge University Press, 2010), 105–41.

Anatolia starting in the eleventh, and northern India in the thirteenth. If conquerors and their allies were the typical agents of conversion in predominantly non-Muslim lands, there are also examples of Muslim subjects converting non-Muslim rulers, as in the case of the Mongols.[48] In addition, we have many examples of conversion outside of imperial or postconquest settings. Oman, for instance, seems to have become predominantly Muslim early on, presumably because of contacts with western Arabia.[49] Finally, history provides numerous instances of conversion through commerce, including in parts of West Africa, Indonesia, and Malaysia; through the efforts of charismatic holy figures, such as Sufis among the Turkic tribes of the Central Asian steppe and in large parts of South Asia; and through Ismāʿīlī missionaries among remote mountain communities in Iran, Afghanistan, India, and elsewhere.[50]

What should the reader take away from this broad survey of conversion and its themes in premodern Islamic history? First and foremost, conversion occurred across a broad spectrum of human experience. Indeed, this reader contains texts that portray conversion as a life-changing event, one that could cause individuals and groups to make a clean break between the old and the new. Other texts, meanwhile, portray conversion as something far messier, as a kind of fence-sitting in which a formal change of creed did not necessarily lead to the adoption of new identities, beliefs, or practices. The distinction leads into a bigger academic debate over whether it is better to understand conversion primarily as an event, isolated in time and leading to a visible change in status, or as a process enduring for years, if not generations, in which the old gradually becomes the new, and the new the old. Neither model categorically excludes the other, and both find support throughout the sources translated in this book.

MODERN HISTORIOGRAPHY ON CONVERSION TO ISLAM

Conversion to Islam in premodern times has received considerable attention in contemporary academic scholarship, both in the context of broad historiographic accounts and in the form of focused thematic discussions. A survey of these studies reveals two overlapping trends: a highly diverse set of questions and methods with which scholars have approached the phenomenon of conversion to Islam and increasingly nuanced perceptions of the act of conversion itself.

48. Peter Jackson, *The Mongols and the Islamic World: From Conquest to Conversion* (New Haven, CT: Yale University Press, 2017).

49. Harry Munt, “Early Islamic Oman: Islamisation and Imperialism in Southeast Arabia,” in *The Reach of Empire*, ed. Stefan Heidemann and Katharina Mewes (Berlin: De Gruyter, forthcoming).

50. On Sufis, see Köse, “Spread of Islam,” 81–84; DeWeese, *Islamization and Native Religion*. For the Ismāʿīlīs, see Daniel Beben, “Islamisation on the Iranian Periphery: Nasir-i Khusraw and Ismailism in Badakhshan,” in Peacock, *Islamisation*, 317–35.

When and Why

Two of perhaps the most salient questions that have featured, and still feature, in modern studies of conversion are when the major waves of conversion to Islam took place and what the reasons behind these conversions really were. Modern scholars have offered divergent estimates of the timing of the major waves of conversion, noting differences in rates in various parts of the broader Islamic world. At the root of this notable interest is the conviction that the emergence of a numerical Muslim majority in Islam-dominated lands constituted an important milestone. Modern scholars have gone as far as to argue that a Muslim majority led to the consolidation of Islamic political authority and social and religious institutions.[51] Most recent estimates commonly theorize that in certain parts of the Middle East a Muslim majority was achieved as late as the fourteenth century. These quantitative estimates are based on assessments of the qualitative character of conversion to Islam, recognizing the progressive nature of the process and variations among nomadic, rural, and urban populations in different historical periods.[52]

Conversion rates differed also on account of the varying motivations for conversion. Accordingly, attempts at quantifying conversion to Islam go hand in hand with efforts to establish the reasons that motivated it. The question has been addressed time and again in different contexts, all producing different explanations, many of which are the products of particular methods and perspectives. Conclusions have seemingly hinged on identifications of initiative on the part of either Muslims or non-Muslims. The former have been depicted as missionizing, preaching, drawing, inducing, or coercing, the latter as inspired, enchanted, opportunistic, dependent, culturally embedded, or communally feeble.[53] What spans most discussions, however, is the consensus view that individuals and groups chose to join the ranks of Islam for various reasons, but the prevailing cir-

51. See especially Bulliet, "Conversion to Islam," 3. See also Michael G. Morony, "The Age of Conversions: A Reassessment," in Gervers and Bikhazi, *Conversion and Continuity*, 135–50, at 137.

52. Carlson, "Contours of Conversion."

53. For the former perspective, see, for example, Thomas Walker Arnold, *The Preaching of Islam: A History of the Propagation of the Muslim Faith* (London: Constable, 1913); Marshall G. S. Hodgson, *The Venture of Islam*, vol. 2, *The Classical Age of Islam* (Chicago: University of Chicago Press, 1974), 533–37; Donald P. Little, "Coptic Conversion to Islam under the Baḥrī Mamlūks, 692–755/1293–1354," *Bulletin of the School of Oriental and African Studies* 39, no. 3 (1976): 552–69; Yaacov Lev, "Persecutions and Conversion to Islam in Eleventh Century Egypt," *Asian and African Studies* 22, nos. 1–3 (1988): 73–91; Milka Levy-Rubin, "New Evidence Relating to the Process of Islamization in Palestine in the Early Muslim Period: The Case of Samaria," *Journal of the Economic and Social History of the Orient* 43, no. 3 (2000): 257–76. For the latter focus, see, for example, Nehemia Levtzion, ed., introduction to *Conversion to Islam* (New York: Holmes and Meier, 1979), 7–12; Richard W. Bulliet, "Introduction: Process and Status in Conversion and Continuity," in Gervers and Bikhazi, *Conversion and Continuity*, 1–12, at 4–5; El-Leithy, "Coptic Culture and Conversion," 35, 65, 362–63; Wasserstein, "Conversion and the *Ahl al-Dhimma*," 185–87; Carlson, "Contours of Conversion."

cumstances in each historical moment rendered certain factors more prominent than others.

The question of motive is closely tied to that of agency. Thus, for example, some scholars have emphasized the importance of active proselytization in the initial spread of Islam, investigating the efforts of missionaries, preachers, spiritual heroes, and merchants in propagating the faith.[54] In instances when social pressures are seen to be at play, agency is often portrayed as coming from the direction of governmental officials.[55] But these explanations give the impression that pressure, at times violent and usually exerted by Islamic institutions, played an important role in winning converts and opposing confessional rivals. Recent scholarship has drawn attention to less formal levels of agency, taking place, among other locations, in popular centers of cult and within different social circles.[56] Moreover, converts themselves are also presented as important agents of conversion in their roles as prominent communal leaders, intellectuals, spouses, siblings, children, and slave owners whose conversion to Islam had an impact on their former coreligionist dependents.[57]

How

The quest to determine the precise reasons for conversion to Islam, as well as the scale of the phenomenon in different periods, has been abandoned in more recent studies that advocate for the importance of examining the process of conversion, specifically the cultural and social mechanisms that facilitated or impeded conversion.[58] Recognizing the cultural diversity of the peoples who came under Muslim rule, these studies often portray conversion to Islam as an uneven process, an act that was either triggered or followed by different forms of acculturation, including the adoption of the Arabic language, Islamic naming practices, and dress codes.[59] Thus, for example, the conversion process that took place in garrison towns during the late seventh and early eighth centuries is often cast as a consequence of an initial phase of Arabization among non-Muslims. In other regions and in later

54. Levtzion, *Conversion to Islam*, 15–17.

55. Little, "Coptic Conversion to Islam."

56. Carlson, "Contours of Conversion."

57. Ragnhild Johnsrud Zorgati, *Pluralism in the Middle Ages: Hybrid Identities, Conversion, and Mixed Marriages in Medieval Iberia* (New York: Routledge, 2012), chs. 4, 5; Uriel Simonsohn, "Conversion to Islam: A Case Study for the Use of Legal Sources," *History Compass* 11, no. 8 (2013): 647–62; Simonsohn, "Conversion, Exemption, and Manipulation: Social Benefits and Conversion to Islam in Late Antiquity and the Middle Ages," *Medieval Worlds* 6 (2017): 203–6; Sahner, *Christian Martyrs under Islam*.

58. Gervers and Bikhazi, *Conversion and Continuity*, 5; Mercedes García-Arenal, *Conversions islamiques: Identités religieuses en Islam méditerranéen* (Paris: Maisonneuve et Larose, 2002), 8.

59. Wasserstein, "Conversion and the *Ahl al-Dhimma*," 200; Sahner, *Christian Martyrs under Islam*, 30.

periods, conversion to Islam is seen as occurring in lockstep with Islamization, the latter referring to the process whereby political, social, cultic, and other communal institutions took on an Islamic veneer. Here, the adoption of an Islamic confessional affiliation became a by-product of socialization.[60] Both acculturation and socialization speak to the progressive or gradual nature of conversion to Islam as a transformative act that was often slowed by former allegiances or sentiments. It is in this context that special attention has been given in modern scholarship to the phenomenon of backsliding, or conversion and reversion. The movement of converts back and forth between their former and new confessional communities highlights, among other things, their liminal position as well as their hybridity.[61] Thus, the passage from one confession to another is also a process of transculturation that overrides definitions of formal communal affiliation.[62]

Responses

The process of conversion to Islam was very much affected by the different responses that the act of conversion set in motion on the part of both the convert's former coreligionists and his or her new ones. Perhaps the most tangible kind of response that has drawn the attention of modern scholarship came from the legal sphere. Legal regulations and opinions, of both Muslim and non-Muslim origin, reflect attempts to formalize the act of conversion and to regulate it on the part of Muslim jurists, to circumvent it on the part of non-Muslim legal authorities, and to address the variety of legal problems that arose in the course of, and following, the act.[63] These endeavors stemmed partially from the mistrust directed toward those who joined the Muslim fold and those who sought to revert back to their former religions. Modern scholars point to a variety of literary genres that expressed suspicions toward converts to Islam, questioning the sincerity of their motives and their integrity as Muslims.[64] Suspicion has been identified as contrib-

60. Carlson, "Contours of Conversion"; Andrew C.S. Peacock, ed., introduction to Peacock, *Islamisation*; Tannous, *Making of the Medieval Middle East*, 363.

61. Simonsohn, "Conversion to Islam."

62. Cyrille Aillet, *Les mozarabes: Christianisme, islamisation et arabisation en péninsule ibérique, IXe–XIIe siècle* (Madrid: Casa de Velázquez, 2010); Zorgati, *Pluralism in the Middle Ages*, ch. 2; Sarah Stroumsa, "Between Acculturation and Conversion in Islamic Spain: The Case of the Banū Ḥasday," *Mediterranea: International Journal on the Transfer of Knowledge* 1 (2016): 9–36.

63. Jean de Menasce, "Problèmes des mazdéens dans l'Iran musulman," in *Festschrift für Wilhelm Eilers: Ein Dokument der internationalen Forschung zum 27. September 1966*, ed. Gernot Wiessner (Wiesbaden: Harrassowitz, 1967), 220–30; Yohanan Friedmann, *Tolerance and Coercion in Islam: Interfaith Relations in the Muslim Tradition* (Cambridge: Cambridge University Press, 2003), chs. 3, 4; Simonsohn, "Conversion to Islam."

64. El-Leithy, "Coptic Culture and Conversion," 29–33, 140–41; Janina M. Safran, "Identity and Differentiation in Ninth-Century al-Andalus," *Speculum* 76, no. 3 (2001): 579; Simonsohn, "Conversion to Islam."

uting to a set of behaviors among converts as well as being emblematic of the liminal aspect of their position. In other instances, we find that the absence of a warm welcome to converts was also the outcome of a social hierarchy that was based on ethnic categories. Thus, for example, in the ninth to eleventh century, against the backdrop of Arab claims to primacy in the Muslim community, Iranian Muslims sought to retell the Islamic past in a manner that highlighted the role of their recently converted forefathers during the early conquests.[65] Other forms of cultural adaptation, albeit of a more mundane type, show up in al-Andalus, where conversion to Islam was accompanied by the adoption of a set of practices that emphasized the integration of converts into an Islamic-Arabian culture.[66] These are only a few of the examples that show up in modern scholarship with regard to the reactions converts received once they joined Muslim communities, and the measures they had to adopt in response. The latter are often seen as strategies of integration and assimilation in societies that frowned upon any compromise along confessional lines, yet at the same time witnessed a great deal of such compromise.

The liminal position of converts to Islam and the lack of trust they often encountered because of their suspected motives may have stemmed from fears of apostasy among many Muslims of the time. Although the theoretical side of the phenomenon has been long noted, recent research into documentary and narrative sources has brought the phenomenon to new historical light.[67] Apostasy is also attributed to the endurance of kinship ties between converts and their former coreligionists. The trend is evidenced in the so-called neomartyr acts that were composed in al-Andalus, Egypt, Palestine, Syria, Iraq, and the Caucasus and that speak of Christian converts to Islam whose reversion to Christianity was attributed to their continued ties with their Christian kinsfolk.[68] Such images find much resonance in legal sources of diverse confessional backgrounds.[69] The utility of these sources for reconstructing Islamic social history is particularly remarkable with regard to matters pertaining to the private domain. Legal sources speak of the overlapping and conflicting spheres of communal and family attachments. They underscore the dangers of apostasy as well as the opportunities for drawing

65. Sarah Bowen Savant, *The New Muslims of Post-Conquest Iran: Tradition, Memory, and Conversion* (Cambridge: Cambridge University Press, 2013).

66. Jessica A. Coope, "Religious and Cultural Conversion to Islam in Ninth-Century Umayyad Córdoba," *Journal of World History* 4, no. 1 (1993): 47–68.

67. Joel L. Kraemer, "Apostates, Rebels, and Brigands," *Israel Oriental Studies* 10 (1980): 34–73; David Cook, "Apostasy from Islam: A Historical Perspective," *Jerusalem Studies in Arabic and Islam* 31 (2006): 248–88; Christian C. Sahner, "Swimming against the Current: Muslim Conversion to Christianity in the Early Islamic Period," *Journal of American Oriental Society* 136, no. 2 (2016): 265–84.

68. Sahner, *Christian Martyrs under Islam*.

69. Simonsohn, "Conversion to Islam."

apostates back to their communities. It is also in the context of lasting family ties that the central role of women has slowly come into view.[70] The importance of mothers, wives, and even sisters in conversion to Islam is gradually taking center stage in modern scholarship.

Impact and Significance

The evident links between conversion to Islam and broad trends such as Islamization, Arabization, and the consolidation of Islamic political power as well as the more minute aspects of daily life justify exploring its broad effects. The significance of conversion to Islam in the formation of Islamic society has already been noted with regard to the continuous interest in the chronological tipping point leading to a numerical Muslim majority. The underlying premise is that conversion to Islam was to a great extent a social act that, with time, gave the Muslim community its distinctive character.[71] In order to accommodate the social, cultural, and even spiritual sentiments of those who joined the Muslim ranks, Islam as a religion was in a constant state of flux.[72] Other effects, of a more local scale, have been noted as well. Thus, in the case of Egypt, scholars have argued that the slower pace of conversion facilitated wide-scale Arabization, in contrast to instances in which bilingualism persisted owing to faster rates of conversion.[73] At the same time, in Iran, where Islam spread at a much earlier stage, yet local Iranian culture continued to flourish, conversion to Islam is seen to have encouraged a unique historiography that emphasized Islam's Iranian past.[74] A consideration of the broader effects of conversion to Islam finds support in the appreciation of the liminality of converts to Islam. Converts were often shrouded with ambiguity, and this has been seen as a sign of their intermediate position, allowing them to cross-pollinate ideas, norms, and practices across confessional boundaries.[75]

The centrality of conversion to Islam in the lives of Muslim and non-Muslim communities alike has also rendered it meaningful for broader historical debates. This fact has much to do with the considerable role confessional divisions played as markers of social boundaries in premodern times. Thus, to a large extent, the choice of individuals or groups to shift their confessional affiliations took place within a social structure that was not only delimiting but also prone to manipulation, exploitation, and, conse-

70. Maya Shatzmiller, "Marriage, Family, and the Faith: Women's Conversion to Islam," *Journal of Family History* 21, no. 3 (1996): 235–66; Elizabeth Urban, "The Early Islamic *Mawālī:* A Window onto Processes of Identity Construction and Social Change" (PhD diss., University of Chicago, 2012), ch. 4; Zorgati, *Pluralism in the Middle Ages*, chs. 4, 5.

71. Bulliet, "Conversion to Islam," 37.

72. García-Arenal, *Conversions islamiques*, 8.

73. El-Leithy, "Coptic Culture and Conversion," 25.

74. Savant, *New Muslims*.

75. Tannous, *Making of the Medieval Middle East*, 387, 398.

quently, modification. Recovering the manner in which conversion to Islam was negotiated, performed, and responded to has enabled modern scholars to address questions pertaining to communal life, including aspects such as social hierarchies, tensions between temporal and clerical leaderships, visions of ideal communities, and paradigms of orthodoxy. In the Iberian context, for example, conversion to Islam has been studied through legal sources, where it is portrayed as a mechanism for the creation or removal of social boundaries.[76] With regard to converts of Iranian origin, the topic has been enlisted for exploring notions of communal belonging.[77] Christian martyrologies, depicting the miraculous achievements of Christian converts to Islam, have proved highly useful for telling the history of Christian communities that fell under Islamic rule.[78] And probing into the manifestations of conversion to Islam among so-called simpleminded Christians, that is, the masses or nonelites, has produced intriguing conclusions regarding what it meant to be Muslim or Christian in the early Islamic period.[79] Conversion narratives emanating from fourteenth- to twentieth-century Central and Inner Asia, which speak of the conversion of the Khan Özbek, provided the grounds for these tribes' claims to political legitimacy.[80] And with regard to the Ottoman Empire, scholars have noticed the utility of the notion of conversion in various literary genres for promoting visions of orthodoxy in moments of Sunni-Shiʿi conflict and the erection of modern group boundaries.[81]

Meaning

The phenomenon of conversion to Islam in premodern times has been approached from many angles, stimulating a variety of historical questions. Only seldom, however, have modern scholarly endeavors ventured beyond isolated case studies focusing on a particular period, region, or group. The shortcomings of these approaches have found a corrective in comparative studies that explore the phenomenon of conversion to Islam across time and geography in order to grasp its relative, contingent nature.[82] To that end, there has also been growing interest in case studies on areas that are often considered to lie beyond the heartlands of Islam, in Africa and Southeast Asia.[83]

76. Zorgati, *Pluralism in the Middle Ages.*

77. Savant, *New Muslims.*

78. Sahner, *Christian Martyrs under Islam.*

79. Tannous, *Making of the Medieval Middle East.*

80. DeWeese, *Islamization and Native Religion,* 11.

81. Krstic, *Contested Conversions to Islam*; Marc David Baer, *Honored by the Glory of Islam: Conversion and Conquest in Ottoman Europe* (New York: Oxford University Press, 2011).

82. Levtzion, *Conversion to Islam;* Carlson, "Contours of Conversion"; Peacock, *Islamisation.*

83. See, for example, Richard Eaton, "Approaches to the Study of Conversion to Islam in India," in *Approaches to Islam in Religious Studies,* ed. Richard C. Martin (Tucson: University of Arizona Press, 1985), 106–23. More generally, see Wasserstein, "Conversion and the *Ahl al-Dhimma,*" 200.

At the same time, the question of the nature of the act has for the most part remained either untouched or only marginally addressed. This inattention does not mean there is a lack of understanding as to what conversion to Islam meant and entailed. Studies concerned with the causes of conversion to Islam, the scope of the phenomenon, responses to it, and its effects on society reflect the diverse ways in which scholars have understood the process. Some have treated conversion to Islam as an act charged with spiritual meanings, echoing a Christian paradigm of change of heart, whereas others have seen it mainly as the adoption of a confessional label, with purely social consequences.[84] Scholars have also attempted to nuance our understanding of conversion by distinguishing between the conversions of individuals and groups, adults and children, men and women, freedmen and captives, and monotheists and polytheists. Others have sought to complicate the debate by investigating the motives for conversion and the circumstances in which conversion took place.[85] To that end, we find attempts to differentiate sincere conversions from outward ones on the basis of A. D. Nock's famous division between conversion in the sense of a reorientation of the soul and conversion as adhesion, which entails the adoption of external practices.[86]

The theme of conversion to Islam as a cultural phenomenon has opened the way to updated accounts of the impact of pivotal cultural transformations in the lives of individuals. At the level of single communities, notice has been taken of the daily dilemmas engendered by conversion and its social implications for the lives of individuals and families. Here, special attention has been given to the wide variety of experiences, including acculturation, adhesion or hybridity, syncretism, and transformation of sociocultural practices and systems of belief. Nuances and growing sensitivities to the different manifestations of religious conversion in general and conversion to Islam in particular have given rise to an expanding body of scholarship that seeks to theorize the act and explore its diverse dimensions.[87]

84. Peacock, *Islamisation*, 4.

85. Morony, "Age of Conversions," 139; Levy-Rubin, "New Evidence," 261, 269.

86. Arthur Darby Nock, *Conversion: The Old and the New in Religion from Alexander the Great to Augustine of Hippo* (London: Oxford University Press, 1961), 5–7; Levtzion, *Conversion to Islam*, 21; Lev, "Persecutions and Conversion," 88.

87. See especially David A. Snow and Richard Machalek, "The Sociology of Conversion," *Annual Review of Sociology* 10 (1984): 167–90; Carole M. Cusack, "Towards a General Theory of Conversion," in *Religious Change, Conversion, and Culture*, ed. Lynette Olson (Sydney: Sydney Association for Studies in Society and Culture, 1996), 1–21; Talal Asad, "Comments on Conversion," in *Conversion to Modernities: The Globalization of Christianity*, ed. Peter van der Veer (London: Routledge, 1996), 263–73; Lewis R. Rambo and Charles E. Farhadian, eds., introduction to *The Oxford Handbook of Religious Conversion* (New York: Oxford University Press, 2014). For a useful overview, see Yaniv Fox and Yosi Yisraeli, eds., introduction to *Contesting Inter-Religious Conversion in the Medieval World* (London: Routledge, 2016).

Yet these distinctions have been challenged by those who argue that Islamic doctrine deems an external adoption of Islam as meaningful as the internal embrace of the religion. In both cases, conversion to Islam resulted in new communal membership, but not necessarily in the complete abandonment of one's former beliefs and practices.[88] More recently, historians have proposed approaching the question of the meaning of conversion to Islam by inquiring about what it meant to be a Muslim and how this was different from being a member of a non-Muslim community in particular historical contexts.[89]

The realization that being Muslim is a state not restricted to matters of belief and praxis has rendered past attempts unsatisfying for understanding conversion as a lived experience with more than one dimension.[90] Although it has been postulated that converts to Islam may not have been aware of the meaning of their act, it seems clear enough that their decision to become Muslims entailed a certain measure of change in their daily lives.[91] How substantial these changes were, and which aspects of the convert's life they affected, are questions that remain open for constructive debate. A recent revisiting of the question endorses such a complex approach but at the same time advocates for the abandonment of former criteria for assessing conversion, such as sincerity, authenticity, and wholeness. The argument rests on the claim that these criteria reflect the agendas of those who sought to set the norms for conversion, rather than the conceptions of those who experienced it.[92] Instead, a useful way of comprehending the phenomenon of conversion is to pay attention to breaking points in the life of the convert, whether spiritual, cultural, social, or even political. They may take place on a spectrum of levels and in different combinations.[93] Although these disruptions are, of course, often construed by those who report them, the call to approach historical questions with as few essentialist categories as possible is a step forward.

OUTLINE OF SOURCES

As the previous section shows, many studies of conversion to Islam address broad social and demographic trends, focusing on when and how Islam entered different regions, when a critical mass of the population converted to Islam, who the agents

88. DeWeese, *Islamization and Native Religion*, 27; Crone, *Nativist Prophets*, 14; Peacock, *Islamisation*, 5.

89. Sahner, *Christian Martyrs under Islam*, 33; Tannous, *Making of the Medieval Middle East*, 361.

90. García-Arenal, *Conversions islamiques*, 9.

91. Wasserstein, "Conversion and the *Ahl al-Dhimma*," 199–200.

92. Arietta Papaconstantinou, introduction to *Conversion in Late Antiquity: Christianity, Islam, and Beyond; Papers from the Andrew W. Mellon Foundation Sawyer Seminar, University of Oxford, 2009–2010*, ed. Arietta Papaconstantinou, Neil McLynn, and Daniel L. Schwartz (Farnham: Ashgate, 2016), xxi.

93. Tannous, *Making of the Medieval Middle East*, 361.

of conversion were, and what happened in the societies that witnessed large-scale Islamization. In recent years, however, a number of studies have appeared that turn their attention to converts themselves and their contemporaries. The present book builds on this new trajectory of research by concentrating on the individuals who converted, the difficulties they faced, the lives of the families and communities that they left behind, and the Muslim societies that they entered. Their personal stories touch on what drove them to convert as well as the obstacles that they confronted as they attempted to become part of Muslim communities. They also reveal the emotions and ambivalence that conversion often stirred among converts and the people surrounding them. In so doing, these stories shed new light on the gradual nature of conversion and how it was experienced.

By turning their attention to the diverse ways in which converts and the people surrounding them experienced conversion, scholars can approach the topic from new vantage points. For example, close readings of personal stories can alter scholars' perspective on one of the classic questions of the field: How were whole societies converted to Islam? This topic—which was illustrated in the beginning of this introduction through a comparison of the small number of Muslims that an imaginary eighth-century traveler would have encountered with the predominantly Muslim societies through which the fourteenth-century traveler Ibn Baṭṭūṭa passed—stands to benefit from an approach that examines acts of conversion through the eyes of the men and women who converted to Islam as well as through those of their contemporaries. These reports and stories enable scholars to reconstruct the emotions and motives of the converts and, in the process, learn about the challenges they faced. It is through a better understanding of the tensions between converts, the relatives they left behind, and the communities they entered that we can learn about their ambivalence, backsliding, zeal, and other forms of behavior that made conversion so complex a phenomenon. At the same time, the information and insights that can be gleaned from contemporaries will also enable scholars to revisit broader questions pertaining to the dynamics of conversion to Islam, which has so profoundly changed the demography of Asia, Africa, and Europe.

This reader brings together nearly sixty texts spanning those regions that witnessed large-scale conversion to Islam. However, it is worth noting that although we have included texts from a wide array of areas—ranging from West Africa to Indonesia—the reader does not offer equal coverage of these areas. Indeed, it is particularly focused on the Middle East and the eastern Mediterranean. In part this is an outcome of the importance we ascribe to Arabia and adjacent regions during the formative decades of Islamic history. It also reflects the availability of superb texts from this region that we were inclined to include.

The texts shed light on conversion to Islam from four different angles. The first is the authoritative discussion found in the Qur'ān and legal sources. The second is the viewpoint of the converts themselves. The third is that of the Muslim society they entered. And the fourth is that of the communities they abandoned. Each of them elaborates a very different narrative, and together they depict the diverse paths by which converts entered Islam.

Qurʾān and Law

A handful of the selections that appear in this reader touch on the foundational religious and legal texts of Islam. These genres greatly shaped much of the thinking and behavior related to conversion, and many of the events and attitudes concerning conversion to Islam were influenced by or reflected in the sacred texts of Islam—the Qurʾān and *ḥadīth* (sayings and deeds ascribed to the Prophet), as well as the accompanying legal discourse. (On the Qurʾān, see selection 1; on *ḥadīth*, see selections 7 and 8.) A critical point often made regarding the Qurʾān is that it rejects coercion in matters of religious conscience. In contrast to this clear-cut statement, the legal discourse contains a multiplicity of views on any given question. Accordingly, jurists articulated varied opinions regarding relations within "mixed families" and demonstrated flexibility in matters related to the act of conversion, about which we learn from the evolving depictions of sociolegal practices of conversion. This divergence in legal views and sociolegal practices reveals that Muslim jurists and societies espoused a range of views about conversion and that only a few rulings were set in stone.

The Converts

As we move from authoritative texts to accounts about converts themselves, we begin to learn how they viewed conversion or, more accurately, what emotions and motives the written tradition ascribes to them. For many, conversion was depicted as the outcome of a spiritual journey, which was often prompted by a powerful religious experience. One such experience was hearing or reading the words of the Qurʾān. Converts sometimes testified that through their encounters with the Qurʾān, they realized its nobility and holiness and therefore recognized the truth of Islam. Others joined the faith, we are told, after witnessing miracles. In the initial stage of Islam such miracles were often ascribed to the Prophet Muḥammad. Centuries later, they were also attributed to Sufi shaykhs, who helped convince their followers that Islam was the path of truth (see selection 40). Another religious experience that moved individuals to convert was the piety of the Muslims whom they met. From these converts' point of view, conversion was thus an outcome of unmediated encounters with the holy.

Other selections in this reader, however, reveal a contrasting take on conversion to Islam. Whereas converts themselves sometimes emphasized spiritual motives, various observers ascribed to them a range of markedly different intentions. In their writings, the observers stressed the social circumstances that made it increasingly difficult to remain a non-Muslim, pointing out that conversion seemed the most sensible way to survive in a new social and political order that accorded rank on the basis of confessional belonging (see selection 28). In other cases, they described how economic interests lured converts away from their original faiths. In still others, they observed, the pressure to convert or the encounter with Islam was conveyed through relatives.

The most powerful form of pressure was outright physical coercion. Although it is widely acknowledged that Muslim ruling elites did not usually force their subjects to convert, there were situations in which non-Muslims were indeed coerced into accepting Islam. Several texts in this reader assert that in certain instances, conversion was linked to political interests, and forcing leaders to convert marked an important step in subduing rebellions (see selection 29). Other selections portray ambivalence that led to backsliding, an act that Muslim jurists regarded as apostasy, demanding that offenders come back to the fold or be executed. This perspective, which tells of the believers' uncertainty and their persecution, is better represented in Christian sources, such as hagiographies and martyrologies, than in Muslim accounts (see selection 14).

Thus, the counternarrative to the Muslim depiction of converts joining the true faith and attaining paradise was the Christian narrative that asserted that the highest spiritual experience that believers could attain was the ultimate act of self-sacrifice—that is, refusing to join the Muslim faith and dying as martyrs. In the first narrative, individuals altered their lives as they embraced Allah, whereas in the second, individuals gave up their lives to remain with their Lord.

Interestingly, one of the texts in this reader (see selection 36) shows that a different narrative evolved among Jewish jurists. Much less heroic or spiritual, it was a theologico-legal discussion that attempted to explain how individuals could lawfully feign conversion to Islam. Viewing Muslims as true monotheists, some Jewish jurists argued that it was legitimate to pretend to convert when one's life was under threat.

Alongside accounts about individual converts, this reader includes reports about collective conversion to Islam. Numerically speaking, it is likely that most converts made the transition in groups, not as individuals. From the experiential perspective, which is at the center of this book's interest, the emotions and spiritual journeys of people involved in collective conversion were probably different from those of individuals who converted alone. In contrast to most individual converts, who are likely to have been knowledgeable about Islam before they converted because of exposure to Islamic rituals, lifestyles, and intellectual culture, many of those who converted in groups knew much less about the religion they were entering. As a consequence, in the years and generations following their conversion they sometimes oscillated between communal identities and only gradually acquired doctrinal knowledge and internalized the ideals of Islam.

The Society Entered

Our sources reveal that the Muslim societies that the converts entered reacted in different ways to their new coreligionists. Whereas in some cases conversion opened new opportunities, such as the chance to join the highest echelons of society as courtiers, administrators, or members of the social elite, in other instances converts felt unwelcomed in their new communities (see selection 15).

The best-known and most significant case of such disappointment occurred during the Umayyad era, in which new converts were denied the rights that Muslims theoretically enjoyed, such as reduced taxes (see selection 12). In other cases the converts' sincerity was doubted, triggering social unrest and legal discussions.

The Society Left Behind

Some of the most moving texts in this reader were written by the kin and community members who were left behind when converts adopted a new confessional community, and who thus felt hurt and vulnerable, lamenting the lost souls of their friends and fearing the extinction of their own community. Therefore, behind the exuberance of the converts who saw the light lies the darkness of those they abandoned, whose writings express sorrow for lost friendships and anxieties over their communities' fates.

As the texts in this reader illustrate, some of the most heated and painful exchanges and dilemmas triggered by conversion took place between converts and their relatives. These difficulties surface in texts written by brothers who exchanged polemical letters or by husbands and wives who battled over their children (see selection 22). Clearly, a convert's abandonment of his or her previous faith and family could prompt feelings of bitterness and aggravation. Furthermore, the controversies and conflicts that arose within mixed families, in which one member converted but others remained true to their original religion, were echoed in legal writings, with jurists of all confessional backgrounds attempting to regulate how family members ought to conduct themselves in the changed circumstances.

The sentiments of those left behind are found in a range of sources, including poignant poetry that depicts extinct cultures, as well as touching verses about a lost friend (see selection 21). Other sources are historical accounts that describe stalwarts of the Muslim community who succumbed to pressures that were applied to them. Perhaps the most painful admissions were written about individuals who chose to leave their faith even though they were not subjected to outright threats or pressure (see selection 13). The writers of such accounts alluded to a variety of temptations, and some of them conjured up the ultimate seducer, Satan.

The dozens of texts that appear in this reader show that conversion to Islam was a multifaceted process, reflecting a wide range of significantly different experiences expressed in diverse narratives. An example of contrasting narratives is

Muslim triumphalism and its counternarrative, driven by Christian, Jewish, or Zoroastrian fears of communal extinction. Accompanying these emotions are radically different descriptions of the motivations to convert: whereas Muslims spoke of spiritual journeys resulting from powerful religious experiences, members of other communities pointed to cynical calculations and powerful seductions on the part of the converts.

BETWEEN MICRO- AND MACROHISTORIES

Most of the accounts and reports that appear in this book focus on individuals or small groups. Some are a few lines long, others a few pages. This is a microscopic scale that invites questions that are often asked of microhistory: Can short and personal anecdotes tell us something of significance about larger historic developments? If we think they can, how do we link individual experiences or specific legal issues with broad topics in Islamic history?[94]

One way of answering these questions is through contextualization: situating small-scale accounts within the larger scheme of historic developments. This reader places the translated texts within three contextual frameworks. The first is an introduction to each text, which links the text to the region and period in which the conversion occurred, as well as discussing the author's background and the genre of the text. By identifying the region, time, and genre of the texts and inquiring about their authors, we learn about the forces that shaped the texts, be they the authors' potential biases or the constraints imposed by literary convention. Of particular importance to understanding a text is awareness of its genre, since genre determines the kind of information that is included, the style in which a source is composed, the criteria of authenticity that are applied to it, and the stylistic features within which historical facts must be presented. In order to shed light on conversion from a variety of angles, we have chosen to include in the reader a wide array of genres, including chronicles, biographies of the Prophet, biographical dictionaries, poetry, books of law, hagiographies, and martyrologies. The introductions to the selections also address the contents of the texts and explain how they are connected to major literary, social, and political issues.

The second contextual framework is provided by the introductions to each of the three chronological parts of the book (seventh–tenth, tenth–thirteenth, and thirteenth–sixteenth centuries CE). These chronological limits are dictated by the goal of providing illustrative sources on conversion to Islam in the premodern

94. For a discussion on the advantages and constraints of microhistory, see Giovanni Levi, "On Microhistory," in *New Perspectives on Historical Writing*, ed. Peter Burke, 93–113 (University Park: Pennsylvania State University Press, 1992). For an outstanding example of such a study, see Carlo Ginzburg, *The Cheese and the Worms: The Cosmos of a Sixteenth-Century Miller* (New York: Penguin, 1984).

world, that is, prior to the early modern Islamic "gunpowder empires" of the Ottomans, Safavids, and Mughals at their heights, and to the epochal ascendancy of European power with which they were contemporary.[95] The book's three section introductions zoom out and situate the translated texts against their wider premodern historical backgrounds. They highlight major historical developments that are related to conversion and that occurred during the respective periods. For example, the introduction to part 1 touches on the unique difficulties that the early Muslim community faced during its persecution by the Meccan elite, and the radical change in policy toward converts that took place when the ʿAbbasids replaced the Umayyads. The introduction to part 2 points out that it was during this period that Muslim-controlled societies also became Muslim-majority societies, and it discusses a variety of themes that became salient in this period, such as the importance of enslavement and the conversion of soldiers, legal discussions of mixed marriages, and the role of agents of conversion, particularly outside areas dominated by Muslims. The introduction to part 3 stresses the expansion of Islam to regions distant from the religion's Middle Eastern birthplace, such as West Africa, Southeast Asia, and China, while recognizing that many of the trends operative in earlier eras and in the heartlands of the Islamic world remained constant. The role of merchants and charismatic Sufi shaykhs is especially prominent here. All three introductions also dwell on such issues as the conversion policies of rulers, the conduct of agents of proselytization, and the obstacles that stood in the way of integrating new Muslims into Muslim societies. They pay close attention to the communities that lost adherents to Islam, noting the grief of families, the blow to their self-confidence, and the fear of communal extinction.

The aim of the introductions to the three chronological parts of the reader is to make explicit the connections between the translated texts and the wider historical developments of which they were a part. By highlighting the links between the texts and their historical contexts, the introductions bring the historical significance of each text into relief.

The third contextual framework is this introduction, which has surveyed the broadest issues related to conversion: major historical dynamics in Islamic history, key analytic themes related to conversion, and the relevant historiography. These presentations enable the reader to observe conversion to Islam in its widest historical, historiographical, and analytical contexts. The three introductory themes—textual, chronological, and historiographical—allow the reader to shift between

95. Douglas E. Streusand, *Islamic Gunpowder Empires: Ottomans, Safavids, and Mughals* (New York: Routledge, 2011); Marshall G. S. Hodgson, *The Venture of Islam*, vol. 3, *The Gunpowder Empires and Modern Times* (Chicago: University of Chicago Press, 1974). In a few instances in part 3, texts from the sixteenth century and later were also included when these illustrated premodern conditions and were the best sources available for a particular region.

three very different vantage points and examine conversion to Islam as a personal matter, as part of collective historical developments, and as a major issue in Islamic and world history. Through these three angles, the imaginative reader can connect the private experiences of individuals to the epoch-making dynamics that transformed Islam into the world's second largest religion in the modern era.

PART ONE

The Prophet and the Empires of the Caliphs

(ca. seventh–tenth centuries)

Nimrod Hurvitz and Christian C. Sahner

IN THE OPENING DECADES OF THE SEVENTH century, the Middle East experienced a religious and political revolution. In less than thirty years, the Muslim community evolved from a fragile, persecuted sect into a true world power. In the subsequent three centuries covered in this section, large segments of the population living in the Iberian Peninsula, North Africa, the Middle East, and vast swaths of Central Asia gradually converted to Islam. This introduction surveys the causes and consequences of conversion to Islam and the sentiments that it triggered from the perspectives of converts themselves, the communities they joined, and the communities they left behind. For every party involved, the experience of conversion was charged with emotions: for some it was a moment of inspiration, for others a sea change that opened new social and economic opportunities, and for still others a cause of depression and remorse.

The narratives that address these conversions do not simply recount events and emotions, however. They are also laden with ideological agendas. Perhaps the most important of these is Islamic triumphalism, which views conversion as an indication of the superiority of Muslims over members of other religions. Such accounts emphasize the tumultuous spiritual drama, the assertive change in beliefs, and the profound conviction of converts. Despite this confident rhetoric, the reality is that many converts were wracked by doubt, ignorant of their new faith, and prone to return to their original ones. The narratives were often written at a considerable chronological distance from the events they describe, and they thus reflect the interests and agendas of later generations of Muslims. These individuals strove to depict the conversion of their forefathers in a positive light and, in the process, to establish social capital for themselves in the present by tracing their families' Islam back to exceptionally early moments in the history of the religion. The social prestige and economic benefits that early conversion to Islam bestowed go a long way toward explaining the distortions and disagreements we find in many narratives about these first generations of Muslims.

The use of conversion narratives to promote ideological agendas is not limited to Muslim authors. Christians also articulated narratives of "heroic resistance," which told of the terrific pressure to convert and of the price paid by those who reneged on their new faith (see selections 14 and 17). Through such accounts, they constructed hagiographic images of martyrs and others; these were designed to set an example for fellow Christians and to inspire them to resist the temptations and threats associated with conversion.

To understand the fuller meaning and significance of these anecdotes and agendas, it is necessary to weave them together into a larger historical tapestry. Therefore, this introduction places the specific selections included in part 1 of this reader within a wider framework consisting of the formative political, social, and economic developments that occurred at the origins of Islam.

ESTABLISHING A COMMUNITY

Social, political, and religious movements tend to be most vulnerable during the earliest stage of their development, when they must attract enough followers to establish a community, when the members of this community may face persecution, and when they desperately seek allies to defend them. The Islamic tradition is very candid about the tribulations of the early Muslims. Islamic sources include numerous accounts of the Prophet's self-doubt and hesitation, the early converts' fears, the growing physical dangers they confronted, and their flight from their native city to a new refuge in Medina. Many of these stories serve to build up triumphalist narratives of Islamic origins, which highlight the courage and perseverance of the first Muslims in the face of terrific odds against them. Interestingly, these accounts also reveal some of the more controversial moments and failures in the history of the early Muslims.

One of the most moving scenes from the earliest stage of Islamic history is the description of the Prophet's confusion after receiving his first revelations. It is at this point that the tradition introduces the first convert to Islam, Khadīja bt. Khuwaylid, the Prophet's first wife and counselor (see selection 2). She is portrayed as advising and encouraging Muḥammad in his moment of uncertainty as he sought to determine whether he had experienced genuine revelations or had simply been possessed. Interestingly, women appear at numerous points in early Islamic history as bold and independent converts who stand up to their non-Muslim families and advocate conversion. One example is Arwā bt. ʿAbd al-Muṭṭalib b. Hāshim, who tries to convince her half-brother Abū Lahab to join the burgeoning Islamic faith (see selection 4). Another example of a woman who confronts her family is Fāṭima bt. al-Khaṭṭāb, who is attacked by her brother, the future caliph ʿUmar b. al-Khaṭṭāb, when he, still a pagan, finds out that she and her husband have converted to Islam and kept it a secret.

Two particularly interesting points come up in these descriptions of the foundational stages of the Muslim community. The first is women's depiction, by later Muslim historians, as tenacious agents of conversion. The second is the tension and confrontations that occurred within families who found themselves split between the new religion and the old. According to these narratives, the appearance of Islam generated a great deal of friction and hostility between the early converts and the pagans of Mecca. As a consequence, the first Muslims suffered from social sanctions and persecution and were forced to flee from Mecca so as to escape their tormentors. The best-known examples were the two waves of immigration (Ar. *hijra*) from Mecca, the first to Ethiopia in ca. 614–15 and the second and more famous to Yathrib, later known as Medina, in 1/622.

In Medina, the fate of the Muslim community quickly changed, and it evolved from a small, persecuted sect into a powerful force in Arabian politics. Two years after their arrival, the Muslims felt sure enough of themselves to confront the Jewish tribes of Medina, most of which had refused to recognize Muḥammad's standing as a prophet and to join the new faith. Muḥammad banished two of the tribes and massacred a third in one of the bloodiest and most divisive episodes in early Islamic history. Nonetheless, sources indicate that small groups of Jews did convert to Islam at this time (see selection 3). A few years later, as the Muslims were growing even more powerful, tribes began to send delegations to Muḥammad, some to forge political alliances with the Muslims and others to convert (see selection 5). These delegations reflect the importance of collective or group conversion in this phase of Islamic history, which would endure well into later periods. (For another text on group conversion, see selection 11.) At this point, the emerging Muslim community became the most powerful political and military force in all of the Arabian Peninsula.

THE RIGHTLY GUIDED CALIPHS AND THE UMAYYADS

The death of the Prophet in 11/632 brought about the first major political and spiritual crisis for the new Muslim community. The Prophet's successor in political leadership, Abū Bakr (d. 13/634), faced large-scale desertion by Arab tribes in what came to be known as the Ridda Wars, or the Wars of Apostasy. Islamic historiography presents Abū Bakr's opponents as backsliders who abandoned the Islamic faith, whereas some modern historians argue that these tribes never actually converted but simply allied themselves with the Muslim community during Muḥammad's lifetime and ceased paying taxes to his successors once he had died and the alliance had dissolved. Although the Qur'ān does not address the issue of apostasy directly, it is very likely that the Ridda Wars moved later Muslim jurists to make strong statements prohibiting apostasy. Whatever the religious identity and motives of the tribes that left the Muslim community at this time, the rebels were swiftly defeated by Abū Bakr's forces and integrated into the growing Islamic state based in Arabia.

After their unification, the Muslims became a powerful military force, and their new leader, ʿUmar b. al-Khaṭṭāb (d. 23/644), channeled their energies into conquering large swaths of territory outside of Arabia. Most of the new territory had once belonged to the two world powers of that era, the Byzantine and Sasanian Empires. Within a decade, the Muslims came to rule over millions of subjects, including large numbers of Christians, Jews, Zoroastrians, Manicheans, Buddhists, and pagans. It is from these populations that new converts began entering Islam in droves. The converts, who were generally not Arabs, came to be known as *mawālī*, meaning "clients" or "freedmen," because the process of conversion also entailed their becoming affiliate members of Arab tribes. Despite their growing numbers, the *mawālī* were treated as second-class citizens, and in the ensuing decades, their subordinate status prompted them to rebel against the Arab-dominated state. Indeed, in 132/750, a coalition of various aggrieved groups—including *mawālī*, Shiʿis, and frustrated Arabs on the periphery of the empire in Khurāsān—toppled the first Muslim dynasty, the Umayyads of Syria.

When it came to the conquered territories, the Muslims generally did not coerce their subjects to convert to Islam. In the early period, at least, the Muslims viewed themselves as a divinely sanctioned military elite, entitled to live off war booty and the tax payments of their subjects. What is more, the Qur'ān seemed to preach against forced conversion, including in the famous passage at 2:256: "There is no coercion in matters of religion" (on Qur'ānic statements about conversion, non-Muslims, and the call to convert, see selection 1). That said, the Qur'ān does encourage conversion to Islam, as many verses call on humankind to recognize the Prophet's mission and to abandon polytheism.

Despite these Qur'ānic calls to Islam, the conversion of increasing numbers of people created an economic dilemma for the ruling class. This dilemma was caused by the fact that non-Muslims paid additional taxes (known variously as the *jizya* and the *kharāj*), and when they converted, they traded these for lower taxes that were specific to Muslims. The prospect of evading the higher taxes created a strong incentive for some non-Muslims to convert. But because conversion entailed a loss in taxes, the economic base of the caliphate threatened to contract, complicating the Arabs' enthusiasm for proselytizing their subjects.

The Umayyads handled this economic crisis in a controversial manner: they simply continued to tax the *mawālī* as if they had remained non-Muslims. As a consequence, the *mawālī* continued to pay large sums of money to the state. Given this situation, it is hardly surprising that growing numbers of new Muslims became frustrated and, over time, gravitated toward rebel movements that worked to overturn this discrimination and the power of the state.

Against this background, one Umayyad ruler stood out. ʿUmar b. ʿAbd al-ʿAzīz (d. 101/720), also known as ʿUmar II, opposed the extra tax burden that was placed on the *mawālī* (see selection 12). His approach was to impose land taxes on anyone who farmed lands belonging to the Muslim community, but to extract the heavier poll tax only from non-Muslims. This policy steered a middle course between the needs of the empire's treasury and the rights of the newly converted Muslims to enjoy financial relief. ʿUmar b. ʿAbd al-ʿAzīz ruled for less than three years, and it seems that his policy did not have a strong influence on the actions of the Umayyad caliphs after him. His line of thinking, however, was later adopted by the ʿAbbasids, who developed it further.

The Arab conquests occurred in two major waves. In the first, in which the Muslims conquered the Middle East and parts of North Africa, they overcame the Byzantines and the Sasanians. In the second, they expanded to the Maghrib and the Iberian Peninsula in the west and deep into Central Asia in the east. They even did battle with the Chinese at Talas, on the border of today's Kazakhstan and Kyrgyzstan, in 133/751. But whereas the conquests were fast-paced, conversion to Islam occurred much more slowly. For the most part, the new converts were individuals who had joined the regime or moved into newly founded garrison cities (Ar. *amṣār*) such as Basra, Kufa, and Fustat. It was probably during the tenth century that large numbers of the Muslims' subjects converted to their rulers' faith. It is also around this period that we learn of individuals and groups in Africa and Asia who were not under Muslim rule but converted to Islam nonetheless.

THE ʿABBASIDS

In 132/750, approximately ninety years after the start of Umayyad rule (in ca. 41/661), the dynasty paid the price for its exclusionary policy toward non-Arab Muslims, who joined other disaffected groups to topple the regime. The central role of the *mawālī* in the ʿAbbasid revolution was not lost on the new rulers of the empire, who adopted a different policy toward converts.

The caliph who laid the foundation of the ʿAbbasid dynasty, al-Manṣūr (d. 158/775), reversed the Umayyads' discrimination against converts to such an extent that Muslim historians have described his regime as preferring *mawālī* over Arabs. The tenth-century historian and littérateur al-Masʿūdī writes of the caliph's relations with the *mawālī* in the following way: "Al-Manṣūr was the first ruler to distribute public offices among his freedmen (*mawālīhi*) and pages. He employed them in matters of importance and advanced them over the Arabs" (al-Masʿūdī, *Murūj al-dhahab*, in Paul Lunde and Caroline Stone, trans. and eds., *The Meadows of Gold: The Abbasids* [London: Kegan Paul International, 1989], 388). Judging by the individuals who were invited to al-Manṣūr's court, such as the formerly Zoroastrian astrologer al-Nawbakhtī and the formerly Buddhist family of viziers known as the Barmakids, this observation seems to reflect an actual shift. The ʿAbbasid caliphs who followed him continued his approach: al-Maʾmūn (d. 218/833), for example, invited al-Faḍl b. Sahl, a Zoroastrian convert to Islam, to join his entourage (see selection 15).

That said, not all who were invited to join the faith of the ruling elite accepted the offer. Some, like Ḥunayn b. Isḥāq, the renowned translator of Greek philosophy into Arabic, declined the invitation to embrace Islam (see selection 18).

The ʿAbbasids implemented their more inclusionary stance toward converts immediately upon coming into power, making room for them at the highest echelons of society. But a second major shift occurred sixty years later, after the fourth civil war between the half-brothers al-Amīn and al-Maʾmūn (ca. 197–204/809–13). It was at this time that the ʿAbbasids began to restructure the army, relying increasingly on Turkic soldiers from Central Asia who had been converted to Islam as part of their training. The need for a change in military policy had become clear in the course of the civil war, as the rulers of the ʿAbbasid empire realized that the Arab troops who had been living comfortably in Baghdad for two generations had lost their battlefield edge and were no longer capable of serving the empire's needs. The army's weakness threatened to become a major crisis, since effective armies are among the basic requirements of any empire, then or now. The solution adopted by the regime was to recruit slave warriors from the periphery of the ʿAbbasid state.

The Turks—a catchall appellation for various peoples of Turkic origin living to the east of the ʿAbbasid caliphate—were brought into the service of the ʿAbbasids after being captured in raids or bought from slave traders. They were often very young, knew no Arabic, and were not at all familiar with Islam. Under the ʿAbbasids, however, they were trained as soldiers, taught the language of their masters, and introduced to the basics of the Islamic faith. It seems that their conversion and acculturation were often not very successful, and as a consequence many Muslims in the ʿAbbasid heartlands looked down on them (see selection 19). Despite this slow start, within a generation or two the descendants of these slave soldiers had become full-fledged Muslims.

Although conversion to Islam may have guaranteed success for many who joined the faith, it sowed misery, regret, and consternation within the non-Muslim communities left behind by the converts. Christians living in various parts of the caliphate produced rich records of this process. For example, some of the earliest Christian witnesses to the rise of Islam in the seventh and eighth centuries deliberated about conversion and puzzled over how to explain it; so disgusted and perplexed were they that they sometimes attributed the phenomenon to demonic possession (see selection 9). Other Christians saw conversion as a thoughtless, insincere decision driven by economic and social self-interest. Indeed, one Syriac author of the early ʿAbbasid period likened swarms of Christians converting to Islam to "sheep rushing to drink water" (see selection 13). The same author later described the conversion of a deacon as an act of spiritual suicide, for the man allegedly witnessed his soul escaping through his mouth as he bent down toward Mecca in prayer. This view is not atypical of non-Muslims in this period more broadly. As Armenian sources from the same time also make clear, conversion affected all levels of society, though perhaps especially Christian elites, who had the most to lose in the new Islamic order and thus were sometimes the most tempted to apostatize (see selection 17).

In most cases, the Islamic sources are indifferent to converts' pre-Islamic beliefs, but they occasionally show flashes of interest and even sympathy for the lives that the converts have abandoned. This is the case in a series of poems in which early Muslims reminisce about the gods and practices of the *jāhiliyya*—the pre-Islamic "age of ignorance" (see selection 6). It is also the case in a unique poem of the tenth century in which a Muslim author, addressing his Christian friend, acknowledges the grief brought about by the conversion of the Christian's nephew (see selection 21). The poem is a remarkable statement of cross-confessional understanding at a moment of increasing religious change.

SOCIAL DIMENSIONS OF CONVERSION

The far-reaching demographic changes caused by conversion also generated a sophisticated legal discourse on both the Muslim and the non-Muslim sides. Somewhat more sober than the historiographic accounts mentioned above, legal texts were written to regulate relations between Muslims and non-Muslims in instances of conversion. On the whole, jurists sought ways to enable coexistence. It is evident, however, that Muslim jurists were also concerned with maintaining the superior status of Muslims. Christian legal texts of this period focus on ways of preserving communities and enabling them to persist under their Muslim rulers, while also protecting the integrity of Christian communities in the face of conversions.

One of the most socially complex and emotionally charged settings for conversion was religiously mixed families, in which parents and children found themselves practicing different religions. Islamic sources that go back to the early eighth century—that is, a century or less after the conquests—already mention dilemmas regarding relations within mixed families. For example, Muslim jurists discuss the case of a non-Muslim woman (a Christian, a Jew, or a Zoroastrian) who is the wife or concubine of a non-Muslim man and who then converts to Islam. The question that Muslim jurists sought to address is whether the couple may continue to have sexual intercourse or, indeed, remain married. The most common answer was that continued sexual relations in such situations were prohibited and that the marriage had to be dissolved (see selection 7). Once a woman converted to Islam, she could not remain with a non-Muslim man, for Islamic law views marriage as analogous to slavery, and thus a Muslim woman cannot be subordinate to an infidel man.

Another issue of concern among Muslim jurists was the motivations of converts. Legal texts reveal that many jurists were not comfortable with conversions driven by expediency. Hence, they wrote critically about converts who accepted Islam after being offered financial rewards, or even to save their lives (see selection 8). On the whole, however, the tendency among the jurists was to be inclusive and embrace all converts, even if the reasons behind their conversions were often dubious.

Whereas Muslim jurists seemed to demonstrate a winner's generosity, the subject populations showed a loser's remorse; indeed, they were concerned mainly with protecting the dwindling number of members still in their communities. Thus, whereas Muslims sought to defend those who had crossed religious lines, in particular women, communities under Muslim rule that were losing members to Islam sought to find ways to safeguard those who remained. One community whose numbers seem to have diminished with great speed and which may have formed a minority in Iran by the eleventh century was the Zoroastrians. Prior to the Islamic conquest Zoroastrianism was the official religion of the Sasanian Empire, but Islamic rule changed its status dramatically. We learn about the concerns of the Zoroastrians who continued to cling to their faith from their legal writings, which, like Jewish, Christian, and Islamic legal texts, were structured around questions and answers. In particular, many of these questions touched on the challenges of living alongside Muslims in everyday settings.

Like Muslim jurists, Zoroastrian priests also focused on the difficulties posed by mixed families (see selection 20). How, for example, could a woman whose whole family had converted to Islam be married when it was expected that a Zoroastrian male relative would serve as her guardian and thus help arrange her marriage? How should inheritances be divided? How might converts who wished to return to Zoroastrianism be reintegrated into the fold?

Mixed families caused by interreligious marriage or the conversion of a spouse posed a threat to Christian communities, too (see selection 10). Accordingly, the issue appears in Christian legal responsa along with other matters that revolve around social interactions with Muslims, including the sharing of food and schools. And like writers from other religions, Christian authors worried about what to do with converts to Islam who subsequently decided to return to their original faith.

Conversion to Islam reconfigured all the societies that had been conquered by Muslims over the course of the seventh and eighth centuries. The changes that conversion brought about and, more importantly, the diverse ways in which contemporaries reacted to it are reflected in the texts translated in this sourcebook. Thus, one of the most interesting aspects of these texts is their reflection of the emotions of both the victors and the vanquished.

1

Conversion in the Qur'ān

The Qur'ān

Abdullah Saeed

Language: Arabic

INTRODUCTION

The issue of conversion to Islam in the Qur'ān is not an easy topic to address. There are many reasons for this. The most important is that the Qur'ān does not explicitly say what conversion is, how it should take place, and whether there are particular rituals that ought to be performed. Because of this ambiguity, we must explore this topic by looking at a range of issues that the Qur'ān does deal with and how they may be connected to the notion of conversion.

The Qur'ān calls on the Meccans to whom the Prophet was sent to recognize the One God, the Creator and the Sustainer; to move away from their polytheistic beliefs and the worship of multiple gods; to accept the prophethood of Muḥammad; and to believe in the messages of God. The Prophet, Muḥammad, is presented as a warner to his people in Mecca.

The Qur'ān provides a number of pointers to help the Meccans to recognize the One God. These are communicated primarily through creation: the sun, the moon, the earth, the heavens, other human beings, and the like. This simple recognition of God was, perhaps, what was initially expected as a kind of conversion. Later, other expectations were added to it, as the notion of what constituted a believer evolved. Over time, the distinction between believers in God and the Prophet Muḥammad, on the one hand, and "nonbelievers," on the other, gradually became starker.

By the time the Prophet migrated to Medina in 622 CE, there was a clear sense of who belonged to the "believers." Believers were now also expected to make the sacrifice of emigration to Medina (the *hijra*) as a mark of their membership in the believing community. In Medina, a strong sense of a distinct community of believers emerged, separate from the monotheistic Jews of the town as well as from the polytheists of Mecca and, later, also from Christians.

In the late Medinan period it is evident that the Qurʾān's mood toward nonbelievers changed significantly. The Qurʾān's tone became stronger and harsher when addressing or referring to the nonbelievers, who now included polytheists as well as those monotheists (local Jews and Christians) who violently opposed the Prophet. A significant political dimension was also added to the understanding of submission to God: a believer must recognize not just the One God, the Prophet, and the scripture but also the rising power of the believing community of Muslims. Those who were not prepared to accept the Muslim polity headed by the Prophet or to live in peace with it, and who instead chose to fight it, were to be subdued and brought under the Muslim state's control. Still, conversion by coercion was not considered an option, given the view that belief cannot be coerced. Accordingly, the Qurʾān rejects conversion by force.

A number of other ideas in the Qurʾān are also associated with conversion.

From the Qurʾān's point of view, every human being comes into this world in the original state of *fiṭra* (natural disposition). In this state, everyone and everything submits to God. Thus, God's message, conveyed through the Prophet, is a way of bringing human beings back to their original state of submission to God. A key aspect of this "bringing back" is the influence of God's guidance (*hudā*). It is only God who can guide people, and He guides whomever He wills and leads astray whomever He wills. Even the Prophet does not have this power. God sends His prophets to invite (*daʿwa*) people to the way of God. The invitee is free to either accept or reject this call.

Human beings are expected to reject the status they had before they received God's guidance. This rejection involves repentance (*tawba*) for old beliefs, deeds, and attitudes that were antithetical to belief in the One God. Through repentance, a person converts or returns to his or her original status at the moment of creation. If human beings do not return to this original status, severe punishment awaits them. By contrast, those who accept the invitation to reclaim their original status earn God's favor and blessings in the life to come. Conversion is thus connected to a person's ultimate success or failure, both in this world and in the next.

Note: In translating the Qur'ānic verses I have benefited from the translations by Marmaduke Pickthall, Muhammad Asad, Arthur J. Arberry, and M. A. S. Abdel Haleem.

TEXTS

[Faith does not come from compulsion]

There is no coercion in matters of faith. (2:256)

Say [O Muḥammad]: "O humankind! I am only a warner [sent by God] to you." (22:49)

We have sent you [Muḥammad] with the truth as a bearer of glad tidings and a warner. (2:119)

[People have chosen to reject the One God]

Have you considered [the false deities] al-Lāt and al-ʿUzzā and Manāt, the third, the other? Why—for yourselves [you would choose only] male offspring, whereas to Him [you assign] female. That, then, would indeed be an unfair division! These [false deities] are nothing but empty names which you have invented, you and your forefathers. God has not revealed any warrant for them. (53:19–23)

And the Jews say, "Ezra is the son of God," and the Christians say, "The Messiah is the son of God." That is their saying with their mouths. They imitate what the unbelievers of earlier times used to say. (9:30)

[God guides people back to Him]

And [know that] God summons to the abode of peace, and brings whom He wills to a straight path. (10:25)

[God restores humankind to their original state so they can know and worship Him]

So direct your face toward the [true] faith, turning away from all that is false, in accordance with the natural disposition (*fiṭra*) which God has instilled into human beings. There should be no change in the creation of God. That is the correct faith, but most people do not know. (30:30)

And [tell them that] I did not create the *jinn* [invisible beings] and the human beings except for the purpose that they should [know and] worship Me [God]. (51:56)

Have they not seen how God creates [life] in the first instance, and then restores it? Surely that is easy for God. Say: "Go all over the earth and observe how He [God] originated creation. Then God will bring into being your second life. Truly God has power over all things." (29:19–20)

[True religion is islām (self-surrender)]

For if one seeks a religion other than *islām* [self-surrender to God], it will never be accepted from him, and in the Hereafter he shall be among the lost. (3:85)

So if they dispute with you [O Prophet], say, "I have submitted myself to God, and [so have] all who follow me." And say to those who have been given scripture and to the unlettered people, "Have you [too] submitted [to God]?" And if they submit to Him, they are rightly guided; but if they turn away, your duty is only to deliver the message: for God sees all that is in [the hearts of] His creatures. (3:20)

Today, those who disbelieve have despaired of [defeating] your religion; so do not hold them in awe, but stand in awe of Me! Today I have perfected your religion for you and bestowed upon you the full measure of My blessings, and have chosen for you as religion *islām* [self-surrender to God]. (5:3)

[True faith requires commitment and sacrifice]

Truly those who believed and emigrated [to Medina] and strove with their wealth and their lives for the cause of God, and those who provided refuge and assisted—they are the allies [and friends] of one another. And those who believed but did not emigrate, you have no duty to protect them until they emigrate. (8:72)

[Some ways in which believers distinguish themselves]

Forbidden to you [for food] are dead meat, blood, the flesh of swine, and that which has been dedicated to [deities] other than God, and the animal that has been strangled, or beaten to death, or killed by a fall, or gored to death, and those from which a wild animal has eaten, except what you [are able to] slaughter [before its death]; and [forbidden to you is] all that has been slaughtered on idolatrous altars. And [you are forbidden] to seek to learn through divination what the future may hold in store for you. This is sinful conduct. (5:3)

[The opponents of the believers are to submit to Muslim authority, not to convert]

[And] fight against those who do not [truly] believe in God nor in the Last Day, and who do not forbid what God and His Messenger have forbidden, nor do they follow the religion of truth [as God has commanded them to] from amongst those who were given the scripture, until they pay the *jizya* [tax] readily, being subdued. (9:29)

FURTHER READING

Bulliet, Richard W. *Conversion to Islam in the Medieval Period* (Cambridge, MA: Harvard University Press, 1979).

Levtzion, Nehemia, ed. *Conversion to Islam* (New York: Holmes and Meier, 1997).

Watt, W. Montgomery. "Conversion in Islam at the Time of the Prophet," *Journal of the American Academy of Religion* 47, special issue (1979): 721–31.

2

The Conversion of Khadīja bt. Khuwaylid

Muḥammad b. Isḥāq (d. 150/767)

Sean W. Anthony

Title: *Kitāb al-Maghāzī* (The book of expeditions)
Genre: Didactic and entertaining literature (literary biography)
Language: Arabic

INTRODUCTION

The cultural memory of the early Muslim community accords a special place to Khadīja bt. Khuwaylid, Muḥammad's first wife and the first person to believe in his prophethood. Before her marriage to Muḥammad, Khadīja was reputedly a widow and a wealthy merchant of Mecca. She would hire trustworthy men to undertake trade journeys on her behalf, and it was after she employed Muḥammad as one such hired hand that he first caught her attention. Their marriage followed soon thereafter.

The story of Khadīja's conversion takes place after their marriage. Muḥammad's realization of his prophethood and Khadīja's conversion are uniquely and inextricably intertwined in the earliest narratives. Khadīja not only believes in his message; she also interprets and vets Muḥammad's first revelatory experiences, employing several clever strategies to do so. She ranks, therefore, as the first convert to Islam, but she is also more. Khadīja acts as Muḥammad's counselor and consoler, convincing Muḥammad of the veracity of his experience and sustaining him in his distress.

The following account of Khadīja's conversion derives from the *Kitāb al-Maghāzī* (The book of expeditions) of Muḥammad b. Isḥāq (d. 150/767). The account, like Ibn Isḥāq's book in general, does not survive in a single version; rather, it survives in numerous versions preserved through his students. Three of these students are best known to scholars: Ziyād al-Bakkāʾī (d. 183/799) and Yūnus b. Bukayr (d. 199/815), who studied under Ibn Isḥāq in Kufa in southern Iraq, and Salama b. al-Faḍl (d. after 190/805), who studied under Ibn Isḥāq in Rayy in northern Iran. Hence, the most famous version of this story appears in the *Sīrat Rasūl Allāh* (The life of the Messenger of God) of Ibn Hishām (d. 218/834), who learned the *Kitāb al-Maghāzī* from Ibn Isḥāq's student Ziyād al-Bakkāʾī. Because Ibn Hishām notoriously abridged and edited Ibn Isḥāq's earlier accounts, I have chosen to translate below a longer version of Ziyād al-Bakkāʾī's transmission of Ibn Isḥāq's story of Khadīja's conversion found outside Ibn Hishām's *Sīra*. After Ziyād's version, I have included two stories about Khadīja's conversion found in the transmission of another student of Ibn Isḥāq, Yūnus b. Bukayr, preserved in a unique manuscript in the library of the famed Qarawiyyīn Mosque in Fez, Morocco.

TEXTS

(1) From Ziyād al-Bakkāʾī's recension (as preserved in Ibn ʿAsākir, Dimashq, *63:12–14)*

Ibn Isḥāq said: Wahb b. Kaysān, a freedman of the house of al-Zubayr, related the following story to me. Wahb said: I overheard ʿAbd Allāh b. al-Zubayr say to ʿUbayd b. ʿUmayr b. Qatāda al-Laythī, "ʿUbayd, tell the story of when Gabriel came to the Messenger of God and how the beginning of his call to prophethood came about!" Now, I was present to hear the story told to ʿAbd Allāh b. al-Zubayr and among those persons present at his court. ʿUbayd answered:

Every year the Prophet used to spend a month in seclusion at Mount Ḥirāʾ. Such was the sort of *taḥannuth* practiced by Quraysh in the era of barbarism before Islam—*taḥannuth* means pious devotion. The Messenger of God would enter into seclusion during that month of each year while feeding the destitute who came to him.

When he had completed his time in seclusion for that specified month, the first thing he would do before going home once he left his seclusion was to head for the Kaʿba, which he would circumambulate seven times (or however many times God so willed). After that, he would return to his home.

Eventually there came the month of that year in which God desired to exalt him and to send him forth. That month was the month of Ramaḍān. The Messenger of God set out for Ḥirāʾ as he was accustomed to do during the time of his seclusion, and his family came along with him. When the night came that God exalted him to become His Messenger and thus showed mercy to His servants, Gabriel came to him with God's command.

The Messenger of God said:

He came to me while I slept, bringing a sheet of silken brocade upon which was a piece of writing (*kitāb*). He said, "Read!" "I cannot read!" I said. Then he pressed against me, and I thought I was dying. He released me and said, "Read!" "I cannot read!" I said. Then he pressed against me, and I thought I was dying. He said, "Read!" I said, "What shall I read?" but I only said this to be rid of him lest he do to me once again what he did before. He then said, "Read in the name of your Lord who did create / created Humanity from coagulate / Read for your Lord is Magnanimous / Who, through the use of the calamus / Has taught Humanity of that which it was ignorant" [Q. 96:1–5]. I read it—all of it—and then he finished and withdrew from me. I woke up from my dream, but it was as though a book (*kitāb*) had been inscribed upon my heart.

Now, of all God's creation nothing was more loathsome to me than a poet or a man inspired by *jinn* (*shāʿir aw majnūn*). I said, "Far be it from me to be a poet or a man inspired by *jinn*! Quraysh will never say this about me! I shall head for the peak of the mountain and cast myself down, end my life, and be spared of this!" I set out with the full intention of doing so, but when I reached the middle of the mountain suddenly I heard a voice cry out from the sky and say, "Muḥammad! You are the Messenger of God, and I am Gabriel." I raised my head to look toward the sky, and there before me stood Gabriel in the form of a man with his legs astride the horizon of the sky, saying, "Muḥammad! You are the Messenger of God, and I am Gabriel." I stood there looking, too overwhelmed to do what I had intended. I could not take a step forward or backward. I began to turn my head toward another part of the horizon, but whichever direction I looked I found him there. I remained standing there, taking not a single step forward or a single step backward, until at last Khadīja sent her servants to track me down. They reached Mecca and then returned to her, but I remained standing transfixed. Gabriel withdrew from me, and only then did I leave and return to see Khadīja.

I sat next to her, leaning against her lap, and she said, "Abū al-Qāsim, where have you been? I had sent my servants to track you down, even to Mecca!"

"Far be it from me to be a poet or man inspired by *jinn*!" I said.

"God preserve you, Abū al-Qāsim!" she replied. "God would never allow anything but good to befall you, for I know you are a man who only speaks the truth, whose word is his bond, whose morals are upright, and who honors bonds of kinship. What is it, my cousin? Perhaps you saw something?"

"Yes," I said to her, and I told her the story of what I saw. She said, "My cousin, rejoice and remain steadfast! By Him in whose hand Khadīja's soul resides, I hope that you will be the prophet of this people (*umma*)!"

She then wrapped herself in her outer garment and set out to see Waraqa b. Nawfal b. Asad, who was her cousin. Waraqa had become a Christian. He read the scriptures (*al-kutub*) and studied under the scholars of the Books of Moses and of the Gospel (*samiʿa min ahl al-tawrāt wa-ahl al-injīl*). She told him the story of what the Messenger of God had seen and heard just as he had related it to her.

Waraqa exclaimed, "Holy! Holy! By Him in whose hand my soul resides, if you have told me the truth, Khadīja, then he is a prophet! Let him be steadfast!"

Khadīja returned to the Messenger of God and gave him the news of what Waraqa had said. The matter became easier for him and removed his worries about what had happened to him. When he completed the time of his seclusion at Ḥirāʾ, he acted as he usually would, and he started for the Kaʿba and circumambulated it. Waraqa b. Nawfal met him while circumambulating the Kaʿba and said, "Dear nephew, tell me what you have seen." The Messenger of God told him the story, and Waraqa replied, "By Him in whose hand my soul resides, you are the prophet of this people (*umma*)! The Great Law (*al-nāmūs al-akbar*) that came to Moses now comes to you! They will call him a liar, persecute him, banish him, and make war against him, but if I live to see the day, I will surely aid God in a manner known to Him" Then Waraqa brought his face close to his and kissed him on the brow. The Messenger of God subsequently departed, and the words of Waraqa greatly reassured him and dispelled much of the anxiety in his heart.

(2) Yūnus b. Bukayr (al-Siyar wa-l-Maghāzī, *124, 132–34*)

Ibn Isḥāq said: ʿAbd Allāh b. Abī Bakr related to us on the authority of Abū Jaʿfar, who said:

In Mecca, the Messenger of God had been stricken by the evil eye (*al-ʿayn*), which had come upon him suddenly before the revelation descended upon him. Khadīja bt. Khuwaylid used to send after an old crone who would cure him [of the evil eye] with charms. When the Qurʾān was revealed to him, he was stricken with the evil eye as he had been before, and Khadīja said to him, "Messenger of God, shall I send for that old crone so that she can cure you with her charms?" "Not anymore," he replied.

[. . .]

Ibn Isḥāq said:

Khadīja was the first to have faith in God and His Messenger and to believe in what he brought forth. Thus did God ease the Messenger of God's burden. Whenever he heard a hateful reply or a denunciation of his message that grieved him, God provided him succor through her. When he came to her, she strengthened him and eased his burden. She testified to the truth of his message and held no regard for what the people said against him, may God show her mercy.

[. . .]

Ibn Isḥāq said: Ismāʿīl b. Abī Ḥakīm, the freedman of [the family of] al-Zubayr, related to me that he was told the following story about Khadīja bt. Khuwaylid:

Among the things she said to the Messenger of God to strengthen his resolve regarding how God had honored him with prophecy was, "Dear cousin, can you tell me when this companion of yours who appeared to you arrives?" "Yes," he agreed. "When he comes, then," she said, "let me know."

While the Messenger of God was with her one day, Gabriel suddenly came, and the Messenger of God saw him. "Khadīja," he said, "this is Gabriel who has come to me!"

"Do you see him now?" she asked.

"Yes!" he said.

"Sit to my left side!" she said, and he sat down. Then she asked, "Do you see him now?"

"Yes!" he said.

"Now sit to my right side," she said, and he went to the other side and sat down. She asked again, "Do you see him now?"

"Yes!" he said.

"Move again and sit in my lap," she said. The Messenger of God moved and sat down, and she said, "Do you see him now?"

"Yes!" he said.

Then she uncovered her hair and cast aside her veil as the Messenger of God remained seated on her lap. "Do you see him now?" she asked.

"No!" he said.

"This is not the Devil," she said. "He is certainly an angel, dear cousin. Be strong and rejoice!" Then she believed in him and testified that he brought the Truth.

Ibn Isḥāq said: I related this story to ʿAbd Allāh b. Ḥasan, and he said, "I heard [my mother] Fāṭima bt. al-Ḥusayn tell this story from Khadīja, except I heard her say, 'She placed the Messenger of God inside her chemise (*dirʿ*), and at that moment Gabriel departed.'"

FURTHER READING

Ali, Kecia. *Lives of Muḥammad* (Cambridge, MA: Harvard University Press, 2014), 114–54.

Kister, Meir J. "The Sons of Khadīja," *Jerusalem Studies in Arabic and Islam* 16 (1993): 59–95.

Schoeler, Gregor. *The Biography of Muḥammad: Nature and Authenticity*, trans. Uwe Vagelpohl, ed. James E. Montgomery (London: Routledge, 2011), 38–79.

3

On Three Jewish Converts to Islam from the Banū Qurayẓa

Ibn Hishām (d. ca. 218/833)

Michael Lecker

Title: *al-Sīra al-Nabawiyya* (The life of the Prophet)
Genre: Didactic and entertaining literature (literary biography)
Language: Arabic

INTRODUCTION

The following text is found in the most popular medieval biography of the Prophet Muḥammad, compiled in the first half of the ninth century by Ibn Hishām. It is an abridged version of a biography compiled several decades earlier by Ibn Isḥāq (d. ca. 151/768). Ibn Isḥāq had a wide range of interests, and he collected accounts wherever he could find them. His interest in *mathālib* or "vices" (usually such that were related to genealogy) antagonized many in his hometown, Medina, in addition to the Umayyad governor himself. When the ʿAbbasids came to power, Ibn Isḥāq became one of the court's favorite intellectuals. Ibn Hishām, on the other hand, was a grammarian. According to his own testimony, he left out, inter alia, "matters that either are disgraceful to talk about or may distress certain people." His self-censorship created a more palatable text and probably helped to make the epitome a bestseller. In recent years it has become even more significant as new movements seek in it inspiration for present-day situations: the fate of the Qurayẓa women, for example, is referenced in discussions of ISIS-captured Yazīdī women in the mid-2010s.

The following text purports to be the unedited record of a conversation between an old man from the Jewish tribe of Qurayẓa and an informant of Ibn Isḥāq who was the grandson of one of Muḥammad's companions. Ibn Isḥāq's origin may be relevant for us here: his Jewish grandfather was captured in Iraq at the very beginning of the Islamic conquests. Two main themes are discernible in the text. The first is the topos of "proofs of the veracity of Muḥammad's prophethood" (*dalā'il al-nubuwwa*): the Jewish saint who appears in the text foretold the imminent appearance of the Arabian prophet. The Jews failed to follow his command (and later denied that Muḥammad was the foretold prophet), and paid with their lives. The second is the survival of the three men who "saw the light" and saved themselves, their families, and their orchards. Their survival was a by-product of their conversion, not the incentive for it.

However, a totally different scenario is suggested by a record in an unpublished manuscript on "vices" (*mathālib*). Muḥammad's tribe, Quraysh, considered marriage outside of the tribe a "vice," and the manuscript in question has a list of Qurashī women who married non-Qurashī husbands. Two of the three men named in the following text were married to two sisters, ʿĀtika and Sukhayla, who were Muḥammad's third cousins ("ʿĀtika and Sukhayla were, respectively, married to Thaʿlaba and Asīd, sons of Saʿya from the Qurayẓa"). No date is given, but if we are to choose between a last-minute conversion and earlier marriage bonds as an explanation for the men's survival, the latter should be given priority. Put differently, the choice is between a widespread polemical story with a moral and a rather embarrassing genealogical detail tucked away in a book on "vices."

TEXT

Ibn Isḥāq said: ʿĀṣim b. ʿUmar b. Qatāda transmitted to me on the authority of an old man from the Banū Qurayẓa what follows. He [the old man, turning to ʿĀṣim,] said: "Do you know the reason for the conversion to Islam of Thaʿlaba b. Saʿya, [his brother] Asīd b. Saʿya, and Asad b. ʿUbayd ([a scribe adds:] a group from the Banū Hadl, the brothers of the Qurayẓa who had been their clients in the *jāhiliyya* [i.e., the three men had been clients of the Qurayẓa] and then became their lords under Islam [*kānū maʿahum fī jāhiliyyatihim thumma kānū sādatahum fī l-islām*])?" I [ʿĀṣim] said, "No." He said: "A Jew from Palestine (Shām) called Ibn al-Hayyabān came to us several years before the advent of Islam and dwelt among us. We have never seen a non-Muslim [literally, one who does not pray the five daily prayers; anachronistic as a reference to a person who died before Islam] better than him. He stayed with us. At the time of drought we used to say to him: 'Go out [with us], Ibn al-Hayyabān, and pray for rain.' He said: 'Not unless you give alms before you go out.' We would say to him: 'How much?' And he would say: 'One *ṣāʿ* [ca. 2.5 liters] of dates or two *mudds* [ca. 1.3 liters] of barley.' We would duly grant them, and then he would lead us to the outward side of our *ḥarra* [stony volcanic tract] and pray for rain on our behalf. By Allah, hardly had he left his place when a cloud passed and it rained. He did it more than once or twice or thrice. When he was about to die among us, he said: 'O Jews, what do you think made me leave a land of wine and bread and come to a land of hardship and hunger?' We said: 'You know better.' He said: 'I only came to this town expecting the emergence of a prophet whose time was at hand. This town is where he will migrate, and I was hoping that he would be sent [in my time], so that I would follow him. His time is at hand; do not let anyone get to him before you, O Jews. Indeed, he will be sent to shed blood and to take captive the women and children of those who oppose him. Let that not keep you back from him.'

"When the Messenger of Allah was sent and [in due course] besieged the Qurayẓa, those young men (*fitya*)—they [the old man is probably referring to himself and to other survivors from the Qurayẓa who witnessed the event] were youths—said: 'O Banū Qurayẓa, by Allah, this is the prophet whom Ibn al-Hayyabān commanded you [to follow].' They [the Qurayẓa] said: 'He is not.' They [the three men] said: 'Of course he is. By Allah, it is him, according to his description (*bi-ṣifatihi*).' So they came down [from the besieged fortress of the Qurayẓa], converted to Islam, and saved their lives, their orchards, and their families (*wa-aḥrazū dimāʾahum wa-amwālahum wa-ahlīhim*)."

FURTHER READING

Lecker, Michael. "Biographical Notes on Abū ʿUbayda Maʿmar b. al-Muthannā," *Studia Islamica* 81 (1995): 71–100.

———. "Ibn Isḥāq (*Sīra*)," in *Encyclopaedia of Islam*, 3rd ed.

———. "Were There Female Relatives of the Prophet Muḥammad among the Besieged Qurayẓa?," *Journal of the American Oriental Society* 136 (2016): 397–404.

Pellat, Charles. "Mat͟hālib," in *Encyclopaedia of Islam*, 2nd ed.

4

Women Converts and Familial Loyalty in the Time of the Prophet

Muḥammad b. Saʿd (d. 230/845)

Keren Abbou Hershkovits

Title: *Kitāb al-Ṭabaqāt al-Kabīr* (The great book of generations)
Genre: Historical writing
Language: Arabic

INTRODUCTION

Ibn Saʿd's biographical dictionary, *The Great Book of Generations* (*Kitāb al-Ṭabaqāt al-Kabīr*), is dedicated to outstanding Muslim personalities, primarily from the first two generations of Islam. It comprises ten volumes, the last of which is concerned solely with women (600 women are represented in the work's total of 4,250 biographies). Ibn Saʿd's biographical dictionary is one of the richest sources on women's lives in the Islamic Middle Ages. Thanks to this work, we can learn about the contributions that women made to the Muslim community in its earliest stages.

Several women were among the first converts to Islam. Some of them are anonymous or mentioned by name only, whereas others are discussed in some detail. Some chroniclers do not include women in their accounts of early converts. Hence, our information on female converts is patchy, and we do not know their actual numbers. However, the female conversion stories that do survive are fascinating and typically provide details on the person who converted as well as her surroundings. Such stories may serve as a platform for the study of power relations in the nascent Islamic community, and they may help us further understand the practice of conversion in early Islam and the social implications of this step.

Let us examine the conversion story of Muḥammad's paternal aunt Arwā bt. ʿAbd al-Muṭṭalib b. Hāshim and its aftermath. Arwā probably converted around 615 CE after a conversation with her son (who had himself converted to Islam in the house of al-Arqam, a meeting place for early Muslims), but she went public only after a talk with her half-brother Abū Lahab. In this conversation, she encouraged Abū Lahab to join Muḥammad, his nephew. Arwā's argument was that should Muḥammad win, Abū Lahab could join the new religion. However, should Muḥammad lose, Abū Lahab could always rescind his conversion and say that he was only doing his duty as an uncle by helping out his nephew.

Arwā's conversion brings up two crucial points. The first concerns the strong social framing of the conversion of Muḥammad's relatives. Whereas Ḥamza was the only one of the Prophet's uncles to convert to Islam, among his aunts there were several converts. It is very likely that two of Arwā's sisters also converted, as Ibn Saʿd mentions acts of devotion on their part. The status of other women in Muḥammad's family, such as Barra, Umayma, and Umm Ḥakīm (Muḥammad's paternal aunts), is less clear, although the biographical details imply that they lived among Muslims and indeed might have converted to Islam. It should be noted that this information must be deduced from the social context, since very little is explained to the reader.

By contrast, Arwā explicitly sets out her perception of conversion, which is one of strategic social ties. Thus, it is to family loyalty that she refers when she speaks to her son about his conversion: "It is most fitting that you help and support your uncle." Her conversation with Abū Lahab is similarly framed in social and political terms. Theological considerations hardly figure in these conversations or in her biography.

A second point of interest concerns her striking assertiveness. Arwā is shown assisting her nephew in the face of her fierce half-brother. Arwā's is not the only case of a woman who converted against her family's wishes. Another example is Fāṭima, ʿUmar b. al-Khaṭṭāb's sister (Ibn Saʿd, 3:248). Fāṭima converted even though her brother ʿUmar was one of Muḥammad's greatest opponents in the early years of Islam.

Yet another interesting female convert is Umm Kulthūm bt. ʿUqba b. Abī Muʿayṭ, who is mentioned as the first person to leave Mecca and follow Muḥammad to Medina. Her case is of particular interest because her brothers subsequently asked Muḥammad to respect the treaty of Ḥudaybiyya and send her back to Mecca. However, Umm Kulthūm approached Muḥammad and pleaded with him not to do so: "O Messenger of God, I am but a woman, and women are weak. Should you send me back to the infidels, they will lead me astray, as I have no ability to endure pain" (Ibn Saʿd, 10:219). Muḥammad agreed to let her stay, informing the community that he had received a revelation that excluded women from the treaty.

These cases illustrate an interesting phenomenon: the early converts included women who converted without their families and at times against their families' wishes. Some of them faced danger, while others received help from Muḥammad and members of the Muslim community. On the whole, the Muslim tradition depicts them as displaying impressive independence of mind.

TEXT

Arwā bt. ʿAbd al-Muṭṭalib b. Hāshim

Her mother was Fāṭima bt. ʿAmr b. ʿĀʾidh of Makhzūm. In the *jāhiliyya* she married ʿUmayr b. Wahb b. ʿAbd Manāf. She bore him Ṭulayb. Then, after him, she married Arṭā b. Shuraḥbīl b. Hāshim and bore him Fāṭima. Then Arwā became Muslim in Mecca and emigrated to Medina.

Muḥammad b. Ibrāhīm b. al-Ḥārith al-Taymī said, "Ṭulayb b. ʿUmayr became Muslim in the house of al-Arqam b. Abī al-Arqam al-Makhzūmī. Then he left and went to his mother, Arwā bt. ʿAbd al-Muṭṭalib. He said, 'I have pledged allegiance to Muḥammad and submitted to God.' His mother said to him, 'It is most fitting that you help and support your uncle. By God, if we were able to do what the men do, we would follow him and defend him.' Ṭulayb said, 'And what prevents you, mother, from becoming Muslim and following him? Your brother Ḥamza has become Muslim.' Then she said, 'I will see what my sisters are doing and then I will be one of them.' Ṭulayb said, 'I ask you, by God, won't you come and submit to him and believe him and testify that there is no god but God and that Muḥammad is the Messenger of God?' Then she supported the Prophet with her tongue and encouraged her son to help him and support him."

Barra bt. Abī Tajra said, "Abū Jahl and a number of unbelievers of Quraysh accosted the Prophet and injured him, and Ṭulayb b. ʿUmayr went to Abū Jahl and dealt him a blow which exposed his skull. They seized him and put him in chains. Abū Lahab had him released. Arwā was asked, 'Do you see that your son Ṭulayb has made himself a target instead of Muḥammad?' She said, 'The best of his days are the days in which he defends the son of his uncle. He has brought the truth from God.' They said, 'And do you follow Muḥammad?' She said, 'Yes.' Some of them went to Abū Lahab and told him, and he went to visit her. He said, 'I am astonished at you that you follow Muḥammad and abandon the religion of ʿAbd al-Muṭṭalib.' She said, 'That is the case. Take the side of your cousin and support him and defend him. If he is victorious, you will have the choice of either joining him or keeping your religion. If he fails, you will have an excuse, as he is your cousin.' Abū Lahab said, 'Do you think that we have power over all the Arabs? He has brought a new religion.' Then Abū Lahab left."

Other people besides Muḥammad b. ʿUmar mentioned that Arwā said on that day, "Ṭulayb has helped his cousin. I exhort him to be steadfast in life and property."

FURTHER READING

Bulliet, Richard W. "Conversion Stories in Early Islam," in *Conversion and Continuity: Indigenous Christian Communities in Islamic Lands, Eighth to Eighteenth Centuries*, ed. Michael Gervers and Ramzi Jibran Bikhazi (Toronto: Pontifical Institute of Mediaeval Studies, 1990), 123–33.

El Cheikh, Nadia Maria. *Women, Islam, and Abbasid Identity* (Cambridge, MA: Harvard University Press, 2015).

Simonsohn, Uriel. "Conversion to Islam: A Case Study for the Use of Legal Sources," *History Compass* 11, no. 8 (2013): 647–62.

5

Reports on Tribal Delegations to the Prophet

Muḥammad b. Sa'd (d. 230/845)

Ella Landau-Tasseron

Title: *Kitāb al-Ṭabaqāt al-Kabīr* (The great book of generations)
Genre: Historial writing
Language: Arabic

INTRODUCTION

Muḥammad b. Sa'd was a non-Arab Muslim historian, resident of Baghdad, and secretary to the also famous historian al-Wāqidī. Ibn Sa'd focused on biographies of transmitters of the Prophet's words and deeds. His *Kitāb al-ṭabaqāt al-kabīr* became a repository of information about thousands of the Prophet's companions (*ṣaḥāba*) and their successors (*tābi'ūn*), classified according to regions and generations. In time, the *ṭabaqāt* literature came to comprise biographies of transmitters, poets, exegetes, linguists, mystics, jurists, and physicians.

The first part of Ibn Sa'd's *Ṭabaqāt* is dedicated to the biography of the Prophet (*sīra*, a disparate literary genre focusing on the events of the Prophet's life). One part of this includes reports of delegations that came to see him (*dhikr wifādāt al-'arab 'alā rasūl allāh*). Two types of narratives may be discerned in these reports: (1) visits of individuals or small groups of close relatives, and (2) delegations representing tribal groups, mostly in the year following the conquest of Mecca (8/630), also known as the "Year of the Delegations" (*'ām al-wufūd*).

Thus, conversion—here construed as the act of joining Muḥammad's community—was sometimes done on an individual basis, at other times in groups. Sometimes it was done under military threat, sometimes in response to a letter or missionaries sent by the Prophet. Delegates came to the Prophet to negotiate or to announce or promise the conversion of their group. The numbers of visitors are not known beyond formulaic figures (e.g., four hundred men); the actual numbers could be much smaller, since even splinter tribal groups were in the habit of acting independently in political matters. As a rule, no ceremony is mentioned except for the phrase "they gave allegiance (*bay'a*)," on their own behalf and often on behalf of their tribal groups.

Themes featured in delegation reports include manifestations of the Prophet's special powers; promises of security (*amān*) by the Prophet, or other political arrangements; gifts, appointments, assignments of land, or other documents given by Muḥammad; instructions about Islam; changes of pagan personal names to Islamic ones; changes of un-Islamic habits in matters such as clothes or modes of greeting; and destruction of pagan deities by the converts when they returned home. In the few reports about Jews and Christians, polemical themes are also included.

The following reports concern (1) the delegation of Banū 'Abd b. 'Adiyy, a splinter group of the Kināna tribe, which lived in the vicinity of Mecca; (2) the delegation of Fazāra, a powerful tribal group from Najd, which was, strangely, headed not by the main Fazārī leader of the time, 'Uyayna b. Ḥiṣn, but by his brother, Khārija; and (3) the delegation of Ju'fiyy, a part of the powerful Yemeni tribe of Madhḥij.

The Ju'fiyy report includes two disparate stories, one about delegates and the other about an individual visit. The latter is a typical visit report, whereas the former has some singular elements. First, the Prophet makes the delegates break a tribal taboo. Second, the report raises the issue of the destiny of virtuous pre-Islamic ancestors, which rarely features in delegation reports. The virtuous one in this story is the deceased mother of the delegates, which is remarkable for two reasons: first, pre-Islamic (*jāhilī*) tribesmen usually took pride in their fathers' accomplishments, not in those of their mothers, secondly, the pagan mother's virtues correspond to good deeds recommended by Islam: setting prisoners free, feeding the poor, and having compassion for the unfortunate. Such a description of a *jāhilī* woman contradicts the stereotypic Islamic view of the *jāhiliyya* as a time of barbarism, lawlessness, cruelty, and selfishness. Nevertheless, many pre-Islamic values, such as solidarity among family members, were Islamized. This virtuous woman, however, had committed one unforgivable sin: she had buried alive a baby daughter. This *jāhilī* custom epitomizes all that was evil in that period.

The Prophet's position is unequivocal: both she and the baby will end up in hell. He emphasizes that his own mother will be there, too, since she was pagan when she died. This declaration makes the delegates renege on their conversion, an unusual element in delegation stories. The Prophet's position here is also unusual. Islamic tradition regards the Prophet's parents as residents of heaven even though they died as pagans (a source of ongoing controversy, as witnessed by the death sentence issued in the case of a Pakistani Muslim in 2001 for doubting that Muḥammad's parents had died as Muslims; see Yohanan Friedmann, *Prophecy Continuous* [Oxford: Oxford University Press, 2003], xv).

On the whole, the delegation reports should not be taken as reflecting what really happened.

TEXTS

(1) The delegation of Banū ʿAbd b. ʿAdiyy

[The narrators] reported: The delegation of Banū ʿAbd b. ʿAdiyy came to see the Prophet. Among its members were al-Ḥārith b. Uhbān, ʿUwaymir b. al-Akhzam, Ḥabīb and Rabīʿa, sons of Mulla, and a few others of their tribal group. They said, "O Muḥammad, we are people of the sacred territory, where we live; we are the strongest group around, but we do not want to fight you. If you fight tribes except the Quraysh, we will fight at your side, but we shall not fight the Quraysh. We like you and yours. [Let us agree that] if you kill one of us unintentionally, you will pay blood money, and if we kill one of yours [unintentionally], we shall pay blood money." The Prophet accepted, and they converted to Islam (*fa-aslamū*).

(2) The delegation of Fazāra

Muḥammad b. ʿUmar transmitted to us from ʿAbd Allāh b. Muḥammad b. ʿUmar al-Jumaḥī, from Abū Wajza al-Saʿdī, the following: When the Messenger of God, peace be upon him, returned from the [military expedition to] Tabūk, in the year 9/631, the delegation of Fazāra came to see him; they were between ten and nineteen men, among them Khārija b. Ḥiṣn and al- Ḥurr b. Qays b. Ḥiṣn, who was the youngest of them. They came mounted on lean camels, announcing their acceptance of Islam. The Prophet asked them about their land. One of them said, "O Messenger of God, our land is affected by drought, our herds perished, our region is dry, and our families are starving. Please pray to your God on our behalf."

The Prophet ascended the pulpit and uttered [the supplication for rain]: "O Lord, water Your land and livestock, pour Your mercy and give life to Your dead country; O Lord, give us rain that is beneficial, delicious, productive, abundant, wide-ranging, soon without delay; [let it be] constructive, not destructive. O Lord, provide us with water of mercy, not of punishment, devastation, flood, and annihilation. O Lord, send us rain and support us against the enemy." Rain started to pour and the skies could not be seen for six days. The Prophet ascended the pulpit and prayed, "O Lord, around us, not on us! [Let the rain fall] on the hills, and the mountains, and the streambeds, and the sites where trees grow." The clouds cleared away from Medina like a garment that is taken off.

(3) The delegation of Ju'fiyy

Hishām b. Muḥammad transmitted to us the following from his father and from Abū Bakr b. Qays al-Ju'fiyy: the Ju'fiyy people had a custom in the *jāhiliyya* to abstain from eating the heart [of slaughtered animals]. Now, two of them came to see the Prophet as delegates: Qays b. Salama b. Sharāḥīl from the Murrān clan of Ju'fiyy and Salama b. Yazīd b. Mashja'a b. al-Mujammi'. They were half-brothers, sharing the same mother, whose name was Mulayka bt. al-Ḥilw b. Mālik from the clan of Ḥarīm b. Ju'fiyy. They both accepted Islam, whereupon the Prophet said to them, "I heard that you abstain from eating the heart [of slaughtered animals]." They said, "That is correct." He said, "Your Islam will not be complete unless you eat it." The Prophet ordered that a roasted heart be brought for them and he served it to Salama b. Yazīd. When the latter took it his hand trembled, but the Prophet said, "Eat it," which he did. Then he said the following:

> Nay, I ate a heart aversely / My fingers trembled when touching it.

[The narrator said] that the Prophet drafted for Qays b. Salama a document worded thus: "A document from Muḥammad, the Messenger of God, to Qays b. Salama b. Sharāḥīl: I appoint you over [the clans of] Murrān, Ḥarīm, and al-Kulāb and the clients affiliated with them; that is, those of them who perform the ritual prayer, give alms, and purify their possessions [by paying all their dues]." [The narrator said] that al-Kulāb included the tribal groups Awd, Zubayd, Jaz' b. Sa'd al-'Ashīra, Zayd Allāh b. Sa'd, 'Ā'idh Allāh b. Mas'ad, and Banū Ṣulā'a from [the tribe of] Banū al-Ḥārith b. Ka'b.

The two [delegates] said, "O Messenger of God, our mother, Mulayka bt. al-Ḥilw, used to set captives free, feed the hungry, and have mercy on the poor. She died having buried alive a baby girl that she had. What will her destiny be?" The Prophet answered, "Both the burier and the buried one will go to hell." They stood up, angry. The Prophet said, "Come back here; my mother will be with your mother." They rejected [his words] and went away, saying, "By God, a man who made us eat a heart and claims that our mother is in hell should not be followed."

They departed, and somewhere on the way they came upon a companion of the Prophet leading camels to be handed over [to the Prophet] as alms; they tied the man up and collected the camels. The news reached the Prophet and he cursed them, together with others whom he used to curse, saying, "May God curse the tribes Ri'l, Dhakwān, 'Uṣayya, Liḥyān, and the two sons of Mulayka [from the clans of] Ḥarīm and Murrān."

The narrator said, I was informed by Hishām b. Muḥammad, who was told by al-Walīd b. 'Abd Allāh al-Ju'fiyy, who transmitted from his father, who transmitted from the [tribal] elders, the following: Abū Sabra Yazīd b. Mālik b. 'Abd Allāh b. al-Dhu'ayb b. Salama b. 'Amr b. Dhuhl b. Murrān came to see the Prophet with his sons Sabra and 'Azīz [the latter name means "powerful" and "exalted"]. The

Prophet asked ʿAzīz, "What is your name?" "ʿAzīz," he said. "There is no exalted one but God," said the Prophet, "[From now on] your name will be ʿAbd al-Raḥmān" [meaning "servant of the Compassionate One," i.e., God]." They became Muslims. Abū Sabra said, "O Messenger of God, I have a swelling on the back of my hand which prevents me from binding the halter on my camel's nose." The Prophet summoned for an arrow to be brought before him and then started to strike the swelling and rub it until it disappeared. The Prophet prayed for him and his two sons. [Then Abū Sabra] said, "O Messenger of God, assign to me the valley of my people in the Yemen"; it was called Ḥurdān. The Prophet did so.

FURTHER READING

Donner, Fred McGraw. *The Early Islamic Conquests* (Princeton, NJ: Princeton University Press, 1981), 62–75.

Landau-Tasseron, Ella."Asad from Jāhiliyya to Islām," *Jerusalem Studies in Arabic and Islam* 6 (1985): 1–28.

———. *The Religious Foundation of Political Allegiance: A Study of Bayʿa in Pre-Modern Islam* (Washington, DC: Hudson Institute, 2010).

Watt, W. Montgomery. *Muhammad at Medina* (Oxford: Clarendon Press, 1956).

6

The Spread of Islam in Arabia: Expressing Conversion in Poetry

Khuzāʿī b. ʿAbd Nuhm al-Muzanī, ʿAbd ʿAmr b. Jabala al-Kalbī, ʿAdī b. ʿAmr b. Suwayd al-Aʿraj al-Maʿnī al-Ṭāʾī, Kaʿb b. Zuhayr b. Abī Sulmā al-Muzanī, and Tamīm b. Ubayy b. Muqbil

Peter Webb

Genre: Didactic and entertaining literature (poetry)
Language: Arabic

INTRODUCTION

Since medieval Muslim traditions conceptualize the Arabs as a people of poetry, we might expect the earliest Arabian converts to Islam to have left us substantial descriptions of their conversions in verse. Unfortunately, relatively little poetry of this kind is extant today. The few relevant conversion poems are not prominent in poetry collections; rather, they are scattered across disparate sources about pre-Islamic Arabian religion and in biographies of the Prophet's companions. This selection presents five poems ascribed to Arabian converts during Muḥammad's lifetime.

Questions of authenticity temper the conclusions about conversion to Islam in Arabia that might be drawn from this material. All the poems below were first recorded only in the late eighth or early ninth century by Muslim narrators in ʿAbbasid Iraq. Those narrators broadly embraced the opinion that all of Arabia's population had converted to Islam during Muḥammad's lifetime, and there is a risk that the Iraqi narrators transported their own notions of Islam backward in time, placing them into the mouths of earlier poets in order to substantiate ʿAbbasid-era opinions. But some poetry has survived the process of historical transmission, and it is remote that all of the verses ascribed to early Muslims constitute later forgeries. Hence, the passages of poetry included here do perhaps reflect the different ways in which Arabians interpreted conversion. There are some threads of commonality, and the poetry's general emphasis on allegiance to Muḥammad may be particularly instructive in this respect. There is current debate among scholars about the importance of Muḥammad in the caliphate's version of Islam before the eighth century; but, at least in the poetic voices below, allegiance to the person of Muḥammad emerges as a key element of belief upon entering the new faith.

TEXTS

(1) Khuzāʿī b. ʿAbd Nuhm al-Muzanī
(*from Ibn al-Kalbī,* Kitāb al-Aṣnām)

I went to Nuhm to slaughter before it,
Ritual offering as I used to do.
But I said to my soul as its reason returned,
You fools! Is this god true?
I refused. Today my faith is Muḥammad's:
Of heaven's Glorious Lord, the Giver of grace.

[*Ibn al-Kalbī (d. 204/819 or 206/821) narrates the poem in his* Kitāb al-Aṣnām *as evidence that "Nuhm" signified an idol worshipped by the Muzayna in the pre-Islamic period. The poet, Khuzāʿī, was memorialized as the idol's custodian. On its face, the poem depicts Islam as the religion of Muḥammad and of an Almighty God; Islam itself is experienced as a rational belief system, articulated via the binary opposition to the expressly irrational worship of idols.*

*Ibn al-Kalbī does not explain why the poem was composed, but context may be augmented via the historian Ibn Saʿd (d. 230/845), who relates that Khuzāʿī was a member of the Muzayna's delegation to the Prophet in 5/626 (*al-Ṭabaqāt al-Kubrā, *1:222–23). The members of the delegation converted and promised to convert their clan, too, but upon their return, their people did not comply as expected. The Prophet ordered his poet Ḥassān b. Thābit to compose a gentle reminder, and upon hearing it, Khuzāʿī addressed his people and secured their conversion. When the Muslims conquered Mecca in 8/630, the Prophet appointed Khuzāʿī leader over the Muzayna.*

While the poem may be a fabrication to explain the end of Arabian paganism for Iraqi Muslim audiences, there is also logic in seeing it as authentic by linking its composition to the process of a public performance. If Ibn Saʿd's narrative is accurate, the poem might be readable as a reply to Ḥassān's verse, a public confirmation of the successful conversion of Khuzāʿī's clan. The poem's switch to the second person plural—"You fools"—suggests reference to the poet's people and lends itself to the interpreta-

tion that the verses were part of disseminating the political statements incumbent on Khuzāʿī to curry favor with Muḥammad and to ensure his appointment as the clan's leader under Islam.]

(2) *ʿAbd ʿAmr b. Jabala al-Kalbī* (*from Ibn Saʿd,* al-Ṭabaqāt al-Kubrā)

The Messenger of God came with right guidance; I complied:
And after praising God I have become abstemious.
Farewell to pleasures of the cup!
All my life I inclined toward play, an addict;
Now I believe in God, illustrious on high,
And I shall reject idols evermore.

(3) *ʿAdī b. ʿAmr b. Suwayd al-Aʿraj al-Maʿnī al-Ṭāʾī* (*from al-Marzubānī,* Muʿjam al-Shuʿarāʾ)

When the morning prayer's announcer rises,
I leave poetry aside and replace it
With the Book of the One God.
Farewell to drink and carousing!
I abstain from wine though
All my life I was its addict.

[*ʿAbd ʿAmr b. Jabala (also known as ʿAmr b. Jabala) is unknown beyond his mention in a story narrated by Ibn al-Kalbī in which ʿAbd ʿAmr and another member of the Kalb are reported to have visited the Prophet, who invited them to convert, and ʿAbd ʿAmr professed his faith via this poem.*

Al-Aʿraj is likewise obscure: the poetry specialist al-Tibrīzī labeled him a Kharijite on account of a bellicose poem ascribed to him in Abū Tammām's al-Ḥamāsa (Sharḥ Dīwān al-Ḥamāsa, *ed. Gharīd Shaykh [Beirut: Dār al-Kutub al-ʿIlmiyya, 2000], 1:251), but al-Aʿraj may instead be an earlier convert from the time of Muḥammad's prophecy, and Ibn al-Kalbī is again the narrator of this conversion poem, explaining that al-Aʿraj composed it upon his conversion (see the report in Ibn al-Athīr,* Usd al-Ghāba fī Maʿrifat al-Ṣaḥāba *[Beirut: Dār Ibn Ḥazm, 2012], 480, biography 3619).*

Like Khuzāʿī's poem above, ʿAbd ʿAmr's conversion is expressed as submission to the Prophet and the emphatically monotheistic God, with explicit rejection of idols. Al-Aʿraj's monotheism strikes a similar tone, but what is most salient is both poets' pointed profession of rejecting alcohol as proof of their new faith. They present drinking as emblematic of pre-Islamic life, and their emphasis constructs drinking as the binary opposite of Islam's way.

The presence of the phrase wa-qad arānī/urā bi-hā sadikan *(I was addicted to wine) in both poems raises intriguing questions of authorship. Is this a stock phrase ascribable to an array of "conversion poems," which implies the possibility that later Iraqi narrators possessed a "conversion poem archetype" that they could muster to embellish any conversion narrative? In this case, do these poems express what the poets experienced when converting to Islam in early seventh-century Arabia, or are they retrojections of later narrators expressing what they felt conversion should have meant?*

The poets' obscurity fuels equivocal interpretation. On the one hand, famous poets were the most common targets of fabricated verse, and thus verses ascribed to otherwise unknown figures may be genuine survivals; on the other hand, narrators could deftly insert obscure figures into narratives to make new meanings from old historic events. The identity of al-Aʿraj is particularly uncertain. What is certain is that the biographical tradition, via the hand of Ibn al-Kalbī, included variations on a form of poetry in which poets expressed their adherence to Islam both by belief in the monotheistic God and His prophet and by explicit rejection of traditions of drinking and idol worship.]

(4) Kaʿb b. Zuhayr b. Abī Sulmā al-Muzanī (d. ca. 11/632)
(from Ibn Hishām, al-Sīra al-Nabawiyya)

I'm told God's Messenger threatens me,
But from the Messenger of God one can seek pardon.
Go easy! Be directed by the One who blessed you
With the Qurʾān, its warnings and guidance.
Never condemn me on rumors,
Much they may say, but I have not sinned.
If an elephant stood where I stand,
And if it saw or heard what I hear,
Then it would tremble—unless the messenger
With God's will—gave a graceful nod.
. . . .
The Messenger is a sword of Indian steel,
Unsheathed, its flashes guide the swords of God.
Among a band of the Quraysh: when they converted,
One in the valley of Mecca cried: "Be gone!"
And they left, but in strength:
Armed, armored, and ready for the fight.

[*The above is an excerpt from Kaʿb b. Zuhayr's celebrated fifty-seven-line poem* Bānat Suʿād, *which was widely recorded and whose context was detailed in the version of the Prophet's biography* (sīra) *compiled by Ibn Hishām (d. 213/828 or 218/833). According to the story, Kaʿb's brother converted to Islam around 7–8/628–29 and invited Kaʿb to do likewise, but Ka ʿb refused and composed poetry disparaging his brother and belittling Islam. Muḥammad heard Ka ʿb's verses and declared Ka ʿb's murder to be permissible, but Ka ʿb eluded danger. Around 9/630–31 he entered Medina, approached Muḥammad, and recited this poem as an expression of his conversion, which was accepted.*

Ka ʿb's conversion poem is somewhat unlike those considered above. Although it echoes their emphasis on Muḥammad and reference to the Qur ʾān, the poem does not praise the new belief system, nor does Ka ʿb repudiate his past lifestyle. Instead, Ka ʿb expresses allegiance to Islam via praise of the formidable warrior skills of the Prophet and his Quraysh companions. Overall, Bānat Suʿād *reflects pre-Islamic poetic conventions, and Ka ʿb makes no statement to suggest that he intends to change his pre-Islamic ways, either.*]

(5) Tamīm b. Ubayy b. Muqbil (from Ibn Sallām al-Jumaḥī, Ṭabaqāt Fuḥūl al-Shuʿarāʾ)

[Ibn Sallām al-Jumaḥī (d. 231/845–46) reports:] Ibn Muqbil was unsettled in his faith. During Islam, he would lament the people of pre-Islam, and reminisce. Once it was said to him: "How is it you cry over the people of pre-Islam, yet you are a Muslim?" And he replied:

> Why shouldn't I weep over vanished abodes and their people?
> The kings of Ḥimyar and ʿAkk used to visit them.
> From everywhere sand grouse descended on our good wells,
> They exhausted our camels' refuges, and took off.

[*The Iraqi poetry specialist Ibn Sallām al-Jumaḥī recorded this comment in his biographical treatise on the great Arabic poets. He counted Ibn Muqbil in the fifth-highest tier, notwithstanding the misgivings over Ibn Muqbil's faith. The precise meanings of the poem and its "sand grouse" metaphor can be interpreted in various ways, but the thrust is clear: the poet laments the new order in which the noble camel is pushed toward privation by a multitude of thirsty grouse. Muslim traditions accept the presence of hypocrites within Muḥammad's own community, and some Islamic-era poets were celebrated for their transgressive verses, but Ibn Muqbil is particularly chastised for what Ibn Sallām's source considered the poet's perplexing refusal to reject positive memory of pre-Islam upon his conversion. This narrator (and perhaps Ibn Sallām, too) evidently deemed conversion to be the radically transformative experience articulated by the first three poets above, whereas Ibn Muqbil appears to have objected to the expectation that he should triumphantly disavow the past.*]

FURTHER READING

Donner, Fred McGraw. *The Early Islamic Conquests* (Princeton, NJ: Princeton University Press, 1981) [on the conversion of Arabia and the spread of Islam].

Stetkevych, Jaroslav. "A Qaṣīdah by Ibn Muqbil," *Journal of Arabic Literature* 37 (2006): 303–54 [on poetry at the dawn of Islam].

Stetkevych, Suzanne. "Pre-Islamic Panegyric and the Poetics of Redemption," in *Reorientations/Arabic and Persian Poetry,* ed. Suzanne Stetkevych (Bloomington: Indiana University Press, 1994), 1–57 [on poetry at the dawn of Islam].

Webb, Peter. "Poetry and the Early Islamic Historical Tradition: Poetry and Narratives of the Battle of Ṣiffīn," in *Poetry and Warfare in Middle Eastern Literatures,* ed. Hugh Kennedy (London: I. B. Tauris, 2014), 119–41 [on poetry's functions in early Arabic historiography].

7

Early *Ḥadīth* Touching on Marriage and Conversion

Ibn Abī Shayba (d. 235/849)

Christopher Melchert

Title: *al-Muṣannaf* (Topically arranged traditions)
Genre: Religious instruction (*ḥadīth*)
Language: Arabic

INTRODUCTION

Abū Bakr b. Abī Shayba (d. 235/849) was a major Kufan *ḥadīth* collector (see Lucas). The *Muṣannaf,* from which the following excerpts are translated, comprises almost thirty-nine thousand *ḥadīth* reports, of which about a fifth go back to the Prophet, a third to the Prophet's companions, and almost half to followers of the generation after (with practically none going back to later authorities). As it happens, though, almost none of the reports below go back all the way to the Prophet, presumably because they have to do with the conversion of Jewish and Christian spouses of Muslims, whereas during the Prophet's lifetime, it was not supposed that any of the Muslims were married to Jews or Christians. How far back the *ḥadīth* provide us with accurate quotations, as opposed to back-projection of current ideas, is up for debate. That being said, almost all specialists would agree that this selection reliably exposes questions that eighth-century Muslim jurisprudents discussed. How far these discussions reflect actual practice is less certain, inasmuch as jurisprudents were naturally attracted to hypothetical questions. Occasional citations of actual practice are sometimes contradictory (as below of the caliph ʿUmar), which makes them evidence mainly that later jurisprudents were attributing their own positions to various early authorities.

It was essential for *ḥadīth* collectors such as Ibn Abī Shayba to present the chains of authorities (*isnāds*) by which reports had reached them. For the sake of brevity, I have reproduced his chain only for the first report in the series, identifying each transmitter along with the city in which he lived. The chains suggest that Kufan jurisprudents tended to be friendlier than Basrans were to cross-religious marriage and concubinage.

The following reports from Ibn Abī Shayba document that some questions about conversion and interreligious relations were still disputed in the eighth century, although they were largely subject to consensus in the later period of the classical schools (notably, whether a Muslim woman can ever be married to a non-Muslim man). The reports also highlight the different regional attitudes of scholars.

In the *ḥadīth* below, the description "client" (*mawlā*) indicates that someone was descended from a freedman and was not Arab by ancestry. Biographers indicate that it was an important category in the eighth century but ceased to be so over the course of the ninth. When captives are said to be forced (*ujbirna*), the reference is probably to involuntary sex. "Treading" and "falling on" are normal euphemisms for sex in medieval Arabic sources, not indicating any special degradation of concubines. The "house of emigration" (*dār al-hijra*) is evidently an archaic term for the realm in which Muslims rule and to which Muslims are supposed to emigrate, as opposed to the "house of war" (*dār al-ḥarb*), which they should fight to subjugate. This report apparently predates the spread of the prophetic report that there is to be no more emigration after the conquest of Mecca (see Crone). The significance of a single divorce is that the couple's remarriage is possible before the expiry of the woman's "waiting period" (*ʿidda*), whereas a triple divorce rules out remarriage until there has been a consummated marriage between the woman and another man. The "divorce of separation" called for by al-Ḥasan al-Baṣrī and the caliph ʿUmar b. ʿAbd al-ʿAzīz is presumably of the latter sort. The waiting period during which a woman may not remarry is three months or three menses for divorcées, four months and ten days for widows (see Spectorsky, chapter 3).

TEXTS

(1) The book of marriage, section on Christian and Jewish slave girls: May a man tread on [i.e., have sex with] them or not?

Jarīr [b. ʿAbd al-Ḥamīd, Kufan, lived in Rayy, d. 188/804] related to us on the authority of Mughīra [b. Miqsam, blind Kufan client, d. 134/751–52?] on the authority of Ḥammād [b. Abī Sulaymān, Kufan, d. 120/737–38] on the authority of Ibrāhīm [al-Nakhāʿī, Kufan, d. 96/714?], who said, "When Jewish and Christian women are captured and offered Islam, they are forced. Whether they convert to Islam or not, they are trodden on and made into servants."

Kufan chain to Mujāhid [b. Jabr, Meccan client, d. 104/722–23?]: "When a man acquires a polytheistic slave girl, let him have her confess that there is no god but God. If she refuses and does not testify, that does not prevent him from falling on her."

Kufan/Basran chain to Mu'āwiya b. Qurra [Basran, d. 113/731–32]: "'Abd Allāh [b. Mas'ūd, companion, d. 32/652–53?] used to force his polytheistic slave girl."

Basran chain to Ibn Mas'ūd concerning the female captive: "One does not tread on her till she says 'There is no god but God' and converts."

Basran chain to Jābir b. Zayd [Abū al-Sha'thā', Basran, d. 104/722–23] concerning whether a man who buys a captured slave girl falls on her: he said, "No, not until he teaches her the ritual prayer, the ritual ablution for major impurity, and shaving the pubic hair."

(2) The book of marriage, section on a Jewish or Christian man who has a Christian woman under him, then converts to Islam before he has gone into her: Is she owed the bride price?

Basran chain to al-Ḥasan [al-Baṣrī, client, d. 110/728]: "When a woman converts to Islam and she has a Jewish, Christian, or Magian [i.e., Zoroastrian] husband who has not converted, she is owed nothing and he does not go into her."

Kufan chain to Ibrāhīm: "She is owed nothing."

Basran chain to al-Ḥasan: "They are to be separated. She is owed half a bride price."

Basran/Kufan chain to Ḥammād: "She is owed half a bride price."

Basran chain to Jābir b. Zayd, on being asked about a man who has under him a Christian woman who has converted to Islam—what if her husband refuses to convert? He said, "I think they should be separated. If he has already gone into her, she is owed a complete bride price. If he has not gone into her, she returns whatever he has given her."

Basran chain to Qatāda [b. Di'āma, Basran, d. 117/735–36?]: "She is owed half a bride price."

(3) The book of divorce, section on what they have said about a woman who converts to Islam before her husband: those who say they are to be separated

Mixed chain to Ibn 'Abbās ['Abd Allāh, companion, d. 70/689–90?]: "When a Christian woman converts to Islam before her husband, she has the better claim to possess herself."

Basran chain to al Ḥasan and 'Umar b. 'Abd al-'Azīz [caliph, d. 101/720], who both said of a Christian woman who converts under her husband, "Islam has put her away from him."

Kufan chain to ʿAṭāʾ [b. Abī Rabāḥ, Meccan client, d. 115/733–34?] concerning the Christian woman who converts to Islam under her husband: he said, "They are to be separated."

Kufan chain to ʿAṭāʾ, Ṭāwūs [b. Kaysān, Yemeni client, d. 106/724–25?], and Mujāhid concerning the Christian woman who is under a Christian man and then converts to Islam: they said, "If he converts to Islam with her, she is his wife, but if he does not convert, they are to be separated."

Kufan chain to Dāwūd b. Kurdūs [fl. first/seventh century]: "There was a man of the Banū Taghlib called ʿUbāda b. Nuʿmān b. Zurʿa. He had a wife of the Banū Tamīm. ʿUbāda was a Christian. His wife converted to Islam, but he refused to convert, so ʿUmar [b. al-Khaṭṭāb, caliph] separated them."

(4) The book of divorce, section on those who say that if she converts to Islam but he does not, she is not taken from him

Kufan/Basran chain to ʿAlī: "If a Christian woman converts to Islam while she is wife to a Jewish or Christian man, he has the greater claim to her genitals, for he has a pact."

Mixed chain to ʿAlī: "He has the greater claim to her so long as he is in the House of Emigration."

Mixed chain to ʿAbd Allāh b. Yazīd al-Khaṭmī that ʿUmar wrote, "They [the women] are to be given the choice."

Kufan chain to al-Shaʿbī: "He has the greater claim to her so long as she is in the city."

Kufan chain to Ibrāhīm: "The two of them are confirmed in their marriage."

Kufan/Basran chain to al-Ḥakam [b. ʿUtayba, Kufan client, d. 114/732–33?] that Hāniʾ b. Qabīṣa al-Shaybānī, a Christian, had four wives who converted to Islam. ʿUmar b. al-Khaṭṭāb decreed that they were to be confirmed as his.

Basran chain to al-Ḥasan that a Christian woman converted to Islam, being under a Christian. They wanted to take her from him; so they went to ʿUmar, who gave her the choice.

(5) The book of divorce, section on what they have said about a situation in which someone converts to Islam while she is in her waiting period: those who say that he has the greater claim to her

Kufan/Medinese chain to al-Zuhrī that the wife of ʿIkrima b. Abī Jahl converted to Islam before he did, then he converted during her waiting period, so she was returned to him. That was in the time of the Prophet.

Kufan/Basran chain to Mujāhid: "When he converts to Islam while she is in her waiting period, she is his wife."

Meccan chain to ʿAṭāʾ: "If he converts to Islam while she is in her waiting period, he has the greater claim to her."

Mixed chain to ʿUmar b. ʿAbd al-ʿAzīz: "He has the greater claim to her so long as she is in her waiting period."

Kufan chain to ʿAṭāʾ: "If he converts to Islam while she is in her waiting period, she is his wife."

Mixed chain to ʿUmar b. ʿAbd al-ʿAzīz: "When a husband converts to Islam after his wife does, he gives her the choice so long as she is in her waiting period" or "he has the greater claim to her so long as she is in her waiting period."

Basran chain to al-Zuhrī: "If a Jew or a Christian converts to Islam, and then his wife converts, they remain married unless the ruler has separated them."

FURTHER READING

Crone, Patricia. "The First-Century Concept of *Hiğra*," *Arabica* 41 (1994): 352–87.

Lucas, Scott C. "Where Are the Legal *Ḥadīth?* A Study of the *Muṣannaf* of Ibn Abī Shayba," *Islamic Law and Society* 15 (2008): 283–314.

Sadeghi, Behnam. "The Traveling Tradition Test: A Method for Dating Traditions," *Der Islam* 85 (2010): 203–42.

Schacht, Joseph. *The Origins of Muhammadan Jurisprudence* (Oxford: Clarendon Press, 1950).

Spectorsky, Susan A. *Women in Classical Islamic Law: A Survey of the Sources* (Leiden: Brill, 2010).

8

Practicalities and Motivations of Conversion as Seen through Early *Ḥadīth* and Law

ʿAbd al-Razzāq b. Humām al-Ṣanʿānī (d. 211/827) and Abū Bakr Aḥmad b. Muḥammad al-Khallāl (d. 311/923)

Yohanan Friedmann

Titles: al-Ṣanʿānī, *al-Muṣannaf* (Topically arranged traditions); al-Khallāl, *Aḥkām Ahl al-Milal min al-Jāmiʿ li-Masāʾil Aḥmad b. Ḥanbal* (Legal judgments regarding people of different creeds, taken from the collection of Ahmad b. Ḥanbal's *masāʾil*)

Genres: Religious instruction (*ḥadīth*); legal writing (responsa)

Language: Arabic

(1) IS CONVERSION TO SAVE ONE'S LIFE VALID? (FROM AL-ṢANʿĀNĪ, *AL-MUṢANNAF*, 10:173–74 [NO. 18720])

Introduction

This passage is taken from a very early collection of prophetic traditions (*ḥadīth*) by al-Ṣanʿānī, a major Yemeni scholar of *ḥadīth*. *Ḥadīth* is a huge corpus of Arabic literature that contains sayings attributed to the Prophet Muḥammad. *Ḥadīth* collections are classified according to one of two methods: by transmitters (*musnad*) or by topic (*muṣannaf*). Though al-Ṣanʿānī's collection is not included in the genre of canonical *ḥadīth*, it precedes the canonical books of al-Bukhārī (d. 256/870) and Muslim b. Ḥajjāj (d. 261/875) by half a century.

The passage reflects the conditions of conversion in the earliest layer of Muslim tradition, in which the pronouncement of only the first part of the declaration of faith (*shahāda;* "There is no god except God") was sufficient for conversion. The tradition indicates that the declaration of faith should be taken at face value and no attempt should be made to assess its sincerity or lack thereof. This view is expounded by the Prophet explicitly and implied by the story of the earth's refusal to accept the body of a companion of the Prophet who killed a polytheist who had uttered the declaration, which indicates that the killing was wrongful: the companion should have accepted the polytheist's declaration and desisted from killing him.

Text

ʿAbd al-Razzāq informed us on the authority of Maʿmar, on the authority of al-Zuhrī, on the authority of ʿAbd Allāh b. Mawhib, on the authority of Qabīṣa b. Dhuʾayb, of the following: A companion of the Prophet, may God bless him and grant him peace, attacked a defeated group of warriors. He overpowered a polytheist belonging to it. When he was about to smite him with the sword, the man said: "There is no god except God" (*lā ilāha illā Allāh*). [The companion] did not desist and killed him. Then he had qualms because of the killing and mentioned the story to the Prophet, saying: "He said it [i.e., 'There is no god except God'] only to seek protection." The Prophet said: "Have you opened his heart?" [The Prophet] said: "The tongue conveys only what is in the heart."

After a short while, the companion died and was buried. In the morning his body was found above ground. His family came to the Prophet, may God bless him and grant him peace, and informed him of this. He said: "Bury him." He was buried again, but in the morning the body was found above ground [again]. His family informed the Prophet, who said: "The earth refused to accept him." And they threw him into one of the caves.

(2) CAN A CHRISTIAN BE CONSIDERED A MUSLIM? (FROM AL-ṢANʿĀNĪ, *AL-MUṢANNAF*, 10:316 [NO. 19220])

Introduction

This passage reflects two different understandings of the term "Islam" and of conversion to Islam. The Prophet asks for the conversion of a Christian man, who maintains that he has already converted. In effect, the Christian claims that Christianity is also Islam. This understanding is possible because some parts of the Muslim tradition can be interpreted as saying that Islam is not only the religion established by the Prophet Muḥammad in the seventh century CE but also the primordial monotheistic faith associated with Abraham, whom the Qurʾān explicitly calls a Muslim (Q. 3:67) because he "submitted" (*aslama*) to God. The Prophet Muḥammad, on the other hand, wants the Christian to embrace the new religion of Islam that includes not only the belief in one God but also the rejection of wine and pork and the denial of the Christian idea that God has a son.

Text

ʿAbd al-Razzāq informed us that Ibn al-Taymī informed us on the authority of his father: Qatāda informed me that the Prophet, may God bless him and grant him peace, said to a Christian: "Embrace Islam (*aslim*), O Abū al-Ḥārith!" The Christian said: "I have submitted (*aslamtu*)." The Prophet said to him [again]: "Embrace Islam, O Abū al-Ḥārith!" The Christian said: "I have submitted." The Prophet said to him, for the third time: "Embrace Islam, O Abū al-Ḥārith!" The Christian said: "I have submitted before you have." The Prophet became angry and said: "You are lying! Three things stand between yourself and Islam: your acquisition of wine (he did not say your drinking of wine), your consumption of pork, and your claim that God has a son."

(3) IS IT APPROPRIATE TO OFFER FINANCIAL INCENTIVES FOR CONVERSION? (FROM AL-KHALLĀL, *AḤKĀM*, 10)

Introduction

This tradition appears in a book of responsa (*masāʾil*) attributed to Aḥmad b. Ḥanbal (d. 241/855). *Masāʾil* (responsa) is a genre of Islamic legal literature in which jurists respond to questions addressed to them pertaining to specific legal matters. It should be contrasted with comprehensive books of jurisprudence, which aspire to include all chapters of Islamic law. This collection of responsa, compiled by Ibn Ḥanbal's disciple Abū Bakr al-Khallāl, deals with the relationship of Muslims with non-Muslims. The passage should be read in conjunction with Qurʾān 9:60, which specifies the social groups and religious purposes that may be supported from alms money. The verse allows the use of alms money to support people who waver in their attitude to Islam; the financial incentive is expected to strengthen their commitment. The commentators of the Qurʾān differ on the question of whether such use of alms was allowed solely in the initial stages of Islam or may be continued also in later periods.

The passage also discusses the question of what happens if the converted Jew reneges on his conversion because the Muslim has not honored his promise to give him one thousand dirhams. Ibn Ḥanbal maintains that although the Muslim should have honored his word and should have given the money to the Jew, the conversion is nonetheless considered valid; the Jew should therefore be executed as an apostate if he reneges on it. The rule requiring the execution of an apostate prevails over the Muslim's failure to fulfill his promise.

Text

A man said to a dhimmī: "Embrace Islam and you will have this and that."

Aḥmad b. Ḥanbal (Abū ʿAbd Allāh) was asked about a man who said to a Jew: "Embrace Islam and I will give you one thousand dirhams." The Jew embraced Islam, but the man did not give him anything. [Ibn Ḥanbal] said: "The Prophet used to give financial incentives to encourage people to embrace Islam. I would like him to fulfill his promise." I said: "And if the Jew says: 'I will not embrace Islam until you give me what you stipulated'?" Aḥmad b. Ḥanbal said: "If he reneges on Islam, I will strike his neck, but the man should have fulfilled his promise."

(4) THE RELIGIOUS AFFILIATION OF MINORS (FROM AL-KHALLĀL, *AḤKĀM*, 39–40)

Introduction

This passage deals with two main issues: the influence of parents on the religion of their minor children, and the age at which a minor becomes responsible for his actions. According to a famous *ḥadīth*, "Every newborn is born in the natural condition (*fiṭra*); it is his two parents who transform him into a Jew, a Christian, or a Zoroastrian." Though the tradition does not mention Islam, the latter can certainly be included in the list. This "natural condition" was explained as Islam, or at least as a sound nature prepared for its acceptance. The idea expressed in this tradition is the reason that the minor children of a woman who embraces Islam are considered Muslims and should be forced to embrace it if they resist.

The other issue is the age at which a minor is able to make decisions regarding his religious affiliation and is no longer dependent on the religion and the wishes of his parents. Since the Prophet ruled that at the age of ten a boy should be beaten to make him perform the prayer, Ibn Ḥanbal draws the conclusion that at this age a boy is responsible for his actions and his conversion to Islam is to be accepted even if his parents object.

Text

A boy aged ten embraces Islam.

Muḥammad b. ʿAlī informed us that Muhannā related to us the following: I asked Aḥmad [b. Ḥanbal] about a Jewish or Christian boy who embraces Islam. Is his conversion valid if he has parents and they object to his conversion? He said: "If he understands what Islam is, it is valid; if not, it is not valid." I said: "What do you mean by understanding?" He said: "He knows how to pray and has a desire for Islam." I said: "How old does he have to be?" He said: "Ten years old." I said: "Should he be killed if he reneges on Islam at the age of ten?" He said: "He should not be killed, but he should be beaten because the Prophet, may God bless him and grant him peace, said: 'When a boy is ten years old, he should be beaten to make him perform the prayer.'"

Ibn Ḥāzim informed us that Isḥāq b. Manṣūr related to us that he said to Abū ʿAbd Allāh: "[What about] a woman who embraces Islam while having children?" He said: "If they are minors, they should be forced to embrace Islam; if they are grown up, they should not." I said: "What is the definition of [being grown up]?" He said: "Ten years."

I said to Aḥmad [b. Ḥanbal]: "What about a boy aged ten who embraces Islam?" [Aḥmad b. Ḥanbal] said: "I would force him to [cling] to Islam because he is [old enough] to be ordered to perform the prayer."

FURTHER READING

Adang, Camilla. "Islam as the Inborn Religion of Mankind: The Concept of *Fiṭra* in the Works of Ibn Ḥazm," *Al-Qanṭara* 21 (2000): 391–410.

"Al-Muʾallafa Ḳulūbuhum," in *Encyclopaedia of Islam,* 2nd ed.

Friedmann, Yohanan. "Conditions of Conversion in Early Islam," in *Patterns of Repentance: Judaism, Christianity, Islam,* ed. Adriana Destro and Mauro Pesce (Leuven: Peeters, 2004), 96–106.

———. *Tolerance and Coercion in Islam: Interfaith Relations in the Muslim Traditio* (Cambridge: Cambridge University Press, 2003), 87–120.

Kister, Meir Jacob. "... *Illā bi-ḥaqqihi* ... : A Study of an Early *ḥadīth,*" *Jerusalem Studies in Arabic and Islam* 5 (1984): 33–52.

9

Christian Conversions to Islam in the Wake of the Arab Conquest

Anastasius of Sinai (d. ca. 80/700)

Yannis Papadogiannakis

Title: *Diegēmata psychōphelē kai steriktika* (Edifying and supportive tales)
Genre: Religious instruction (hagiography)
Language: Greek

INTRODUCTION

Anastasius (d. ca. 700) lived through the Muslim conquest in Sinai, and his works offer a precious glimpse into its impact on the lives of ordinary Christians. Along with his other better-known and more accessible works, such as the *Questions and Answers* (*Erotapokriseis*), the stories from his *Edifying Tales* highlight his intimate knowledge of Syria, Palestine, and Sinai and the tensions created within Christian communities by the Islamic conquest. Often, Anastasius purports to be an eyewitness to the stories that he recounts. As well as being an effort to document early examples of Christian holiness in the Sinai Peninsula, Anastasius's *Edifying Tales* aimed to support Christians who were facing pressures to convert to Islam, to help them cope with this challenge, and to encourage them to hold fast to their faith. To achieve this, Anastasius focused on Christians who became martyrs, praising them as examples of steadfastness in their faith. Anastasius expressed his praise against the background of early Christian martyrdom traditions, which identified the motives of those who converted to demonic agency. In doing so, Anastasius portrayed Islam as being tantamount to the religion of the Devil. More broadly, Anastasius highlighted the phenomenon of flip-flopping between Christianity and Islam, and the fact that many early conversions occurred within the context of slavery and captivity. Anastasius's account of the martyrdom of George the Black is the oldest surviving account of a Christian martyrdom under Islam.

TEXTS

(1) Moses, the apostate from Clysma

We spoke a little earlier about Sartabias the possessed, and the kind of things the demon told him, calling the Arabs his companions. The tale that is now going to be told for our edification and benefit confirms that previous one.

There was a man in Clysma [at the head of the Gulf of Suez in Egypt] named Azarias, who was the first among those called the *doukatores* [from Lat. *ducator, ductor:* leaders or guides for the army]; he is a friend and well known to us. He has a son called Moses, who is still alive and lives in [the town of] In. It so happened that this Moses was subject to possession from his infancy. After his father, who was a good Christian, died five years ago, being free [to do so], he erred and renounced his faith in Christ. Then when he was reprimanded by his fellow citizens, he became a Christian again. A short time later, he renounced our faith again, and as he did it multiple times, he was scolded by his fellow citizens.

When I came to In last year I found him to be an apostate. And as an old friend of his father's and of his, I reprimanded him and admonished him for having renounced the faith of Christ multiple times. Then Moses groaned and said to me: "And what can I do, my lord abba, because each time I convert and become Christian, the Devil disturbs me severely, and when I become an apostate again, he does not bother me at all. But the spirit appeared to me many times and commanded me with the words: Do not venerate Christ and I will not bother you; do not confess him as God and Son of God and I will not come near you; do not take the communion and I will not harass you; do not make the sign of the cross and I will love you." I was not the only one to hear this from Moses, but the poor man evidently brought himself to say the same also to others of our brothers who are faithful in our mysteries.

Let the church of Christ hear this, and rejoice. Let the children of Christians hear this and let them dance in celebration and let them preserve it indelibly. Let the children of the Jews and of the infidels hear them and be put to shame. Let those who do not confess Christ as God be put to shame, and let them register that, since the demons do confess as much [i.e., that Christ is God], they exceed the demons in their insult to Christ. Demons tremble before the cross of Christ, and yet those demons incarnate mock the cross. This present tale has proved that the demons are often vanquished by the sign of the cross, and the one told immediately after will confirm it.

(2) The slave Euphemia of Damascus

A Saracen, a most impious woman who lived in Damascus in the church of Saint Cyprian, acquired a Christian slave who was already of an advanced age. And she hindered her from [going] to church and from the holy communion by making an agreement with her that each time she took communion she would receive two hundred lashes. And, as the Lord in glory is my witness, this trophy-bearer of Christ never failed, even on a single Sunday, to receive holy communion. And one could see her come from the holy church and immediately, before even having a drink of water, receive the two hundred lashes.

One day, when it was a feast and when the slave of Christ had come from the gathering, as she was being flogged in the usual way by her fellow slaves, she, the terrible Jezebel, ordered them not to change the spot on the body of the Holy Euphemia of Christ [upon which they would lash her], but instead to inflict the two hundred lashes unflinchingly and pitilessly on the same part. And once this had happened, after she had been flogged, some Christ-loving women of the court took her in the usual way to anoint and tend to her wounds, and when they undressed her in private, they didn't find any bruising at all, nor any sign of a wound on her holy body, and they marveled and praised God.

These things did not happen long ago and are not ancient or without witnesses; rather, they are things that we saw with our own eyes, things that we saw and that our hands touched in order to tell this good tale. God, however, who never forsakes those who hope in Him, did not forsake our new holy martyr Euphemia either. For a man of those who love Christ, and who has often succeeded in catching such prey, was deemed worthy of possessing this treasure, too. Even though he was without means then, he used all means to ransom the holy martyr and, by the grace of God, succeeded in this. And since she departed for [heaven] first, he [being still in the land of the living] has her as protector and ambassador to God on his behalf.

(3) Martyrdom of George the Black

The memory of the victorious martyr George the Black is celebrated to this day in Damascus. He was a slave of a Saracen in Damascus. He had renounced his faith as a child when he was taken prisoner when he was eight. When he reached puberty and became aware of this, he converted again and became an exemplary Christian, defying any human fear.

One day one of his fellow slaves, a Christ-hating apostate, went to the mosque and denounced him to this master, saying that "so-and-so has become a Christian." He [the master] sent to have him brought before him and interrogated him and exhorted him to pray together with him. In spite of many exhortations and threats, he could not persuade him to apostatize from his faith in Christ. He then ordered four of the Saracens who were gathered there to seize hold of his two hands and his legs and suspend him in the air belly downward. And once this was done, his master cut him in half with his own hands with his sword. The inhabitants of Damascus took his remains and deposited them reverently in a special monument before the city gates, where nobody rests save for the slave and martyr of Christ, George.

FURTHER READING

Caner, Daniel, trans. *History and Hagiography from the Late Antique Sinai: Including Translations of Pseudo-Nilus' "Narrations," Ammonius' "Report on the Slaughter of the Monks of Sinai and Rhaithou," and Anastasius of Sinai's "Tales of the Sinai Fathers"* (Liverpool: Liverpool University Press, 2010).

Flusin, Bernard. "Démons et Sarrasins: L'auteur et le propos des *Diègèmata stèriktika* d'Anastase le Sinaïte," *Travaux et Mémoires* 11 (1991): 381–409.

Haldon, John. "The Works of Anastasius of Sinai: A Key Source for the History of Seventh-Century East Mediterranean Society and Belief," in *The Byzantine and Early Islamic Near East: Papers of the First Workshop on Late Antiquity and Early Islam*, ed. Averil Cameron and Lawrence I. Conrad (Princeton, NJ: Darwin Press, 1992), 107–47.

Papaconstantinou, Arietta. "Saints and Saracens: On Some Miracle Accounts of the Early Arab Period," in *Byzantine Religious Culture: Studies in Honor of Alice-Mary Talbot*, ed. Denis Sullivan, Elizabeth Fisher, and Stratis Papaioannou (Leiden: Brill, 2011), 323–38.

Papadogiannakis, Yannis. "Christian Identity in Seventh-Century Byzantium: The Case of Anastasius of Sinai," in *Motions of Late Antiquity: Essays on Religion, Politics, and Society in Honor of Peter Brown*, ed. Helmut Reimitz and Jamie Kreiner (Turnhout: Brepols, 2016), 249–67.

Reinink, Gerrit. "Following the Doctrine of the Demons: Early Christian Fear of Conversion to Islam," in *Cultures of Conversions*, ed. Jan N. Bremmer, Wout J. van Bekkum, and Arie L. Molendijk (Leuven: Peeters, 2006), 127–38.

Sahner, Christian C. *Christian Martyrs under Islam: Religious Violence and the Making of the Muslim World* (Princeton, NJ: Princeton University Press, 2018).

10

Jacob of Edessa's Canonical Responsa about Conversion and Islam

Jacob of Edessa (d. 89/708)

Jack Tannous

Title: Questions and Canons
Genre: Legal writing (juridical responsa)
Language: Syriac

INTRODUCTION

Jacob of Edessa (d. 708) was a Miaphysite bishop of the Umayyad period. Among Jacob's literary remains is what Herman Teule has termed his "juridical" correspondence. In these letters, Jacob answers questions that were sent to him by correspondents; at times, non-Miaphysite Christians, pagans, Jews, and Muslims appear in these questions.

Several points in Jacob's juridical material stand out for the history of conversion. Apostasy to Islam was a phenomenon that church leaders were confronting already in Jacob's day, but Jacob's canonical letters also suggest that Christians were joining the pagan community. Jacob's canonical material shows that some of those who moved out of the Christian community had regrets and wished to rejoin it. A conversion to Islam was not necessarily a permanent change.

One of the major engines of Islamization in the Middle East was likely interreligious marriage: when Muslim men married Christian women, it was most typical for their children to be Muslims. In Jacob's correspondence, we can see that intermarriage was already creating social dilemmas that church leaders had to deal with.

When considering conversion, the question of the social relationships between Christians and Muslims and the question of just what a shift from Christianity to Islam entailed in terms of everyday religious behavior should be addressed, and Jacob's correspondence contains precious evidence about these subjects as well.

The medieval canonical tradition would take Jacob's juridical letters and edit his responses, sometimes eliminating the original question he was posed and condensing his answers into stand-alone canons. In what follows, I have given the translation of the original question-and-answer between Jacob and his correspondent and in a few instances also supplied a later, edited version. In one case, when two different versions of the same question-and-answer differ slightly in the way they have been transmitted, I have given both versions. Finally, because there is no standard edition or ordering of Jacob's juridical responsa and canons, I have elected to simply arrange the extracts below thematically. The Syriac texts are found in a variety of sources; the specific source used is indicated at the end of each paragraph.

TEXTS

§ Addai: Whether a priest has the authority to give absolution to one who has become a Hagarene [i.e., Muslim] or a pagan who is afflicted to the point of dying? Jacob: If he is pressed to the point of death and there is no bishop nearby, then [the priest] has the authority to grant him absolution and give him the Eucharist and bury him if he dies. If, however, he is alive, let him be brought to the bishop and let [the bishop] set a punishment in accordance with what he knows [the person] is able to bear. (Vööbus, *Synodicon I,* Syriac text 261, no. 21)

§ John: If an individual becomes a Hagarene or a pagan and, after a time, turns back and feels regret and comes out of his paganism, should he be baptized or not? I want to learn. Has he been stripped of the grace of baptism by becoming a Hagarene? Jacob: A Christian who becomes a Hagarene or a pagan should not be baptized [again] on the grounds that he was at one time born from water and Spirit, according to the statement of our Lord [John 3:5–6]. But there should be a prayer for him by the head priest, and an appropriate period of penance should be defined for him. After the period of penance, let even the taking of the Mysteries be permitted to him. We can find this [view] validated by those who were baptized in water, but the Holy Spirit did not accept them, and then afterward they were counted worthy of it only through the prayer and laying on of hands of the head priest [Acts 8:16–17]. Now concerning the question of whether or not he has been stripped of the grace of baptism because he has become a Hagarene, I have this to say: About those things of which God is the giver, it is not for us to say whether or not they are taken away or stripped off from those who receive them. This is, rather, for God alone. For He waits for their return and repentance [cf. 2 Pet. 3:9], because He does not take pleasure in the death of a sinner, but rather wants them to turn back and be made holy [Ezek. 18:23, 33:11]. Here in this world and in this present life, He will not take from him the grace, but there, at the Last Day of the Resurrection, He will strip him of the grace and will take from him the talent, as from the wicked servant, and will cast him into the eternal fire [Matt. 25:26–30]. (Vööbus, *Synodicon I,* Syriac text 253, no. 15)

§ We do not baptize anew the Christian who becomes a Hagarene or a pagan and then returns. Instead, let the prayer of the penitents be said over him by the head priest and let a period of penance be appointed for him; when it is completed, let him take the Eucharist. (Kayser, *Die Canones Jacob's,* 8)

§ So far as a Christian who becomes a Hagarene and then returns is concerned, or a Christian who becomes a pagan and returns: let there be a prayer over him from the head priest, and once the period of penance is complete, let him take the Eucharist. (Kayser, *Die Canones Jacob's,* 13)

§ Addai: Concerning a Christian woman who of her own will marries a Hagarene: Should priests give her the Eucharist? Is there a specific canonical punishment concerning this? And if her husband threatens the priest, that he will kill him if he does not give her the Eucharist: Should he agree for a time while [the husband] is seeking to have him put to death, or should he consent and have it be considered a sin for him? Or is it preferable that he give her the Eucharist and she not become a Hagarene and her husband be kind to Christians? Jacob: You have resolved your perplexities in this question with what you have said: "Is it right that the Eucharist be given to her and she not become a Hagarene?" For the sake of her not becoming a Hagarene, therefore, even if the priest sins when he gives it to her and even if her husband does not make threats, he should give her the Eucharist [and he will not have a sin on account of giving it to her]. Now, as for the last thing you spoke of, namely, whether there is a specific canonical punishment concerning this, you should be guided in this way: if it is that there is no fear about her apostatizing and her husband is not making threats, she should fall under canonical discipline to the extent she seems to those in authority to be able to bear it, so that there will be fear among other [women], so that they themselves do not stumble, and for the sake of her own admonishment. (*Church of the Forty Martyrs* 310, 424–25)

§ So far as a woman who has married one of the Hagarenes is concerned: if it is that she says she will become a Hagarene because the Eucharist is not being given to her, let it be given to her, but along with a just canonical punishment that she receives. (Kayser, *Die Canones Jacob's,* 13)

§ Addai: Is it appropriate for a priest to teach the children of the Hagarenes, who have the power to harm him if he does not give instruction? Jacob: Along with the fact that necessity permits this person to do so, I myself say that this does no harm to the one who teaches, nor to the faith, and neither would it do so if they did not have the power to do harm, for from situations like these many things that bring profit have often emerged. (Lamy, *Dissertatio,* 158)

§ Whether it is appropriate for a priest to teach the children of the Hagarenes, who have the power to harm him if he does not give instruction? Jacob of Edessa says: "Along with the fact that necessity permits this person to do so, I myself say that this does no harm to the one who teaches, nor to the faith, and neither would it do so if they did not have the power to do harm, for the occurrence of such things has often brought profit to many." (Kayser, *Die Canones Jacob's,* 28)

§ John: Is it right that a priest give the blessings of the saints to Hagarenes or pagans who are afflicted by evil spirits so that they smear [them on] themselves and be healed, or that [he give them] *ḥnānā* [a mixture of oil, water, and dust compounded with saints' relics] for a similar purpose? Jacob: It is by all means right, very right, that we not hold something like these back from people, but that they rather be given to them. Concerning all illness, whatever it be, I am allowed to say that God's granting them healing even as you are giving them some of the blessings [of the saints] is a clear proof. You should give to them without impediment. (Vööbus, *Synodicon I,* Syriac text 249, no. 6)

§ John: Is it right that a priest give the blessings of the saints to Hagarenes or pagans who are afflicted by evil spirits so that they smear [them on themselves] and be healed, or that [he give them] *ḥnānā* for a similar purpose? Jacob: It is by all means right, very right, that we not hold back from one of them something like this, but that it be given to them for the sake of illness, whatever it be. For I am allowed to say that God's giving them healing even as you are giving them the blessings [of the saints] is a clear proof. You should give to them without impediment (Rignell, *Letter from Jacob of Edessa,* 52)

§ Addai: An emir ordered a man who was the steward of a monastery to eat with him from a [single] plate. Should he eat or not eat? Jacob: It is not I who permits such a one: necessity does. (*Church of the Forty Martyrs* 310, 405–6)

§ John: Whether it is necessary that the doors of the church be shut at present when the Eucharist is being celebrated? Jacob: This is a necessary thing, especially on account of the Hagarenes, so that they not enter and mix with the faithful and bother them and mock the Holy Mysteries. (Vööbus, *Synodicon I,* Syriac text 237, no. 9)

§ John: Now if an entire village of heretics returns to the true faith, what should we do with their Mysteries? Jacob: Let them be sent to the members of their confession. This also happened to me: Once some Hagarenes brought a Eucharist that they had taken from the land of the Greeks [i.e., Byzantium]. When they had been shamed by their conscience, they brought it to me. I sent it to members of the same confession as those Greeks. (Vööbus, *Synodicon I,* Syriac text 243–44, no. 23)

FURTHER READING

Hoyland, Robert G. *Seeing Islam as Others Saw It: A Survey and Evaluation of Christian, Jewish, and Zoroastrian Writings on Early Islam* (Princeton, NJ: Darwin Press, 1997), 160–68, 601–10.

Tannous, Jack. *The Making of the Medieval Middle East: Religion, Society, and Simple Believers* (Princeton, NJ: Princeton University Press, 2018).

Teule, Herman G. B. "Jacob of Edessa and Canon Law," in *Jacob of Edessa and the Syriac Culture of His Day*, ed. Robert Bas ter Haar Romeny (Leiden: Brill, 2008), 83–100.

Vööbus, Arthur. *Syrische Kanonessammlungen: Ein Beitrag zur Quellenkunde*, vol. 1, *Westsyrische Originalurkunden*, 1, A–B (Louvain: Secrétariat du CorpusSCO, 1970), 202–16, 273–98.

11

A Multireligious City in Khurāsān Converts to Islam?

Shaykh al-Islām Abū Bakr ʿAbd Allāh al-Wāʿiẓ al-Balkhī (fl. 610/1214)

Arezou Azad

Title: *Faḍāʾil-i Balkh* (The merits of Balkh)
Genre: Historical writing
Language: Persian

INTRODUCTION

The *Faḍāʾil-i Balkh* (*FB*) was written in Arabic by Shaykh al-Islām Abū Bakr ʿAbd Allāh b. ʿUmar b. Muḥammad b. Dāwūd al-Wāʿiẓ al-Balkhī in 610/1214 and was adapted into Persian by ʿAbd Allāh [b. Muḥammad] b. al-Qāsim al-Ḥusaynī in 676/1278. Only the Persian version survives. The published edition by Ḥabībī is based on three manuscripts, the oldest of which is Persan-115 at the Bibliothèque nationale de France, dated to the fifteenth century (its folio numbers are indicated here in angle brackets). A revised edition, based on these manuscripts as well as a fourth manuscript previously held in private hands and acquired in 2019 by Āstān-i Quds-Raḍawī Library in Mashhad (M54324) and dated to the seventeenth century, along with a translation into English, is in press with the Gibb Memorial Trust Series. The translation provided here emanates from the upcoming publication.

According to the author, *FB* was simplified and translated for a nonscholarly audience, and it resulted from a series of sermons transmitted orally by the Shaykh al-Islām and transcribed by a student. The text often retains purported sayings of the Prophet (*ḥadīth*) and other reports (*akhbār*) in Arabic (rendered in italics in the translation) and then adapts these into Persian. The importance of Persian for

Islamization is emphasized and provides an important corrective to the idea that Arabization necessarily goes hand in hand with Islamization. The language in *FB* is simple, and no extraneous or complicated terms or concepts appear in the text beyond technical terms in Islamic scholarship (Ar. *ʿilm*), asceticism and early mysticism, in particular. *FB* was written at a time when local history-writing had become part of the literary and scholarly repertoire, and scholars in the eastern Islamic lands were translating Arabic historical texts into Persian to make them accessible to a wider audience.

The excerpts reveal that narratives about conversion to Islam were often contradictory and varied, reflecting the maxim of contradictions between authorities (Ar. *ikhtilāf*) in Islamic historiography—namely, that there is no single narrative. Thus, while in some instances the author is at pains to emphasize the immediate conversion of Balkh to Islam, there are other instances where we read of continuities in previous religious practices in Balkh. The text also reveals that the concept of "conversion," which has no lexical equivalent per se in Arabic or Persian, may be quite different in this context from Judeo-Christian notions. The latter see conversion as an individual act that represents a change of heart: the convert gives up a previous religion and replaces it with a new one. In *FB*, on the other hand, the "convert"—whom the Persian text describes as "bringing Islam" (Pers. *Islām āwardan*) or "accepting Islam" (*Islām qabūl kardan*), while the converter is described as "offering Islam" (*Islām arḍa kardan*)—first rejects Islam (*irtidād āward*) several times. Although previous scholars may have labeled such conversions insincere or opportunistic, it cannot be ruled out that people simply attached themselves to more than one religion at a given point in time and did not see this as a major contradiction.

Readers should pay especially close attention to the accounts of the Hephthalite ruler Nīzak Ṭarkhān and his "renunciation" in the eyes of his captor, the Umayyad general Qutayba b. Muslim (d. ca. 96/715). Also of interest is the account of the Barmakid ruler Faḍl b. Yaḥyā b. Khālid b. Barmak (d. 193/809), the foster brother of the ʿAbbāsid caliph Hārūn al-Rashīd (r. 170–93/786–809) and governor (Ar. *wālī*) of Khurāsān in 176/792. Through an Islamic normative and doctrinally based narrative he is shown to have pacified his ancestors' pre-Islamic past as the keepers of Balkh's Naw Bahār Buddhist complex. Accounts of the sacred tombs of the city, such as the famous Naw Bahār temple and monastery, and the construction of the city in Islamic times appear to have been corrupted by an amalgamation of Zoroastrian and Buddhist traditions. They provide insight into how the author, a senior Islamic scholar of the late twelfth century, weaves into his narrative Islamic concepts of conversion and pre-Islamic notions of (sacred) landscape. In this way, the narrative becomes a mechanism of communal conversion, evoking both Islamic paradigms and non-Islamic religious themes.

TEXT

Part 1: The merits [of Balkh] attested in texts

[P-13b] Muqātil b. Sulaymān is quoted as saying, "With his own blessed hand, he [possibly the Prophet Muḥammad] pointed to those two mounds where Job's shrine lay."

Ḥaṣan Baṣrī is quoted as saying, "Job the Forebearer is in a city called Balkh, and he lies in a place called Maydan. And they say that Job the Forebearer and Gushtāsp are both at rest in Maydan."

And one of the famous mosques is the Mosque of the Tomb. And they say that there is the tomb of a prophet in that mosque. Mutawakkil b. Ḥumrān used to sit in the ʿAbd al-Azīz Maqbarī Mosque and say, "In this mosque lies the dust of a prophet, and I am receiving blessings from my proximity to it." They relate of Abū Muṭīʿ that he said, "That tomb is underneath our minaret." [P-14a] Kathīr b. Ziyād said, "In the Mosque of Karānisī's [or Kawānisī's] Friend in Dashtak [a district of Balkh] there is a prophet's tomb. And several times I have seen a light shining from that place, that is, from under the minaret." . . .

It is mentioned in certain works that the angels surrounding the throne of God speak Fārsī-Darī. Ḥaṣan Baṣrī says that the language of heaven's residents [P-15a] is Pārsī. Naḍr b. Shumayl says that Pārsī-Darī is the language of the people of Balkh. . . .

After that, Qutayba b. Muslim reached the town of Bulūriyān in the environs of Balkh during the governorship of Ḥajjāj. In the year 87/705–6, he proposed to the chief (*dihqān*) of the place to accept Islam. The *dihqān* said, "I will not accept Islam until Nīzak Ṭarkhān, who is the ruler of Balkh, does." Thus, they made peace with him in exchange for some gold and silver. When they handed over the gold and silver, [Qutayba's army] broke the golden vessels that were there and seized more than the agreed amount. The infidel *dihqān* said, "Did you need to bring thousands of troops just for this meaningless gold and silver?"

Qutayba built the first mosque in Bulūriyān, and then he set off for [the valley of] Bahār Darra. Near this valley there was a castle (*kūshk*) with a lot of water [P-16b] around it. Nīzak had fortified himself there. ʿAṭāʾ b. Abī Sāyib of the Muslim army, the namesake of the "bridges of ʿAṭāʾ," said to Qutayba: "This infidel (*gabr*) relies on a castle and water. Why is it that we do not rely on God Almighty?" At once, he whipped his horse and crossed the water unscathed. He seized the fortress gate and pulled it down. When Nīzak saw this, he came down. They captured him and brought him to Qutayba, and Nīzak accepted Islam.

Subsequently, in the winter, Qutayba returned to Bukhara. Once [Qutayba] had settled in Bukhara, Nīzak rejected Islam. The news reached Qutayba, and he mobilized his troops once again and set off towards him by the Chaghāniyān road, and Chaghāniyān was conquered by him. He made Mutawakkil b. Ḥumrān the judge (*qāḍī*) and governor of that land, and the people of Tirmidh accepted Islam. Qutayba asked for their [P-17a] assistance so that he could subdue Nīzak and take Balkh. The people of Tirmidh responded favorably and obeyed, and crossed the Oxus. They captured Nīzak, and he accepted Islam once again. After that, he [Nīzak] rejected Islam again and headed for Khulm and Siminjān, and from there he went to Ishkamish. Qutayba destroyed the residences and his followers and laid siege on Ishkamish. He swore that he would not eat any food until he had made a stream out of the blood of Nīzak and his followers, turned a water mill with that blood, and made food out of the flour from that mill. The people of that land built a watermill and dug a millstream. They ordered that the necks of six thousand Nīzak's companions be severed. Then they channeled the blood toward the watermill and made food from that flour. On the second and third days they did the same, until they found Nīzak. [P-17b] They captured him, cut his throat, killed all his children and troops, and left none of his followers alive.

When Qutayba returned from the battle with Nīzak Ṭarkhān, he made Barūqān the capital and ordered the construction of the Jāmiʿ Mosque in Barūqān. He was the first to pray and hold the Friday service there. Qutayba was martyred in Dhū al-ḥijja 96/714–15 in Ferghana. He waged holy war (*ghazw*) sixteen times until he brought the religion of Islam as far as the borders of China. Qutayba's shrine is in Ferghana in a place called Kulīj. . . .

In the year 175/791–92, which was at the time of the apogee of the Barmakids, when Balkh's *ʿulamāʾ* and great people from the time of Hārūn al-Rashīd spread to all parts of the world. Faḍl b. Yaḥyā, who was of the Barmakid family, summoned the religious leaders and great people amongst Balkh's *ʿulamāʾ* to the Naw Bahār gateway. [P-19b] He said, "The original Barmakids were from Jibākhān in Balkh. My ancestors are known to have built Naw Bahār. Naw Bahār was the sanctuary and temple of the Magians. Today I am ashamed of that. Instruct me to do something that can absolve me of this disgrace." The religious leaders reached a joint decision that he should build a watercourse through the city to enhance his dignity and secure him a good name. He did that in the months of the year 178/794–95.

Shaykh al-Islām [al-Wāʿiẓ] says, "I have heard from reliable transmitters that when Asad b. ʿAbd Allāh was [re]building the city of Balkh, he endowed fifty waterskins of the kind that are used in Balkh province for carrying and distributing water (*az barā-yi saqqāʾī-hā wa ābrāh-hā*)."

It is attributed to Shādhān b. Faḍl al-Ḥāfiẓ [possibly Abū Bakr Shādhān, the thirty-eighth shaykh listed in the *FB*] that he said, "I saw the Prophet in my sleep. And in his blessed hand [P-20a] was a book. I said, 'O Messenger of God! What book is this?' He answered, 'It contains the names of the denizens of heaven who are from Balkh.' I said, 'Can you show it to me?' And he did. The first words were 'In the name of God, the most merciful.' The first name was that of Faḍl b. Yaḥyā. The religious leaders of Balkh jointly agreed that this was because he had built the water canal for the city of Balkh, thus giving relief to] the weak and those who lacked the strength to carry water and were inconvenienced because of that. And this is the verification of the Prophetic tradition concerning bearing and offering water."

From part 2: The special qualities [of Balkh] that are perceptible to the senses

The first religious blessing that is characteristic of this city is that it was built in the time of Islam, and that its people were firm and solid in [their belief in] Islam. It is for this reason that they called this place the "dome of Islam." Thus, it was said in the introduction to this book that the city of Balkh was in ruins until the eve of Islam and was rebuilt in the Islamic period in the time of Asad b. ʿAbd Allāh al-Qasrī. This means that most of the quarters had Arabic names.

The first house and quarter coming from the Naw Bahār gate is the House of Ḥarb b. ʿIrwān al-Saʿīd, after whom the Ḥarb Mosque is named. Today they call it the Spindlemakers' Quarter. The second quarter is the House of Muhallab b. Rāshid, which they call the Chequewriters' Quarter. The third is the House of Farāwaja. The fourth is the House of the Euphrates. The fifth is the House of the Sugarmakers. The sixth is the House of Muqātil b. Sulaymān, and today they call it the Nawand Quarter. The seventh is the House of ʿAbd al-ʿAzīz Maqbarī. [P-23b] The eighth is the House of Muqātil Maqbarī. The ninth is the House of Muhallab. The tenth is the House of Abū Faṭima, and the eleventh the House of Ijtihād. All these [names] are proof that [the quarters] were built in the Islamic period.

The second blessing is that all the people [of Balkh] were Muslims, and it was devoid of people who came from other lands, such as Jews, Christians, Zoroastrians, *dhimmīs*, and so on. There was no one from outside the community of the true [monotheistic] religion (*millat-i ḥanafī*). This good fortune and blessing sufficed [for this city] because no one in this place was an idolator or polytheist (*kasī dar way butparast nabūda wa mālik al-mulūk-rā shirk nayāwarda ast*). The third blessing is that other than the doctrine of the Sunnis (*juz az madhhab-i sunnat wa jamāʿat*), and there was no bad doctrine or innovation. Even though the people of Balkh were gentle, warm, generous, and patient, they were severe and uncompromising on matters of religious doctrine. The fourth blessing is that on all occasions they maintained the proper reliance and trust (*tawakkul wa iʿtimādī*) in their Creator, [P-24a] and in all important matters they sought the right recourse in none other than God. They limited their freedom of choice (*ikhtiyār*) and bridled their desires according to the decree of God. Therefore, the omnipotent God with His abundant grace took care of their important affairs....

Their nobles and common people, for the most part, were learned and strong in their religious beliefs. And they taught all things to the common people in Pārsī so that all could benefit from [Islamic] knowledge. The seventh blessing is that they were humble, gentle, beneficent, and generous, and they never remained in the hands of an oppressor or tyrant [for long], because when they turned to the most exalted [P-24b] and almighty God, he took care of their important matters. The eighth blessing is that they displayed miracles (*yad-i bayḍā*, literally the miracle of light that emanated from the hand of Moses) in their discourses and sweet allusions, and in their Arabic compositions, metaphors, subtleties, and intricacies. And they knew all the sciences well.

Another special aspect of this city is that it is more ancient than all the other cities, and its fame and renown has reached all corners and regions of the world. [Balkh] is famous in the region of Ṭurkistān and all the lands around it, and from India all the way to the very remotest lands. Even in Byzantium (*Rūm*) all the history books of that land and the comings and goings of [their] merchants speak of [Balkh]. And the favor [bestowed upon Balkh by] Muslim rulers and the legitimately designated caliphs needs no further elaboration.

But in the non-Arab lands during pre-Islamic times, it was the sanctuary (*ka ʿba*) and temple of the Magians. It is attributed to Ibn Shawdhab that the devil has his home in Khurāsān, and they call it "the Naw Bahār of Balkh." Every [P-25a] year, he dons a white garb (*iḥrām*) and makes a pilgrimage (*ḥajj*) to that house. Previously it was the sanctuary of the Magians and the temple of worship of the non-Arab lands. They also relate from Ibn Shawdhab that when the new solar year began, the great and noble ones of Ṭukhāristān [lit. Ṭakhīristān], India, and Turkistān and the lands of Iraq, Syria, and Greater Syria would come to this city and celebrate for seven days at the Naw Bahār site.

FURTHER READING

Azad, Arezou. *Sacred Landscape in Medieval Afghanistan: Revisiting the Faḍā ʾil-i Balkh* (Oxford: Oxford University Press, 2014).

Cribb, Joe, and Georgina Herrmann. *After Alexander: Central Asia before Islam* (Oxford: Oxford University Press and British Academy, 2007).

Paul, Jürgen. "Balkh, from the Seljuqs to the Mongol Invasion," *Eurasian Studies* 16 (2018): 313–51.

Vaissière, Étienne de la. "De Bactres à Balkh, par le Nowbahār," *Journal Asiatique* 298, no. 2 (2010): 517–33.

12

ʿUmar II and the Treatment of the *Mawālī*

Aḥmad b. Yaḥyā b. Jābir al-Balādhurī (d. 279/892), Muḥammad b. Jarīr al-Ṭabarī (d. 310/923), and Abū Muḥammad ʿAbd Allāh b. ʿAbd al-Ḥakam (d. 214/829)

Gerald Hawting

Titles: Ibn ʿAbd al-Ḥakam, *Sīrat ʿUmar b. ʿAbd al-ʿAzīz* (The life of ʿUmar b. ʿAbd al-ʿAzīz); al-Balādhurī, *Kitāb Futūḥ al-Buldān* (The book of the conquests of the lands) and *Ansāb al-Ashrāf* (The genealogies of the nobles); al-Ṭabarī, *Taʾrīkh al-Rusul wa-l-Mulūk* (The history of prophets and kings)
Genres: Historical writing; didactic and entertaining literature (biography)
Language: Arabic

INTRODUCTION

In the time of ʿUmar b. ʿAbd al-ʿAzīz (ʿUmar II, caliph from 99/717 to 101/720), conversion to Islam was both a social and a religious process. Those who came under Muslim rule as a result of the conquests could join Islam through the institution of clientage (*walāʾ*). Under this system, a client (*mawlā*, pl. *mawālī*) could seek to attach himself to a Muslim patron, effectively assuming a position between that of a free man and a slave. The client and the patron had obligations and duties toward one another, and the relationship offered advantages to both. The client attached himself to the patron's family or tribe, and generally assumed his religious identity.

By the time of ʿUmar's caliphate, in Iraq at least, most of those seeking to become clients were former landholders and agriculturalists who had migrated to the conquerors' garrison towns (*amṣār*) in the hope of finding employment and of avoiding the taxes they would have been subjected to had they remained on their lands.

These converts posed a great difficulty for the rulers. Whereas Muslims were liable only for certain alms payments as required by Islamic law, the non-Muslim conquered population supported the regime by the payment of tribute in the form of taxation. Large-scale conversion may have gained souls for Islam, but it also shrank the numbers of the possible tribute-payers.

In addition, the transfer of land from non-Muslim to Muslim hands diminished the main resource on which the government could levy tribute. After the conquests, the majority of the agricultural land in a place like Iraq had been left to be occupied and worked by the non-Muslim population. Under Islamic law, it was designated as *fayʾ* (unmovable booty or spoils) and was to be exploited by the ruler for the benefit of the Muslims. Exploitation meant taxing those who worked the land—namely, the non-Muslims. But when these peasants converted, the land they farmed became tax exempt, for as Muslims, they now had to pay only the obligatory religious contributions.

Thus, a tension developed between two priorities: the need to honor the rights of all who wished to become Muslims and the need to maintain the finances of the empire. Several of the extracts translated here illustrate this tension. ʿUmar II is portrayed as wishing to encourage conversion, whereas most other Umayyads are shown trying to protect state finances by preventing non-Muslims from abandoning their lands and migrating to the towns. The emblematic contrast is between ʿUmar II and al-Ḥajjāj b. Yūsuf, the famous governor of Iraq between 695 and 715.

The details of the fiscal system in force in the various provinces of the empire remain obscure. That being said, in the century or so following ʿUmar's reign, a reasonably consistent distinction developed between two kinds of tax. The first was a land tax, generally called *kharāj,* which was to be paid by anyone, Muslim and non-Muslim alike, who owned land that was considered *fayʾ* (that is, land taken by conquest and regarded as the property of the Muslims as a whole). The second was a tax levied on the heads of non-Muslims (the *ahl al-dhimma* or *ahl al-kitāb*) and usually called *jizya.* The *jizya* is often referred to as a poll tax.

It is not clear, however, how far that system had developed by the time of ʿUmar II. Although *kharāj* is often mentioned in the sources in connection with the land, the difference between it and *jizya* is not always obvious, since flight to the *amṣār* would allow one to escape taxes on one's land and head alike. In extract 5, in response to the complaint that those who had accepted Islam were still being forced to pay the *kharāj,* ʿUmar responds by asking for the *jizya* to be lifted from them.

There is also a somewhat bewildering variety of names for the alms that Muslims were supposed to contribute, and for the land and other things on which they were to be paid at specified rates. In extract 1, for instance, land owned by a Muslim and exempt from *kharāj* is first referred to as *ʿushriyya* (subject to a tithe) and then as *ṣadaqa,* a word that sometimes refers to the obligatory alms payment required of a Muslim (also called *zakāt*) and at other times to voluntary alms. In extract 4, the plural form of *ṣadaqa* (*ṣadaqāt*) is mentioned together with the *akhmās* (lit. "fifths"), apparently with reference to the obligatory alms to be paid by a Muslim. The singular form of *akhmās, khums,* is usually used in Sunni Muslim law to indicate a share of the captured booty to be paid to the ruler, whereas in Shiʿi usage it normally refers to all sorts of property. Therefore, the distinction between it and *zakāt* is blurred. Its sense in ʿUmar's "fiscal rescript" seems closer to the Shiʿi usage.

The first two extracts in this selection illustrate the nature of the problems confronting ʿUmar, his predecessors, and his successors and the different ways in which various caliphs and governors tried to deal with them.

The third extract shows the danger faced by the Umayyad empire when religious discontent caused by the government's attempt to stem the migration into the garrison cities fused with a revolt in the army. Ibn al-Ashʿath was a high-ranking commander who led a major, although ultimately unsuccessful, revolt against the Umayyads in the first years of the eighth century. The identity of the *qurrāʾ* (lit. "readers" or "reciters"), the religious activists referred to in the extract, has been the subject of scholarly debate.

The fourth extract is taken from a long document included in Ibn ʿAbd al-Ḥakam's hagiographical biography (*sīra*) of ʿUmar II. The document was translated and analyzed by the historian H. A. R. Gibb, who called it "the fiscal rescript of ʿUmar II" and treated it as authentic. The problem is that the document is made up of various parts for which there are parallels or similar versions in other sources. ʿUmar clearly became idealized as a Muslim ruler, and it is likely that many of the letters and other judgments attributed to him in the sources are later creations. That does not mean that none of them are genuine or that the views attributed to him do not reflect his own, but we should be cautious about treating the "fiscal rescript" or the other letters translated here as genuine documents of ʿUmar. Generally, we see him attempting to grant new converts exemption from the financial impositions they continued to suffer from their time as non-Muslims, and less often concerned with preserving their land for the benefit of the Muslims in general.

The fifth extract, from the chronicle of the historian al-Ṭabarī, refers to the discontent felt by clients in Khurāsān in northeast Iran under the governor al-Jarrāḥ. The extract tells us that al-Jarrāḥ attempted to stem the tide of conversion by insisting on the circumcision of aspiring converts, but ʿUmar rejected this condition. It is striking that the slogan attributed to ʿUmar here ("God sent Muḥammad to call to Islam; He did not send him to circumcise") is nearly identical in Arabic to that which is more commonly attributed to him ("God sent Muḥammad to call to Islam; He did not send him to impose taxes"). "Circumcising" (*khātinan*) and "taxing" (*jābiyan*) have the same ductus in Arabic, and only the dots (often omitted when writing Arabic) distinguish the meaning.

In the final extract—which consists of three letters sent by ʿUmar to his governors taken from the chapter devoted to ʿUmar in al-Balādhurī's *Ansāb al-Ashrāf*—

ʿUmar takes circumcision for granted as a sign of Islam and again insists that his governors allow converts all their rights as Muslims. In the third of these letters, there is the interesting idea that converts from a Christian background and those from a Jewish one would have different beliefs or points of view. Christians would focus on the Qurʾān's description of Jesus as servant, word, and Messenger of God, while Jews would concentrate on its reference to ʿUzayr (usually identified as the biblical Ezra).

All of the extracts translated here are from texts authored considerably later than the time of ʿUmar himself, although some of them are introduced with chains of transmitters (*isnāds*, omitted here) that claim to document the transmission of the material over more than a century. Even if those chains are accurate, they cannot guarantee the absence of subtle evolution of the material in the course of its transmission. In this respect, the development of the image of ʿUmar II as a model Muslim ruler has already been mentioned.

Given the shortness of his caliphate, it seems unlikely that ʿUmar's measures had much lasting effect. At the same time, the consistency with which the sources refer to him in connection with taxation and the *mawālī* (or, more accurately, would-be *mawālī*) is probably not merely a result of ʿUmar's hagiographic image: it reflects the fact that by his day the issue of the conversion of non-Muslims had become a critical problem for the Muslim rulers of the greater Middle East.

TEXTS

(1) *Al-Balādhurī,* Futūḥ, *368*

There were lands on the Euphrates whose people accepted Islam when the Muslims arrived, and lands which passed from the hands of those who occupied them to some Muslims—by gift and through other measures taken by the rulers. Thus, they became tithe lands (*ʿushriyya*), whereas previously they had been *kharāj* lands (*kharājiyya*). Al-Ḥajjāj reimposed the *kharāj* on them, and then ʿUmar b. ʿAbd al-ʿAzīz restored them to the *ṣadaqa*. ʿUmar b. Hubayra [governor of Iraq, 102–5/721–24] subsequently again made them *kharāj* lands, but when Hishām b. ʿAbd al-Malik became ruler [in 105/724], he made some of them *ṣadaqa* land again. Then, al-Mahdī, the Commander of the Believers [caliph, 158–69/775–85], included all of it in the lands of the *ṣadaqa*.

(2) *Al-Balādhurī,* Futūḥ, *73*

When Muḥammad b. Yūsuf [d. not long after 91/710], brother of al-Ḥajjāj b. Yūsuf, governed Yemen, he acted badly and oppressed his subjects. He seized the people's land unjustifiably, including al-Ḥaraja [or perhaps "the thicket"]. He imposed on the people of Yemen a *kharāj,* which he made a burden for them. When ʿUmar b. ʿAbd al-ʿAzīz ruled, he wrote to his financial intendant (*ʿāmil*), ordering the removal of that burden and its limitation to the tithe (*ʿushr*). ʿUmar said, "If I did not receive even a handful of *katam* [a plant which provided oil for lamps] from Yemen, I would prefer that to confirming this imposition." But when Yazīd b. ʿAbd al-Malik ruled, he ordered its restoration.

(3) Al-Ṭabarī, Taʾrīkh, *part 2, 1122–23*

Al-Ḥajjāj's financial intendants wrote to him, "The *kharāj* is in ruins. The non-Muslims (*ahl al-dhimma*) have accepted Islam and settled in the garrison towns." He, therefore, wrote to Basra and other places, saying that whoever had come from a settlement must go back to it. The people left and set up camps, and they began to weep and to cry out, "*Yā Muḥammadāh, yā Muḥammadāh!*" They had no idea where to go. The pious activists (*qurrāʾ*) among the people of Basra started going out to them, wearing veils [signifying mourning?] and weeping because of what they heard and saw of them. Ibn al-Ashʿath emerged at this time [ca. 83/702], and the *qurrāʾ* of the people of Basra considered joining ʿAbd al-Raḥmān b. Muḥammad b. al-Ashʿath to fight against al-Ḥajjāj.

(4) Ibn ʿAbd al-Ḥakam, Sīrat ʿUmar b. ʿAbd al-ʿAzīz, *83–84*

ʿUmar b. ʿAbd al-ʿAzīz wrote: From ʿAbd Allāh ʿUmar, Commander of the Believers, to the governors:

"Now, God sent Muḥammad (God bless him and give him peace) 'with the guidance and the religion of truth to make it victorious over all religion, even though those who worship others together with God reject it' [Q. 9:33]. . . .

"Whoever accepts Islam among those who today pay the *jizya,* whether Christian, Jew, or Magian [Zoroastrian], and associates with the company of Muslims in their land, abandoning his previous abode, is to have what the Muslims have and to be subject to what they are subject to, and it is the Muslims' duty to associate with him and support him.

"However, his land and his abode are part of what God has given as spoils (*fayʾ*) for the Muslims in general. If he had accepted Islam there before God opened it up to the Muslims, it would be his, but [now] it is God's *fayʾ* for the Muslims in general.

"As for him who today is at war [with the Muslims], let him be called to Islam before he is fought. If he accepts Islam, he is to have what the Muslims have and the obligations they are subject to, and he keeps the household and wealth he had when accepting Islam. If he [remains] one of the subject 'People of the Book' (*ahl al-kitāb*), brings the *jizya,* and refrains from opposition to the Muslims, we accept that from him."

(5) Al-Ṭabarī, Taʾrīkh, *part 2, 1353–54*

Al-Jarrāḥ [governor of Khurāsān, 99–100/717–19] wrote to ʿUmar and sent a delegation—two Arabs and a *mawlā* of the tribe of Ḍabba, whose patronym was

Abū al-Ṣaydāʾ and personal name Ṣāliḥ b. Ṭarīf and who was meritorious in his religion. It has been said that the *mawlā* was Saʿīd, the brother of Khālid or Yazīd al-Naḥwī.

The two Arabs spoke while the *mawlā* sat. ʿUmar said to him, "Aren't you part of the delegation?" "Yes, indeed." "Then why don't you speak?"

He replied, "O Commander of the Believers, twenty thousand of the *mawālī* fight without any pay or provisions. A similar number of the non-Muslim subjects (*ahl al-dhimma*) have accepted Islam, but the *kharāj* is still taken from them. Our governor is crudely partisan toward his own tribal group. He stands on our pulpit saying, 'I came to you with consideration for you, but now I take the part of my own people. By God, one of my own people is more to me than a hundred others.' He is so coarse that the sleeve of his hauberk reaches only halfway down his arm. Furthermore, he is one of the swords of al-Ḥajjāj. He rules with oppression and hostility."

ʿUmar said, "In that case, let those like you come in delegation." He wrote to al-Jarrāḥ, "Look to see who is in front of you praying toward the *qibla* [the direction of Mecca and the Kaʿba faced by Muslims in prayer], unburden him of the *jizya,* and hurry the people into Islam."

Al-Jarrāḥ was told, "The people are rushing into Islam, but only to escape the *jizya,* so put them to the test of circumcision." He wrote about the matter to ʿUmar, who replied, "God sent Muḥammad to call people [to Islam]; He did not send him to circumcise them."

(6) Al-Balādhurī, Ansāb, *8:146, 152–53, 163*

ʿAdī b. Arṭāt [governor of Baṣra, 99–101/717–20] wrote to ʿUmar, saying that a group of non-Muslim subjects (*ahl al-dhimma*) had sought refuge in Islam to escape the *jizya* and asking him to write back with his views on the matter.

ʿUmar replied, "God sent His prophet to call people [to Islam] and not to tax them. Whoever enters among the Muslims is to have what they have and to be subject to what they are subject to. So, observe those of the subject people who [now] profess Islam, have been circumcised, and recite chapters from the Qurʾān. Remove the *jizya* from them, God willing; so farewell. . . . "

[. . .]

ʿAbd al-Ḥamīd b. ʿAbd al-Raḥmān [governor of Kufa, 99–102/717–20] wrote to ʿUmar b. ʿAbd al-ʿAzīz, "Some of those subject to the payment of *kharāj* have sought to escape it by fleeing from one district to another, so I have ordered that the land of those who fled should become *ṣafiya* [abandoned land that has passed to the state]. I hope that, God willing, that will make them stop what they are doing."

ʿUmar replied, "I have received your letter. By my life! If you do not leave alone those who have left their district for another, and their settlement for another, and instead you seize their land and then are removed from office or die, you will have separated the owner of the land from the land and assumed the burden of his offense. People abandon their land only when they are imposed on beyond their capacity. Beware, lest you and your financial officers act like [al-Ḥajjāj] Ibn Yūsuf. He and his officials were miscreants against whom God has passed judgment to the effect that their acts will be of no avail. Support those who work the land, for their land and their region are dearer to them than flight, if you treat them with justice and kindness, God willing. And farewell."

[. . .]

ʿUmar wrote to one of his governors, "God has graciously bestowed Islam on His people, and with it removed abasement and humiliation from them. So, look to anyone who espouses Islam, bears witness that there is no god but God and that Muḥammad is His messenger, believes in God, His angels, and His messengers, and affirms that Jesus is the servant of God, His word, and His messenger (if he was a Christian) or that ʿUzayr was God's servant (if he was a Jew), observes the number of prayers and their times, recites the opening chapter (*al-Fātiḥa*) and more from the Qurʾān, and performs the ritual ablutions well, and whom you have found to be circumcised—and remove the *jizya* from him.

FURTHER READING

Encyclopaedia of Islam, 2nd ed. [substantial articles concerned with topics mentioned here, including, in particular, "ʿUmar b. ʿAbd al-ʿAzīz" (Paul Cobb), "Mawlā" (Patricia Crone), "Umayyads" (G. R. Hawting), "Djizya" (Claude Cahen), and "Kharādj" (Claude Cahen), and providing guides to further reading].

Levy-Rubin, Milka. *Non-Muslims in the Early Islamic Empire* (Cambridge: Cambridge University Press, 2011), chapter 3.

Wellhausen, Julius. *The Arab Kingdom and Its Fall* (Calcutta: University of Calcutta Press, 1927; repr., London: Routledge, 2016), 267–311.

13

Mass Conversion of Christians in Northern Mesopotamia

Joshua the Stylite of Zuqnīn (d. mid-second/late eighth century)

Christian C. Sahner

Title: *The Chronicle of Zuqnīn* (*Ktābā hānā d-ʿuhdānā hānā d-zabnē d-bīshātā*, Book of this record of evil times)
Genre: Historical writing
Language: Syriac

INTRODUCTION

The *Chronicle of Zuqnīn* is a history of the world written in Syriac by a monk in northern Mesopotamia, in a region that is today located in southeastern Turkey. The author belonged to the Syrian Orthodox, or Miaphysite, Church, one of the largest Christian communities in the early medieval Middle East.

The *Chronicle* is an exceptionally rich source about daily life in the early ʿAbbasid period, when Muslim officials imposed numerous financial hardships on the local Christian population. The most important of these was the *jizya*, a poll tax that non-Muslims paid to the Islamic state in exchange for basic protections. The author explains that large numbers of Christians converted to Islam to escape such burdens.

In the translated passage, we see how Christians of all social classes—including clergy—went en masse to the Muslim-dominated cities to convert. There, former Christians were apparently called *aydūlī*, possibly a garbled allusion to the Arabic term *mawālī*, meaning "clients," or non-Arab converts to Islam. Such individuals were often reviled as second-class citizens in the Arab-dominated society of their day.

The *Chronicle* also describes the conversion of an individual deacon in the city of Edessa. His story gives a good idea of how conversion may have worked, especially the manner in which converts had to publicly renounce core tenets of their old faith (in this case, the divinity of Jesus) and to profess core tenets of their new faith (Jesus's status as a prophet, Muḥammad's role as the Messenger of God). Converts also signaled their change of faith by removing a belt known in Arabic as the *zunnār*, which Christians were required to wear in public to distinguish themselves from Muslims (for a Zoroastrian parallel, see selection 20 in this volume).

The author of the *Chronicle* portrays conversion as a kind of spiritual suicide. This is evidenced by the dramatic scene in which the deacon's soul is portrayed as escaping from his mouth as he prays toward Mecca for the first time. The chronicler also compares converts to Judas Iscariot, who betrayed Jesus to the Jewish authorities, playing on the fact that the Syriac words for "traitor" and "Muslim" are in fact homonyms (*mashlmānā*).

The numbers in angle brackets refer to pages in Chabot's edition of the *Chronicle*.

TEXT

The year 1081 (AD 769–70):

<381> When this wicked and godless kingdom began to rule and hold dominion, great and innumerable evils fell across the entire land because of the bitter, harsh, and merciless tributes [imposed by the state]. They began persecuting the Christian people without pity, and work of any kind ceased in every place in which the tyrants stopped giving grain and rations to the Arabs (*ṭayāyē*), as was customary. Because of this, currency became scarce throughout the land. The Arabs bought for themselves estates, vineyards, and yokes, and they became farmers. The tributes and the poll tax (*gzītā*, from Ar. *jizya*) burdened the Christian people without measure, and they started to spread desolation throughout the land. . . .

They had not yet learned to flee from place to place, so the door to paganism (*ḥanpūtā*, i.e., Islam) was opened for them. Bit by bit, all the wanton and dissolute people slipped toward the pit and gulf of perdition. <382> Their souls perished along with their bodies, that is to say, everything which they possessed, including their faith in our Lord Jesus Christ, baptism, the holy seal of our Lord, the living body, and the absolving blood. . . .

<383> Therefore, when they broke their trust in the help of Christ, they turned to paganism faster than sheep rushing to drink water. . . .

<385> For even without scourges and lacerations, they slipped toward [unbelief] with great enthusiasm. They would do this in groups of twenty, thirty, a hundred, two hundred, three hundred men, without any compulsion [forcing them] to it. They would go down to Ḥarrān and to the prefects and convert to Islam (*w-mahgerīn*). . . . [Satan] assembled a great crowd from the regions of Edessa, Ḥarrān, Tella, Resh ʿayn, . . . Dara, Nisibis, Sinjar, and Callinicum. Error and slander intensified beyond measure among the people from these regions, since there were in a village fifty or a hundred, or half or a third of this. They were different

from the believing people in both their persons and their names—in person because their once-happy persons became repellent, such that they were recognized by the intelligent ones by their persons, their odor, and the look in their eyes. This also happened to Judas the betrayer (*mashlmānā*) and their first father, in that his appearance and his name were revealed when he departed the rank of the disciples and when the Holy Spirit left him and a foul spirit came to dwell in him. . . .

<387> Along with their appearance, the name of Christians—and even that of Muslims (*mashlmānā*)—was taken away from them. They lost one name, that of Christ, but they did not snatch another, that of Muḥammad. Instead, as a result of their apostasy (*kfūryāhūn*), they discovered a name which they despised, by which they were called "Aydūlī," and by which they could be distinguished from the gentiles (*ʿammīn*) and their faith.

<388> . . . Many people have turned to paganism and renounced Christ, baptism, the Eucharist, and the cross upon which salvation was secured for every man. They renounced everything related to the providence of Christ. They acknowledged only that Christ was the word and the spirit of God [Q. 4:171].

<389> Whenever someone asked them, "This word and spirit of God which is with ʿĪsā [i.e., the Islamic name for Jesus], what is it?" they blasphemed and said, "He is like Moses, Elijah, and Muḥammad, their prophet who established for them the faith—a prophet like one of the prophets, a man like me or you." But they also professed that [ʿĪsā] was not born of a human seed, like all men. Rather, they denied him any divine substance. They claimed he was the word and the spirit of God and a prophet, and that he was not born of a man's seed. Instead, God commanded Mary and she conceived him, just as the trees are pollinated to produce fruit without a male, since they are pollinated by the wind. The prophet Jeremiah proclaimed weak faith like this to be like a leaky cistern [Jer. 2:13]. This was done not only by the young but also by adults, the elderly, and, worst of all, even by senior priests and so many deacons they could not be counted. . . .

It happened that at that time, I was in Edessa because of some matter that was taking place there. While I was there, several people appeared and said before us and everyone there that a certain deacon from <390> the plain of Edessa had slipped into the chasm and pit of this perdition. When the idea to apostatize came to him, all the nobles and priests of the village seized him and at length tried to persuade him [not to apostatize], but he was not persuaded. After beseeching him with doleful tears and gifts to repent of the wicked choice which he had set for himself, above all on account of the rank of holy priesthood which was upon him, since he did not yield to them, they left him alone. Meanwhile, he went to seek refuge with a certain man of the Arabs who was there. [The Arab] beseeched him to convert to Islam at his hands. He did not force him to do it; in fact, he asked him not to do it, lest he regret it on the same day and return to his original faith, causing them to inflict great tortures upon him. But he said, "If repentance comes to my mind, I shall not return from your faith, for God has shown me a sign!"

Therefore, [the Arab] said to him, "Do you renounce Christ?" He said, "Yes."

Then he said to him, "Do you renounce baptism?" He said, "I renounce it."

Then he said to him, "Do you renounce the cross, the Eucharist, and everything which the Christians confess?" He said, "I renounce them."

Along with these, the Slanderer [i.e., the Devil] said words of disgrace which were not among the demands of the Arabs. When this happened, he compelled him to apostatize. Then he demanded of him, "Do you confess that Muḥammad is the Messenger of God (*rasūleh d-alāhā*, Ar. *rasūl allāh*), and that the scripture [i.e., the Qur ʾān], which is from heaven, came down upon him?" He said, "I confess these."

Then he said, "Do you confess that ʿĪsā is the word and the spirit of God [Q. 4:171], that he is a prophet, and that he is not God?" He replied, "Yes."

Thus he compelled him to renounce everything by his own free will. Not a single one of them was forced to renounce his faith by compulsion, except by their father, the Slanderer, for many <391> of them apostatized without cause of any kind.

Then [the Arab] ordered him, "Remove your belt and pray toward the south [i.e., toward Mecca]!" . . . When he removed his belt and bent down to pray, his body became tense. When he bowed down, there went forth from his mouth some beautiful white object in the shape of a dove, which ascended to heaven. When that wretched man beheld this, he wailed bitterly like a woman and terrified everyone there. Then he said, "Woe is me! Woe is me! Woe is me! What has happened to me?"

When he had stopped his bellowing, he told everyone what he had seen and what had happened to him. He recounted this publicly before everyone, with many tears. Some people related to me these things which they heard from [the apostate's] own mouth. But because I was not particularly concerned with this matter at the time, I forgot the name of the man, that of his father, and that of his village.

Regarding this wretched man and those who behave as he does, the scripture says, "Howl, mourn, and make lamentations like a jackal" [Micah 1:8]. In this way, the Holy Spirit, a mistress, went out [from him], and a foul spirit, a mere handmaid, went in, as the scripture says.

FURTHER READING

Harrak, Amir. "Christianity in the Eyes of the Muslims of the Jazīrah at the End of the Eighth Century," *Parole de l'Orient* 20 (1995): 337–56.

———, trans. *The Chronicle of Zuqnīn, Parts III and IV, A.D. 488–775* (Toronto: Pontifical Institute of Mediaeval Studies, 1999), esp. 1–33.

Robinson, Chase F. *Empire and Elites after the Muslim Conquest: The Transformation of Northern Mesopotamia* (Cambridge: Cambridge University Press, 2000).

14

Conversion and Martyrdom in ʿAbbasid Damascus

Anonymous (second–third/eighth–ninth century)

Johannes Pahlitzsch

Title: *Hypomnēma kath' historian tēs athlēseōs tou hagiou megalomartyros Hēlia tou neou* (Memorial according to the account of the martyrdom of the holy great martyr Elias the Younger)

Genre: Religious instruction (martyrology)

Language: Greek

INTRODUCTION

Nothing is known about the anonymous writer of the *Martyrdom of Elias of Helioupolis*, except that he must have been a native of Syria. The vita he authored is transmitted in a unique manuscript (Cod. Paris. Coislin. Gr. 303) from the tenth or eleventh century, though the surviving text is presumably a reworking of an older, shorter version. Whether this original vita was written in Greek, Syriac, or Arabic cannot be determined. The text was likely authored after the eighth-century events it purports to describe, because the author makes no reference to eyewitnesses and describes the cult of Elias as having already existed for some time. It has been suggested that certain details in the life reflect a tenth-century rather than an eighth-century context.

According to the vita, Elias was born in 759 to a Christian family in Helioupolis (Baalbek in modern Lebanon) and trained as a carpenter. Together with his mother and two brothers, he left his native town for Damascus, where for two years he was employed by a Syrian who had renounced his Christian faith. After Elias was falsely accused of having converted to Islam—under highly contentious circumstances, involving a dance and a belt—he left Damascus to live in his hometown. Elias returned eight years later to Damascus to open his own workshop, obviously believing that the incident had been forgotten. However, he was denounced by his former employer and executed on the orders of the eparch al-Layth (in Greek, Leithi) in 779.

The text is of interest because of its emphasis on the laity, and it thus contrasts sharply with the otherwise overwhelmingly monastic character of Greek hagiography from this period. It presents a lively picture of daily coexistence between Christians and Muslims in Damascus during the eighth century. It also demonstrates how religious change could be contested, particularly given that conversion was often signaled through ambiguous gestures, such as the removal of a belt. In this context, Elias's belt is meant to represent an article of clothing known in Arabic as the *zunnār,* which Christians were obliged to wear in public spaces so as to distinguish themselves from Muslims, according to Islamic law.

TEXT

Elias, this holy neomartyr and athlete for Christ, stemmed from the exceedingly pious inhabitants of Helioupolis in the Lebanon range of Phoenicia Secunda, received a Christian upbringing and led a normal life. He practiced the trade they term carpentry, working with medium-sized pieces of wood. With his indigent mother and two brothers he left his homeland of Helioupolis and moved to the large metropolis of Damascus, in which he hoped [to find] a more suitable living. There he was hired by a certain sycophant (*parasitos*), who was of Syrian extraction and devoted to one of the Arabs, and from then on he endured two years spent practicing this same trade with him. Through the Devil's dealing and with the approval of the Arab, however, the sycophant Syrian renounced the faith of Christ, yet continued to practice his craft. The child Elias, however, already at that point a great martyr (*megalomartyros*), ignored the designs of the wicked one and remained with the apostate, earning wages through [his] trade.

Yet shortly thereafter the Arab, the patron of the apostate, died after he had contracted his son to be married. And afterward his son sired a child [and] at the advice of his friends celebrated the birthday of the child by putting on a feast. After the feast had concluded and the apostate had also celebrated, they called the great martyr Elias to attend to them. And Elias was about twelve years old. And so he served at the dinner, all the while bantering and enjoying the feast because he was an innocent child. The clients of the [deceased] patron turned to the martyr and said: "Where do you come from, child, since we see that you are clever and are celebrating with us?" But the apostate, answering in his stead, replied: "He is employed in my trade, since he is good, as you can see." And so with each of them laying hold of him they said to the saint: "If you so desire, child, should you not also abandon the Christian faith and become like us, so that you shall not continue to be a laborer for your master, but rather a son?" At once the saint answered: "You have gathered to feast, not to lecture; stop saying such things to me." They answered in return: "Then come and eat with us." And the saint, coming without guile and eating, continued to serve them, and some of them, standing up from the feast, danced, and forced the saint to prepare to dance with them, pressed around him to loosen the saint's belt (*zōnē;* cf. Ar. *zunnār*) and ripped it from his side. This was so that the movement of his body would not be constrained while dancing. Then the feast of the wicked intrigue dissolved.

After the night had passed, the holy great martyr Elias arose in the morning. Since all those who had celebrated with him were still sleeping in the house, he girded himself according to the custom of the Christian community with his own belt, and after washing his face he left the house and set out to pray to God. But someone still groggy from the previous night's drinking called out to him and said: "Elias, where are you going?" The saint answered: "I am going to pray." Grasping him, someone else said to the saint: "Did you not deny your faith last night?" The saint paid no heed to this talk and did not turn to the speaker, but went on his way to pray; then, upon returning, he arrived at the workshop and found the apostate. And the latter said to him: "Truly, Elias, had I not hindered my companions, they would have vexed you today, because they say that last night you denied Christ. But work and be unafraid." After he had heard these things the saint wondered at them, was silent for a time, and then at breakfast time departed and came to his brothers and told them the things that had happened to him. Following the opinion of the older brother and together with his mother, they went to the apostate and said to him: "See here, sir, [our] brother has been here a year with you and nothing of his salary has been paid by you. Give us what is rightfully ours and our brother will leave you, because we have decided to send him to Helioupolis, our native city." The apostate answered: "You shall have nothing paid from the wages of the child. Moreover, I will not allow your child to leave me, because he has renounced the faith of the Christians, and I have witnesses against him."

There then arose a dispute between the two, wherein the saint narrated what had been said during that wicked feast, while the apostate reiterated that he would bring the saint to the governor. Then the brothers of the saint renounced his wages that they had sought and seemed to placate the apostate. Taking the saint aside, his brothers said: "Brother, we have resolved that you should withdraw to Helioupolis, our homeland, because there you can earn a living by working for a time, until this story passes. For we fear that if you are seen, the apostate will be stirred up again and arrange a further attempt. Since he desires to have you as his slave, he had arranged such things." Mollified, the saint then turned back to Helioupolis and made his living among its inhabitants by working for eight years. Afterward he decided to go to Damascus. His brothers, who were in agreement, said to the saint:

"A period of eight years has already passed and the apostate has forgotten that intention he had regarding you. For from the time you departed from him, he has said nothing to us about you, though we have met and come across him by chance often. Therefore now we have resolved that you should not be apart from us, especially as this grieves our mother. But you are, after all, finally a youth. For already you have reached your twentieth year and, having begun to grow a beard, you might be trusted as a man in his craft: open a workshop and be with us in Damascus."

And so the saint was convinced, and after he had realized his intention, he endeavored in his workshop to make camel saddles, which he then sold. But upon learning this, the apostate became envious of the saint. And since he was very much in the vicinity of the workshop, he came to the saint and said to him: "Friend, where have you been all these years? Why do you admonish me, as I come to you today? Instead come now and work again with me as a partner." The saint said with a smile: "You have done me wrong by withholding my wages. Do you wish to injure me again?" The apostate was stung by this and said to the saint: "I have in fact done you wrong by allowing you to remain in your faith, even though you renounced it." And after summoning the son of the deceased Arab who had been his patron, whose wicked feast was previously described, he said to him: "Do you not testify that this Elias left after renouncing Christ on that night?" And he answered: "Yes." And the apostate said to the saint: "Let us go to the eparch."

FURTHER READING

Foss, Clive. "Byzantine Saints in Early Islamic Syria," *Analecta Bollandiana* 125 (2007): 93–119.

McGrath, Stamatina. "Elias of Heliopolis: The Life of an Eighth-Century Syrian Saint," in *Byzantine Authors: Literary Activities and Preoccupations; Texts and Translations Dedicated to the Memory of Nicolas Oikonomides*, ed. John W. Nesbitt (Leiden: Brill, 2003), 85–107 [with separate English translation].

Sahner, Christian C. *Christian Martyrs under Islam: Religious Violence and the Making of the Muslim World* (Princeton, NJ: Princeton University Press, 2018), esp. 53–59.

Sizgorich, Thomas. "The Dancing Martyr: Violence, Identity, and the Abbasid Postcolonial," *History of Religions* 57 (2017): 2–27.

15

Three Accounts of Zoroastrian Conversion to Islam

Muḥammad b. ʿAbdūs al-Jahshiyārī (d. 331/942), ʿAlī b. Yūsuf al-Qifṭī (d. 646/1248), and Abū al-Faraj al-Iṣfahānī (d. early 360s/970s)

Michael Cooperson

Titles: (1) al-Jahshiyārī, *Kitāb al-Wuzarāʾ wa-l-Kuttāb* (The book of viziers and scribes); (2) Ibn al-Qifṭī, *Taʾrīkh al-Ḥukamāʾ* (Biographies of philosopher-scientists); (3) al-Iṣfahānī, *Kitāb al-Aghānī* (The book of songs)

Genres: (1) historical writing (administrative); (2–3) didactic and entertaining literature (scientific and literary biography)

Language: Arabic

(1) FROM THE OUTSIDE

Introduction

In this text al-Jahshiyārī sets out to explain how al-Faḍl (d. 202/817–18), a bright young Zoroastrian from a provincial family, came to join the entourage of al-Maʾmūn (r. 198–218/813–33), the seventh caliph of the ʿAbbasid dynasty. The account is unusually thorough: it traces al-Faḍl's ascendancy back to the murder of his uncle. It explains how al-Faḍl's father, Sahl, seeking justice for his brother's murder, became a client of the Barmakid family of viziers. As it follows Sahl's quest, the report gives us a ground-level view of patron-client relationships in the ʿAbbasid period. As we learn, *mawlā*s (conventionally "clients," though probably better translated as "affiliates") might have possessed their own *mawlā*s, who in turn had their own *mawlā*s, and so on up to at least five tiers of patronage. In Sahl's case, conversion made it easier for him to press his case up to the next tier. (What remains unclear is why a Zoroastrian such as Sahl would reach out to former Buddhists such as the Barmakids.) Sahl's conversion is presented as a solo exercise, not a collective act: his sons embraced Islam later, and for reasons of their own. (Strikingly, though, the sons had Muslim names even before they converted.) We can also glimpse what was in it for the patrons: sponsoring a conversion gained them a grateful affiliate. Finally, even if all the parties were aware of the calculations involved, none seems to have taken conversion any less seriously, nor did they imagine that the act was any less valid or sincere by virtue of its immediate practical benefits.

Text

Al-Faḍl b. Sahl b. Zādhānfarrūkh came from a town in al-Sīb called Ṣābarnītā [near Kufa]. He had an uncle on his father's side called Yazīd b. Zādhānfarrūkh. Yazīd had the care of a woman [*jāriya*, here apparently a valued slave, or perhaps a freeborn daughter] who belonged to the household of ʿĀṣim b. Ṣubayḥ, an affiliate of Dāwūd b. ʿAlī, in al-Sīb. Yazīd and his family themselves had a house and an estate there. In addition to carrying out the responsibilities assigned to him, he managed his property well. He grew wealthy, and the lady came to value him enormously. Suspicious of the favor shown to Yazīd, ʿĀṣim summoned him and, while drunk, killed him with a blow of his sword. He then sent agents to secure the house and the estate.

Soon thereafter Yazīd's brother Sahl b. Zādhānfarrūkh, who was still a Zoroastrian (*wa-hwa majūsiyyun baʿdu*), presented himself at the gate of Yaḥyā b. Khālid [of the Barmakid family of viziers]. He asked him to help him regain the house and the estate and see justice done to ʿĀṣim b. Ṣubayḥ for killing his brother. Establishing a connection with Yaḥyā's affiliate Sallām b. al-Faraj, Sahl asked him to help right the wrong that had been done. Sallām agreed to take his side. He sent one of his own affiliates (*mawlā lahu*), a man called Murshid al-Daylamī, who with his crew wrested the estate from ʿĀṣim's agent, restored it to Sahl, and saw to the safety of the latter's children and possessions. It was at Sallām's hands that Sahl b. Zādhānfarrūkh converted to Islam (*aslama*).

Soon enough, ʿĀṣim b. Ṣubayḥ went to Yaḥyā to lodge a complaint against Sallām. Yaḥyā sent for him and rebuked him. In response, Sallām explained what had happened and had Sahl brought in to corroborate his account. Seeing that Sahl was the injured party, Yaḥyā took his side against ʿĀṣim. Sallām stayed on to provide protection to Sahl and look after the estate, with Sahl serving him and becoming a member of his entourage. Sahl thus came to mix with the Barmakid family. His two sons, al-Faḍl and al-Ḥasan, joined the household as well. The former established a connection with al-Faḍl b. Jaʿfar and took over the management of his household, while the latter established a connection with al-ʿAbbās b. al-Faḍl b. Yaḥyā. Having entered the service of the Barmakids, the two sons of Sahl came to the attention of Yaḥyā b. Khālid, who appreciated their loyalty and asked of them only nominal service ([?] *wa-kāna yuḥāfiẓu ʿalā yasīr al-khidma*).

At one point, al-Faḍl b. Sahl translated a document for Yaḥyā from Persian to Arabic. Impressed with his acuity and power of expression, Yaḥyā said: "I can see that you're intelligent and you have a bright future ahead of you. I can bring you on board with us and make sure you do well for yourself, but you'll need to convert to Islam."

Al-Faḍl thanked him and offered to convert at his hands.

"No," said Yaḥyā. "I'd rather set you up where you'll do as well for yourself as we have."

Summoning his affiliate (*mawlāhu*) Sallām, Yaḥyā told him to take the young man by the hand and bring him to Jaʿfar, and to tell Jaʿfar to introduce him to his pupil al-Maʾmūn and have him convert at the latter's hands. Jaʿfar did as he was asked, and so it was that al-Faḍl became a Muslim at the hands of al-Maʾmūn. The latter treated him very generously and included him among his stipendiaries. Sahl continued as a member of al-Faḍl b. Jaʿfar's entourage until the fall of the Barmakid family, at which point he joined the entourage of al-Maʾmūn.

(2) FROM THE INSIDE?

Introduction

If al-Jahshiyārī's account opens a window onto the sociology of conversion, this second passage, by the biographer Ibn al-Qifṭī, might be said to supply the phenomenology. It purports to tell us how al-Faḍl, the bright young man of al-Jahshiyārī's tale, felt about his new religion. The report is fitted with a plausible transmission history. Al-Faḍl's confidant, the Christian physician Jibraʾīl b. Bukhtīshūʿ (d. 212/827), was an affiliate of the vizier Jaʿfar al-Barmakī and may therefore have been aware of al-Faḍl's conversion. We know Jibraʾīl to have been in Baghdad at the same time as Ibrāhīm b. al-Mahdī (d. 224/839), the ʿAbbasid prince to whom he supposedly told the story. Whatever its authenticity, the report seems to be a joke made at al-Faḍl's expense. The words he exchanges with Jibraʾīl are given in Persian (italicized in the passage below) but translated into Arabic, as if intended for an audience suspicious of what the *ʿajam* (non-Arabs, usually Persians, and often non-Muslims) might be saying among themselves. In this case, what they are described as saying suggests that al-Faḍl knew little about Islam before he adopted it. Moreover, he was incapable of finding the Qurʾān any more sublime than *Kalīla wa-Dimna,* a collection of Sanskrit animal fables translated from Middle Persian into Arabic by Ibn al-Muqaffaʿ (d. 138/756?). Even if intended to mock the convert, this report may preserve some memory of what actually happened when Zoroastrians of the patrician class (and, *mutatis mutandis,* members of other non-Muslim communities) converted to Islam: they attempted to salvage elements of their former self-understanding.

Text

While speaking one day with Ibrāhīm b. al-Mahdī, Jibraʾīl reported that he had once called upon al-Faḍl b. Sahl, the Dual Authority [a title later granted to him by the caliph al-Maʾmūn to indicate his command over civil and military affairs], after his conversion to Islam. He found al-Faḍl freshly circumcised, reading a copy of the Qurʾān that lay before him.

Said Jibraʾīl: "I asked him, '*Chun bīnī nām-i Īzad?*'

'*Khush,*' he replied, '*u chun Kalīla wa-Dimna.*'"

The translation (*tafsīr*) of what they said is:

Said Jibraʾīl: "I asked him, 'How do you find (*kayfa tarā*) the Book of God?'

'Good,' he replied, 'like *Kalīla wa-Dimna.*'"

(3) CONVERSION BY DEFAULT?

Introduction

This excerpt from the biography of the famous singer Ibrāhīm al-Mawṣilī (d. 188/803 or 804) reports that he was born into a Zoroastrian family but joined an Arab Muslim household as a child and thus grew up Muslim. Unlike the preceding texts, it does not mention a formal conversion. His father, Māhān, does not seem to have converted: he was given a Muslim name only posthumously, as the first report explains. The excerpt also shows what happened when the adult Ibrāhīm met a fellow Persian who was not a Muslim: apparently, each could identify the other for what he was based on his appearance.

Text

[His name was] Ibrāhīm b. Maymūn, or Māhān, b. Bahman b. Nask. The way he became known as "the son of Maymūn" was that he once wrote a letter to a friend and headed it "From Ibrāhīm b. Māhān." One of his Kufan gang brothers (*fityān*) asked, "Aren't you ashamed of that name?"

"It's my father's," replied Ibrāhīm.

"Change it!"

"How?"

The young man took the letter, rubbed out "Māhān," and wrote "Maymūn." And the name stuck.

Ibrāhīm's son Isḥāq quoted him as saying: "Our family came originally from Fārs. Among the non-Arabs, ours was a noble house. My grandfather Maymūn was driven out by an oppressive Umayyad governor. He settled in Kufa, among the tribespeople of ʿAbd Allāh b. Dārim." Ibrāhīm's parents then exchanged nurslings (*kāna* [*baynahum*] *raḍāʿ*) with the children of Naḍla b. Nuʿaym.

Ibrāhīm's mother came from a family of provincial landowners (*dahāqīn*) who had fled Fārs at the same time as his father, Maymūn. Her family settled among the

ʿAbd Allāh b. Dārim as well. She and Maymūn were married, and she bore him Ibrāhīm. While Ibrāhīm was still a child, his father died in an epidemic. . . . The boy was taken into the care of Khuzayma b. Khāzim and his family . . . and later went to Qurʾān school with Khuzayma's sons. This is how he entered a relationship of clientage (*walāʾ*) with the tribe of Tamīm.

[. . .]

[Ibrāhīm:] I was told there was a man in Ubullah named Jāvanuwayh who was a skillful [music teacher]. I went to see him but didn't find him at home. So I waited for him. When he saw me he made a display of deference, as he was a Zoroastrian (*iḥtashamanī wa-kāna majūsiyyan*).

FURTHER READING

Bulliet, Richard W. "Conversion Stories in Early Islam," in *Conversion and Continuity: Indigenous Christian Communities in Islamic Lands, Eighth to Eighteenth Centuries*, ed. Michael Gervers and Ramzi Jibran Bikhazi (Toronto: Pontifical Institute of Mediaeval Studies, 1990), 123–33.

Choksy, Jamsheed K. *Conflict and Cooperation: Zoroastrian Subalterns and Muslim Elites in Medieval Iranian Society* (New York: Columbia University Press, 1997).

Cooperson, Michael. "An Early Conversion Story: The Case of al-Faḍl ibn Sahl," in *Essays in Islamic Philology, History, and Philosophy*, ed. Alireza Korangy, Roy P. Mottahedeh, and William Granara (Berlin: de Gruyter, 2016), 386–99.

Morony, Michael. "Madjūs," in *Encyclopaedia of Islam*, 2nd ed.

Savant, Sarah Bowen. *The New Muslims of Post-Conquest Iran: Tradition, Memory, and Conversion* (Cambridge: Cambridge University Press, 2015).

16

Conversion to Islam among the Armenian Elite

T'ovma Artsruni (Thomas Arcruni, d. ca. 292/904)

Tim Greenwood

Title: *Patmut'iwn tann Artsruneats'* (History of the house of Artsrunik')
Genre: Historical writing
Language: Armenian

INTRODUCTION

T'ovma is an elusive figure, unattested outside his *History* and a reluctant presence within it, referring to himself only once. He was a cleric with close connections to several members of the Armenian princely family of Artsruni, which controlled lands to the east and south of Lake Van. He reveals that he was asked to write a history of this princely family by one of its leading figures, Grigor Derenik. He continued it under the patronage of Grigor's second son, Gagik. The *History* breaks off in midsentence, with the Artsruni lands under threat of invasion in the year 904 CE.

The extracts below derive from an extensive narrative reporting the campaigns of the Turkish warlord and general Bughā al-Kabīr across the lands of the Caucasus between 851 and 855 CE, undertaken at the command of the 'Abbasid caliph al-Mutawakkil. Ashot Artsruni, the father and grandfather, respectively, of T'ovma's patrons, was one of the leading princes who was led away into captivity to Samarra, then the 'Abbasid capital, with several members of his family, including his son Grigor Derenik. It is therefore striking that T'ovma does not gloss over Ashot's conversion but acknowledges it, together with the conversions of members of other princely families, notably Bagarat Bagratuni.

Two features of the passage merit particular comment. First, Tʿovma's description of the tribunal is modeled closely on passages in Ełishē's earlier account of Armenian rebellion, persecution, and apostasy in the middle of the fifth century, when several princes reportedly feigned submission to Zoroastrianism at the court of the Persian king. The portrait of al-Mutawakkil is based on the Sasanian king Yazdgerd II and that of Bughā on Yazdgerd's vizier Mihrnerseh. Tʿovma's account of forced conversion is therefore a literary reconstruction, based on older Armenian tradition. Unlike that earlier text, however, Tʿovma agonizes about the consequences of his subjects' actions, indicating that some form of conversion took place and that it was a real issue at the time of writing.

The central question is whether conversion under duress should be treated differently from voluntary conversion. Tʿovma reflects on the example of the heretical Elkesites of the early Christian period and their conviction that one could apostatize with impunity during a time of persecution. This illustration and the response of the Roman priest Novatian to it derive from Eusebius's *Ecclesiastical History*, although Tʿovma maintains that Novatian changed his mind on readmitting lapsed believers, leaving the teaching unclear. His uncertainty is also a striking feature of the final extract, in which he meditates on Ashot's eternal fate in the light of his temporary denial and subsequent conduct.

The numbers in angle brackets refer to pages in Gēorg Tēr-Vardanean's edition of the text.

TEXT

<178> All the recollections in this narrative are intense, sad, and filled with bitterness at the concession of our great nobles and princes. This account is filled with tears, and I am incapable of describing the circumstances of their ruinous error in straying from the orthodox and pure apostolic confession of faith in the Father and the Son and the Holy Spirit of the Catholic Church. And I do not want to apply myself to describing and setting down in writing the destruction of our princely lords and whatever misfortune they brought upon their souls rather than their bodies, yet unwillingly I am compelled to write down and organize, briefly and in short, a summary, assembling in a few words a history of what transpired, because it is impossible to cover it up in silence, to hide or not disclose the unfathomable and terrible troubles and misfortunes which came upon us. . . .

[*Tʿovma then explains that while Ashot Artsruni and his family were in prison in Samarra, the caliph arrived in the city and summoned them before a public tribunal. They began to converse, and the caliph accused them of violent resistance and of failing to pay their taxes. Tʿovma quotes the caliph as follows:*]

<180> "But I now see that you are indeed of fine appearance and handsome, with your noble faces, seemly and becoming, that you are indeed the sons of kings

of that country and worthy of pity, and that you are indeed men of valor, and it is clear from your presence that you are powerful because you have done so much harm to me. Yet you have presented yourself before me in the tribunal with untroubled and joyful faces, like innocent men who do good deeds, eager to oblige us in every way, with complete sincerity. So I will spare you and will not put an end to your lives, as your wicked deeds and the harm which you have caused me deserve. Without experiencing torments or violent tortures, accept us and our legislator Mahumat, receive this faith and divinely given religion, far from falsehood, filled with everything which is the opposite of falsehood; reject completely that useless and false worship of yours in relation to Christ to whom you, in your stubbornness, have lashed yourselves. Then we shall ignore your damaging acts against us, your lives will be spared, and you will live and rule over your country and your houses, you and your sons." . . .

[*T'ovma then explains that the bishop of Artsrunik' rejected the offer, maintaining that the unsupported testimony of the Prophet Muḥammad cannot withstand comparison with the 111 witnesses to the divinity of Christ. The caliph responded by repeating his offer to the Artsruni princes.*]

<181> Although they had not wanted to turn in the slightest from worshipping the Son of God, since the faith of the holy apostles had settled in their hearts, because it did not have roots, it withered before the heat of the Devil. For at his bellowing, sparks fell and smoke of the fiery furnace came out through his nostrils, as is written in the book of Job [Job 41:21]. And on account of their weakness of spirit and unstable and wavering minds, they loved the glory of man <182> more than the glory of God, since "This people," he says, "worship me with [their] lips, but their hearts were removed and separated from me." And [as they were set apart] from the love of God, fear of death [took hold of] them, especially as they did not want to leave the vain life of this transitory world, and they said, "We accept the royal commands," having resolved that outwardly they would satisfy the intentions of the king but inwardly they would hold fast to their confession in Christ. But it is impossible for one person to hold both positions, and no one can serve two masters, as the Savior said, which I shall be required to illustrate in its own place.

Then straightaway they were circumcised as Muslims (*mslimanak*), following Bagarat Bagratuni, who was seized by another commander in the city of Khlatʿ, and he was prince of Taron; he was brought to Samarra and became an apostate and he opened the broad and wide road, the path of destruction which leads to unfathomable destruction, as Jeroboam, son of Nabat, who sinned and caused Israel to sin. . . .

[*T'ovma then comments on the willing conversion of Vasak Artsruni before describing in some detail the steadfast resistance of Yovhannēs, the bishop of Artsrunik'; Grigor the priest; and lord Grigor Artsruni. He also reflects on Bagarat Bagratuni's later defense of his actions:*]

<200a> In relation to his apostasy, Bagarat said that apostasy under threat of affliction causes no harm if one keeps secretly in one's heart the confession of faith. . . . Let us turn to the Elkesites, those who at the time of persecution fell into the error of idolatry. And this man had the notion that if anyone should turn to the worship of idols under threat of affliction, it would count for nothing if his heart held genuinely to the faith of Christ. At this time, Novatian, a priest in Rome, dispatched people to refute the Elkesites, and at the ending of the persecution, he did not receive those who repented of sacrificing to idols. And this man prevented many from idolatry, although he caused those who had turned back in repentance to wander in despair, and he ruined the whole world by being a stickler for unimportant things, although later on he did admit those who repented. . . .

[*T'ovma then reports the eventual return of Ashot Artsruni from Samarra and his struggle to reestablish himself in his former domains:*]

<227> Now when Ashot had reached the age of nineteen years, he exercised princely power for a further sixteen years, down to the Armenian captivity. He spent five years in captivity and lived for six years after his release. On returning to this country, he openly practiced the Christian religion, repenting that he had denied Christ.

But what should I say here? For although on returning they openly came back to the worship of Christ our God, they did not perform the canonical regulations in the correct manner, not only Ashot but all the Armenian princes who had been released. They rejected completely the corruption of apostasy but remained outside the canonical regulations, leading lives that were inconsistent with Christianity in terms of debauchery and drunkenness, of adulterous and disgusting behavior, in terms of appalling and revolting <25v> homosexual acts which surpassed the bestial acts associated with Jericho and the brazen conduct associated with Sodom, with man shamelessly lusting after man, incurring cascades of everlasting fire from heaven, worse than the deadly destruction of the Flood. Some of them strayed in pursuit of women, having intercourse with the daughters of Cain, and were destroyed by water; others, who engaged in disgraceful acts with men, were burned with a sulfurous fire, securing for themselves the certain prospect of the eternal fire.

But Ashot, when he reached the time for leaving this world, was plunged into the deepest remorse and regret; with copious tears he made confession, trusting for intercession in the mercy of Christ, repeating the last words of the tax collector and the thief, looking in faith to the saving body and blood of the Son of God for the forgiveness of sins, trusting in God's kindness. I do not despise or mock his remorse and regret, for "whoever shall call on the name of the Lord shall live" [Acts 2:21]. But it is unclear if they were effective, for with difficulty are scars removed, according to the holy injunctions. Yet, in the house of the Father of Christ, there are many mansions. Perhaps they shall live and stay without torments, although they shall not enjoy the wedding with the bridegroom. And so this man departed not without hope, looking to God's kindness.

FURTHER READING

Thomson, Robert W., trans. *Thomas Artsruni: History of the House of Artsrunik'* (Detroit: Wayne State University Press, 1985).

———. "T'ovmay Arcruni's Debt to Ełišē," *Revue des Études Arméniennes* 18 (1984): 227–35.

Vacca, Alison. "Conflict and Community in the Medieval Caucasus," *Al-ʿUṣūr al-Wusṭā: The Journal of Middle East Medievalists* 25 (2017): 66–112.

17

Conversion and Martyrdom in Córdoba

Eulogius of Córdoba (d. 244/859)

Kenneth Baxter Wolf

Titles: *Memoriale sanctorum* (Memorial of the saints) and *Liber apologeticus martyrum* (The apologetic book of the martyrs)
Genre: Religious instruction (martyrology)
Language: Latin

INTRODUCTION

Between the years 236/850 and 244/859, forty-eight Christians were executed in the Muslim city of Córdoba for religious offenses against Islam. The majority of the victims—thirty-eight to be exact—were condemned for blasphemy, most of these having deliberately flouted well-known proscriptions against public expressions of disrespect for the Prophet Muḥammad. The rest were executed for apostasy, most often because they were products of mixed marriages who had opted to live as Christians despite the fact that they were legally Muslims.

Practically everything we know about the circumstances surrounding the "Córdoban martyrs" comes from the pen of one man: a priest named Eulogius (d. 859), who took it upon himself to write two extended martyrologies that presented the dead Christians as martyrs analogous to the ancient Roman ones. Four of Eulogius's martyrs—Felix, Witesindus, Rudericus, and Salomon—happen to have been Christian converts to Islam who later decided to return to their natal religion. Thus, although they died as apostates for rejecting Islam, it was their earlier conversion to Islam that rendered their ultimate desire to live as Christians illegal. A fifth convert to Islam, mentioned by Eulogius though not as one of his martyrs, was an unnamed Christian official who worked for the Muslim administration of Córdoba. It is likely that he was Qūmis (Count) Ibn Antūnyān, who is referred to in Arabic sources as holding such a position at that time. In any case, when he was deprived of his position because of a government purge orchestrated by the emir, Muḥammad I, in 238/852, he converted to Islam and was reinstated to his position.

Texts 1–4 below describe the circumstances of each of the four conversions to Islam that led to execution. Eulogius treats the case of Rudericus in some detail because it involved an act of inadvertent apostasy that, as far as he was concerned, only enhanced Rudericus's eventual status as a Christian martyr. The other three such cases are mentioned only in passing. Text 5, describing the apostasy of the unnamed government official, shows Eulogius at his most caustic, which is not surprising because this official had personally attacked him in a church council that was convened to address the crisis caused by the spontaneous blasphemers.

TEXTS

(1) *The conversion of Felix*

There was also a certain kinsman of blessed Aurelius by the name of Felix who was joined to him as well by a holy love. Having vacillated in his faith as the result of some diabolical ploy, Felix was no longer able to practice the religion of Christ in public even though he regretted his apostasy deeply. He also took in marriage a daughter of secret Christians by the name of Liliosa and worshipped Christ secretly in hidden places. Clinging to one another unshakingly, [Aurelius and Felix] always maintained the same familiarity and bore the same sweetness toward one another. . . . This great bond of piety between the two brothers conferred on them the perfection of love to the point that they, whom the occasion of religion had joined, would be separated neither in life nor in death. (*Memoriale sanctorum* 2.10.4)

(2) *The conversion of Witesindus*

In that time there was a certain man of advanced age named Witesindus from the province of Cabra, who as the result of some unknown persecution had incurred a lapse of the holy faith. Yet when he was encouraged to practice his recently acquired worship, he refused to remain infected by such a sacrilege, which he had accepted suddenly due either to the weakness of the flesh or to a trick of the Devil. (*Memoriale sanctorum* 3.14)

(3) *The disputed conversion of Rudericus*

The blessed priest Rudericus was born in the village of Cabra and in that same town he merited both instruction in the holy law and the rank of priest. He had two brothers, of whom one rightly held the faith of Christ while the other, corrupted by gentile error [i.e., Islam], had spurned the Catholic religion. The latter brother, who remained at odds with the holy faith, was moved to conflict with the other Catholic brother whenever occasion arose. One night, when both brothers were engaged in just such a spontaneous argument—the circumstances of which I know not—and were raging with foul enmity toward one another, the holy priest [Rudericus] intervened with the intention of settling the quarrel. But both his brothers were so ignited with fury that they turned on him in their blind indignation and, not really knowing what they were doing, practically beat him to death.

When he, having been pounded by this beating and deprived of all his strength, laid his broken body on a bed, his profane brother put him on a litter and had him dragged back and forth through the streets and neighborhoods on the arms of porters. Like a true imitator of the Devil, he fabricated with his fraudulent machinations a confession of iniquity on behalf of the unconscious priest, saying: "Here is my brother the priest who, made remorseful by a divine visitation, has opted for the worship of our faith [i.e., Islam]. Close to death, as you can see, he did not want to leave this world before this was made known to you." Wandering through various places with him, this one recounted such things and others like them with slanderous words, while his brother remained totally unaware—in fact he was not even conscious—of what this evil man had contrived against him.

After a few days the priest recovered his condition, restored to his faculties by the dispensation of God. When he became aware of the deceitful actions of his nefarious brother, he—following the example of the Lord, who avoided the trap set by Herod for the sake of our own instruction [Matt. 14:13], and not being a deaf hearer of the gospel, by which we are commanded to seek refuge from city to city for the sake of avoiding persecution [Matt. 10:23]—abandoned his homeland and went elsewhere, where he could serve Christ freely, as if he could evade the temporal punishment by which he, divinely predestined from the creation of the world, would be prepared for martyrdom; as if he, deceiving the profane persecutor by hiding himself for a time, could remove himself from the sight of his pious Redeemer, the one summoning him to heaven. (*Liber apologeticus martyrum* 21)

(4) Salomon the apostate

In jail, Rudericus encountered blessed Salomon, whom the cruelty of the persecuting ones had confined there some time before on account of his profession in the name of Christ. He was accused of a similar crime because, spurning the cult of the holy religion, he had for a time adhered to the Muhammadan sect. Immediately the two were joined by an indivisible vow. Ministering to one another in turn with the support of their consolation, they mutually armed each other to complete the struggle, agreeing to do it together so that, with their affections for this world trampled, they might adhere to God in pious servitude each day. (*Liber apologeticus martyrum* 25)

(5) The conversion of a Christian official

Many [Christians], turning away from Christ of their own free will, clung to the wicked ones and honored the sect of the Devil [i.e., Islam] with the greatest affection, just like that bastard—unworthy of the blessing of the saints—about whom we made mention in book 2. Placing the pomp of worldly reverence over heavenly matters and venerating his office [as a minister working for the emir] instead of God with an unheard-of wantonness, he was—in the twelfth month after decreeing that the Christians were to be anathematized and after attacking us with foul insults—removed from his position. Thanks to his ability in the Arabic language, in which he was quite gifted, he alone of the Christians had been kept on by the consuls in the office of *exceptor,* but after some months he, too, was expelled from the palace and his service. He did not take what had been done to him lightly. When he saw that he was being removed, he, deeply grieved at being deprived of such a dignity, opted to die to God rather than not live for the world. Immediately spurning the faith of the Holy Trinity, he yielded to the sect of perversity, no longer wishing to be seen as a Christian. As a result of this, he who had never reflected on the simple things turned toward worse ones, becoming an exile to the Christians as he was joined to the gentiles. With his constant wanderings, he frequently entered that temple of impiety [that is, the mosque] as if he were one of the ministers of the Devil, expelled from the temple of the Lord, which, even when he was still one of the faithful, he would visit only on occasion and without enthusiasm. Thus it is written: "He shall not dwell in the midst of my house, he who does pride; he that speaketh unjust things did not prosper before my eyes" [Ps. 100:7]. After this betrayal, he was restored to his former honor and brought back to the palace, where he, who had become a trap for himself for the sake of temporal glory, could become a shackle and a hook for enticing others, an inducement to apostasy. (*Memoriale sanctorum* 3.2)

FURTHER READING

Safran, Janina. *Defining Boundaries in al-Andalus: Muslims, Christians, and Jews in Islamic Iberia* (Ithaca, NY: Cornell University Press, 2013).

Sahner, Christian C. *Christian Martyrs under Islam: Religious Violence and the Making of the Muslim World* (Princeton, NJ: Princeton University Press, 2018).

Wolf, Kenneth Baxter. *The Eulogius Corpus* (Liverpool: Liverpool University Press, 2019).

18

A Christian Intellectual Declines to Convert to Islam

Ḥunayn b. Isḥāq (d. 260/873)

Barbara Roggema

Title: *Kayfiyyat Idrāk Ḥaqīqat al-Diyāna* (How to discern the truth of a religion)
Genre: Religious instruction (apologetics)
Language: Arabic

INTRODUCTION

Ḥunayn b. Isḥāq was a famous East Syrian Christian polymath in ninth-century Baghdad. He is remembered first and foremost as one of the most prominent figures of the ʿAbbasid translation movement, but he was also the author of numerous scientific works and the chief physician at the court of the ʿAbbasid caliph al-Mutawakkil (r. 232–47/847–61). His career knew some ups and downs: he argued with his teachers and left for Byzantium for some years, and he was accused, in a court intrigue, of being an insincere believer. On the whole, however, his life shows that it was possible for a Christian to achieve high standing among the Muslim elite. Whether he was directly affected by the discriminatory measures against *dhimmīs* introduced by al-Mutawakkil is not known, but if we believe the texts that have come down to us, Ḥunayn was invited to abandon his original religion and join Islam. This occurred when the courtier and patron of scholars ʿAlī b. Yaḥyā b. al-Munajjim sent him his "undeniable proof" of the truth of Islam (*al-Burhān*). In this text Ibn al-Munajjim focused on the inimitability of the Qurʾān, of which he thought the Prophet Muḥammad must have had supernatural certainty. In his response, rather than replying to all the arguments of Ibn al-Munajjim's treatise, Ḥunayn describes in a purposely distant manner how one can distinguish between the various truth claims of religions by looking at the motives for which people choose to convert to them. Islam and Christianity are never mentioned explicitly, nor are the names of their respective founders, but the text is clearly a comparison of these two faiths. A personal note can perhaps be detected in Ḥunayn's claim that kinship ties should not be an argument for religious choice. As a native Arabic speaker, he was probably expected to recognize the supernatural beauty of the Qurʾānic text even more easily than was Ibn al-Munajjim, who was of Persian ancestry. Yet Ḥunayn declines the latter's powerful invitation and argues that the true faith is not wrapped up in rhetorical ploys. He also includes a thinly veiled critique of people who convert to Islam in order to increase their social mobility. In the generation before him, the Arab Christian apologists ʿAmmār al-Baṣrī and Abū Rāʾiṭa al-Takrītī had made similar lists of wrong motives for conversion and, just like Ḥunayn, claimed that the socially least attractive religion is the only one that is true.

TEXT

How does a person know that what he believes is the truth and what someone else believes is false?

If someone were to say that it is because it came down to him from his forefathers, or from a scripture, or from a prophet who performed signs, or from his own opinion, if he has reflected on it, and that his religion is therefore true according to him, then followers of opposing religions will claim the same as he does. And if this is the answer common to all followers of religions, then anyone who accepts his religion on the basis of such proof should necessarily accept—rather than reject—another religion, precisely because of this proof. And if he does not accept the proof of his opponents, then such proof should not be accepted by his coreligionists either.

To someone who maintains this, we say:

The truth and falsehood of all assertions can be known from the grounds on which they have been accepted from the beginning. The grounds on which falsehood is accepted are different from those on which the truth is accepted. The grounds on which falsehood is accepted are six:

The first is that the recipient is forced to accept what is imposed upon him against his will.

The second is that a person decides to escape from hardship and oppression, when he cannot bear it any longer, and moves on from there to what he hopes will bring him comfort and affluence.

The third is that might is preferable to lowliness, a high rank to inferiority, and power to weakness, and therefore someone leaves his religion and converts to another.

The fourth is that the religious propagator is a manipulator who uses ploys in his speech and thus deceives and misleads the people whom he invites to his religion.

The fifth is that he exploits the ignorance and lack of education of the people he calls to his religion.

The sixth is that there is natural kinship between the propagator and another person and [the latter] does not like to rupture that kinship between him and his coreligionist.

As for the grounds on which the truth is accepted, these are four:

The first is that the person embracing a religion sees miraculous signs of which all of humankind is incapable.

The second is that the visible reality of that which the religious propagator preaches gives evidence of its invisible reality.

The third is rational proof that compels one to accept it.

The fourth is that the latter-day state [of the religion] is in agreement with its origin and that the origin is the truth, in the sense that what happens later, after the truth of what precedes it, is not subject to doubt, in the sense that what happens later serves as an authentication of what happened before.

This may suffice for us to determine how we know that all other religions were accepted on the basis of the six characteristics, and the true religion on the basis of the four. It would take me a long time to mention every single religion—the ancient ones among them which disappeared because of the falsehood on which they were founded, and the ones that came into being later and which are constructed on the same foundations as those that have disappeared. To the extent that we know that this element [i.e., the foundation] in them is false, they are false, just like the religions before them were false.

Anyone who wants to understand the grounds on which his religion was embraced at its inception—whether it was on the grounds on which falsehood is accepted or on the grounds on which the truth is accepted—needs to determine on which grounds those who embrace the religion today accept it, whether on the grounds of truth or the grounds of falsehood, in order to understand the adoption of what has come down to him in his time through how it was adopted before him, at its inception; and he needs to be aware that the truth is accepted spontaneously, whereas falsehood requires grounds that confirm it for the recipient. When one contemplates this, one becomes aware which forms of worship are the true ones and which ones are the false ones.

As for me, I will leave aside all other forms of worship and clarify my own, which was accepted on the grounds on which the truth is accepted, either completely or partially. And I maintain that it is impossible to think that people would adopt a certain religion without any of the grounds on which all religions are adopted, and that it is not possible to imagine any ground beyond the ten characteristics we have listed: six on the basis of which falsehood is accepted, and four for the truth. And if it is indeed the case that the ground on which the worship of God was embraced was not one of those on which falsehood is adopted, then it is necessarily the case that the grounds for adoption were several or all of the four on the basis of which the truth is accepted. If no ground for the adoption of our worship of God were found to be a ground on which falsehood is accepted and we rather found its grounds to lie at the opposite extreme, its truth would be firmly established and inescapable. And that is how we found it to be.

Contemplating each one of the grounds:

The first is that it was not adopted through the might of a king or the force of a ruler. All the kings and rulers of the earth were hostile to it and made it prohibited for all the people, using all kinds of torture and atrocious killings, and they banished it from the land. And yet it vanquished them all and became firmly established.

Second, it did not promote abandoning a tough and oppressive situation for one of ease and comfort. On the contrary: it promoted abandoning all ease and comfort for a situation of hardship and difficulty, and yet it was accepted splendidly.

Third, it promoted abandoning neither lowliness for a high rank nor submissiveness for might. On the contrary: it promoted abandoning might for submissiveness, and yet it was accepted to the point that people would rather die than live for its cause.

Fourth, it was not adopted from people using ploys and clever discourse. On the contrary: it was taken from ignorant, inarticulate people, fishermen who were dumber and less capable than the fish, so to speak.

Fifth, the people who embraced it were not ignorant, inarticulate people, nor were they the uneducated masses. They were among the best logicians and philosophers of the whole world, sophisticated thinkers, scientists, and those who outshone all others in wisdom.

Sixth, among the people who embraced it, no one made closer connections with their loved ones and friends thereby. On the contrary: by embracing it, they separated themselves from all the people with whom they had a bond, whether it was a bond of family or one of friendship.

If you would like, you could add a seventh characteristic, which is conducive to certainty: the apostles disseminated something which, on the face of it, could not be less probable.

It is not necessary for anyone at all to claim that if this all happened in this way, the acceptance of what we adhere to took place without the appearance of signs and miracles. This is not possible, except for an adversary adducing his "expertise." If this is what you claim, then probe your soul about your religion and that of others with regard to what we have described to you, and you will know.

FURTHER READING

Griffith, Sidney. "Ḥunayn ibn Isḥāq and the *Kitāb Ādāb al-Falāsifah:* The Pursuit of Wisdom and a Humane Polity in Early Abbasid Baghdad," in *Malphono w-Rabo d-Malphone: Studies in Honor of Sebastian P. Brock,* ed. George A. Kiraz (Piscataway, NJ: Gorgias Press, 2008), 135–60.

Roggema, Barbara. "Ḥunayn ibn Isḥāq, *Kayfiyyat Idrāk Ḥaqīqat al-Diyāna,* 'How to Discern the Truth of a Religion,'" in *Christian-Muslim Relations: A Bibliographical History,* vol. 1, *600–900,* ed. David Thomas and Barbara Roggema (Leiden: Brill, 2009), 775–79 [with full bibliography].

Swanson, Mark. "A Curious and Delicate Correspondence: The *Burhān* of Ibn al-Munajjim and the *Jawāb* of Ḥunayn ibn Isḥāq," *Islam and Christian-Muslim Relations* 22 (2011): 173–83

19

The Religious Commitment of the ʿAbbasid "Slave Soldiers"

Muḥammad b. Jarīr al-Ṭabarī (d. 310/923) and Aḥmad b. Yūsuf ("Ibn al-Dāya," d. ca. 335/946)

Matthew Gordon

Titles: al-Ṭabarī, *Taʾrīkh al-Rusul wa-l-Mulūk* (The history of prophets and kings); Ibn al-Dāya, biography of Aḥmad b. Ṭūlūn

Genres: Historical writing; didactic and entertaining literature (biography)

Language: Arabic

INTRODUCTION

Conversion is seldom, if ever, simply a matter of embracing a new faith tradition. The evidence regarding individual and collective acts of conversion in the early and medieval Islamic Middle East is fragmentary. It suggests very clearly, however, that decisions of this kind reflected as much social, economic, and political calculations as purely "religious" ones.

The comments that follow concern the "Turkish" military forces of the ninth-century ʿAbbasid Empire. These were soldiers of Central Asian and Turkic origin, brought into the Arab/Islamic heartland as slaves and freedmen and incorporated into the imperial armed forces. Modern historians know these men as "the slave military" of the early ʿAbbasid period. The term is perhaps misleading on two counts: first, it appears that most of these troops were manumitted and thus became freedmen; and, second, the imperial state furnished at least the upper ranks of these forces with salaries, properties, and slave women. In other words, even if these men were enslaved at an early point in their lives, many "slave soldiers" were accorded privileges and rank that Western readers might find surprising, given that slaves are often thought as having abject social and economic standing.

The two texts in this selection raise a pair of questions to which there is no clear answer: Did the "Turkish" soldiers convert to Islam, either as required by the ʿAbbasid state or of their own accord? And in what manner did they convert? Both texts clearly suggest that the extent and nature of their attachment to Islam was a matter of dispute in contemporary (ninth-century) Islamic society. Both texts refer to the "Turks," a catchall term used by Arab/Islamic sources to refer collectively to these men as not properly belonging to the Islamic community. The second text concerns Aḥmad b. Ṭūlūn, a second-generation "Turk" (his father is reported to have been acquired by an ʿAbbasid governor in 200/815) and founder of the short-lived Tulunid dynasty of Egypt (254–92/868–905). In praising Ibn Ṭūlūn—the text in which the passage occurs is largely hagiographic—its author uses his subject's religious commitment to set him apart from his peers.

TEXTS

(1) Al-Ṭabarī, on the year 249/863

When word reached the people of Baghdad, Samarra, and the adjoining Muslim cities of the deaths of ʿUmar b. ʿAbd Allāh [or ʿUbayd Allāh] al-Aqṭaʿ and ʿAlī b. Yaḥyā al-Armanī, the shock was widespread. The two men had been great champions of Islam, highly esteemed and widely praised in the frontier districts (Ar. *al-thughūr*) where they served. Their grief was compounded by the fact that news of one death followed so closely upon that of the other. Already their distress was running high because of the murder of [the caliph] al-Mutawakkil [in 227/842] at the hands of the Turks and the manner in which these men were lording it over the Muslims. The Turks murdered any caliph they desired to kill and replaced him with whomever they wished, with no regard for religious sensitivities or recourse to the views of the Muslims. The populace of Baghdad gathered to voice their anger and demand a response.

(2) Ibn al-Dāya

The Turks held Aḥmad b. Ṭūlūn in high regard and esteem; he, however, felt toward them only deep contempt. He disparaged their intelligence and behavior and argued that they scarcely deserved the ranks to which they had been promoted. He charged that they routinely violated the sanctity of religion and neglected its obligatory duties. He said one day to [his close friend and adviser] Aḥmad b. Muḥammad b. Khāqān: "Brother, how much longer do we put up with this situation? We are ridiculed for everything we do!" "The way out is to petition the vizier to allow us to transfer to the Byzantine frontier, where we can be compensated for good deeds and commit ourselves to righteous warfare (Ar. *jihād*)." [Aḥmad b. Muḥammad added:] "We followed up and presented our case to ʿUbayd Allāh, who saw to our transfer to the frontier. Once we were settled in

Tarsus, and Ibn Ṭūlūn could see firsthand how well its inhabitants devoted themselves to 'upholding the good and shunning wrongdoing' [a central Qur'ānic principle], his spirits lifted and his anguish fell away. He kept company with the traditionists (Ar. *muḥaddithūn*) to such an extent that he seldom returned home from his activity with them before nightfall. . . . [But], seeing him in this state, I grew anxious that he would neglect his duties to the state. When it came time for us to return [to Iraq], he said, 'Do not delay on my behalf, I will remain here.'"

FURTHER READING

Bonner, Michael. "Ibn Ṭūlūn's Jihad: The Damascus Assembly of 269/883." *Journal of the American Oriental Society* 130, no. 4 (2010): 573–605.

Gordon, Matthew. *The Breaking of a Thousand Swords: A History of the Turkish Military of Samarra (A.H. 200–275/815–889 C.E.)* (Albany: State University of New York Press, 2001).

Kennedy, Hugh. *The Armies of the Caliphs: Military and Society in the Early Islamic State* (London: Routledge, 2001).

20

Zoroastrian Priests Offer Legal Advice about Conversion

Ādurfarnbag son of Farroxzād (ca. third/ninth century) and Ēmēd son of Ašawahišt (ca. fourth/tenth century)

Christian C. Sahner

Title: The *Rivāyats* (Responsa) of Ādurfarnbag ī Farroxzādān and of Ēmēd ī Ašawahištān

Genre: Legal writing (responsa)

Language: Pahlavi

INTRODUCTION

Zoroastrianism was the official religion of the Sasanian Empire in Late Antiquity. After the Arab conquest, Zoroastrians continued to form a majority of the population in many parts of Iran and Central Asia. This majority, however, was gradually reduced by the effects of conversion, such that scholars speculate that by the tenth or eleventh century, Iran had transformed into a largely Muslim society. This transformation seems to have occurred faster and more comprehensively in Iran than it did in other parts of the greater Middle East, such as Egypt, where the Christian majority may have endured as late as the fourteenth century.

Zoroastrian sources from the early Islamic period offer an underutilized window into this process of religious change. Written in Pahlavi, a late form of Middle Persian (the language of the Sasanian Empire, which continued to serve as a sacred language of the Zoroastrian clergy after the conquests), these sources testify to Iran's conversion from the perspective of the Zoroastrian community. One of the most important genres of Pahlavi literature is responsa (Pahl. *pursišnīhā*, "questions"), commonly known as *rivāyat*s, in which high-ranking priests fielded questions on an array of legal, ritual, and theological matters of everyday concern. During the ninth and tenth centuries, many questions pertained to the challenges of living alongside Muslims and other non-Zoroastrians (known in the sources as *anēr,* "non-Iranians," or *ag-dēn,* "adherents of the Evil Religion," "infidels"). In this sense, they paralleled the contemporary responsa of Christians and Jews, who were forced to grapple with similar issues, such as intermarriage, commercial exchange with the religious other, and the sharing of food (see, for example, selections 10 and 37 in the present volume).

A major theme of the Pahlavi *rivāyat*s is conversion. As ever larger numbers of Zoroastrians became Muslims, priests had to develop rules for interacting with those who had left the community behind; for family members most directly affected by conversion, such as spouses and children; and for those who wished to return to the fold. Zoroastrians believed in a pervasive dichotomy between good and evil, light and darkness, and purity and pollution. Consequently, Islam and other non-Zoroastrian religions were regarded as the work of demons. Anyone who converted risked an eternity of damnation unless he or she repented.

Attitudes about conversion to Islam were shaped by earlier waves of Zoroastrian conversions to Manicheism and Christianity in Late Antiquity. Therefore, it is not always clear whether Islamic-era texts are speaking about Muslims or about other groups who threatened the community with apostasy. Given the period in which these responsa were written, however, most scholars believe they refer to Islam.

The following texts are taken from the *rivāyat*s of two prominent priests active during the ʿAbbasid period: Ādurfarnbag son of Farroxzād (ca. ninth century), the leader of the Zoroastrian community of Baghdad; and Ēmēd son of Ašawahišt (ca. tenth century), a more obscure figure, who was active in Iraq and the Jibāl region of western Iran.

TEXTS

(1) Rivāyat of Ādurfarnbag son of Farroxzād

On the fate of a Zoroastrian woman whose relatives convert

[The following passage sheds light on the socially precarious position of a woman whose entire family has left Zoroastrianism. The concern here is whether her relatives' apostasy has made it impossible for her to enter into a normal pādixšāy *marriage, since the guardians who would normally consent to such a marriage have left the community.* Pādixšāy *was the highest form of marriage in Zoroastrianism: a* pādixšāy *wife fell under the guardianship of her husband; she had to obey him; she was entitled to a portion of his inheritance; and their children were considered legitimate under the law. A* xwasrāyēn *marriage, by contrast, was lower in rank, and a* xwasrāyēn *wife was not entitled to inheritance from her husband. It usually took place when a man*

and a woman decided to marry without the consent of the woman's guardian. Ādurfarnbag proposes an alternative solution in which Zoroastrian clergy and learned men may step into the role of the woman's male relatives to ensure her guardianship.]

Question: When all the people in a family become non-Iranian except one woman, can that daughter become a *pādixšāy* wife or [only] *xwasrāyēn?*

Answer: As far as I know, when not even a single one of her ancestors whose lineage can be enumerated is a Zoroastrian (*weh-dēn*, lit. "an adherent of the Good Religion"), [then] a guardian should be appointed [for her] before the *rads* [religious judges], the *mowbeds* [highest-ranking Zoroastrian priests], or the *dastwars* [religious teachers or consultants]; or someone [already] designated should be made [guardian] for her in order to give her in marriage.

When no *rad* [or] *dastwar* is present, he in the town who is the foremost examiner of the law and knows more of the Avesta [the Zoroastrian sacred scripture] and the Zand [the Middle Persian translation and commentary on the Avesta] by heart should identify a guardian, [and] that guardian should give her in marriage, [being] authorized to give her [away].

On a Zoroastrian convert who then repents and returns to the community

[As Christian and Jewish sources also attest, it was not uncommon for first-generation converts to renege on Islam and return to their old beliefs. The following passage details the actions returnees had to undertake in order to wipe away the sin of apostasy, including some requirements unique to Zoroastrianism. Ādurfarnbag shows a lenient attitude toward those who return within a year of conversion, guaranteeing they could die as Zoroastrians in good standing. The text also hints at the need to accommodate converts who wished to return but could not do so for fear of their safety, presumably because apostasy was considered a capital offense under Islamic law. The kustīg *mentioned in the account is the sacred girdle worn around the waist by all adult Zoroastrian men; converts to Islam sometimes signaled their change of faith by removing this girdle, and returnees likewise signaled theirs by refastening it. A Christian-specific girdle knwn as the* zunnār *served a similar purpose among converts (see selection 13 in the present volume).* Xwēdōdah *refers to next-of-kin marriage (i.e., between a father and a daughter, a mother and a son, or a brother and a sister), which Zoroastrians in the premodern period considered the most virtuous form of human relationship. There is debate, however, over how widespread the practice really was.]*

Question: A man unties the *kustīg* [i.e., becomes a non-Zoroastrian]; within a year he becomes repentant, [but] fearing for his body, he is not able to tie on the *kustīg*. After that, he commits few sins, is diligent in other activities and good deeds, performs acts of *xwēdōdah*, and performs other work and good deeds, whatever he can. Do those activities and good deeds become his own or not? And when he dies, they carry that corpse (*nasāy*) of his [by] force onto water and fire. What, then, is his legal position?

Answer: The activities and good deeds he performs will be in the usual way, but he will have the sin of "running around [with the *kustīg*] untied." When they do not wash and bury [the corpse] and he, when he dies, is in repentance, [the demons] will perform the "three-nights punishment" [in which demons punish the soul for its sins for three nights before it proceeds to heaven] but not put him in hell. When they wash and bury [the corpse], there was one who said that he is in a state of sinfulness. And when he does not withdraw [from the non-Zoroastrian religion] because he is unable to, there was one who said that [the title] "repentant" will work.

I know the following: a *margarzān* [a sin theoretically punishable by death] incurred in such a way will always go to [his] account [even] after death. [But] when he has informed somebody by [the following] message—"If they wash and bury me, express my repentance before the *dastwar*s as my intercessor with my message!"—and when he is repentant by a message from an intercessor on his behalf in this manner, his repentance is in order. And after a three-night period they should perform the "three-nights ritual" in the usual way. [In any case] he should perform the other work and good deeds as best he can!

(2) Rivāyat of Ēmēd son of Ašawahišt

Concerning the inheritance of a Zoroastrian convert

[Here, the author addresses one of the thorniest problems facing religiously mixed families in the early Islamic period: Were converts entitled to inheritance after leaving their original community? Ēmēd states decisively that converts who do not return within a year of their apostasy forfeit their inheritance, which passes into the hands of the converts' family instead. Still, in an interesting admission of the difficult conditions facing Zoroastrians in the ʿAbbasid period, Ēmēd states that it is not always possible to deny converts such inheritance, presumably because of the status they enjoy as Muslims. Indeed, Ēmēd hints that he is talking about Muslims specifically and not non-Zoroastrians generally, given the reference to circumcision.]

Question: Regarding a son who has converted to the Evil Religion, does he inherit everything he would have inherited from his father and mother while he was a Zoroastrian (*pad weh-dēnīh*), whether or not he is in the Evil Religion?

Answer: If a man has converted from Zoroastrianism to the Evil Religion and remains in the Evil Religion, he shall be considered to have committed a *tanābuhl* [a sin entailing forfeiture of the offender's body]. If, within a period of a year, he abandons Zoroastrianism [for good], it shall be a *margarzān*.

If he bears a brand on his member as the infidels do (*pad handām drōš ī čiyōn ag-dēnān*), and if they bury in the earth that which they severed from his member [i.e., if he is circumcised in the Islamic manner and his foreskin is disposed of], it will eventually reach the water and the fire [thereby polluting them]. The lowest grade of his sin shall be *margarzān*.

If he has any property, the "law of primitive man" shall apply. The ruling of the "law of primitive man" is this: the property shall fall under the personal control of whomever among the Zoroastrians first seizes that property. Today, however, this custom is difficult to observe (*ēn ēwēnag kerdan dušwār*). . . .

As for a son who belongs to the Evil Religion, if he remains in the Evil Religion for a period of a year and no one holds him back, his inheritance goes to his father's family, [which is to say] the share of the infidel (*ag-dēn*) does not remain with him. Then all his property is removed and placed in the sort [of arrangement] written about above. As for the Zoroastrian property, if they are able to seize the share of the infidel by the "law of primitive man," keep it in their possession, and not give it to the infidel, then they are acting lawfully, and their taking it is legal.

If it is not possible to fulfill this custom to your benefit, there is no [other choice than] for them to give [the inheritance] to him [i.e., the convert]. Therefore, they ought to arrange things in the most careful and least harmful way.

FURTHER READING

Choksy, Jamsheed K. *Conflict and Cooperation: Zoroastrian Subalterns and Muslim Elites in Medieval Iranian Society* (New York: Columbia University Press, 1997).

Crone, Patricia. *The Nativist Prophets of Early Islamic Iran: Rural Revolt and Local Zoroastrianism* (Cambridge: Cambridge University Press, 2012).

Kiel, Yishai, and Prods Oktor Skjærvø. "Apostasy and Repentance in Early Medieval Zoroastrianism," *Journal of the American Oriental Society* 137 (2017): 221–43.

21

A Muslim Poet Consoles a Christian Friend Whose Nephew Has Converted to Islam

al-Qāsim b. Yaḥyā al-Maryamī (d. 316/928 or 929)

Luke Yarbrough

Genre: Didactic and entertaining literature (poetry)
Language: Arabic

INTRODUCTION

The lines below were composed by a Muslim poet of late ʿAbbasid Egypt called al-Qāsim b. Yaḥyā al-Maryamī. Reportedly a descendant of one of the Prophet's companions, he belonged to the inner circle of Egypt's Turkic ruler, Abū al-Jaysh Khumārawayh (d. 282/896), whose father, Ibn Ṭūlūn, had shrugged off the waning authority of the ʿAbbasid caliph to seize power in Egypt. Al-Qāsim addresses the poem to his Christian friend, Isḥāq b. Nuṣayr al-ʿIbādī. Isḥāq was a learned Arab Christian from Iraq. As Egypt's highest chancery secretary, he, too, was close to Khumārawayh. In the brief introduction provided by the renowned Iberian scholar Ibn ʿAbd al-Barr (d. 463/1071), whose literary anthology is the only source in which the poem appears to survive, we learn that Isḥāq's nephew, al-Walīd, has recently converted to Islam.

In the poem, al-Qāsim sets out to comfort Isḥāq. The first four lines are typical of Arabic consolation poems; the grieving addressee is reminded that fate cannot be avoided and is advised to take courage. This suggests that conversion to Islam was legible to both Muslims and non-Muslims in this historical setting as a kind of social death. The poet then expresses his conflicting emotions upon hearing of al-Walīd's conversion. He describes his elation as a Muslim whose community has gained a "star," as well as his profound sorrow at the sadness he knows his Christian friend must feel. In the poem's final two lines, al-Qāsim alludes to a prominent, unnamed young Muslim who has converted to Christianity, dismaying Muslims much as the Christian Isḥāq is now dismayed. He implies a kind of equivalence between the two converts, describing their conversions as an exchange between their communities. This description may reflect a poet's imaginative license, and the question of whether so flexible an ethic reflected contemporary social norms or contravened them is an open one. The meaning of the poem's final phrase is uncertain.

This unusual poem demonstrates that early Muslims' reactions to conversion could be complex, ambivalent, and affected by their many social and professional ties to non-Muslim friends, family members, and colleagues. In gesturing to Muslim conversion to Christianity, the poet both affirms and transcends the stern disapproval with which such conversions are usually portrayed by Muslim writers, treating conversion to and from Islam as equivalent acts.

TEXT

The following lines are by the poet al-Maryamī, whose name was al-Qāsim b. Yaḥyā. He was a descendant of Abū Maryam al-Sulamī, the companion of the Prophet, God bless and keep him. Al-Maryamī addressed the poem to Abū Yaʿqūb Isḥāq b. Nuṣayr, the Arab Christian official, when the latter's nephew al-Walīd converted to Islam. This Isḥāq was the secretary of Abū al-Jaysh b. Ṭūlūn, the ruler of Egypt.

Take solace! Even the best of us wears out in time;
For good and ill alike are all men made.
Reprieves from the ravages of Fate are gifts;
Some profit by them, others are deprived.
It is altogether prudent for a good and upright man,
drowning in a sea of cares, to steel himself.
If he finds no way out
then it is fitting and most proper that he bear up.
Sorrow came to me by some joyful news I heard,
and now I am neither enchained nor free.
I rejoice at the conversion of al-Walīd,
But anguish at the knowledge of your anguish.
My heart is cleft in twain at it; half exuberant,
Half saddened, scorched for your sake.
We have claimed a star of yours, radiant and luminous;
You have one of ours just like him, radiating light.
How it alarms us whenever a Muslim turns Christian!
Very well then, this one for that one,
and happy is he whom God will grant success.

FURTHER READING

Bianquis, Thierry. "Autonomous Egypt from Ibn Ṭūlūn to Kāfūr, 868–969," in *The Cambridge History of Egypt*, vol. 1, *Islamic Egypt, 640–1517*, ed. Carl F. Petry (Cambridge: Cambridge University Press, 1998), 86–119.

Yarbrough, Luke. "A Christian Shīʿī, and Other Curious Confreres: Ibn ʿAbd al-Barr of Cordoba on Getting Along with Unbelievers," *al-Masāq* 30 (2018): 284–303.

PART TWO

The Islamic Commonwealth

(ca. tenth–thirteenth centuries)

Uriel Simonsohn

THE SO-CALLED MIDDLE ISLAMIC period, dated in this reader to between 333–34/945 and 648/1250, witnessed a series of changes, some of them radical, in the arrangement of Islamic politics and the composition of Islamic societies. These changes should be seen in light both of processes that had begun in earlier centuries and of events that are unique to the middle period. One of the most important of these processes was conversion to Islam—a trend that in the middle Islamic period took on characteristics that were to a large extent dictated by contemporaneous circumstances.

The year 333–34/945 marked the takeover of the central government of the ʿAbbasid caliphate by the Buyid dynasty (333–34–447/945–1055). These Shiʿi warlords from Daylam ended what was left of the political sway of the ʿAbbasid caliph, retaining him as a figurehead, a reminder of the Islamic political model conceived in seventh-century Arabia. Earlier, the caliph al-Mutawakkil (r. 232–47/847–61) had resolved decades of fierce confrontations between the ʿAbbasid court and a group of resolute theologians. His decisive intervention had led to the triumph of the traditionist camp (*ahl al-ḥadīth*) over the rationalist Muʿtazilī theologians and scholars, thus stripping religious authority from subsequent caliphs. These signs of drastic decline in the status of the caliph occurred in conjunction with broader trends across the Islamic world. The tenth century witnessed, among other developments, new forms of social mobility among Muslim converts, the rise to power of military elites, the consolidation of Islamic scholarly power, the emergence of local strongmen and dynasties, the creation of new urban centers and commercial enterprises, and the rapid spread of Muslim sectarian groups. From Córdoba through Qayrawan, Cairo, Damascus, Nishapur, and beyond, local rulers allied with loyal generals, notables, and men of scholarly repute, politically fracturing what had been only a short time ago a unified empire from the Atlantic to the Oxus. At the same time, the period also experienced the vitality of Shiʿi ruling groups and doctrines, whose presence filled the political vacuum that had resulted from the decline of ʿAbbasid government. By the end of the tenth century, vast regions that were formally governed by a Sunni caliph in Baghdad had fallen under the authority of Shiʿi dynasties. Although most Shiʿi political power would dissolve within two centuries, its presence signaled the political and religious diversity of the Islamicate and its permeability to a myriad of local traditions.

This was also a period of unprecedented intellectual and cultural flourishing. The establishment of new centers of learning was accompanied with non-Arabs' pride in their ancient heritages, literary productivity, and the introduction or adaptation of new practices, styles, and fashions in art, architecture, poetry, and modes of governance. Simultaneously, the period witnessed the consolidation of the four Sunni schools of law, the emergence of clearly articulated Shiʿi doctrines, the rise of Islamic mysticism, and the resolution of long-standing Sunni theological disputes (such as the aforementioned debates between the traditionists and the rationalists).

Muslim societies were experiencing a dynamic state of flux, too, thanks to their increasingly multiethnic compositions, which included not only Arabs but also Iranians, Berbers, Arameans, Armenians, Turks, Slavs, and more. At the same time, however, regions that had been ruled by Islamic governments for centuries were conquered, if only for a short time, by the non-Muslim armies of the Crusaders in the West and the Mongols in the East. The unchallenged sovereignty established by the conquering armies of Islam in the seventh and eighth centuries was broken. Its defeat revived questions of divine and temporal power within a social setting that was still very much non-Muslim.

The documents of the Cairo Geniza and a renaissance of Eastern Christian historiography are only two among many signs of the enduring vitality of the communities that had come under Islamic rule centuries earlier. It is also in the middle period that we find hints of a growing interest in the principles of the Pact of ʿUmar, evidenced by new efforts to disseminate the document and others like it, which were famously designed to regulate ties between Muslims and non-Muslims and to restrict the latter's freedoms.

The texts gathered in this section offer vivid testimonies to the multifaceted nature of the act of conversion, and they should be read within these different contexts. They speak of the circumstances in which conversion to Islam took place, the responses it triggered, and the manner in which it was envisioned or represented. Many of these texts also offer a more intimate window into the daily lives of converts, their former and new coreligionists, and their kinsfolk.

THE FRAGILE STATE OF NON-MUSLIM COMMUNITIES

The flow of new adherents into Islam continued or intensified during this period, creating in certain parts of the Middle East a numerical Muslim majority for the first time. Whereas Muslims may have been encouraged by the continuous flow of converts, for non-Muslims the departure of their coreligionists was at times a painful reflection of the dwindling state of their communities. The polemicizing efforts of recently converted Muslims against their former coreligionists celebrated this triumph; indeed, many enlisted their non-Muslim background to further undermine the legitimacy of their former religions (see selections 22 and 33). These attacks constituted a pointed reminder to non-Muslim communities of their fragile status, given the appeal of conversion to Islam. Accordingly, adequate responses on the part of non-Muslim gatekeepers were perceived as necessary in order to stem further conversions. Thus a Coptic apocalyptic text of the period laments the deteriorating state of the Coptic language and warns of the terrible consequences of its decline, reflecting the notion that Arabization paved the way for conversion to Islam (see selection 26). Further to the east, Armenian neomartyr stories were meant to offer Christian converts to Islam a means of resisting conversion by valorizing apostasy from Islam (see selection 35). Later, in the twelfth century, in response to the persecutions initiated by the North African dynasty of the Almohads, Maimonides devised a scheme that would allow Jews who were forced to convert to Islam to retain their religion by feigning recognition of Muḥammad as a prophet of God, thus escaping the death penalty that awaited Muslim apostates (see selection 36). His epistle reflects some of the violent pressures that prompted non-Muslims to convert to Islam during this period. Among these we find occasional waves of fierce persecution and discrimination, as in the time of the notorious Fatimid caliph al-Ḥākim bi-Amr Allāh (r. 386–411–12/996–1021; see selection 28). Persecutions and the fear of losing public office are further attested in eleventh-century Baghdad (see selection 29).

AGENCY AND PROSELYTIZING

Yet conversion to Islam was caused not only by coercion but also by the agency of various figures. A legendary story, depicting the conversion of Christian monks after the miraculous events that followed the death of a Muslim admirer of a Christian girl, highlights the important role that wondrous events, or at least the belief in them, played in Muslim missionary efforts (see selection 23). Sufi orders became a major force in efforts to recruit converts to Islam, especially through the sayings, healings, and charisma of Sufi saints in various parts of Muslim-dominated lands (see selections 27 and 40). The narratives that describe the careers of Sufi saints, legendary though they may be, serve as an important reminder of the significance of influential figures as agents of conversion to Islam and as disseminators of Islamic doctrine and practice. A particularly central role is ascribed to religious scholars who appear to have resorted to the more conventional method of religious instruction in order to attract new believers (see selection 34). In other instances, we find commercial activities driving religious change, as exemplified in the conversion of the Bulgar elite in the tenth century as a result of their ties with Muslim merchants (see selection 24).

MILITARY RECRUITMENT, WAR, CONQUEST, AND SETTLEMENT

Warfare and related factors also seem to have played a major role in conversion. The recruitment of soldiers into Muslim armies through the practice of initially enslaving and converting children, especially from the steppes of Central Asia, had begun already in the first half of the ninth century under the caliph al-Muʿtaṣim (r. 218–27/833–42). The practice continued well beyond his reign, involving not only minors but also adult mercenaries, such as the Turks who took part in Muslim military campaigns. This trend coincided with waves of Turkish migration into the caliphate (see selection 31). At the same time, the arrival of the Crusader armies from Europe in the Middle East at the end of the eleventh century, coupled with the subsequent encounter of these Europeans with local Muslim populations, created multiple opportunities for crossing religious, cultural, and social divides. These encounters facilitated conversion both from Christianity to Islam (see selection 39) and from Islam to Christianity (see selection 34).

SOCIAL CONSEQUENCES AND LEGAL SOLUTIONS

Conversion to Islam aroused a variety of concerns and emotions in both non-Muslim and Muslim communities. Many of these can be seen in the context of religiously mixed families, in which the religious identity of converts' children was contested between members of rival religions (see selection 32). The creation of such mixed families through the conversion of a family member is but one indication of the enduring ties between converts and their former coreligionists (see selection 38). In this familial context, conversion to Islam did not necessarily entail abandoning sentiments and practices that belonged to the convert's former religious world. And given the endurance of family ties between converts and their non-Muslim relatives, conversion to Islam could be a temporary act, followed shortly by reversion. In response, Muslim jurists sought to regulate the act of conversion (see selection 25) and to address the phenomenon of apostasy from Islam (see selection 30). Muslim jurists were not alone in their preoccupation, as non-Muslim legal specialists appear to have been troubled by the flip side of this process—namely, apostasy from a non-Islamic religion (see selection 37).

The texts in this section have been arranged chronologically in accordance with the events they describe, refer to, or result from.

22

A Christian Convert's Examination of His Former Faith

al-Ḥasan b. Ayyūb (d. before 380/990)

Clint Hackenburg

Title: *Risāla ilā Akhī ʿAlī b. Ayyūb fī al-Radd ʿalā al-Naṣārā* (A letter to my brother ʿAlī b. Ayyūb, refuting the Christians)

Genre: Religious instruction (polemics)

Language: Arabic

INTRODUCTION

Al-Ḥasan b. Ayyūb (d. before 380/990) was a Christian convert to Islam. His sole surviving work, *Risāla ilā Akhī ʿAlī b. Ayyūb fī al-Radd ʿalā al-Naṣārā* (A letter to my brother ʿAlī b. Ayyūb, refuting the Christians), has survived in the form of extensive quotations by Ibn Taymiyya (d. 728/1328) in his *al-Jawāb al-Ṣaḥīḥ li-Man Baddala Dīn al-Masīḥ* (The correct response to those who have altered the religion of Christ). Evidence suggests al-Ḥasan was regarded as a lesser-known scholar; his name is conspicuously absent from the *ṭabaqāt* works, and Ibn al-Nadīm (d. 344/995) mentions al-Ḥasan in his *Fihrist* as an essentially unknown, mid-tenth-century Muʿtazilī.

In many ways, al-Ḥasan's *Risāla* is reminiscent of the rationally oriented works of theologians contemporary with him, including al-Nāshiʾ al-Akbar (d. 293/906), Abū ʿAlī al-Jubbāʾī (d. 302/915), al-Māturīdī (d. 332/944), and al-Bāqillānī (d. 403/1013). However, al-Ḥasan also embodies a new type of Christian-turned-Muslim polemicist. His *Risāla* is not entirely characteristic of the earlier works of the convert ʿAlī al-Ṭabarī (d. ca. 246/860), nor does it precisely follow the polemical techniques of al-Qāsim b. Ibrāhīm (d. 246/860), Abū ʿĪsā al-Warrāq (d. ca. 247/861), or Abū Yūsuf al-Kindī (d. ca. 256/870). Instead, al-Ḥasan implements a polemical style in which rationality and scripture, particularly biblical proof texts, operate rather seamlessly in tandem. Moreover, al-Ḥasan attempts to contextualize Trinitarian Christianity and its Nicene formulation within a Roman culture that he and many subsequent Muslim polemicists, notably ʿAbd al-Jabbār (d. 416/1025), characterize as corrosive to Christ's original message.

According to al-Ḥasan, he composed his *Risāla* after an arduous and protracted personal journey rife with significant societal, familial, and psychological challenges. Al-Ḥasan's letter to his brother, like the works of ʿAlī al-Ṭabarī that preceded it, represents an integral component in the growth and development of Christian apostate literature. The writings of several later converts, including Naṣr b. Yaḥyā (d. 558/1163 or 589/1193), Yūsuf al-Lubnānī (d. ca. mid-thirteenth century), and Anselm Turmeda (d. 827–33/1424–30) attest to al-Ḥasan's influence.

TEXT

[Let me start by] informing you, may God guide you, that the doubt which came upon me while I was a Christian and the distaste to confess such beliefs began more than twenty years ago when I examined them in a treatise concerning the corruption of the oneness of God, may He be exalted and glorified, which was caused by the doctrine of the three hypostases and other beliefs constituting the law of the Christians as well as the arguments put in place, which do not justify or validate such beliefs. Whenever I delved into these beliefs and pondered them, their shortcomings became obvious, but I kept myself from acknowledging them. However, when I contemplated the religion of Islam, which God has bestowed upon me, I found its sources verifiable, its doctrines true, and its law beautiful.

No one among you or anyone else who understands God, may He be exalted and glorified, disagrees that the basis of Islam is faith in God, the Living, the Self-Sustaining, the Hearing, the Seeing, the Indivisible, the One, the King, the Holy, the Munificent, the Just; the God of Abraham, Ishmael, Isaac, Jacob, and the tribes; the God of Moses, Jesus, and the remaining prophets; the God of all creation, who has no beginning and no end, who has neither counterpart nor equal, who has taken no consort, who has no children, who created everything—not from something, and not based on a previous example, but rather as He willed it. When He said, "Be," it was, just as He designed and just as He wanted. He is the Omnipotent, the Omniscient, the Compassionate, and the Merciful, whom nothing resembles; He is the All-Conquering who is never conquered, the Munificent who is never miserly; no request is ever overlooked by and no secret hidden from Him. He knows the treachery of the eyes and what hearts conceal; He knows what is hidden in the world and what comes forth from it; and He knows what descends from heaven and what ascends to it. All that has been mentioned or that has been conceived of is from Him and through Him. All are obedient to Him.

Furthermore, we believe that He sent Muḥammad, His servant and His messenger, with guidance and the religion of truth, so that He may grant it victory over all religions, although the polytheists may be averse [Q. 9:33]; we believe in Moses, Jesus, and the rest of the prophets, may God's prayers and peace be upon them, and we do not make any distinction between them; we believe in the Torah, the Gospel, the Psalms, the Qurʾān, and the rest of the books which have been revealed by God, may He be exalted, to His prophets; we believe that the time is coming about which there is no doubt, that God will resurrect those who are in graves, that the innocent will be in bliss, and that the dissolute will be in hell, where they will be burned alive on the Day of Judgment. This is on account of what their hands have earned, for God is not unjust to his servants [Q. 3:182].

[Know that] it was the familiarity with my religion, the time spent in it, the commitment I had to it, and the sense of community among fathers, mothers, brothers, sisters, relatives, neighbors, acquaintances, and friends that allowed me to postpone my decision and delay the inevitability of the matter [i.e., conversion]. It was during this period of indecision that I deepened my investigation and redoubled my examination. Therefore, I did not shelve a single one of the prophetic books, including the Torah, the Gospel, the Psalms, the Books of the Prophets, and the Qurʾān, without having contemplated it and scrutinized it; nor did I set aside a single one of the treatises of the Christians without having pondered it. As a result, when I did not find any means to defend my belief, to alleviate my doubt, or to justify enduring or lingering any longer, I went forth alone as an emigrant to God, may He be exalted and glorified, and with my new religion, I left behind comfort, communal stability, my home, respect, and the ability to earn a living. I openly professed [Islam] with a sincere motivation, a clear conscience, and an absolute conviction. Praise be to God, who has guided us to this, for if God had not guided us, we would not have been guided. Certainly the messengers of our Lord came with the truth [Q. 7:43]. We ask Him, may He be exalted, that He not avert our hearts after He has guided us, and that He give to us of His mercy. Truly He is the All-Giving.

[At this point in the text, al-Ḥasan presents a comparative, albeit formulaic, description of Arian, Jacobite, Melkite, and Nestorian doctrines.]

If they [i.e., the Christians] persist in such fallaciousness and continue to defend this vile doctrine, and if they continue to actively embellish their beliefs with speciousness and casuistry, which they then offer to those whose knowledge is inadequate, we will establish for them a testimony which they themselves cannot refute. We are speaking, of course, of the creed that the leaders, including the patriarchs, the metropolitans, the bishops, the clergy, and the erudite men of their religion, who gathered from the ends of the earth, composed for them in the presence of the king in the city of Constantinople, where 318 men described that they were speaking by means of the Holy Spirit. This is the creed which, apart from their disagreement over the articles therein, the community did not dispute. Moreover, no Eucharist is complete without a profession of it in the following manner:

We believe in God, the Father, master of everything, creator of what is seen and what is not seen; and in the one Lord, Jesus Christ, the only son of God, the first-born of all of creation; who is not made, true God from true God, from the substance of his Father, by whose hand the worlds were perfected and everything was created; who, on account of us, the community of mankind, and on account of our salvation, descended from heaven, was incarnated by means of the Holy Spirit, and became a man; was carried and born of the Virgin Mary; was tortured and crucified in the days of Pontius Pilate; was buried and rose on the third day, as it is written; ascended to heaven and sat at the right of his Father; he is ready to return once again in order to judge the dead and the living. We believe in the one Holy Spirit, the Spirit of Truth who proceeds from the Father, the life-giving Spirit; in one baptism for the forgiveness of sins; in one holy apostolic Catholic Church; in the resurrection of our bodies; and in everlasting life, for ever and ever.

They agree upon the faith in this creed. They would give up their life for it. The souls of countless Melkites, Jacobites, and Nestorians would be lost without it. They confess in it completely that the Lord Christ, whose description corresponds with that which they have precisely delineated, is true God from true God; he descended from heaven, was incarnated by the Holy Spirit, became a man, was carried and born of the Virgin Mary, was tortured, and was crucified.

Is there any doubtful point in this statement or any loose end to which some cryptic meaning might attach that could defend such an argument? Ponder this doctrine, O community of Christians, for none of you can escape it nor deny that which is articulated in it. Certainly, if you say that the killed and crucified is God, then Mary, according to your belief, gave birth to God, may He be praised and exalted above that which they say; whereas if you say that he is a man, then Mary gave birth to a man. And herein lies the totality of the falsity of your creed. Choose whichever of the two statements you wish, for either will invalidate your religion.

It is necessary for rational men to refrain from worshipping a god who was born of Mary, a mortal woman, and who subsequently remained on the earth for thirty years, living a conventional mortal life. He was fed and nurtured; he experienced health and sickness, fear and contentment; he received knowledge and granted knowledge. You cannot presume to claim that during this time he was divine in any way, given that he possessed no means to escape the limitations of mortal men: their needs, their demands, their concerns, their trials, and their behaviors. Then, after this long period of time, he began to manifest the will of God, may He be exalted, express splendid prophecies, and perform astonishing miracles by the power of God, may He be exalted. However, there were others among the prophets who accomplished comparable wonders as well as even more remarkable marvels. Moreover, this stage of his life was less than three years; then his mission was completed, as they have described. That is to say, he died. They claim that he was imprisoned, beaten, scourged, crucified, and killed. Can rational minds accept what they have said?

FURTHER READING

Accad, Martin. "The Gospels in the Muslim and Christian Exegetical Discourse from the Eighth to the Fourteenth Century: A Thematic and Chronological Study of Muslim and Christian (Syriac and Arabic) Sources of the Crucial Period in the History of the Development of Arab Christianity" (PhD diss., University of Oxford, 2001).

Ebied, Rifaat, and David Thomas, eds. *The Polemical Works of ʿAlī al-Ṭabarī* (Leiden: Brill, 2016).

Hackenburg, Clint. "Voices of the Converted: Christian Apostate Literature in Medieval Islam" (PhD diss., Ohio State University, 2015).

23

A Monk's Conversion to Islam

Abū al-Faraj al-Iṣfahānī (d. 356/967)

David Cook

Title: *Kitāb al-Diyārāt* (The book of monasteries)
Genre: Didactic and entertaining literature (collection of anecdotes)
Language: Arabic

INTRODUCTION

This text was written by the renowned Abū al-Faraj al-Iṣfahānī (d. 356/967), best known for his monumental *Kitāb al-Aghānī* on the Arabic poetic heritage and for his martyrology of the Prophet Muḥammad's family, *Maqātil al-Ṭālibiyyīn*. By contrast, the *Kitāb al-Diyārāt* is a minor work, a collection of anecdotes about the various monasteries scattered through Iraq and Syria (Egyptian monasteries are not prominent in this collection). Most of these anecdotes relate to visits by prominent political or literary Muslim personalities to the monasteries, and they do not provide much description of the structures themselves, let alone their inhabitants.

However, this selection, cited from the otherwise unknown Abū Bakr Muḥammad al-Anbārī, is not only much longer than the other anecdotes in the work but also has a ring of historicity about it. The description of travel to Amorium (in the center of Anatolia) is entirely plausible for the middle ʿAbbasid period, precise names are given throughout, and the ultimate cause for conversion is compatible with the overall flow of the story. While one can assume that details have been embellished, the idea that monks would be moved by a contest of spiritual power is not so far-fetched. However, one should note that there is a Christian legend dating (apparently) from the 223/838 sack of Amorium by the Muslims that describes forty-two people from the town who were taken captive to Iraq, refused to convert to Islam, and were martyred. It is thus interesting that the total number of people featured in the present text is also forty-two (the lovelorn ʿAbd al-Masīḥ, the forty monks, and the girl).

TEXT

Abū Bakr Muḥammad al-Anbārī: I departed from al-Anbār on one of my trips to Amorium in the land of the Byzantines, and I overnighted along the way at a monastery called Dayr al-Anwār, close to Amorium. The head of the monastery, the leader of the monks in it, whose name was ʿAbd al-Masīḥ, came out to me. He caused me to enter the monastery, and I found in it forty monks. They honored me that evening with good hospitality, but then I left them in the morning. I had seen in their spiritual exertions and worship that which I had never seen from anybody previously.

I finished off my errand in Amorium and returned to al-Anbār. When it was the following year, I performed the *ḥajj*, and while I was circumambulating the Noble House, I suddenly saw ʿAbd al-Masīḥ the monk circumambulating also, and with him five of his fellow monks. When I had ascertained that it was him, I approached and said: "Are you ʿAbd al-Masīḥ the monk?" He said: "No, I am ʿAbd Allāh, the one who desires the clemency of God."

So I began to kiss his gray hair and weep, and took his hand, turning to one side of the sanctuary and saying: "By the truth of the One who guided you, will you not tell me of the circumstances of your conversion to Islam?" He said: "It was an amazing experience. There was a group of Muslim ascetics and devotees who passed by the village in which [I was], so they sent one of their youths to buy food for them; he saw a Christian girl in the market selling bread, and she was the most beautiful and perfectly formed of women. When he gazed upon her, he was tempted by her, fell down, and fainted. When he came to [consciousness], he returned to his fellows and told them what had occurred, and he said to them: 'Go on your way; I will not be going with you.' They reproved him and exhorted him, but he did not turn toward them, so they departed and left him. He entered the village and sat at the entrance of that woman's shop (*ḥānūt*). So she asked him what he needed, and he told her that he was infatuated with her, but she turned away from him. So he stayed in his place for three days, without eating food, while his eyes were fixed on her. When she saw that he had not departed from her, she went to her family and neighbors and told them, so they set young boys on him to stone him. They stoned him until his head was crushed, his face was bruised, and his limbs were bleeding. But in spite of all that, he did not depart, so the people of the village decided to kill him.

"A man from among them came to me and told me of his situation, so I went out to him and saw him cast aside. I then wiped the blood from his face, carried him to the monastery, and healed his wounds. He stayed with me for fourteen days. Then, when he was able to walk, he left the monastery, went to the front of the woman's shop, and sat, gazing at her. When she saw him, she rose and said to him: 'By God, I have mercy on you; will you enter my religion so that I can marry you?' He said: 'God forbid that I would strip off the religion of monotheism and enter the religion of polytheism!' So she said: 'Rise and come into my house, and fulfill your desire, then go well guided.' He said: 'I am not the sort to let go of twelve years' worship for the lust of one moment!' She said: 'Then get out!' He said: 'My heart will not allow me to do that,' so she turned away from him, whereupon the young boys perceived him and approached him to stone him. He fell upon his face and said: 'The One who takes care of me is Allah, who caused the Book to be revealed, and He will take care of the righteous!' I then came down from the monastery and approached him, chasing away the young boys. I lifted his face from the ground, and I heard him say: 'O God Almighty! Join me and her in paradise!' So I took him toward the monastery, but he died before I could get him there. I took him away from the village and dug a grave for him and buried him.

"When the night came, after half of it was over, that woman screamed in her bed a mighty scream so that all of the people of the village gathered around her, asking her about the reason. She said: 'While I was sleeping, this Muslim man came to me and took my hand, leading me to paradise. When he had brought me to its gate, the gatekeeper forbade me to enter and said that it is forbidden to infidels. So I converted to Islam at his [the man's] hand and entered paradise together with him. I then saw palaces and trees in it which I cannot rightly describe to you. He took me to a palace of jewels and said: "This is my and your palace, but I will not enter it without you. Within the next five nights you will be with me in it, God willing." Then he reached out his hand to a tree at the gate of the palace, plucked two apples, and said: "Eat this one, but save the other for when the monks see you." So I ate an apple—never have I seen a better one—whereupon he took my hand and had me leave until I came upon my house.' Then she took out the other apple from her inner garment so that it shone in the dark night as if it were a twinkling star. They brought the woman to us in the monastery together with the apple, but we had never seen anything like it from the fruits of paradise. I took a knife and divided it among a number of my fellows, and we had never tasted anything more pleasurable than it, nor [smelled] a more pleasant smell.

"We [presumably the monks] said: 'Perhaps Satan appeared in disguise to her to deceive her from her religion.' But then her family took her and departed. She would not eat or drink, and on the fifth night, she rose from her bed and left her house to go to his grave. She threw herself on it and died, yet no one of her family knew of it. By morning, two Muslim shaykhs [i.e., elders] arrived at the village, wearing clothes of hair, with two women [wearing] the same, and said: 'God has a female *walī* [devotee] in your presence, who died as a Muslim, and we would like to take care of her without you.' The people of the village sought that woman and found her [lying] dead on the grave. They said: 'This is the one; she died according to our religion, so we will take care of her.' The disagreement heated up between them [i.e., between the two groups], so one of the two shaykhs said: 'The sign of her conversion to Islam is that forty monks of the monastery will try to pull her out of the grave together. If they succeed, she is a Christian. One of us will also set forth and try to draw her away from it. If she is drawn away with him, she is a Muslim.' The people of the village were satisfied with that.

"The forty monks of the monastery assembled and we all approached her to carry her, but we could not carry her. We tied a rough rope around her waist, and all of the forty monks pulled it together, but the rope snapped and she did not move. The people of the village tried also, but she did not move from her place, and we were unable to move her with anything we thought of.

"We said to one of the two shaykhs: 'Come and carry her.' So he came and pulled her by her clothes and said: 'In the name of God, the Merciful, the Compassionate, upon the community of the Messenger of God'—then he carried her clasped to him, went to a cave there, and put her in it. The two women came and washed her [body] and wrapped it. Then the two shaykhs approached her and buried her in the grave of that ascetic. We departed, having borne witness to all this.

"When we were apart, we said among ourselves: 'It is more worthy that we should follow the truth, and the truth has become clear to us by personal eyewitness experience. There is no clearer proof concerning the correctness of the Islamic religion than what we have seen.' I then converted to Islam and the forty monks of the monastery likewise converted to Islam, as well as all of the people of that village. Then we sent to the land of al-Jazīra, asking for a knowledgeable jurisprudent (*faqīh*) to teach us the laws (*sharāʾiʿ*) of Islam and the rules (*aḥkām*) of the religion. Thereupon a man, a righteous jurisprudent, came to us, to teach us the essence of piety and the rules of Islam, so today we are doing well."

FURTHER READING

Kazhdan, Alexander, ed. *Oxford Dictionary of Byzantium* (Oxford: Oxford University Press, 1991), s.v. "Forty-Two Martyrs of Amorium."

Kilpatrick, Hilary. "Monasteries through Muslim Eyes: The *Diyārāt* Books," in *Christians at the Heart of Islamic Rule,* ed. David Thomas (Leiden: Brill, 2003), 19–37.

Sizgorich, Thomas. "The Dancing Martyr: Violence, Identity, and the Abbasid Postcolonial," *History of Religions* 57, no. 1 (2017): 2–27.

24

The Conversion of the Volga Bulgars

Aḥmad b. Faḍlān b. al-ʿAbbās b. Rāshid b. Ḥammād (fl. fourth/tenth century)

Gerald Mako

Title: *Risāla* (Epistle)
Genre: Didactic and entertaining literature (travel account)
Language: Arabic

INTRODUCTION

The Volga Bulgars were a Turkic-speaking people who established the second Muslim state in Europe (after the Emirate of Córdoba) in the early fourth/tenth century and ruled over extensive lands and a wide array of people around the middle Volga and Kama Rivers between the second/ninth and early seventh/thirteenth centuries. The Bulgars acted as middlemen between Central Asian merchants and the Rus, and the northern, mainly Finno-Ugric tribes whose main trading commodity was fur, which was greatly valued as a luxury item throughout the Islamic world. The slave trade was also of great significance. Because of these commercial activities, an enormous quantity of dirhams streamed into Bulgaria. Even though the Bulgars were originally pastoral nomads, they developed a flourishing urban civilization. Their strong ties with Muslim merchants led to the gradual conversion of their elite to Sunni Islam during the early fourth/tenth century, and in 308/920 their ruler, Almiş, sent a legation to Caliph al-Muqtadir (r. 295–320/908–32), asking him to send missionaries to the Bulgars. As a result, the new Muslim Volga Bulgaria was born. This development was not a mere historical curiosity. Although the Mongol campaigns swept the Bulgar state into the ash heap of history, the Bulgars' conversion to Islam paved the way for a flourishing Islamic culture in what is now Tatarstan in the Russian Federation.

We possess comparatively detailed information regarding the circumstances of the Bulgars' conversion to Islam thanks to a member of the caliph's embassy to the Bulgars: Aḥmad b. Faḍlān b. al-ʿAbbās b. Rāshid b. Ḥammād (fl. fourth/tenth century), an Arab writer and traveler, who probably wrote his *Risāla* as private correspondence or with the aim of providing useful information to merchants. Though Ibn Faḍlān was hardly the swordsman par excellence blessed with almost feline dexterity that Antonio Banderas depicted in the film *The 13th Warrior*, his *Risāla* is an invaluable account of the fourth/tenth-century Pontic-Caspian and Great Steppes. This is chiefly because unlike most Muslim authors of his age, Ibn Faḍlān mainly (though not exclusively) wrote about things he himself witnessed. His work sheds interesting light on the finer details of the conversion of the Bulgars, who, like their ruler, had a rather vague understanding of Islam and its teachings. What makes the *Risāla* (or *Kitāb*, lit. "book," as the work is also known, since it survived without a title) a fascinating read in this regard is that it paints a candid picture of the problems and confusion that inevitably arose during the transitionary period when the permeation of Islam into local culture was only skin-deep.

TEXTS

The letter

In the letter of Almiş, son of Yiltawar, the king of the Ṣaqāliba [Slavs], which al-Muqtadir, the Commander of the Faithful, received, the king asked al-Muqtadir to send people to instruct him in the laws of Islam, to build a mosque, and to construct a *minbar* from which he could proclaim al-Muqtadir's name throughout his kingdom. Moreover, he also asked the caliph to build a fortress which would defend him against those kings who harbor hostility toward him. His requests were granted.

Addresses

Prior to my arrival, the proclamation from the *minbar* for him during the Friday prayer was worded, "O God, keep King Yiltawar, king of the Bulgars, in prosperity!" I told the king, "God is the king, and none but He alone, the majestic and the glorious, should be addressed in this manner from the *minbar*. Your master, the Commander of the Faithful, is satisfied with being referred to from his *minbar*s in the east and the west in this manner: 'O God, safeguard Jaʿfar al-Muqtadir bi-llāh, the *imām*, your humble servant, caliph, and Commander of the Faithful!' And it was the same with his forefathers, the caliphs who ruled before him. The Prophet (God's blessing and peace be upon him) said, 'Refrain from praising me in the manner in which the Christians praise Jesus, son of Mary, for I am a humble servant and Messenger of God.'" The king then asked me, "What address can be used for me in the Friday prayer?" and I replied, "Your name and that of your father." "But," he said, "my father was an unbeliever, and I do not want his name to be mentioned from the *minbar.* In fact, I do not wish to have even my own name mentioned, for it was given to me by an unbeliever. What is the name of my liege, the Commander of the Faithful?" "Jaʿfar," I replied. "Would it be possible for me to take his name?" "Yes." "Then I shall take Jaʿfar as my name, and ʿAbd Allāh as that of my father. Convey my decision to the preacher." And I did so. From then on the sermon during Friday prayer went thus: "O God, keep in good health your servant Jaʿfar the son of ʿAbd Allāh, the emir of the Bulgars, the client (*mawlā*) of the Commander of the Faithful!"

White nights

One day I entered my yurt with the king's tailor who was from Baghdad and who had ended up in this country by chance. We were conversing, not for long, but for less time than it takes to read halfway through one-seventh of the Qurʾān, as nightfall was approaching, and we were still waiting for the call to the evening prayer. All of a sudden we heard it and as we went outside the yurt, we realized that dawn had broken already. Thus, I asked the muezzin, "Which call to prayer did you make?" "[That for] the dawn prayer." So I asked, "And what about the evening prayer?" "We perform that together with the sunset prayer." "And what of the night [prayer]?" I asked. [He replied,] "The nights are, as you see, very short. They used to be even shorter, but now they have started to grow longer." He mentioned that he had not slept for a month, as he was afraid he would miss the morning prayer: if you put a pot on the fire, by the time you have performed the morning prayer the pot will not have started to boil. Daylight was very long.

Naming issues

Among the Bulgars we observed a group quite similar to them which counted five thousand souls, both men and women, all of whom converted to Islam and are known as the Baranjār. They had built a wooden mosque for themselves where they prayed, but they did not know how to read the Qurʾān. Thus I taught a group among them how to conduct their prayers. A man named Ṭālūt accepted Islam at my hands, and I gave him the name ʿAbd Allāh. However, he said to me, "I would like you to call me by your name, Muḥammad." I agreed. His wife, mother, and children also embraced Islam, and they all took the name Muḥammad. I taught him the *sūra*s "Praise be to God" [Q. 87] and "Say: He is God, the One" [Q. 112], and his delight at having come to know these two *sūra*s was greater than if he had been made king of the Ṣaqāliba.

FURTHER READING

Mako, Gerald. "The Islamization of the Volga Bulghars: A Question Reconsidered," *Archivum Eurasiae Medii Aevi* 18 (2012): 199–223.

Montgomery, James. "Travelling Autopsies: Ibn Fadlān and the Bulghar," *Middle Eastern Literatures* 7, no. 1 (2004): 3–32.

Zimonyi, István. *The Origins of the Volga Bulghars* (Szeged: Universitas Szegediensis de Attila József Nominata, 1990).

25

Notarial Forms for the Conversion of Non-Muslims to Islam

Muḥammad b. Aḥmad al-Umawī, Ibn al-ʿAṭṭār (d. 399/1008)

Linda G. Jones

Title: *Kitāb al-Wathāʾiq wa-l-Sijillāt* (The book of certificates and registers)
Genre: Legal writing (legal documents)
Language: Arabic

INTRODUCTION

Muḥammad b. Aḥmad al-Umawī, known as Ibn al-ʿAṭṭār, was a chief notary public of Córdoba during the later Umayyad period. He was asked by the high judge of Córdoba to compile a complete set of notarial documents and related explanations that could be used to train the judge's grandson in the notarial profession. Ibn al-ʿAṭṭār agreed and gathered together "the best and most complete documents [he] could find, condensing them to their essential points and inserting [jurisprudential and lexical] explanations to facilitate their comprehension by the new student and to reinforce the knowledge of the seasoned [notary public]" (Chalmeta, 29). Ibn al-ʿAṭṭār's compendium served as a model for notary publics for centuries to come: the jurist Abū Isḥāq al-Gharnāṭī (d. 767/1366) considered it "the most useful of the Andalusi notary form compilations" (Chalmeta, 29).

The notary forms for conversion to Islam highlight the legal dimension of religious conversion. Conversion affects the legal status not only of the convert but potentially of his or her family and heirs. The forms begin with the convert testifying that she or he is sound of mind and body, is legally free, has freely chosen to convert to Islam, voluntarily renounces his or her previous religion, and vows to comply faithfully with all the norms of Islam. They include provisions addressing the possible conversion of the convert's spouse and the legal status of any children, which depends on whether they were minors at the time of their parent's conversion. The forms indicate the gender of the convert and explain the legal role of the Muslim witness who acts as the convert's legal sponsor. According to Mālikī law, the Muslim witness becomes the heir of the convert if the latter has no other legally recognized Muslim heirs upon his or her death. Finally, the texts refer to the religious identity of converts, which is specified in the forms to be signed before the notary public. Thus, after bearing witness that "Muḥammad is [God's] servant, messenger, and the seal of His prophets," the Jewish convert must add that "Moses, Ezra, and the rest of the prophets are the servants of God and His messengers," whereas the Christian convert must profess that Jesus, the son of Mary, is God's messenger and prophet.

TEXTS

A notary form for the conversion to Islam of a Jewish man (wathīqat islām al-Yahūdī)

The convert, so-and-so [son of so-and-so], being of sound mind and body, firmly resolved in his mind, and in possession of complete mental faculties and juridical capacity, hereby invokes the testimony of the witness of this act that he abandons the Jewish religion, rejecting it willingly, and embraces Islam of his own free will. He knows that God, Almighty and Sublime, admits no other religion nor derives satisfaction from any other religion, and that this one, Islam, abrogates all previous laws. [The convert] bears witness that there is no god but God, who has no partners, and that Muḥammad, may God bless him and grant him salvation, is His servant and messenger and the last of His prophets, and that Moses and Ezra, along with the other prophets, are His servants and messengers. [He also bears witness] that in the eyes of God the only religion is Islam. He has performed the major ritual of cleansing for the sake of his conversion to Islam [*wa-ightasala li-islāmihi,* i.e., in order to embrace Islam], the minor ablution, and the ritual prayer (*wa-tawaḍḍa ʾa wa-ṣallā*). He accepts all the laws of Islam and the pillars upon which it was founded in their totality: the ablutions, the ritual prayer, the obligatory alms-tax, the annual fast of the month of Ramadan, and the pilgrimage to the House [of God], if he has the means for it. And he has obliged himself to do all of this. He has praised God for inspiring him to do this) *wa-ḥamida Allāh ʿalā mā alhāmahu ilayhi minhu*).

His conversion to Islam took place before so-and-so [son of so-and-so]. And if [so-and-so] were an authority (*ṣāḥib ḥukūma*) he should say, "before so-and-so, the high judge (*qāḍī al-jamā ʿa*) of Córdoba, or the judge of such and such a province (*kūra*), or the chief of the affairs of the police or of the city, the marketplace, or an estate in Córdoba (*ṣāḥib aḥkām al-shurṭa aw al-madīna aw al-sūq aw al-radd bi-Qurṭuba*)," [and his conversion] being done in security and good faith, without guile, not for fear of anything or in expectation of anything in return. He [the witness] has testified regarding the conversion of so-and-so [son of so-and-so], confirming all that has been stated in this act [after verifying the convert's comprehension of everything and his commitment to the obligations imposed upon him], through his own acknowledgment and hearing it [explicitly] from him. And if he wishes, he may say, "From him [the convert] who has understood this exactly, and he is in the condition described above. Dated such and such a month and year, and the act is in two copies or one copy."

Jurisprudence (fiqh) [This section is part of the same form and follows immediately after the above text.]

And we add, "and his conversion to Islam was undertaken at the hands of so-and-so," thus informing how the matter came about. And there was no profit to be gained by it (*lā fā ʾida fīhi*) and no [self-]interest for him, for it is not obligatory that the one who converts to Islam before him be in a relationship of clientage to him (*walā ʾahu*). Yet Mālik [b. Anas] and others believed that one who converted to Islam before someone should designate him as his heir if he does not have a legitimate heir to whom to bequeath his legacy. This is what the [Muslim] people agreed on this matter concerning conversion to Islam in view of the differences of opinion that existed previously. And we therefore make it binding, for if we did not impose it as a duty, perhaps the matter of the binding decision would revert to someone else who would have to rule on it at a later date. Or perhaps he would try to extract some benefit (*manfa ʿa*) from it. Or perhaps he [the convert] will die in a country in which his [non-Muslim] people will decide the matter. Therefore, let the one at whose hands he converted to Islam inherit his [the convert's] estate. For according to Mālik [b. Anas] his estate must indeed go to the Muslims. And if [the convert] does not have [individual] Muslim heirs then [his estate] should go to the entire Muslim community (*fa-li-jamā ʿat al-Muslimīn*). . . . And if a [formerly] Christian man has a Christian wife or a [formerly] Jewish man has a Jewish wife, or if they have slaves in that condition [i.e., Christian or Jewish], the two of them may honor their contract, because a Muslim man may marry a Christian woman or a Jewish woman. Thus the marriage contract between them is not abrogated by the [husband's] conversion to Islam, unless the wife is a slave (*mamlūka*), in which case the marriage contract between them must be nullified (*fa-yufsakhu al-nikāḥ baynahumā*). For a Muslim man may not marry a Jewish or Christian female slave. For as God, Almighty and Sublime, said, "And [lawful to you are] in wedlock . . . women from among those who have been vouchsafed revelation before your time" [Q. 5:5].

A notary form for the conversion to Islam of a Christian man (wathīqat islām al-Naṣrānī)

The convert, so-and-so [son of so-and-so], being of sound mind and body, firmly resolved in his mind, and in possession of complete mental faculties and juridical capacity, hereby invokes the testimony of the witness of this act that he abandons the Christian faith, willingly rejecting it, and that he embraces Islam of his own free will. He bears witness that there is no god but God, who has no partners, and that Muḥammad, may God bless him and grant him salvation, is His servant and His messenger, and that the Messiah, Jesus son of Mary, may God bless him and grant him salvation, is His servant, His messenger, His word, and His spirit, which He has sent into Mary. He has performed the major ritual cleansing for the sake of his conversion to Islam [*wa-ightasala li-islāmihi,* i.e., in order to embrace Islam] and has performed the ritual prayer. He has agreed to the laws of Islam: the ablutions, the ritual prayer, the obligatory alms-tax, the annual fast of the month of Ramadan, and the pilgrimage to the House [of God] if he has the means for it, and he has understood the obligatory punishments (*wa-ʿarafa ḥudūdahā*) and their obligatory times (*wa-mawāqītahā*).

He has committed himself to this, grasping firmly onto Islam, in a state of joy over his entry into it (*ightibāṭan bi-l-dukhūl fīhi*) and he has praised God for inspiring him to do this. He knows that in the eyes of God the [only] religion is Islam, which abrogates all the other religions (*wa-annahu nāsik li-jamīʿ al-adyān*), that it supersedes and is not superseded by them, and that God admits no other religion nor derives satisfaction from any other.

His conversion to Islam is being done in security and good faith, not fleeing from something, without guile, not in expectation of anything in return, before so-and-so [son of so-and-so]. And if [so-and-so] were an authority (*ḥakam*) he should say, "before so-and-so, the high judge (*qāḍī al-jamāʿa*) of Córdoba, or the judge of such and such a place, or the chief of the affairs of the police or of the city, the marketplace, or an estate in Córdoba (*ṣāḥib aḥkām al-shurṭa aw al-madīna aw al-sūq aw al-radd bi-Qurṭuba*)." He [the witness] has testified regarding the conversion of so-and-so [son of so-and-so], confirming all that has been stated in this act [after verifying the convert's comprehension of everything and his commitment to the obligations imposed upon him], through his own acknowledgment and hearing it [explicitly] from him. And he is in the condition described above [and that on this date . . .]

And if you substitute [the statement] "hearing it from him" with "from him [the convert] who has understood this exactly," this is satisfactory. Then you should say, "And this is in such-and-such a month and year, and the act is in two copies or one copy." And if there is one trustworthy copy, that is good, [but] multiple copies of it are better and preferable (*wa-l-ikthār minhā aqwā wa-afḍal*), God willing.

Commentary (tafsīr) [This section is part of the same form and follows immediately after the above text.]

If the name of his father is not known or if it is one of those insufferable, loathsome foreign names (*min asmāʾ al-ʿajam thaqīla al-karīha*), then you should say, "so-and-so son of ʿAbd Allāh," thereby identifying his father as a "servant of God" in accordance with the unanimous agreement that all [humans] are servants of God.

And we say that "al-Islāmī" is correct [to add as a surname] because you [i.e., the Muslim sponsor or witness] have brought him into a relationship with Islam (*li-annaka nasabtahu ilā al-islām*).

Jurisprudence (fiqh) [This section is part of the same form and follows immediately after the above text.]

The Christian must perform the major ritual ablution for his conversion to Islam (*wa-yaghtasilu al-Naṣrānī li-islāmihi*) and he is not permitted to perform the minor ablution (*wa-lā yajzīhi al-wuḍūʾ*) because the Christian is a defiled malignance (*li-anna al-Naṣrānī khubth najas*). As God, Almighty and Sublime, said, "[O you who believe], those who associate others with God are defiled" [Q. 9:28].

A notary form for the conversion to Islam of a Christian woman (wathīqat islām al-Naṣrānīyya)

The convert, so-and-so [daughter of so-and-so] or the daughter of a male servant of God if the name of her father is unknown, being of sound mind and body, firmly resolved in her mind, and in possession of complete mental faculties and juridical capacity, hereby invokes the testimony of the witness of this act that she abandons the Christian religion, which she followed, rejecting it willingly, and embraces Islam of her own free will. She bears witness that there is no god but God, who has no partners, and that Muḥammad is His servant and His messenger and the last of His messengers and prophets, and His chosen one among His created beings. He sent him with guidance and the true religion in order to manifest the religion in its entirety, even though the polytheists despise it. And [she bears witness] that Jesus son of Mary, may God bless all the prophets, is the servant of God, a created being from among His created beings, a messenger from among His messengers, and His word, which He cast into Mary, and a spirit from Him, just as God, Almighty and Sublime, says. She has performed the major ritual cleansing (*wa-ightasalat*) and has performed the ritual prayer (*wa-ṣallat*), and she has accepted all the laws of Islam and its pillars: the complete ablution with sincere intention (*al-wuḍūʾ al-sābigh bi-l-niyya al-khāliṣa*), the ritual prayer, the obligatory alms-tax, the annual fast of the month of Ramadan, and the pilgrimage to the House [of God], if she has the means for it. And she has agreed to all parts of this, has imposed it as an obligation upon herself, and is satisfied with it. She has praised God, Almighty and Sublime, for inspiring her to do this and she has thanked Him for the benefits He has bestowed upon her through it, willingly embracing Islam and being without guile and without expectation of anything in return and without fear of anything. She has converted to Islam before so-and-so [son of so-and-so], in accordance with what has gone before in the contract. Then you should say, "He [presumably the witness] has witnessed (*shahida*)."

Jurisprudence (fiqh) [This section is part of the same form and follows immediately after the above text.]

If she does not have a husband, let the [male Muslim witness] before whom the woman proselyte converted to Islam act as her sponsor (*walīyan*) in marriage and marry her to someone [Muslim] of her liking. If she is married, her marriage to the [non-Muslim] man must be annulled and she must undergo the waiting period (*infasakha nikāḥuhā min zawjihā wa-umirat bi-l-ʿidda*), if he had sex with her [*in kāna dakhala bi-hā;* i.e., consummated the marriage] and paid her living and maintenance expenses. If she is pregnant, this [i.e., the payment] should continue until the termination of her pregnancy. But if she is not pregnant, his maintenance should be terminated. He is obliged to pay the living expenses during the waiting period, especially if she [the female convert] resides in the house of the young woman's family. And if she resides in the house of the [non-Muslim] husband, she must remain there until the termination of the waiting period.

If he [the non-Muslim husband] converts to Islam during her waiting period before three menses have passed since the time of her conversion, if she is a menstruating woman, or before three months have passed, if she is one of the women who do not menstruate, he may take possession of her [i.e., have sex with her] and they may remain married to one another. But if her waiting period passes before his conversion to Islam, there is no way for him to contract marriage with her if he converts afterward. Now, if he converts to Islam after that and becomes one of her suitors, and if she converts before he has sex with her, the purity of the marital consummation between them is abrogated (*inqaṭaʿat ʿiṣmat al-nikāḥ baynahumā*). Then there will be no way for him to [lawfully] marry her if he converts to Islam after her. But if [his conversion] is close [in time] to her conversion to Islam, let him contract marriage with her again, with her approval, through a [Muslim] sponsor and the [Islamic] dowry (*ṣadāq*). And if he converts to Islam along with her, she remains his lawful wife as she was before and the marriage shall not be abrogated.

The Jewish woman converts to Islam under the same binding conditions, and the ruling with regard to her husband is the same as that with regard to the husband of the Christian woman, if it pleases God, Almighty and Sublime.

FURTHER READING

Chalmeta, Pedro. "El matrimonio según el *Kitab al-Wataʾiq* de Ibn al-ʿAttar (s. x): Análisis y observaciones," *Anaquel de Estudios Árabes* 6 (1995): 29–70.

Coope, Jessica A. "Religious and Cultural Conversion to Islam in Ninth-Century Umayyad Cordoba," *Journal of World History* 4, no. 1 (1993): 47–68.

Shatzmiller, Maya. "Marriage, Family, and the Faith: Women's Conversion to Islam," *Journal of Family History* 21, no. 3 (1996): 235–66.

Simonsohn, Uriel. "Conversion to Islam: A Case Study for the Use of Legal Sources," *History Compass* 11, no. 8 (2013): 647–62.

26

A Monk Deploring the Assimilation of the Christians to the Hagarenes

Attributed to a monk called Apollo (fourth/late tenth or fifth/eleventh century)

Arietta Papaconstantinou

Title: *Maqālat Ṣamuʾīl Raʾīs Dayr al-Qalamūn* (The apocalypse [lit. "discourse"] of Samuel of Qalamūn)
Genre: Religious instruction (apocalypse)
Language: Arabic

INTRODUCTION

This is an extract from a longer text in Arabic probably dating to the late tenth or early eleventh century, but with a frame narrative that places it in the late seventh century. The purported author, the monk Apollo, claims it is a prophecy he heard from the mouth of Samuel, his spiritual master and the founder and superior of the monastic community of Qalamūn in the Fayyūm (Egypt), in the presence of all the brothers and of Gregory, bishop of al-Qays. The text is clearly a product of the Qalamūn community, and it shows knowledge of the Coptic *Life of Samuel*, an account of the foundation of the monastery written shortly after the Arab conquest. However, the contents of the text place it much later, at a time of transition for the Christians of Egypt, when the prospect of linguistic and cultural assimilation to the ruling Muslims is becoming threatening in the eyes of the monks of Qalamūn. Indeed, the main aim of the *Apocalypse* is to describe this assimilation and to warn Christians against it by listing the punishments for those who indulge in it and promoting the benefits of keeping to their own traditions.

The new people (*umma*) will initially be friendly to the Christians, we are told, but they will soon start oppressing them financially and religiously. Eventually

God will help the righteous regain their freedom through the intervention of the kings of Rūm (Byzantium) and Abyssinia. The largest part of the text laments Christian imitation of the ways of the Arabs, which entails the loss of ancestral traditions. The author focuses unusually strongly on linguistic assimilation, which for him involves a loss of communal memory and ritual efficiency: Christians no longer understand the books that contain their own history, nor what is said during the holy rites. He castigates the clergy for not resisting this development but instead going along with it. Even though he does not talk about conversion as such, he understands this assimilation as a first step toward it, since it not only is a form of forgetting the teachings of the Gospel and the Fathers but also entails the abandonment of a holy language with a Christian essence (Coptic) in favor of a Muslim one (Arabic).

A few notes about vocalization and terminology:

(1) I have vocalized the Arabic هجر as *hajara*, following John Iskander and especially Khalil Samir, who argued at some length in favor of this reading. Previous translations have vocalized it as *hijra* and translated it as "hegira" or "emigrants."

(2) According to Jos van Lent, who is preparing a critical edition of the text, the other extant manuscripts indicate that the reading *al-gharība* of Paris. Ar. 150 (used by Jean Ziadeh) is a misreading in Arabic for *al-aʿrabiyya*. The same is true further in the text with the expression "Arabic names."

(3) The word *barbar* has often been translated (including by Ziadeh) as "Berbers," who are commonly mentioned as raiders in texts from the Fayyūm. The context of juxtaposing two languages, one civilized and one not, as well as the author's tendency to call the Muslims *al-aʿrāb* (rather than *al-ʿarab*), implying they are uncivilized Bedouin, makes the meaning "barbarians" a more plausible option. Besides, the term Berbers is itself derived from βάρβαρος, which is what the *Life* of Samuel calls them.

The numbers in angle brackets refer to pages and folios in Ziadeh's edition of the text.

TEXT

<379/22r> Woe upon woe! What shall I say, my children, about those times and about the great idleness that will overtake the Christians? At that time they will move away from uprightness and start to assimilate themselves to the Hagarenes (*yatashabbahū bi-l-hajara*) in their actions: they will give their names to their children, discarding the names of the angels, the prophets, the apostles, and the martyrs.

They will also do something else, which, if I were to tell you of it, would greatly pain your hearts: they will abandon (*yatrukū*) the beautiful Coptic language, in which the Holy Spirit has often spoken through the mouths of our spiritual fathers; they will teach their children from an early age to speak the language of the Bedouin (*al-aʿrāb*), and will take pride in it. Even the priests and the monks—they too!—will dare to speak in Arabic and to take pride in it, and that within the sanctuary (*haykal*).

Woe upon woe! Oh, my dear children! What shall I say? At that time the readers in the church will no longer understand what they read nor what they say because they will have forgotten their language (*nasū lughatahum*), and they will truly be miserable and deserving to be wept over because they will have forgotten their language and will speak the language of the Hagarenes.

But woe to every Christian who teaches his son the language of the Hagarenes from an early age, causing him to forget the language of his fathers! He will be responsible for his transgression, as it is written, "Parents will be judged for their sons" [cf. Exod. 20:5; Deut. 24:16; Ezek. 18:20].

What shall I say on account of the moral slackness that is overtaking the Christians: they eat and they drink inside the sanctuary without fear. They have forgotten the fear of the sanctuary, and the sanctuary is nothing to them. The doors of the sanctuary will be forlorn, and no half-deacon <22v> will remain at them, because they will neglect the seven rites [i.e., sacraments] that the Church has and they will not fulfill them. You will see the men of those times look for clerical rank <380> while they are not yet ready to be readers and to read before the people.

Many books of the Church shall fall into disuse (*tabṭulu*), because there shall be nobody among them to take care of the books, their hearts being attracted by the Arabic books. They will forget many martyrs at that time because their biographies will fall into disuse and there will be none left. If the few biographies that will be found are read, many people will not understand what is read because they will not know the language. And many churches, at that time, will fall into ruin, and they shall be deserted on the eves of the feasts and on the eve of Sunday, too. There will be no one among them who will read a book on a pulpit, not even during the forty holy ones [i.e., Lent] that are intended for our salvation. You will find no one to read to the people, or to preach to them, because they will have forgotten the language and will not understand what is read to them or have any knowledge of it. Neither will the readers understand, even in Arsinoe, the great city which is in the Fayyūm, and all of its districts, where the lovely laws of Christ are in their books.

Those who are strong in the knowledge of God, whose Coptic language matched the sweetness of honey in their mouths and spread around them like the smell of perfumes because of their beautiful pronunciation of the Coptic language, all of them, at that time, shall abandon it and speak the Arabic language and take pride in it, to the point that it will be impossible to recognize them as Christians; on the contrary, they will be taken for barbarians. And the remnant remaining in the south (*wa-l-baqiyya allatī tabqā fī al-saʿīd*) who will know the Coptic language and speak in it will be reviled and mocked <23r> by their brothers, the Christians who speak in the Arabic language.

Woe upon woe! How great the sorrow and how afflicting the acts that will be accomplished by the Christians at that time! Truly my heart was in great pain as I brought you these tidings; my eyes shed tears and my body was greatly shaken. Do you think there is for the heart a greater pain than to see the Christians abandon their sweet language (*yatrukū lughatahum al-ḥilwa*) to take pride in the Arabic language and in their names? In truth I tell you, my children, that those who will abandon the names of the saints (*asmāʾ al-qiddīsīn*) <381> to give their children Arabic names—those who will act thus will be excluded from the blessing of the saints; and whoever will dare to speak, within the sanctuary, in the language of the Hagarenes, he will have diverged from the instructions of our holy Fathers.

[. . .]

<384/25r> . . . And now I recommend to you, my dear children, I beseech you humbly to recommend to those who will come after you till the end of times that they watch over their souls perfectly and not let a Christian speak Arabic in this place, because it will bring about an ominous judgment. Many at that time will indeed dare to speak the language of the Hagarenes at the altar (*madhbaḥ*). Woe upon woe on them! As I have myself heard from an old man devoted to the service of God, clothed with the Spirit and accomplished in holiness, when I asked him concerning the Hagarenes, he answered, "Look, my son Samuel, and understand what I tell you. At the time when <25v> the Christians shall dare to speak near the altar in the language of the Hagarenes, through which they will blaspheme against the Holy Spirit and against the Holy Trinity, at that time woe to the Christians! Woe, sevenfold woe!"

[. . .]

<388/28r> Instruct (*awṣū*) your children, who will instruct (*yuwṣū*) those who come after them unto the end of the future times, that no one should speak at the altar in the language of the Hagarenes. For he who acts in this way deserves a curse (*laʿna*).

FURTHER READING

Iskander, John. "Islamization in Medieval Egypt: The Copto-Arabic 'Apocalypse of Samuel' as a Source for the Social and Religious History of Medieval Copts," *Medieval Encounters* 4, no. 3 (1998): 219–27.

Papaconstantinou, Arietta. "'They Shall Speak the Arabic Language and Take Pride in It': Reconsidering the Fate of Coptic after the Arab Conquest," *Le Muséon* 120, nos. 3–4 (2007): 273–99.

Samir, Khalil. "L'Apocalypse de Samuel de Qalamūn et la domination des Hagaréens," in *"Guerra santa" e conquiste islamiche nel Mediterraneo (VII–XI secolo)*, ed. Marco Di Branco and Kordula Wolf (Rome: Viella, 2014), 17–63.

Zaborowski, Jason R. "Egyptian Christians Implicating Chalcedonians in the Arab Takeover of Egypt: The Arabic Apocalypse of Samuel of Qalamūn," *Oriens Christianus* 87 (2003): 100–115.

———. "From Coptic to Arabic in Medieval Egypt," *Medieval Encounters* 14, no. 1 (2008): 15–40.

27

The Foundation of Shaykh Abū Isḥāq Kāzarūnī's Congregational Mosque

Maḥmūd b. ʿUthmān (fl. eighth/fourteenth century)

Neguin Yavari

Title: *Firdaws al-Murshidiyya fī Asrār al-Ṣamadiyya* (Paradise of the righteous leaders and their divine intimations)

Genre: Religious instruction (hagiography)

Language: Persian

INTRODUCTION

Firdaws al-Murshidiyya fī Asrār al-Ṣamadiyya was written in 727–28/1327–28 by Maḥmūd b. ʿUthmān, a fourteenth-century Sufi devotee. The book is written in Persian, and its title implies a double meaning. It refers on the one hand to righteous leaders in general, a literal translation of *murshidiyya,* and on the other to the leaders of the Kāzarūniyya order specifically, as the order was also known as the Murshidiyya, followers of Shaykh Murshid.

The work is a hagiography of Shaykh Abū Isḥāq Kāzarūnī (351–424/963–1033), a celibate, vegetarian Sufi leader and proselytizer active in the eleventh century in the southwestern Iranian province of Fārs, which was at that time under Būyid (319–453/932–1062) rule. Known as *shaykh murshid* (spiritual leader), Abū Isḥāq Kāzarūnī was renowned for his preaching and his pivotal role in strengthening the Muslim community and founding Islamic institutions in the region. *Firdaws al-Murshidiyya* recounts Kāzarūnī's many exploits—real and imagined—against non-Muslim *gabrs* in Kāzarūn and its environs.

In most medieval Persian accounts, *gabr,* like *majūs,* refers to adherents of a variety of native Iranian religions, the most populous of which was Zoroastrianism. On most occurrences, it is distinguished from "unbeliever," often connoted by *kāfir*. *Gabr* is sometimes used in conjunction with "fire-worshipper," another appellation for Zoroastrians, and at times as an equivalent of it. The term is New Persian, probably of Aramaic origin, and in the Sasanian period (224–650) it indicated free Mesopotamian peasants. To preserve its semantic nuances, *gabr* is left untranslated in this text.

Conversion is only a tangential theme in the accounts of Kāzarūnī's exploits. His uncanny ability to win over converts for Islam is strung together with a host of other virtues, including unwavering support for the poor and the downtrodden, unending beneficence to friends and strangers alike, and fearlessness in confronting power. The shaykh is praised for his generosity and humility, as well as strategic planning. His acquisitions comprised both spiritual and material terrain: he collected converts as readily as he opened up new territories to the spread of Islam.

The hagiography pivots around the theme of memory, combining material and miraculous feats to parade the various facets of the shaykh's remembrances. Marked for distinction even before birth, he is reported to have intoned religious chants, audible to those present, while still a fetus in his mother's womb. Even his tomb was associated with magical properties. The centerpiece of his legacy is the Kāzarūniyya Sufi order, founded by his disciples and active in Iran until the early sixteenth century. The Kāzarūniyya spread to India, China, and Anatolia, known variously as the Murshidiyya or the Isḥāqiyya. It survives in Turkey to this day.

The excerpt below is a highly stylized dramatic account of the spiritual journey of a group of non-Muslims toward conversion, symbolized in the narrative by mosque building. Alongside explicit analogies between the shaykh and the Prophet, the prophetic template is also invoked in the several unsuccessful attempts at building the mosque. Like Muḥammad, who secured victory at the Battle of Badr in 13/624 only through the grace of God (Q. 3:13, 123–25; 8:42, 47), the shaykh's efforts are thwarted at every turn, until Muḥammad appears in his dream, signaling divine consent and the coming to fruition of his work. The episode is recounted on the authority of Abū Bakr Muḥammad b. ʿAbd al-Karīm (d. 501/1108), the third leader of the Kāzarūniyya order, who is referred to as a preacher (*khaṭīb*, a common title among Abū Isḥāq's successors, which points to the importance of preaching to the Kāzarūniyya Sufis). The Arabic biography of Abū Isḥāq by the preacher Abū Bakr Muḥammad, no longer extant, is our author's principal source.

TEXT

The preacher Imam Abū Bakr Muḥammad b. ʿAbd al-Karīm, God's mercy upon him, recounts: I heard from Muḥammad b. ʿAlī al-Shīrāzī [otherwise unknown] that he said: "I heard from Shaykh Murshid, God bless his soul, that he said: 'The initial instigation for constructing a mosque was this: at the outset, I gathered some stones and made a replica of a *miḥrāb* [prayer niche] and made the call to prayer (*adhān*) from there and performed the daily worship. One day, the elder of the *gabrs* ordered the *miḥrāb* destroyed. The next day I built it anew, better than the old. The leader of the *gabrs* dispatched his men to demolish it again. The third time, I built an even better one. The leader of the *gabrs* was vexed and said: "An endeavor on this small scale will not cause us any trouble, but if he does build a mosque, I will destroy it and make his life a misery for him.'

"Shaykh Murshid, God bless him, added: 'I continued praying in that location and issuing the call to prayer. The *gabrs* would come by and throw stones and hurl profanities at me. After a few days, I laid down the foundational walls of the mosque. The *gabrs* found out. They came and tore it down. A few days later I rebuilt the walls of the mosque; and once again they came and pulled it down.'"

Muḥammad b. ʿAlī al-Shīrāzī said that each time the *gabrs* tore down the walls of the mosque, Shaykh Murshid, God bless his dear soul, would withdraw without facing them, leaving them free to do as they pleased, and prevented his disciples from confronting them there and then. This time around, when they repaired the mosque, the shaykh's disciples stood their ground and sought to prevent the *gabrs* from destroying it. The *gabrs* had come in great numbers, and they overcame the shaykh's followers, demolished the mosque, and went away. Afterward, the disciples sought an audience with the shaykh and recounted the incident and said: "O Shaykh! How long must we suffer this hardship and endure such humiliation at the hands of the *gabrs*?"

The shaykh, God bless his dear soul, said: "The Sublime Truth has commanded that I be patient, as He had commanded the Prophet, peace and prayers be upon him and his family. The Most Almighty said: 'Therefore patiently persevere, as did [all] apostles of inflexible purpose; and be in no haste about the [Unbelievers]. On the Day that they see the [Punishment] promised them, [it will be] as if they had not tarried more than an hour in a single day. [Thine but] to proclaim the Message: but shall any be destroyed except those who transgress?' [Q. 46:35]. And all prophets have endured hardship at the hands of unbelievers as well as of their own people, and they have persevered with patience until they have found solace. We have no choice but to be patient until the Exalted Truth sends us some relief."

Muḥammad b. ʿAlī al-Shīrāzī said that when Shaykh Murshid, God bless his dear soul, endeavored to build the mosque in 370 [980–81 CE] the *gabrs* prevented him from doing so. [Consequently,] for an entire year he issued the call to prayer and performed his worship in open fields. At the end of the year, the Prophet, peace and prayers be upon him and his family, appeared to him in a dream, holding a rope [*ḥabl*, referring here to the Qurʾānic concept of a rope stretched out by God to hold the believers together and protect them from division and strife; Q. 3:103] and laying the foundation of a mosque. The shaykh, God bless his dear soul, hurried toward the Prophet, peace be upon him, and greeted him. The Prophet, peace be upon him, embraced the shaykh and held him close in affection, and the shaykh exuded the blessed scent of the Prophet, peace be upon him, to his dying day. The shaykh, God bless his dear soul, woke up and knew that the building of the mosque must be resumed, as the Prophet, God's peace and prayers upon him and his family, had signaled. The next day, he began construction and built it so it covered seven *haras* [*haras* is a wooden beam used in roofing; here it must signify the length of the beams], and Aḥmad b. Mūsā al-Ghundijānī [a devotee of the shaykh about whom nothing else is known] underwrote the construction. It took four years for a mosque of this expanse to be completed. The *gabr*s had become despondent and ceased their obstructive actions.

Another account has it that when Shaykh Murshid, God bless his dear soul, built the mosque anew, people informed the leader of the *gabr*s. The leader of the *gabr*s said: "If I demolish the mosque again, I fear that the Muslims will unite and defeat me. The best way forward is that I summon the shaykh, harass him, and then imprison him. Once he is incarcerated, there is not a thing his disciples or his friends can do, and they will disperse in awe." He summoned the shaykh and insulted him and ordered that he should be incarcerated. But when the *gabr*s set upon the shaykh, the emir of the *gabr*s regretted his decision and stood down his men. He said, "I am pondering now that if I jail him, the Muslims will unite and start a war, and we may suffer a defeat, for the shaykh is held in great affection among the Muslims and enjoys their highest esteem." He sent someone to recall the shaykh. When they had brought the shaykh to his presence, the leaders of the *gabr*s and the fire-worshippers said, "O Shaykh, abandon any thoughts of building, and forgo your mosque and *miḥrāb* so that you gain your freedom, and if you won't do this, at least abandon the call to prayer. Grant us this minimal wish, for every time that you issue the call to prayer the fires in our fire temples die out."

They said this and released the shaykh. When he got back to his own home ground, it was time for prayers. He went to the mosque's rooftop and called out the summons to pray in a loud voice, ignoring any fear of the *gabr*s; and each day he strove more for the cause of Islam. Shaykh Murshid, God bless his dear soul, said: "The *gabr*s are dismayed because they have tried to restrain me and failed. I issued the call to prayer and I vanquished them, as the Exalted Almighty has decreed: 'And preserve them from [all] ills; and any whom Thou dost preserve from ills that Day, on them wilt Thou have bestowed mercy indeed, and that will be truly [for them] the highest achievement' [Q. 40:9]." And the *gabr*s were in a constant state of distress and affliction and felt powerless, while the Muslims were gaining superiority over them.

Next, Shaykh Murshid, God bless his dear soul, consulted with his intimate circle and disciples and said: "The mosque is too small, and now that the *gabr*s have become subdued, I can enlarge the mosque for the Muslims. What are your thoughts: Shall I begin construction or should I let it be?" The disciples said, "O

Shaykh, you are in charge and you know best; we are at your service to do whatsoever you command." The shaykh, God bless his soul, had already issued the order to begin construction, but he consulted with his close associates to emulate the Prophet, as the Exalted Almighty had commanded the Prophet, peace and prayers be upon him and his family, "Consult them in the matter" [Q. 3:159]. After that Shaykh Murshid, God bless his memory, expanded the mosque to twenty *haras*, and that status prevailed for a while. After that he expanded the mosque further to fifty *haras*. And another period of time transpired. This time he built the mosque to a full one hundred *haras*. After that Shaykh Murshid, God bless his dear soul, commanded that the Friday communal prayers were to be held in the newly expanded mosque. Prior to that, the people of Nūrd [according to legend, one of the three villages that merged to make up the town of Kāzarūn] had attended Friday prayers in the Old City. Thereafter they never once went to the Old City for the Friday prayers.

And with each passing day Islam gained more might, the Muslims became more victorious, and the *gabr*s grew more despondent. Their religion was weakened by the *baraka* [blessing or indwelling spiritual power believed to be possessed by certain people, objects, or sacred sites] of Shaykh Murshid, God bless his dear soul; and the *gabr*s would seek audience with the shaykh and convert to Islam. And people flocked from all corners to areas adjacent to the shaykh's congregational mosque and his hospice [*ribāṭ*, similar to *khānaqā* or *zāwiya;* a gathering house for members of Sufi orders, where hospitality was offered to pilgrims and travelers], and built their houses there, and Kāzarūn prospered. Before Shaykh Murshid's time, God's blessing on his dear soul, the town did not exist. There was a small village on the south side of the shaykh's hospice called Nūrd, and the town was Balad al-ʿAtīq, which means Old City. The people of the region were mostly *gabr*s and fire-worshippers, and that was their domain. All the elite and notables of Kāzarūn and its environs were *gabr*s. Although subject to Muslim rule, they remained *gabr*s and paid the *jizya* [poll tax] to the Muslims. The reason for this was that one of the bravest and most chivalrous of the Arab emirs, called Qiyāth Wāḍiḥ [otherwise unknown], had brought forth a vast army of Muslims to fight the *gabr*s and had vanquished them all and imposed the *jizya* on them. The *gabr*s paid the *jizya* but remained true to their religion, and the majority were fire-worshippers until Shaykh Murshid, God bless his dear soul, appeared and the Exalted Almighty selected him by His grace and made him a leader of the Muslims; and thanks to the *baraka* of his breath the Muslims became more victorious day by day and the *gabr*s descended deeper into decline.

It is said that there were several fire temples belonging to the fire-worshippers in the environs of Kāzarūn, where for years they had had fires burning day and night and engaged in worship, and the fires had never died down. But each time Shaykh Murshid, God bless his dear soul, made the call to prayer, the fire in all the temples would die down, and the fire-worshippers would all become despondent, powerless to do anything. Gradually, they would seek the presence of the shaykh and become Muslims. And it was during the lifetime of Shaykh Murshid, God bless his dear soul, that the majority of the *gabr*s and fire-worshippers became Muslims through him. It is recorded in the biography that twenty-four thousand men from among the *gabr*s, the fire-worshippers, and the Jews were converted by Shaykh Murshid, God bless his dear soul, and found the true path thanks to his miraculous blessings.

FURTHER READING

Aigle, Denise. "Un fondateur d'ordre en milieu rural: Le cheikh Abū Isḥāq de Kāzarūn," in *Saints orientaux*, ed. Denise Aigle (Paris: De Boccard, 1995), 181–209.

Arberry, Arthur John. "The Biography of Shaikh Abū Isḥāq al-Kāzarūni," *Oriens* 3, no. 2 (1950): 163–82.

Yavari, Neguin. "The Conversion Stories of Shaykh Abū Isḥāq al-Kāzarūnī," in *Christianizing Peoples and Converting Individuals*, ed. Guyda Armstrong and Ian N. Wood (Turnhout: Brepols, 2000), 225–46.

28

Conversion to Islam under the Fatimid Caliph al-Ḥākim bi-Amr Allāh

Michael of Damrū (Mīkhā'īl al-Damrāwī), Bishop of Tinnīs (d. after 442/1050)

Mark Swanson

Title: *Siyar al-Bīʿa al-Muqaddasa* (Biographies of the Holy Church), usually referred to as *The History of the Patriarchs of Alexandria*
Genre: Historical writing (hagiography)
Language: Arabic

INTRODUCTION

The excerpts below are taken from the biography of Coptic patriarch Zacharias (the sixty-fourth patriarch, 394–423/1004–32), written originally in Coptic in about 442–43/1051 by Michael of Damrū (Mīkhā'īl al-Damrāwī), bishop of Tinnīs. A generation later his collection of patriarchal biographies was one of the sources translated into Arabic and knitted together into the work usually called *The History of the Patriarchs of Alexandria.* Bishop Michael, as understood from the excerpts, is especially interested in giving examples of Christians who heroically *resisted* pressure to convert to Islam; but in telling their stories, he gives vivid testimony to what he calls a "time of turmoil."

The Fatimid period in Egypt (358–567/969–1171) is generally remembered as a relatively favorable one for *dhimmī* communities (that is, the "protected" Christians and Jews), with one great exception: the rule of the caliph al-Ḥākim bi-Amr Allāh (r. 386–411/996–1021), who, from about the year 395/1004 onward, began to adopt policies and issue decrees that made the life of non-Muslims very difficult and led to a number of conversions to Islam. The excerpts below bear witness to some of these policies: pressure on non-Muslim civil servants to convert to Islam;

enforcement of policies meant to mark off and humiliate *dhimmīs* through distinctive clothing, insignia, and other regulations; and (from about 400/1010) the widespread destruction of churches.

One may discern from the excerpts below that pressure to convert was "top down," beginning with leading government functionaries, but that it eventually came to be felt more widely. Furthermore, we may note local variations: our excerpts bear witness to Copts in Cairo who managed to pass themselves off as Muslims, but also to intense humiliation of Christians in Tinnīs. Finally, the last excerpt points to the remarkable fact that toward the end of his reign al-Ḥākim seems to have lost interest in enforcing his policies, and he eventually allowed government functionaries who had converted to Islam under pressure to return to their Christian belief.

Like much else about al-Ḥākim, his motivation for the anti-*dhimmī* policies remains a mystery. These should probably not be seen in the light of any earlier Sunni jurisprudence; after all, al-Ḥākim was an Ismāʿīlī caliph, and his word was law. It is not impossible that esoteric speculations about events at the turn of the century (400–401/1010) played some role in his thinking.

TEXT

Excerpt 1

[*Bishop Michael reports that al-Ḥākim began to kill off a number of his associates and army chiefs but then turned his attention to the Coptic financial administrators—"archons and secretaries"—in his administration.*]

Then the archons and secretaries returned, and he [al-Ḥākim] selected ten of them. Among their leaders was Abū Najāḥ "the elder" (*al-kabīr*), who was an Orthodox Christian. He [al-Ḥākim] summoned him and said, "I want you to give up your religion (*dīn*) and return to my religion, and I will make you my vizier so that you can direct the affairs of my kingdom." He [Abū Najāḥ] said to him, "Grant me a respite until tomorrow, so that I may think it over." He [al-Ḥākim] granted him the respite and let him go.

So Abū Najāḥ went to his house, summoned his friends, and informed them of what had transpired between them. He said, "I am prepared to die upon the name of the Lord Christ. My purpose in seeking a respite until tomorrow was not to think it over; I only said that in order to gather with you and with my family, to bid farewell to you and to them, and to give some words of counsel to you and to them . . . "

[*Abū Najāḥ then made his parting exhortation and gave a feast for his friends.*]

When the following day had come, Abū Najāḥ went to al-Ḥākim bi-Amr Allāh, who said to him, "Najāḥ, tell me. Are you feeling at ease?"

He said, "Yes."

Al-Ḥākim said, "With what decision?"

Abū Najāḥ said, "With my remaining in my religion."

Al-Ḥākim strove in every way, with enticement and intimidation, to move him from his religion, but he did not do that; al-Ḥākim was unable to turn Abū Najāḥ's determination away from his faith community (*madhhab*). So he commanded that he be stripped of his garment, stretched out upon the rack, and beaten. . . .

Abū Najāḥ was beaten savagely. After eight hundred lashes he said, "I am thirsty." They quit beating him and informed al-Ḥākim, who said, "Give him something to drink after you say to him that he [must] return to our religion."

When they came to him with water and said what the king had commanded, he said to them, "Return his water to him, for I am not in need of it, because my Lord Jesus Christ has given me to drink." A group of officials and others who were present bore witness that they saw the water that dripped from his beard. And once he had said that, he gave up his spirit.

They informed the hard-hearted king of his death. He ordered that he receive the full thousand lashes, even while dead. Thus took place his martyrdom; may his blessings be with us.

And among them [the archons and secretaries] was another, known as "the chief" (*al-raʾīs*), Fahd b. Ibrāhīm, whom he [al-Ḥākim] had advanced over all the secretaries and bureau heads. He summoned him into his presence and said, "You know that I have chosen you and advanced you over everyone in my state (*dawla*). Listen to me: be with me in my religion, and I shall raise you higher than you already are, and you shall be like a brother to me." He [Fahd] did not comply with his speech, so al-Ḥākim commanded that he be beheaded and his body burned with fire. . . .

[*Fahd's right hand, which had often given alms to the poor, was not touched by the fire.*]

As for the rest of those ten judges who had been brought forward, when he [al-Ḥākim] demanded that they abandon and move away from their religion, they did not do that; they did not obey him. He commanded that they be tortured, so they beat them with whips. When the beating became intense, four of them converted to Islam (*aslamū*). One of these four died that very night. As for the other three, at the end of the time of turmoil they returned to the Christian faith community (*madhhab al-Naṣrāniyya*). The rest of the ten died under torture and obtained everlasting life. (*History*, 122, line 4–123, line 19)

Excerpt 2

[*At this point in the narrative, Christians and Jews have already been burdened with regulations designed to distinguish and diminish them in public; for example, Chris-*

*tians are obliged to wear a distinctive badge (*ghiyār*) and waistband (*zunnār*). Now, however, we hear how the burden literally became heavier.*]

He [al-Ḥākim] commanded, with respect to the wooden crosses of the Christians, that the weight of each cross be five pounds [lit. "five Egyptian *raṭls*"], that each be sealed with a lead seal bearing the name of the king, and that they hang them from their necks with ropes of palm fiber. And likewise the Jews: the measure of the ball that hung from their necks was to be five pounds. Whoever of them was found without the seal would be treated with contempt and assessed a fine. Many Christians and Jews, from their leaders to the least of them, renounced their faith (*jaḥada*) because of this, for they could not bear this humiliation and torment. (*History*, 126, lines 16–20)

Excerpt 3

[*The persecution intensified over the years, perhaps reaching its climax around the year 402/1012. Some Christians converted to Islam; others feigned conversion.*]

Some days later, al-Ḥākim sent out written decrees (*sijillāt*) to all the districts of his kingdom that the churches be destroyed and that whatever vessels of gold and silver were in them be carried to his palace; that [payment?] be demanded of the bishops in every place; and that Christians not engage in selling or buying in any locality. A group of them renounced (*jaḥada*) their religion because of that; but most of the Christians of Cairo (*al-Miṣriyyīn*) took off their badge (*ghiyār*), cross (*ṣalīb*), waistband (*zunnār*), and wooden stirrups (*rukub*) and affected the likeness of the Muslims. No one gave them away, and everyone who saw them assumed that they had converted to Islam (*aslamū*). (*History*, 128, lines 11–16)

[*Bishop Michael tells a story about one of his own saintly mentors—another example of a Copt from the financial administration who came under pressure to convert.*]

There was a deacon named Buqayra, who left the service of the government bureau (*dīwān*) which had been his. He bore his cross, went to the palace, and cried out at its gate, "Christ is the Son of God!" When al-Ḥākim heard his voice, he commanded that he be brought to him; he strove with him to make him deny (*yunkir*) his religion and confess Islam (*ya'tarif bi-islām*), but he did not; he was like a strong rock that would not be shaken. The more he [al-Ḥākim] exhorted him, the more he cried out and said, "Christ is the Son of God!" Al-Ḥākim commanded that he be bound at the neck with a collar and iron chain and cast into the Prison of Blood. (*History*, 128, lines 16–20)

[*We then learn that Buqayra was released from prison and devoted himself to serving prisoners and members of the community who had been reduced to poverty.*]

Excerpt 4

[*Bishop Michael's biography of Zacharias describes how a weak and ineffective patriarch became a saint through his steadfastness in the midst of persecution. Here Patriarch Zacharias speaks the language of the martyrs.*]

As for Anbā Zacharias, he remained imprisoned for three months, during which time they attempted every day to terrorize him with [threats of] being burned with fire or thrown to the wild beasts if he did not enter into the religion of Islam. And they said to him, "If you accede to that, you will obtain great glory: al-Ḥākim will make you chief judge (*qāḍī al-quḍāt*)." But he would not incline or bow to them. There was with him in the prison an evil Muslim man, who said to him, "You wicked old man, why don't you convert (*tuslim*) so that they let you go, and you shall receive great honor from them?" The patriarch said to him, "My reliance is on God, whose is the power, and He shall help me."

When this speech was complete, one of the Turks came in and hit him in the mouth with a mace. The patriarch said to him, "As for the body, it is under your authority to destroy as you will; but as for the soul, it is in the hand of the Lord." (*History*, 131, lines 9–15)

[*According to Bishop Michael's account, Patriarch Zacharias was indeed thrown to the lions but, like biblical Daniel, came through unscathed. He was released and spent nine years in virtual exile in the desert monasteries of the Wādī Ḥabīb, known today as Wādī al-Naṭrūn.*]

Excerpt 5

During those nine years the Christians experienced great distress, expulsion, insult, and cursing from the Muslims, who spat in their faces. The greater part of that was in the city of Tinnīs and its districts. If a Christian passed through them, they insulted him and said to him, "Break this cross and enter into the encompassing religion (*al-dīn al-wāsiʿ*)." If a Christian forgot his cross and walked without it, he would encounter much disgrace. (*History*, 133, lines 3–7)

[*Soon afterward Michael tells a story about his father, who, while being reviled by a crowd, had gone so far as to offer the following prayer:*]

"O my Lord Jesus Christ, if you do not reveal to me something to pacify my heart, so that I know that there is a reward for me in the midst of what I am receiving from these people, then I will deny your religion!" (*History*, 133, lines 19–21)

[*His prayer was answered with a vision of heaven, including a conversation with Christ.*]

Excerpt 6

[*Toward the end of al-Ḥākim's rule, the anti-*dhimmī *measures lost much of their intensity.*]

After that, a group of Christians who had converted to Islam (*aslamū*) stood before him [al-Ḥākim]. He said to them, "What do you want?" They said to him, "That you return us to our religion." Then he said to each one of them, "Where are your waistband, your cross, and your badge?" And they took them out from under their garments. He commanded them to put them on before him and sent with each one of them a mounted escort, writing for him a document (*sijill*) to be in his possession, to the effect that he should not be impeded. Thus many of those who had converted to Islam returned to their religion. (*History,* 135, lines 8–12)

FURTHER READING

Swanson, Mark N. *The Coptic Papacy in Islamic Egypt (641–1517)* (Cairo: American University in Cairo Press, 2010), chapter 4.

Walker, Paul E. "Al-Ḥākim and the *Dhimmīs*," *Medieval Encounters* 21, nos. 4–5 (2015): 345–63.

———. *Caliph of Cairo: Al-Hakim bi-Amr Allah, 996–1021* (Cairo: American University in Cairo Press, 2012).

29

Conversion from Motives of Expediency

Sibṭ Ibn al-Jawzī, Shams al-Dīn Abū al-Muẓaffar Yūsuf b. Qizoghlū (d. 654/1256)

D. G. Tor

Title: *Mir'āt al-Zamān fī Ta'rīkh al-A'yān* (The looking glass of time concerning the history of the notables)
Genre: Historical writing
Language: Arabic

INTRODUCTION

Sibṭ Ibn al-Jawzī (581 or 582–654/1185 or 1186–1256), preacher and writer, was the son of a Turkish freedman of a caliphal vizier and the daughter of ʿAbd al-Raḥmān b. al-Jawzī (d. 596/1200), one of the most important Baghdadi clerics of the hard-line Ḥanbalī stream of Sunnism. Together, the chronicles of Ibn al-Jawzī and his grandson Sibṭ Ibn al-Jawzī constitute two of the most important historical sources for the tenth through twelfth centuries.

The episode narrated in the passage translated here had a broader political context. The decade preceding this particular crackdown on *dhimmī*s (the so-called protected peoples, i.e., Jews and Christians) was rife with caliphal proclamations enforcing the various anti-*dhimmī* strictures enjoined by Islamic law. In 478/1085, for instance, the caliph al-Muqtadī (r. 467–86/1075–94) issued an order for Baghdad that all houses belonging to Jews that were built higher than the houses of Muslims should be destroyed; that their gates near the Friday mosque should be blocked off; and that the Jews were to be obligated "to lower their voices in reading the Bible in their houses, and to show the external signs upon their heads." Two years later, in 480/1088, the caliph is said to have issued similar directives for more distant parts of Iraq.

Since this enforcement of *sharʿī* laws against *dhimmīs* would have entailed the loss of public office as well, Ibn Mūṣilāyā, the Christian secretary of the caliph's chancery, converted to Islam, thus removing any impediment to his political advancement, and was subsequently promoted to the position of vizier. Such conversions also entailed the impoverishment of the convert's original community and family; when Ibn Mūṣilāyā died some years later, no Christian members of his family could inherit from him, and his obituary states specifically that his property went instead to Muslim "pious uses."

TEXT

And in [the month of] Ṣafar in the year 484 [April 7, 1091], the vizier Abū Shujāʿ wrote to the caliph, informing him of the presumptuousness of the people of the *dhimma* toward the Muslims and of the necessity of discriminating [the *dhimmīs*] from [the Muslims]. The caliph commanded that [Abū Shujāʿ] act as he saw fit, so he [in turn] commanded [the *dhimmīs*] to wear the distinguishing badges and sashes [blue for Christians and yellow for Jews], and to hang the lead discs around their necks, with *dhimmī* written upon the discs, and to place these discs upon the throats of their women in the baths, so that they be known by it; and [he commanded] that they [i.e., the women] wear [mismatched] shoes, one black and one red, and that they wear anklets around their legs [with bells on them to warn Muslims that a *dhimmī* was approaching]; and they were humiliated and suppressed (*fa-dhallū wa-nqamaʿū*). At that time, Abū Saʿd b. al-Mūsilāyā, secretary of the caliphal chancery, converted to Islam, together with his brother's son, Abū Naṣr Hibat Allāh, and asked that this be in the presence of the caliph, who acquiesced to it.

FURTHER READING

Peacock, A. C. S. *The Great Seljuq Empire* (Edinburgh: Edinburgh University Press, 2015), chapter 3.

Tor, D. G. "Rayy and the Religious History of the Seljuq Period," *Der Islam* 93, no. 2 (2016): 377–405.

Van Renterghem, Vanessa. *Les élites bagdadiennes au temps des Seldjoukides: Étude d'histoire sociale*, 2 vols. (Beirut: Institut français du Proche-Orient, 2015).

30

Conversion, Confession, Prayer, and Apostasy

Ibn Rushd al-Jadd al-Qurṭubī (450–520/1058–1126)

Maribel Fierro

Title: *Kitāb al-Bayān wa-l-Taḥṣīl wa-l-Sharḥ wa-l-Tawjīh wa-l-Ta ʿlīl li-Masā ʾil al-ʿUtbiyya* (The book of clarification, summation, expounding, guidance, and argumentation to the questions in the *ʿUtbiyya*)

Genre: Legal writing (legal questions, i.e., *masā ʾil*)

Language: Arabic

INTRODUCTION

Abū ʿAbd Allāh Muḥammad b. Aḥmad b. ʿAbd al-ʿAzīz b. (Abī) ʿUtba b. Jamīl/Jumayl (Ḥamīd/Ḥumayd) b. Abī ʿUtba b. Abī Sufyān Ṣakhr b. Ḥarb b. Umayya b. ʿAbd al-Shams al-Umawī al-ʿUtbī al-Sufyānī al-Qurṭubī (d. ca. 255/869) was the descendant of an Umayyad client (*mawlā*). He studied in Córdoba with Yaḥyā b. Yaḥyā (d. 234/848), whose transmission (*riwāya*) of the *Muwaṭṭa* ʾ, the legal work of the Medinese scholar Mālik b. Anas (d. 179/795), became canonical in al-Andalus. In Qayrawān, al-ʿUtbī studied with another Mālikī scholar, Saḥnūn b. Saʿīd (d. 240/854), who compiled in his *Mudawwana* the auditions (*samā ʿāt*) of the three most important Egyptian students of Mālik b. Anas: Ibn Wahb (d. 197/812), Ashhab (d. 204/819), and most especially Ibn al-Qāsim (d. 191/806). In Egypt, al-ʿUtbī studied with Aṣbagh b. al-Faraj (d. 225/839), a student of the three abovementioned Egyptian Mālikī scholars. All of these scholars appear in the text translated here, found in Ibn Rushd al-Jadd's *Kitāb al-Bayān*, a commentary on al-ʿUtbī's *al-Mustakhraja min al-asmi ʿa al-masmū ʿa min Mālik b. Anas* (Auditions of the audible from Mālik b. Anas), var. *al-Mustakhraja min al-asmi ʿa mimmā laysa fī al-Mudawwana* (Auditions of what is not found in the *Mudawwana*), also known as *al-ʿUtbiyya.* In it, the Córdoban jurist compiled materials from the auditions of Mālik's teachings, as recorded by his Andalusi and Egyptian students, materials that were lacking in Saḥnūn's *Mudawwana.*

These materials consist of *masāʾil,* that is, questions and answers on a variety of legal issues. The answers were given according to Mālikī legal reasoning in that period, that is, in accordance with the authoritative opinion (*raʾy*) of Mālik and his students as well as the authoritative precedent of the practice (*ʿamal*) of Medina, the town where the Prophet had acted as statesman, but making almost no reference to prophetic tradition (*ḥadīth*). Al-ʿUtbī's work enjoyed sustained popularity in both al-Andalus and North Africa, and because of its popularity it was abridged and also commented on several times, most notably by Ibn Abī Zayd al-Qayrawānī (310–86/922–96) in his *al-Nawādir wa-l-Ziyādāt ʿalā mā fī al-Mudawwana wa-ghayrihā (Kitāb Ibn al-Mawwāz, Ibn ʿAbdūs, Ibn Ḥabīb, al-ʿUtbiyya) min al-Ummahāt,* and by Ibn Rushd al-Jadd in his *Kitāb al-Bayān wa-l-Taḥṣīl.*

The text translated here from the latter work (16:432–35) exemplifies how the Andalusi Mālikī school had evolved toward a more systematic treatment of legal issues in the almost three centuries that had passed between al-ʿUtbī and Ibn Rushd. Ibn Rushd explains the contents of the *ʿUtbiyya* according to the new ways of legal reasoning that he and other "reformed" Mālikīs support under the influence of Shāfiʿism with its reliance on prophetic traditions (*ḥadīth*) and analogy (*qiyās*).

The legal question presented in the text deals with a topic that concerned early Egyptian Mālikī scholars: how to establish with certainty that someone not born as a Muslim had become a Muslim. Two specific cases are mentioned: a monk who confesses that he converted to Islam but then retracts what he said; and the case of Christians known to have converted to Islam out of duress (for example, by being subject to high taxation) who later reverted to their former religion. Should they be considered apostates?

Mālik b. Anas and his Egyptian pupils Ibn Wahb and Ibn al-Qāsim were of the opinion that apostates were only those who could be proven to have been "real" Muslims. Thus anyone who had not converted willingly should not be executed.

It should be noted that whereas prayer constituted proof of a convert's Muslimness for these early jurists, other religious practices (namely, the profession of faith—which could be pronounced by other monotheists without necessarily implying that they believed in Islam—along with almsgiving, fasting, and pilgrimage) were not considered equally demonstrative of "real" conversion. This was likely because the obligatory prayers tended to be communal, especially the Friday prayer, and were considered specifically Islamic (as opposed to the prayers of Christians and Jews).

By contrast, however, Ashhab, who was also a student of Mālik, as well as other Medinese and Mālikī scholars, held that a reverting convert, whether voluntarily converted or not, was to be executed.

As for the Egyptian Aṣbagh, for him the performance of prayer did not determine whether someone was to be considered a Muslim: if a recent convert died before praying—even if he would have had the time to do it—he was to be treated as a Muslim.

Ibn Rushd succeeds in explaining and summarizing these different positions, introducing order and coherence to the early, unsystematized legal opinions.

TEXT

Yaḥyā [b. Yaḥyā al-Laythī] said that Ibn Wahb posed to Mālik a question regarding a monk who was asked: "You are an eloquent Arabic-speaking man, acquainted with the superiority of Islam and its people over the rest of the religions. What has prevented you from converting to Islam?" The monk answered: "I was a Muslim for a time and became acquainted with Islam, but I did not see any religion superior to Christianity and thus I returned to it precisely because of what I had ascertained of its superiority."

These words reached the ruler in charge of government (*sulṭān*), who sent orders to bring the monk into his presence to question him about what he had said. The monk then said: "I said those words but I was never a Muslim. It was just something that I said." The *sulṭān* imprisoned him and solicited testimonial evidence (*bayyina*) against him to establish that he had converted to Islam. [Yet] no such evidence attesting that he had been a Muslim was found except for those words he had pronounced confessing his conversion to Islam. What is the legal procedure against him (*fa-mādhā yajibu ʿalayhi*)? Mālik answered: "I do not see that he can be executed or that a punishment can be inflicted upon him or that he should be asked to repent as in the case of someone who is considered an apostate (*murtadd*), except if testimony was given against the monk that he was seen praying, even if he prayed just one *rakʿa* [part of the Muslim prayer]."

I [Ibn Wahb] persisted [with Mālik]: "And what if he had pronounced the profession of faith (*shahāda*), acknowledged the prophet (*nabī*), and had been acquainted with the obligatory precepts (*farāʾiḍ*) regarding the performance of alms, pilgrimage, and the fast of Ramadan? That is, what if he had pronounced the Islamic profession of faith after having acquired knowledge on Islam so that he could not be excused on the grounds of ignorance?" [Mālik answered]: "There would still be no basis to start any legal procedure against him (*fa-lam yajib bi-shayʾin*)."

I [Yaḥyā] asked Ibn al-Qāsim regarding this issue, and he answered: "I heard Mālik say that nobody should be executed because of apostasy (*irtidād*) except a person for whom there is clear evidence that he was a Muslim and it is known that he converted willingly, that he prayed, and that he consented to convert to Islam. This excludes anyone who converted to Islam in order to escape from the distress caused by the payment of the poll tax (*jizya*), or something similar, or anyone who was charged with regard to his poll tax with what he could not possibly comply with and this made him resort to conversion to Islam. As for someone who is to be counted among those in similar circumstances because of the suffering inflicted on him by the payment of the land tax (*kharāj*) or because he was imprisoned for a long time: it is said that if he converted to Islam (*aslama*), those circumstances would be deemed to excuse him [in case he reverts to his former religion]." Aṣbagh said: "Ibn Wahb said something similar."

I [Yaḥyā] asked Ashhab, too, about this question, saying: "[What is the status of] a Christian who converts to Islam (*yuslimu*) during a time of hardship and heavy taxation (*ḍayyiq min al-kharāj*), who turns to Islam [and therefore has to pay less taxes] and then reverts [to Christianity], claiming that his conversion was due to the distress that he was suffering, yet this is not known except for his own declaration?" Ashhab gave me this answer: "Even if it is known to be as he has declared [that he converted under pressure], and moreover, if someone else gives testimony in accordance with his declaration [i.e., that the Christian converted to Islam under pressure], I think that he has to be killed if he does not return to Islam." Ibn Wahb did not think that he had to be killed if he had converted out of distress, suffering, or fear. Both gave advice on this issue to Isḥāq b. Sulaymān al-Hāshimī [an Egyptian governor whose name is given by al-Kindī (d. 350/961) as ʿAlī b. Sulaymān al-Hāshimī, an eighth-century contemporary of Ibn Wahb and Ashhab] when [this question] was brought up among us in Miṣr [old Cairo].

The *imām* and judge [Ibn Rushd al-Jadd] explained: regarding the monk who first said, "I was a Muslim for some time," and then, when he was asked to clarify his situation, replied, "I was never a Muslim; it was just something that I said" Ibn Wahb's doctrine that neither execution nor punishment can be applied to him is clear and correct. This is so because the monk testified against himself regarding his conversion to Islam, and it is not correct to execute someone using his own testimony if he has withdrawn it and has subsequently stated that he lied in this previous testimony. This is the same as if two witnesses had testified saying that the monk was a Muslim and then retracted their testimony and said: "We lied in our testimony against him regarding this matter."

When Ibn Wahb was questioned regarding a person who showed satisfaction with his conversion to Islam after having mastered its precepts, acknowledged the Prophet, and pronounced the profession of faith and who then reverted from Islam, Ibn Wahb answered that there is no basis for any legal procedure against him. Ibn Wahb's doctrine (*madhhab*) is that there is no execution on the grounds of infidelity for someone who rejected Islam after conversion if he belonged to the protected religious groups (*ahl al-dhimma*), that is, Christians and Jews, if the only thing that was testified against him is that he verbally professed Islam. This is clear from what he stated. Also, the convert is not asked to repent, as is done in the case of someone who is considered an apostate, except if testimony is given against him that he was seen praying, even if he prayed only one *rakʿa* of the obligatory prayer.

This is similar to Ibn al-Qāsim's narration that he heard Mālik say: "The execution for apostasy is applied only when it has been firmly proved that the person in question had converted willingly to Islam and used to pray [on a regular basis]."

Aṣbagh says: "Regarding a person who converted willingly to Islam and then apostatized—whether a long period of time had passed since his conversion or whether he apostatized immediately after it, and whether he had prayed and fasted or not [*ṣallā wa-ṣāma aw lam yafʿal;* the text here has been amended according to Ibn Abī Zayd al-Qayrawānī's *al-Nawādir wa-l-Ziyādāt,* 14:490–94]—an attempt should be made to bring him to recant his apostasy (*rujjiʿa fī mawqifihi*); that is, he is to be treated in the same way as those who are born into the *fiṭra* [i.e., born Muslims, who are offered the chance to repent and thus avoid execution]. The calling to repentance (*istitāba*) consists of a period of three days during which the person should be filled with fear of being killed and is to be reminded of the Islamic religion and exposed to it. There is no discrepancy of opinion (*ikhtilāf*) regarding the view that someone who has professed Islam in his heart is a Muslim believer (*muslim muʾmin*), because faith is one of the actions of the heart. There is also no discrepancy of opinion regarding the view that he is to be judged according to Islamic norms once he has manifested his profession of faith, so that he is inherited from [i.e., a Muslim can inherit from him], the funeral prayer is said for him, and he is buried in the cemeteries of the Muslims, even if he dies before he has had time to pray or to fast. This is the case even if the times of the obligatory prayers passed before he died and he did not pray, because it is implied of him, regardless of possible omission and neglect that do not affect Islam and belief according to the doctrine of all scholars." The doctrine of Aṣbagh is that he should be given the opportunity to repent, and if he repents, he is fine, and if he does not, he is to be executed [but in Ibn Abī Zayd al-Qayrawānī's *al-Nawādir wa-l-Ziyādāt,* Aṣbagh is said to have stated that if he repents, he is fine, and if he does not, he is to be left alone and cannot be executed]. This is reasoning by analogy (*qiyās*).

To a certain extent, what Ibn Wahb and Mālik [according to the transmission of Ibn al-Qāsim] were pointing at when they said [in the case of the monk] that no repentance is required of him and that he cannot be executed unless he prayed was an external way of following what the Prophet—salutations upon him—had said: "Cut the neck of anyone who changes his religion" (*man ghayyara dīnahu fa-ḍribū ʿunqahu*). That is because nobody is entitled to state that someone belongs to the religion of Islam unless that person has extensively practiced its legal norms, such as prayer, almsgiving, fasting, and pilgrimage according to the saying of the Prophet—salutations upon him—that "Islam is built upon five [pillars]: the profession of faith,

'There is no god but God'; the performance of prayer; the giving of alms; fasting in Ramadan; and performing pilgrimage to the Sacred House of God for those who are able to do it." And it is also because we cannot have certitude regarding the veracity of testimony given about someone's being a Muslim, if such testimony has been disowned on the basis of the witnesses' doubts in what they had testified regarding his faith. Thus, there is a discrepancy of opinion as to whether what was testified against him regarding his apostasy has been subsequently denied. However, if the testimony of the witnesses is verified, then it is obligatory that he be granted the opportunity of repentance; and if he repents, he is safe, but if he does not, he is to be executed, even if he did not pray; and there is agreement (*ittifāq*) on this. And God knows better.

The doctrine of Ibn al-Qāsim and Ibn Wahb that he [the Christian who converted to Islam] should be given the opportunity to excuse himself, given that when he converted, according to what was mentioned, he did so because he was charged beyond his means with the poll tax or was in some other, similar situation that was acknowledged as having existed and therefore as providing an excuse—[this] points to the case in which his claim could not be verified because there was no acknowledgment that such a situation had existed. Abū Zayd [b. Abī al-Ghamr] has narrated from Ibn al-Qāsim on the case of a Christian who converts to Islam and prays but then says, "I converted out of fear of payment of the poll tax or of being oppressed," that Ibn al-Qāsim said that this excuse is to be accepted from the Christian and he is not to be considered an apostate. Ibn Abī Zayd mentioned this transmission in *al-Nawādir.* All this is based on the understanding that such an acceptance applies only if his declaration is considered plausible.

The stipulation of Ibn al-Qāsim and Ibn Wahb that "if the excuse that he [the Christian who converted to Islam] gives regarding his conversion—namely, that it was motivated by a demand for the poll tax beyond what he could pay or some other situation similar to this—can be verified" indicates that they do not accept it as true if it cannot be verified. However, Abū Zayd [b. Abī al-Ghamr] has narrated from Ibn al-Qāsim that the declaration of the Christian who converts to Islam and performs the prayer but states that he converted out of fear of having to pay the poll tax or of being oppressed has to be accepted, as he is not like the apostate. Ibn Abī Zayd included this transmission in *al-Nawādir,* and it has to be understood that this applies in the case that his declaration is considered plausible.

The summary (*taḥṣīl*) of all that has been discussed here is that on this legal question there are two doctrines:

(1) The first one is that he [the Christian who converted out of fear] is not given the possibility of excusing himself; this is the doctrine of Ashhab and Ibn Ḥabīb (d. 238/853), who narrated the same view, taking it from Muṭarrif (d. 220/835) and Ibn al-Mājishūn (d. 212/827).

(2) The second is that such a circumstance is considered exculpatory. But within the doctrine that it is considered exculpatory there is discrepancy on the following

point: Should his declaration be verified to prove that what he claims was correct? There are two positions on this issue:

(2.1) The first is that it should be verified; this is the doctrine of Ibn al-Qāsim and Ibn Wahb in this transmission.

(2.2) The second is that it should not be verified; this is the doctrine of Ibn al-Qāsim in the transmission of Abū Zayd [b. Abī al-Ghamr] from him, but it applies only, of course, if his declaration appears plausible.

At the beginning of this audition chapter, the meaning of this question has already been dealt with, as well as at the beginning of the audition chapter of ʿĪsā [b. Dīnār]. Ponder and reflect on all of this. Success depends on God.

FURTHER READING

Dennett, Daniel C. *Conversion and the Poll Tax in Early Islam* (Cambridge, MA: Harvard University Press, 1950).

Fernández Félix, Ana. *Cuestiones legales del Islam temprano: La ʿUtbiyya y el proceso de formación de la sociedad islámica andalusí* (Madrid: CSIC, 2003).

Friedmann, Yohanan. *Tolerance and Coercion in Islam: Interfaith Relations in the Muslim Tradition* (Cambridge: Cambridge University Press, 2003), 121–59.

Simonsohn, Uriel. "'Halting between Two Opinions': Conversion and Apostasy in Early Islam," *Medieval Encounters* 19, no. 3 (2013): 342–70.

31

The Conversion of the Turks

Michael the Syrian (d. 596/1199)

Maria Conterno

Title: *Maktbonut zabne* (Chronography)
Genre: Historical writing (universal chronicle)
Language: Syriac

INTRODUCTION

Michael the Syrian, also known as Michael the Great (Syr. Mikha'il Rabo), is one of the major Syriac historians. Born in Melitene in 519/1126, he was patriarch of the Syrian Orthodox Church from 561/1166 until his death in 596/1199. He was a very active church leader but also a prolific writer. His only surviving work is a universal chronicle that extends from the creation to 591/1195. The text as it is now preserved is structured in three columns, dealing with civil, ecclesiastical, and various other matters, respectively. The original layout, however, followed more closely the Eusebian model, anchoring the events in a chronological canon parallel to the three columns.

The present passage is interesting in that it discusses a case of collective conversion to Islam and concerns people other than Christians and Jews—the Turks. It is collocated in the middle of the eleventh century, within an excursus on the Turks, their origins, customs, and conquests. The Turks' ancestral religion is referred to as "Tengrism": it had shamanic and animistic traits, and was centered on the worship of the almighty sky god Tengri. Such pagan, yet monotheistic, religion is indeed presented by Michael as one of the factors that eased the Turks' conversion to Islam. Michael indicates as one of the contexts in which the Turks were exposed to

Muslim "proselytism" the military campaigns in which the Arabs employed them as mercenaries. But the conversion process is also given a diachronic dimension in relation to newly arrived groups following the lead of those who had previously converted, which accurately corresponds to the multiple waves of Turkish migration through the centuries. Significantly, Michael presents the conversion of the Turks to Islam as politically beneficial, not only to them but to the Arabs as well: to the former as a means of political legitimation and to the latter as a way for retaining authority over the Turkish rulers.

Michael calls the Muslims either "Arabs" or *ṭayyaye,* the latter being the Syriac word used to indicate people from Arabia since pre-Islamic times. Interestingly, he does not use the common Syriac verbs when he refers to conversion to Islam (all of which are based on the root *h-g-r: hgar, ahgar, ethagar*), but rather periphrases it as "uniting with the Arabs" and "adhering to/accepting their religion."

TEXT

A chapter that relates the union in religion of the people of the Turks with the Arabs

In three ways were the Turks easily united with the Arabs and accepted the religion (*qbalu l-tawdito*) they confessed. First: as we said above, the Turks have always proclaimed one God, already in their land of origin, even though they considered the visible firmament as God. So up until today, when someone asks some ignorant among them, he answers and says, "*Qan ṭangri,*" *qan* in their language meaning "blue" [possibly a mistake for *qak,* closer to the Turkish word *gök,* "sky blue"] and *ṭangri* [meaning] "God." They think in fact that the sky is the unique God. So when they heard that the Arabs speak about one God, they adhered to their religion (*nqapu l-tawdithun*). The second way: the Turks who came first and went to the land of Margiana [the region of Merv in today's Turkmenistan] and settled there arrived at the time of the Persians. After a while Muḥammad appeared and was accepted by the Arabs, and then by the Persians too. The kingdom of the Ṭayyaye became strong and the kingdom of the Persians ceased [to exist], as did all the kingdoms that were in the east, and the former alone prevailed. So the Turks who had migrated to the land of Margiana joined (*etnaqapu*) Islam, just like the Persian people and the race of the Kurds. And when the new Turks who arrived afterward met their people and those who spoke their language, they also turned to the customs they found the others had taken up, following their lead.

The third way of the Turks' union with the Ṭayyaye was the following: since the Arabs used to take the Turks with them as mercenaries in the war against the Greeks, and they would enter these prosperous regions and feed on the booty, they would listen to the Arabs and accept the word of Muḥammad, who said that by giving up the worship of idols and other created things, and [by] confessing his religion, a blessed and beautiful land would be given to them and they would rule it. And because of this desire, they agreed to be circumcised and to observe the customs of the ancient law, [namely,] the ablutions of the genitals before prayer.

On these three accounts the Turks accepted Muḥammad and united with the Arabs and became like one people [with them]. And the Ṭayyaye accepted the Turks so that if one of them would rise to power, he could be called and proclaimed "king of the Muslims" [but] only if the leader of their religion, who is called caliph, would consecrate him king. For these and other, similar reasons, the Turks were united with the Arabs in the religion (*etḥayadu l-arbaye b-tawdito*).

[*The chapter ends with an account of the election of the first Turkish king, who was chosen from among the seventy most noble tribes: the leader of each tribe threw his rods at a circular sign on the ground, and the one whose rod plunged into the very center of it became king, by divine will.*]

FURTHER READING

Debié, Muriel. *L'écriture de l'histoire en syriaque: Transmissions interculturelles et constructions identitaires entre héllenisme et islam* (Leuven: Peeters, 2015).

Weltecke, Dorothea. "A Renaissance in Historiography? Patriarch Michael, the Anonymous Chronicle ad a. 1234, and Bar 'Ebrōyō," in *The Syriac Renaissance*, ed. Herman G.B. Teule, Carmen Fontescu Tauwinkl, Bas ter Haar Romeny, and Jan van Ginkel (Leuven: Peeters, 2010), 95–111.

———. "The World Chronicle by Patriarch Michael the Great: Some Reflections," *Journal of Assyrian Academic Studies* 11, no. 2 (1997): 6–30.

32

The Tribulations of a Converted Man's Daughter

Bar Hebraeus (d. 685/1286)

Maria Conterno

Title: *Eqlesyasṭiqi* (Ecclesiastical history)
Genre: Historical writing
Language: Syriac

INTRODUCTION

Bar Hebraeus (Syr. Bar Ebroyo) is, like Michael the Syrian (see the preceding selection), a major representative of the so-called Syriac Renaissance of the twelfth–thirteenth centuries. Born in Melitene in 623/1226, he was the leader of the Syrian Orthodox Church in the east (Maphrian) from 663/1265 until his death in 685/1286. More than forty works on multiple subjects are ascribed to him, including a work of history. This is a universal chronicle consisting of two parts: one dealing with civil events from the creation to the author's time (called "Chronography") and one focused on ecclesiastical matters (called "Ecclesiastical History"). The latter includes in turn two sections: one dedicated to the history of the Syrian Orthodox Church in the western regions (namely, west of the Euphrates) and one centered on the Syrian Orthodox Church in the eastern regions (east of the Euphrates) and on the East Syrian Church. The history of these three institutions is narrated through the biographies of their leaders: patriarchs, maphrians (the highest Syrian Orthodox authority in the eastern regions), and catholicoi, respectively.

The selected passage comes from Bar Hebraeus's *Ecclesiastical History,* and it relates an episode that took place in 553/1159 in Mosul, at that time governed by the

Zengids (a vassal dynasty of the Seljuq Empire that controlled part of its territories between the twelfth and thirteenth centuries).

The story gives us an insight into the practical hurdles generated by conversion to Islam in the private lives of common people. Notably, it raises questions regarding the status of the offspring of converted individuals and regarding interreligious marriage: Is a daughter born to a man before his conversion to be considered the daughter of a Christian or of a Muslim? Is she allowed to marry a Christian? The text reveals that these were problematic questions from both Christian and Islamic points of view. Although the case was allegedly blown up by a certain priest Abraham (who, we are told, begrudged the maphrian for not allowing him to repudiate his wife), the very fact that such issues were exploited for internal quarrels and brought before the Muslim authorities reveals how thorny they were. Significantly, the maphrian and the Muslim judge give the same response: it all depends on the girl's own confession; her being the daughter of a Muslim does not make a Muslim of her. Conversion, therefore, emerges from this passage as a personal choice that has no impact, from the canonical and judicial points of view, on the offspring's status.

Just like Michael the Syrian, Bar Hebraeus uses the Syriac term *ṭayyaye* (originally an ethnonym) to denote all Muslims, even those who converted to Islam from other religions. For the conversion to Islam, he uses the common Syriac verbs based on the root *h-g-r* (from the Arabic *hijra, muhājirūn*).

TEXT

In those days some priests from Telliʿapar [Talʿafar, a village near Mosul] sent a letter to the Maphrian, asking him: "A certain Christian man among us converted (*hgar*) to Islam long ago. He had a wife, who begot him two daughters, and now one of them has grown up and her mother wants to marry her to a young Christian man. What do you prescribe? [Is] she to receive the blessing within the church or not?" And the Maphrian replied: "If the girl has not converted to Islam (*ahgrat*), she shall receive the blessing."

This response of the Maphrian's fell in the hands of the wretched Abraham, who brought it to the [attention of the] authorities of the *ṭayyaye*, saying: "He [the Maphrian] prescribed that the daughter of a *ṭayyayo* be given to a Christian." Then the troops of the *ṭayyaye* gathered and carried with them stones to stone the Maphrian, and the captain and the bodyguards were hardly able to defend him from them. They [the soldiers?] took him to the judge on the Sunday of Cana [i.e., the first Sunday of Lent], and the judge decreed: "If this girl confesses that she is a *ṭayyayto*, the Maphrian is to be executed." Once she was among them, they began interrogating her cunningly, saying: "Whose daughter are you? [You are the daughter] of a certain *ṭayyayo*, aren't you?" But she stood firm, shouting: "I am a Christian and this is my mother, who raised me. My father, in contrast, I do not know at all."

As they tried to cajole her with gifts and she did not yield, they drew their swords against her, but not even then did she change her word. Therefore, they threw her into jail, and the Maphrian, too, was imprisoned for forty days.

The *ṭayyaye* were astonished that he would constantly stand up in prayer [every] day and night. He ate only a single piece of consecrated bread every second day for nourishment. In those days, while the Maphrian was being kept in prison, the miserable priest Abraham was struck by a violent disease and, after being tormented for three days, died, and his sudden death frightened many. Hearing that, the girl took courage again, and when they brought her three more times before the judge and threatened to throw her into the river or into the fire, she did not shrink in the least. Then the blessed people of Niniveh gave three hundred dinars to the judge and to the other notables, so they released the Maphrian. The girl was saved as well, and she went to Jerusalem, where she took up the monastic robe.

FURTHER READING

Debié, Muriel. *L'écriture de l'histoire en syriaque: Transmissions interculturelles et constructions identitaires entre héllenisme et islam* (Leuven: Peeters 2015), 589–94.

Weltecke, Dorothea. "A Renaissance in Historiography? Patriarch Michael, the Anonymous Chronicle ad a. 1234, and Bar 'Ebrōyō," in *The Syriac Renaissance,* ed. Herman G. B. Teule, Carmen Fontescu Tauwinkl, Bas ter Haar Romeny, and Jan van Ginkel (Leuven: Peeters, 2010), 95–111.

Witakowski, Witold. "The Ecclesiastical Chronicle of Gregory Bar 'Ebroyo," *Journal of the Canadian Society for Syriac Studies* 6 (2006): 61–81.

33

A Polemical Treatise by a Twelfth-Century Jewish Convert to Islam

Abū Naṣr Samawʾal b. Yaḥyā al-Maghribī (d. 570/1175)

Gregor Schwarb

Titles: *Ifḥām al-Yahūd* (Silencing the Jews) and *Qiṣṣat Islām Samawʾal* (The tale of Samawʾal's conversion to Islam)
Genre: Religious instruction (polemics)
Language: Arabic

INTRODUCTION

Abū Naṣr Samawʾal b. Yaḥyā al-Maghribī (518–70/1125–75) was a Jewish mathematician and physician in twelfth-century Iraq and Iran, who converted to Islam in his late thirties (viz. in 558/1163). His father, Yaḥyā b. (Judah ben) Abdūn, was a rabbi and poet of Moroccan origin (from Fez) who had moved to Baghdad in adolescence. His learned mother, Ḥanna, hailed from a distinguished Jewish Iraqi family of scholars from Basra.

Born and educated in Baghdad, Samawʾal was early on introduced to Hebrew, scriptures, and Arab-Islamic lore; in his youth he set out to study mathematics and medicine, among other subjects, with Abū al-Barakāt al-Baghdādī (d. 560/1165). Samawʾal's extant works include several mathematical treatises and at least one medical text. As a practicing physician, Samawʾal consorted with the social elite of the Seljuq Empire.

His embrace of Islam was celebrated in a solemn ceremony during the Friday service at the mosque of Marāgha on 10 Dhū al-ḥijja 558/November 9, 1163 (see the extract from his autobiography below). The polemical tract *Ifḥām al-Yahūd* (Silencing the Jews) was written in Arabic in the immediate aftermath of his conversion and repeatedly revised in subsequent years. As he explains in the introduction, he wrote the *Ifḥām* to advance rational proofs and demonstrations against the validity of Jewish scripture and law "on the basis of the wording of their scripture and in accordance with their own methods":

> The ultimate purpose in writing this work is to refute that obstinate and stubborn people and to reveal with what corruption their tenets are beset. . . . By using scriptural passages current among the Jews, this book clears the way to silencing them. God made the Jews blind when they tampered with the text; so these same passages, possessed by the Jews, might thus serve as evidence against the Jews.

In an open letter he later had to dispel accusations by an unnamed figure who doubted the sincerity of his conversion. Four years after his conversion, in 563/1167, he published an autobiography that describes his intellectual development and expounds the motives for his decision to convert (see Perlmann's ed., 94–120, and trans., 75–88; and the extract below). In it, he also relates that numerous copies of the *Ifḥām* were made under his supervision. A short and a long version of the work—circulating under various titles—enjoyed great popularity in subsequent centuries and became important sources and reference texts for later authors of polemical tracts against Judaism.

Several scholars have argued that Samawʾal al-Maghribī should be identified with the anonymous Jewish apostate mentioned in Maimonides's *Epistle to Yemen* (written in 568/1172). In this epistle, Maimonides refutes and ridicules biblical proof texts (Deut. 18:15/18; Gen. 17:20; Deut. 33:2) that allegedly announce the future emergence of the prophet Aḥmad/Muḥammad. Maimonides's refutation does indeed reflect several compositional peculiarities that—in comparison with earlier anti-Jewish polemical pamphlets in Arabic—are unique to Samawʾal's *Ifḥām*.

The main issues broached in the *Ifḥām* are the following:

1. Abrogation (*naskh*): the first section of the *Ifḥām* aims at "compelling the Jews to accept abrogation," that is, the view that a later divine dispensation may override an earlier one and that the validity of the Mosaic dispensation is therefore terminable.
2. The parity of the probative force in support of Moses's prophethood (i.e., the performed miracles and chains of transmission) with that in support of the prophethood of Jesus and Muḥammad: "From this, it follows that the Jews must accept as true the prophethood of Jesus and of Muḥammad."
3. Verses and pointers (*āyāt wa-ʿalāmāt/ishārāt*) in the Torah hinting at the prophethood of Muḥammad.
4. Blasphemous beliefs (*kufr*) and anthropomorphic heresies (*kufriyyāt al-tajsīm*) in the Torah: "It is true that their scholars, benefiting from Muslim monotheism, have refined much of their ancestors' belief and have

put such an interpretation upon their texts as will shield them from the Muslims' disapproval, even though it is not in accord with the words they interpret and translate."

5. The falsification, fraudulent modification (*tabdīl/taḥrīf*), and interrupted transmission of the Torah (see the extract quoted below).
6. Misinterpretations (*buṭlān ta'wīlātihim*), fanaticism (*ifrāṭuhum fī al-ta'aṣṣub*), contradictions, absurdities, and ignominies in their law and religious practice.
7. Differences between Karaites and Rabbanites.

Of the two extracts translated here, the first offers a glimpse into the social, biographical, and ceremonial contexts of Samaw'al's conversion. The second half of the autobiography contains elaborate accounts of encounters with the prophets Samuel and Muḥammad in two divinely inspired dreams (*manāmāt*) that Samaw'al claims to have had in the night of 9 Dhū al-ḥijja 558 (November 8, 1163) in Marāgha, on the eve of his conversion, but which he preferred to conceal "until the book *Silencing the Jews* had become well known, its copies had become numerous, and it had been read by a great number of people." These dreams, he writes, triggered his decision to convert on the following morning.

The extract from the *Ifḥām* is a key passage from the section on scriptural falsification that had a particularly lasting impact on subsequent polemical tracts against Judaism.

TEXTS

Autobiography (trans. Perlmann, 85–86 [amended in places]; ed., 115–18)

Then I woke up, though it was not yet dawn. I performed the ritual ablution and said the prayer of dawn. I was very eager then to proclaim the creed and to make public my conversion to the faith of Islam (*i'lān al-intiqāl ilā dīn al-islām*). I was at the time in Marāgha in Azerbaijan, guest of the glorious master (*al-ṣāḥib al-amjad*) Fakhr al-Dīn Abū al-'Izz 'Abd-al-'Azīz b. Maḥmūd b. Sa'd b. 'Alī b. Ḥamīd al-Muḍarī, God's mercy upon him. He had suffered from a disease but God had restored him to health. I had been friendly with him even before. I came to him in the early hours of the aforementioned Friday and informed him that God had lifted the veil from me and had granted me his guidance. How great was his joy that day at hearing the news! He said: "By God, this is what I have always wished for and hoped for, and for a long time I have discussed it with the supreme judge (*qāḍī al-quḍāt*), Ṣadr al-Dīn, and both of us have regretted that your scholarship and virtues should adorn a non-Muslim (*lā takūnu islāmiyya*); praise God for the rightness and guidance He has inspired you with, and for thus answering our prayer. But tell me, how did God reveal this to you and how did He facilitate it, after denial and delay?" I said: "This is something that God has injected into my soul by inspiration (*bi-l-ilhām*). However, I had known the idea and its rational proof and demonstration even before—its proof is in the Torah—but out of consideration for my father, and thus shunning divine reproof, I was reluctant to be the cause of his grief. But now this doubt has been lifted. Stretch out your hand: I shall testify that there is but one God and that Muḥammad is the Messenger of God [i.e., the Muslim *shahāda*]." The master, in great happiness, stood up trembling with joy—before that he could stand up only with difficulty. He left me, inviting me to be seated until his return, bestowed upon me the finest of clothes, had me carried on the noblest of steeds, and ordered his retinue to rush to the mosque in front of me. The master himself had gone ahead to the preacher (*khaṭīb*) and ordered him to bide his time and to wait until I appeared at the mosque. For it took the tailors a while to complete the sewing of the *jubba* (a long outer garment) the master had ordered to be cut. I set out for the mosque as the community was waiting for me. Upon my arrival the congregation broke into a loud "God is great!" and the great mosque shook with the prayer for the Messenger of God. Then the *khaṭīb* ascended the *minbar,* and the judge, the prince of preachers, Ṣadr al-Dīn Abū Bakr Muḥammad b. ʿAbd Allāh b. ʿAbd al-Raḥīm al-Marāghī [d. 590/1194], delivered a sermon, speaking at length in my praise and on the praise due to God for having granted me alertness and guidance. His eloquence on the subject was exquisite. For the most part the assembly was occupied with myself.

In the evening of that day, that is, the night of the Feast of Immolation (*laylat ʿīd al-naḥr*), I began writing the arguments for silencing the Jews (*al-ḥujaj al-mufḥima li-l-Yahūd*) and compiled them in a book I entitled *Ifḥām al-Yahūd* (Silencing the Jews). The book became well known, its fame was widespread, and numerous copies (*nusakh kathīra*) of it were made under my supervision in many places in the regions of Mosul, Diyārbakr, Iraq, and Persia. Later I added to it several chapters of objections against the Jews on the basis of the Torah, so that it became an exquisite tract of disputation against the Jews (*kitāb badīʿ . . . fī munāẓarat al-Yahūd*), the like of which had never been produced in Islam.

Silencing the Jews (trans. Perlmann, 53–55; ed., 48–51)

[As to] why the Torah was falsified

None of their [i.e., the Jews'] scholars or rabbis believes that the Torah in their possession is the one revealed to Moses. For Moses guarded (*ṣāna*) the Torah from the children of Israel and did not divulge it to them but delivered it to his tribe, the sons of Levi. Proof thereof is the Torah passage "Moses wrote this law, and delivered it unto the priests, the sons of Levi" [Deut. 31:9].

The sons of Aaron were the judges and rulers of the Jews. They were in charge of the priesthood, the service of sacrifices, and the Temple. Moses did not distribute any part of the Torah among the children of Israel other than half a chapter (*sūra*) entitled "Ha'azinu" [Deut. 32]. It was this chapter of the Torah which Moses taught the children of Israel. It says: "So Moses wrote this song [the same day], and taught it to the children of Israel" [Deut. 31:22, inaccurately rendered]. God also said to Moses concerning this chapter: "This song may be a witness for Me against the children of Israel" [Deut 31:19, inaccurately rendered]. Moreover, God said to Moses concerning this chapter: "For it shall not be forgotten out of the mouths of their seed" [Deut. 31:21]. He meant that this chapter contains a reproof of their character, and that they would violate the precepts of the Torah, and that, subsequently, evil would befall them, their land would be destroyed, and they would be dispersed over the earth. He [God] said: "This chapter will always be in their mouths as a witness against them, certifying the truth of what had been said to them."

As God said: "Shall not be forgotten out of the mouths of their seed," this chapter indicates that God knew that the other chapters would be forgotten. This is also proof that Moses did not give the Israelites any of the Torah, other than this chapter. As to the rest of the Torah, he gave it to the sons of Aaron, depositing it among them and keeping it away from all others (*wa-ṣānahā ʿan siwāhim*). These Aaronid priests, who knew the Torah and had memorized most of it, were slain by Nebuchadnezzar in a massacre during the conquest of Jerusalem. Memorizing the Torah was neither obligatory (*farḍ*) nor common (*sunna*), but each Aaronid used to memorize a section of it. When Ezra saw that the Temple of the people was destroyed by fire, their state disappeared, their masses dispersed, and their book vanished, he collected some of his own remembrances, while some were still retained by the priests, and from these he concocted the Torah that the Jews now possess. That is why they hold Ezra in such high esteem and claim that a light appears over his tomb, situated near the marshes of Iraq, even unto the present day; for he has produced a book that preserves their religion. Now this Torah that they have is in truth a book by Ezra (*kitāb ʿIzrā*), and not a book of God (*kitāb Allāh*). This shows that the person who collected the sections now in their possession was a vain man, ignorant of divine attributes. That is why he attributed anthropomorphism to God—regret over His past actions and the promise of abstention from similar acts in the future—as mentioned above.

FURTHER READING

Amboura, Adel. "As-Samaw'al ibn Yaḥya al-Magribī (d.c. 570 H.)," *al-Machriq* 55 (1961): 89–107.

Chiesa, Bruno, and Sabine Schmidtke. "The Jewish Reception of Samawʾal al-Maghribī's (d. 570/1175) *Ifḥām al-Yahūd:* Some Evidence from the Abraham Firkovitch Collection I," *Jerusalem Studies in Arabic and Islam* 32 (2006): 327–49.

Husain, Adnan A. "Conversion to History: Negating Exile and Messianism in al-Samawʾal al-Maghribī's Polemic against Judaism," *Medieval Encounters* 8, no. 1 (2002): 3–34.

Mazuz, Haggai. "The Identity of the Apostate in the *Epistle to Yemen,*" *AJS Review* 38, no. 2 (2014): 363–74.

34

Anecdotes about Conversion in Twelfth-Century Syria

Shams al-Dīn al-Dhahabī (d. 748/1348), Ibn Rajab (d. 795/1393), and Ḍiyāʾ al-Dīn al-Maqdisī (d. 643/1245)

Daniella Talmon-Heller

Titles: al-Dhahabī, *Siyar Aʿlām al-Nubalāʾ* (The biographies of distinguished men); Ibn Rajab, *Dhayl Ṭabaqāt al-Ḥanābila* (An addendum to the biographical dictionary of Ḥanbalīs [lit. "to the generations of Ḥanbalīs"]); al-Maqdisī, *al-Ḥikāyāt al-Muqtabasa fī Karāmāt Mashāyikh al-Arḍ al-Muqaddasa* (The cited tales of the wondrous doings of the shaykhs of the Holy Land)

Genre: Didactic and entertaining literature (biography)

Language: Arabic

1. THE CONVERSION OF A PERSIAN CLERK

Introduction

Al-Dhahabī's *Biographies of Distinguished Men* is a voluminous encyclopedic compilation of essays on noteworthy Muslims from the age of the Prophet until the time of the author, arranged by generation. It is of great value for modern research on the social and cultural history of the Islamic world, especially of the religious elite and its worldview and discourse.

The entry dedicated to the Ḥanbalī *ḥadīth* expert ʿAbd al-Ghanī al-Maqdisī (d. 600/1204) is quite typically based on the citation of students and colleagues of the shaykh and constructed as a series of anecdotes about, or by, the biographee. ʿAbd al-Ghanī, who was born in a village in central Palestine (then under Frankish rule), studied in Baghdad, and spent most of his life in Damascus, narrates this particular anecdote. It is about the conversion to Islam of a clerk of unclear religious affiliation whom ʿAbd al-Ghanī had allegedly met in person in Isfahan. Like other Persian cities, Isfahan must have had a solid Islamic majority by the late twelfth century. Non-Muslim officials employed in the administration of Muslim states at that time must have been under pressure to convert and free themselves of the restrictions and degradation inherent in the status of *dhimmī*s, perhaps also consequent to an implicit threat to be replaced by Muslims. ʿAbd al-Ghanī's short story adds little new to our understanding of the big historical process, yet it is interesting as a narrative that constructs his piety, charisma, and even sainthood upon his success as a missionary of Islam. ʿAbd al-Ghanī himself humbly attributes the clerk's conversion to the compelling effect of the recitation of the Qurʾān, a well-known early Islamic topos, told and retold in glory of the sacred book. Thus, for example, a widespread version of the conversion of the second caliph ʿUmar b. al-Khaṭṭāb in about 618 CE stresses that he was deeply influenced by hearing verses of the Qurʾān, and until this very day the power of the recited Qurʾānic text is seen as steering hearts toward repentance and conversion to Islam.

Text

He [ʿAbd al-Ghanī] said: "I stayed in Isfahan in somebody's home, and we had dinner with another guest of his. When we rose to pray, that man did not join us. I asked: 'What is it with him?' They said: 'He is a sun-worshipper (*shamsī*).' I was upset and said to my host: 'You had to invite me with an infidel?' He said: 'He is a government clerk (*kātib*), and he treats us well.' I rose to pray at night, and the man awoke and heard my prayer. Upon hearing the words of the Qurʾān, he sighed deeply, and several days later he converted to Islam. He told me: 'When I heard you recite, Islam entered my heart.'"

2. THE CONVERSION OF A CHRISTIAN ORPHAN FROM THE VILLAGE OF JUBBA

Introduction

Ibn Rajab's biographical dictionary is devoted to scholars belonging, like himself, to the Ḥanbalī school of law, from the mid-eleventh century until his own times. Like al-Dhahabī's work, it was compiled according to the conventions of this extremely popular genre of Arabic and Islamic literature as a reference book for scholars of religion, genealogy, and history, with, undoubtedly, the additional agenda of enhancing the prestige and internal solidarity of the Ḥanbalī school. Most of the text before us is also written as a memoir by the main protagonist, with digressions and comments by the author. It is a turbulent life story of the son of a Christian priest from a village in Mount Lebanon, a refugee of the wars of the Crusading era, who was forced to leave his village as a child and was subsequently enslaved by Muslims and moved to Damascus. There, he studied Islam, converted, and regained his freedom. Like the clerk encountered in the preceding text, the boy, too, claims to have been swayed by Qur'ānic recitation and the influence of Ḥanbalī Muslims. Known to have been particularly active in the performance of the Qur'ānic injunction to command right and forbid wrong (*al-amr bi-l-ma'rūf wa-l-nahī 'an al-munkar*), the Ḥanbalīs appear here also as agents of conversion, employing the persuasive force of Qur'ānic recitation. Another interesting point in this text is the social mobility the convert enjoys after his conversion: the former Christian slave of rural descent becomes a respected Islamic scholar thanks to his devotion to religious studies and travels in pursuit of knowledge. This is indeed striking, but not implausible in the world described in *Dhayl Ṭabaqāt al-Ḥanābila* and similar biographical dictionaries. At the time of Ibn Rajab's compilation of this dictionary under the rule of the Mamluks (themselves freed slaves), Muslims constituted a majority in Syria and Egypt. Still, cases of conversion to Islam roused the curiosity and enthusiasm of writers.

Text

'Abd Allāh b. Abī al-Ḥasan b. Abī al-Faraj al-Jubbā'ī al- Ṭarābulsī al-Shāmī the jurist, the ascetic, Abū Muḥammad . . . said: "I was born around 521 [1127 CE]. . . . We come from the village of al-Jubba . . . in the district of Tripoli, Mount Lebanon. We were Christians. My father died when we were young. He was a learned Christian, considered to possess hidden knowledge. When he died, I was sent to a teacher. My mother said: 'My oldest son is the breadwinner; he will work our land. My youngest'—and she pointed at me—'is weak for such work.' We had another brother between us. The teacher said: 'The youngest is not fit for this study; rather, that one is,' and he took my middle brother and taught him to take the place of my father. And God decreed that war broke out; we left our village, and I parted with my family.

"There was, in our village, a group of Muslims who used to read the Qur'ān, and I would weep whenever I heard them. Once I entered the countries of the Muslims, I converted to Islam. I was eleven years old then. Later, I heard that my older brother became a Muslim too, and died defending the frontiers of Islam (*murābiṭ*). Then my younger brother, who was tutored by that teacher, also converted. I came to Baghdad in 540 [1145 CE]."

I [Ibn Rajab] say: Prior to that, he was captured and enslaved. Abū al-Faraj al-Ḥanbalī, from whom I [the author] copied, said: "He was a slave (*mamlūk*), who read the Qur'ān in the Ḥanbalī circle in the Great Mosque of Damascus, and he learned it by heart. He also learned some of the devotions of the Ḥanbalī school. A group went up to the preacher Shaykh Zayn al-Dīn 'Alī b. Ibrāhīm while he was still on the pulpit and said: 'This youngster has memorized the Qur'ān and he is on the good [path]; we would like to buy him and set him free.' So he was bought from his master and set free, and left Damascus. He traveled to Hamadān in search of a teacher, and there he studied the Qur'ān and *ḥadīth* under Abū 'Alī al-Hamadānī and became his teaching assistant. He became known for his learning and piety, traveled to the lands of the Persians, studied a great deal, and returned to Baghdad, where he studied *ḥadīth* and met our shaykhs. . . ."

Shaykh Ṭalḥa [an informant of the author] told me concerning him that he saw the Prophet in his dream and asked him: "O Messenger of God, is there a reward for the recitation of the Qur'ān?" He said: "Yes." He asked: "O Messenger of God, whether one understands it or not?" The Prophet said: "Yes. . . ."

And Ibn al-Jawzī [a prominent Ḥanbalī Baghdadi scholar, d. 597/1201] has written down several of al-Jubbā'ī's dreams and included them in his book. He said that he was one of the righteous. . . . He died in 605 [1208 CE].

3. AN ENIGMATIC CONVERSION TO CHRISTIANITY

Introduction

Ḍiyā' al-Dīn al-Maqdisī (d. 640/1243), the nephew of the abovementioned 'Abd al-Ghanī al-Maqdisī, was a Damascene madrasa professor and author of treatises on the Qur'ān and *ḥadīth.* His *Cited Tales,* compiled in the form of a biographical dictionary arranged in alphabetical order, captures, quite unusually, the lore of Palestinian villagers, inhabitants of Mount Nablus under the rule of the Latin Kingdom of Jerusalem (492–582/1099–1187) or the ensuing Ayyubids (566–649/1171–1252). It portrays the wondrous doings (*karāmāt*) of local shaykhs, exposing facets of rural everyday life and religion. The following, rather enigmatic anecdote mentions the conversion of a Muslim to Christianity. The shaykh demonstrates his *firāsa* (knowledge of hidden things, or mind reading) by foretelling the event. Despite undoubtedly being an embarrassment to the community, this rather juicy story (albeit curtly told one) is not silenced, giving testimony to the divergent crossing of religious boundaries in the Levant in the period of the Crusades and counter-Crusades (twelfth–thirteenth centuries). This phenomenon was noted by Benjamin Z. Kedar and Emmanuel Sivan, who showed that prisoners of war were especially prone to converting to the religion of their captors (some only temporarily), but there were also free men and women who chose to convert under various circumstances.

Text

I heard the venerable shaykh Abū Aḥmad 'Abd al-Hādī b. Yūsuf b. Muḥammad b. Qudāma al-Maqdisī say: "Shaykh 'Abd Allāh of Fundūq [a village in Mount Nablus] . . . was in a good mood and said: ' . . . I can judge things hidden from the eye. So-and-so belongs to the people of paradise, and so-and-so to the people of hell.' Then he bit his finger, as if regretting what he had said. And the man about whom he had said that he belonged to the people of paradise was a rascal; I think he said that this man was known to drink wine; whereas the man about whom he said that he belonged to the people of hell was a muezzin [?], who used to pray. After some time it became known that the man about whom he had said that he belonged to the people of hell entered a church and became a Christian, while the other man made the pilgrimage to Mecca and returned to God, or something to this effect.

FURTHER READING

Kedar, Benjamin Z. "Multidirectional Conversion in the Frankish Levant," in *Varieties of Religious Conversion in the Middle Ages*, ed. James Muldoon (Gainesville: University Press of Florida, 1997), 190–99.

Leder, Stefan. "Charismatic Scripturalism: The Ḥanbalī Maqdisīs of Damascus," *Der Islam* 74 (1997): 279–303.

Talmon-Heller, Daniella. "*ʿIlm, Baraka, Shafāʿa*—the Resources of Ayyūbid and Early Mamlūk *ʿUlamāʾ*," *Mamlūk Studies Review* 13 (2009): 1–23.

Yarbrough, Luke. "'A Rather Small Genre': Arabic Works against Non-Muslim State Officials," *Der Islam* 93 (2016): 139–69.

35

Selections from Two Armenian Martyrologies

Anonymous (composed ca. 566/1170)

Sergio La Porta and Zaroui Pogossian

Title: *Yaysmawurk'* (Synaxarion)
Genre: Historical writing (hagiography)
Language: Armenian

INTRODUCTION

The following two texts are taken from martyrologies published by Yakob Manandean and Hrach'ea Achaṙean in a volume devoted to Armenian neomartyrs. Both accounts are contained within compilations of Armenian lives of saints known as the *Yaysmawurk'*, equivalent to the Greek *Synaxarion* (a collection of saints' lives arranged according to the liturgical calendar). Different versions of the martyrologies exist, but the translation below is based on the text established by the editors. The texts were composed around 566/1170 by unknown authors associated with the Armenian Apostolic Church who possibly belonged to a monastic community. Thus, they may have been produced in a monastic intellectual milieu.

The events in the texts take place near the urban centers of Gandzak and Duin in the southern Caucasus in the late twelfth century during a conflict over control in the region between the Georgian Bagrat'ioni monarchy (ninth–nineteenth centuries) and the Eldigüzid Atabegs of Arrān (Azerbaijan; 540–622/1145–1225).

The martyrologies address two different situations of attempted conversion to Islam. In the first, that of Khosrov of Gandzak (d. 562/1167), the Christian protagonist has been falsely accused of raping a neighbor Muslim girl. In order to escape punishment, the judge implores Khosrov to accept Islam and marry the girl. In the second martyrology, that of Yovsēpʻ of Duin (d. 566/1170), the main character was born and raised a Muslim, but became disillusioned with his faith and turned to Christianity, adopting the name Yovsēpʻ. His apostasy is discovered, and he consequently faces both the chief of his village and the ruler of the region. The latter tries to convince Yovsēpʻ to abandon his new faith and return to that of his parents.

The texts are taken from the interrogation scenes immediately preceding the martyrs' execution. Despite the differences in circumstances, both stories present the future martyr with a choice between many worldly benefits and death. The texts thus emphasize spiritual power over worldly power. The point is further developed in the first text through the martyr's denigration of Muḥammad and in the second by the martyr's observation that Islam lacks a presence in Jerusalem. Indeed, both texts are concerned with resistance—rather than conversion—to Islam, something to be expected from compositions authored by Christian clerics.

TEXTS

(1) Khosrov of Gandzak

[*Khosrov of Gandzak was accused of raping his Muslim neighbor. According to the text, the girl was in fact impregnated by her brother, but she accused Khosrov because she was in love with him and thought the accusation would force him to marry her. Khosrov was brought before a judge and thrown into jail. After a month, his parents visited him and tried to convince him to convert and then flee to Georgia. Khosrov refused to accept their advice. The judge also attempted to persuade him to convert, offering him much money and the girl in marriage.*]

The judge began to speak and said: "Khosrov, don't go astray needlessly. Convert and accept [Muḥammad], and I will give you much gold and that girl in marriage, as well as much other greatness. If you do not wish to listen to me, I will torture you with many and impossible torments."

The saint said: "May your gifts be with you in perdition. I am a believer in Christ my king, who made the heavens and the earth, the sea and everything which is in them."

The judge said: "Spare your youth and do what I say to you. Be with us and you will be called my son and live; otherwise, I will ruin your pleasant beauty."

Saint Khosrov said: "I said to you and again I say, I will not listen to your fabricated deceptions, for sooner or later, I will die."

The judge said: "I will burn you with fire if you do not turn from such obstinacy."

Khosrov said: "You are not able to prepare such a fire as Christ has prepared for those who have sinned and for the impious like you."

The judge said: "At least accept Muḥammad, who gave us this world and paradise there."

The saint said: "Do you want me to deny the living and worship the dead who themselves went astray and led you astray from the straight path?"

[*The judge finally ordered Khosrov to be stoned to death. However, his executioners attempted one last time to convince him to accept Islam. Khosrov again defiantly refused.*]

The saint said: "Whom do you really want me to worship? A sorcerer and a heretic and a dead dog?" And they began to growl like wild beasts and gnash their teeth over him; they came and struck him without care and bound him to a mulberry tree, but before his binding, he fell to his knees in prayer and said: "I glorify you, Christ, with the Father and the all-holy Spirit."

And the barbarians incited each other and threw stones at the saint, but the blessed one stood there like a lamb among wolves. There was no one who had mercy and no one who helped; all of the Persian visitors and inhabitants were rabid like dogs and flung at him arrows of reproach. And from the weight of the stones, which were like drenching rain poured over the saint, all his bones were pounded and his limbs were broken in pieces, and his body began to fall off bit by bit. And the saint commended his soul to the glory of God, in accordance with the writing: "The souls of the righteous are in the hand of God" [Wisd. 3:1].

(2) Yovsēp' of Duin

[*Yovsēp' of Duin was born a Muslim by the name Abū Bakr in the environs of the city of Duin. He became disillusioned with Islam and began to follow Christian teachings and to learn its basic tenets from locals. Having been rebuked by his family, he traveled through the region in order to deepen his faith and changed his name to Yovsēp'. After visiting Jerusalem, he returned home, where his brother denounced him to the authorities. As a result, he was put in jail, where he was interrogated by the head of the village, whom he antagonized with his answers. Finally, when the Atabeg (lit. "father," i.e., tutor, of the prince) of Arrān, Shams al-Dīn Eldigüz, who is referred to here as the* amirapet *(chief emir), encamped near Duin, the head of the village informed him of Yovsēp'. Yovsēp' was then brought before the Atabeg.*]

The great *amirapet* said to him: "Your father and mother are Persian and worship our messenger. By whom were you forced or afflicted that you converted to such a faith or dress in such a shape? Now, listen to me and do not contradict my commands."

But he gave nothing for an answer and only ceaselessly made the sign of the cross on his face. The great *amirapet* said: "He is afraid of us in my presence." But Srjahan [the head of the village], who held him, said to the *amirapet:* "It is not out of fear, but [because] he does not consider it worthy of a response. He has been with me for many days in prison and [endured] tortures, and I heard no word of weakness from him. Give the order to kill [him]."

Then he ordered him to be brought again before him. Again the *amirapet* said to him: "Do not be stubborn and die needlessly. Trust me and I will give you your paternal village as your inheritance." And he placed before him much gold. But the blessed Yovsēpʻ said to him: "I was not constrained or forced by anyone; rather, I came of my own will to this place. I think nothing of that gold and the greatness which you promise. [Even] if you give me any realm or region which is under your authority, I will not exchange it for this faith which I have. If your will is sweet toward me, let me remain in my faith; otherwise give your gold to my killers."

The great *amirapet* said: "Everyone is obedient to my commands, and you are willing to contradict them and insult our guide?"

The saint replied and said to him: "I have been to Jerusalem and I have seen the place of the nativity, and the place of the torments, and of the resurrection, and the ascension, and the place of other champions, and the tomb, but I did not see or find that of your messenger anywhere."

Then he ordered the multitude of the Muslim (*aylasēr̄*, lit. "of another race") army which was surrounding him to kill and stone him. And they growled like bloodthirsty beasts and gnashed their teeth. And they grabbed him from all sides and rushed him to the place of killing. But the blessed martyr did not cease reciting these psalms: "For your sake we are being killed all day long [Ps. 44(43):22; Rom. 8:36], for your sake I shed my blood as You for mine." And they struck him, some with their hands, some with wood, and they said many words of insult. But he said: "Lord, don't reckon them sinners, for they know not what they are saying" [cf. Luke 23:34; Acts 7:60].

And his brother fell at his feet and with many pleas and tears said: "Don't let yourself be killed. Promise to do their command now and afterward live as you will." But the holy one was very angry and said to his brother: "Go away; you are against me. Do not deprive me of my martyr's championship. For the Savior commanded: 'Whoever denies me before others, I will deny before my Father in heaven' [Matt. 10:33]."

And when they moved away a little, the guard who had restrained his right hand stabbed his left side with a knife and slit it across [him] to his right [side]; and he fell on his face and rolled in his own blood. Then those who were around were striking him, some with a sword, some with a stone, and with the bones of the dead, and then they threw over him anything that fell into their hands. And they cut his head off and flayed it so that they might take this thing [i.e., his scalp] to their own realm for [their] collection [lit. "for the sake of collecting"].

And the saint commended his soul into the hands of the living God according to that [verse]: "The souls of the righteous are in the hand of God" [Wisd. 3:1]. And his brother dug the place a bit and buried the saint's body with the head.

FURTHER READING

Bedrosian, Robert. "Armenia during the Seljuk and Mongol Periods," in *Armenian People from Ancient to Modern Times*, vol. 1, *The Dynastic Periods: From Antiquity to the Fourteenth Century*, ed. Richard G. Hovannisian (New York: St. Martin's Press, 2004), 241–71.

La Porta, Sergio. "Re-Constructing Armenia: Strategies of Co-Existence amongst Christians and Muslims in the Thirteenth Century," in *Negotiating Co-Existence: Communities, Cultures, and* Convivencia *in Byzantine Society*, ed. Barbara Crostini and Sergio La Porta (Trier: Wissenschaftlicher Verlag, 2013), 251–72.

36

A Letter of Maimonides about Conversion and Martyrdom

Attributed to Moshe ben Maimon (Maimonides, d. 600/1204)

Ryan Szpiech

Title: *Iggeret ha-Shemad* (Letter on forced conversion), also called *Maʾamar Qiddush ha-Shem* (Treatise on martyrdom/sanctifying the name [of God])
Genres: Legal writing (epistolary responsa)
Language: Hebrew

INTRODUCTION

Maimonides wrote the *Letter on Forced Conversion* (*Iggeret ha-Shemad*), also called in some editions *Maʾamar Qiddush ha-Shem* (Treatise on martyrdom/sanctifying the name [of God]), in Fez in the early 550s/1160s, when he was not yet thirty years old. He and his family had left their native town of Córdoba around 554/1159 to escape persecution by the Almohads, who had recently conquered al-Andalus and replaced the ruling Almoravid dynasty. After fleeing Córdoba, Maimonides settled in Fez but fled persecution again in 560/1165, moving first to Palestine and finally to Fusṭāṭ, near Cairo, where he would remain.

The *Letter on Forced Conversion* is Maimonides's earliest public epistle, and although its authorship has been called into question by some, it is now usually accepted as authentic. The original Arabic version does not survive. The text was translated into Hebrew twice, with one translation (A) made of the whole letter, and the other translation (B) including only the first part. Eight manuscripts are known of translation A, and only one of translation B. All known manuscripts are listed in Yitsḥak Shailat's edition, on which the present English translation is based.

The text addresses the question of *shemad,* which literally means "destruction" or "extirpation" and which is generally translated as "religious persecution," "forced conversion," or "apostasy." Conversion to Islam requires explicit recognition of Muḥammad as a prophet of God, and part of the question discussed in this letter concerns the question of whether one can feign such recognition. In the context of persecutions of Jews by the Almohads, the question of the permissibility of feigning belief in Islamic tenets in order to escape danger or death was not an abstract or academic one. Many Jews who remained in Almohad lands—and Maimonides was probably not an exception—did pretend to embrace Islamic customs and beliefs while continuing to uphold Jewish beliefs and commandments in secret. Others embraced Islam and did not return. Maimonides, who certainly never willingly converted, was probably prompted to flee Fez, which was also under Almohad control, after Judah b. Shoshan, a leading rabbi in Fez, was put to death for apostasy from Islam.

In the letter, offered as an (apparently) unsolicited comment on the response given by another rabbi to an inquiry by a contemporary, Maimonides attempts to counter the stance of the rabbi that recognition of any Islamic beliefs, even under coercion or in order to escape persecution or death, is tantamount to apostasy from Judaism and worthy of punishment. For this unnamed rabbi, any response besides martyrdom is unacceptable. Maimonides attacks this argument first by impugning the knowledge and logic of its author and then by providing textual proof that supports a distinction between feigned and willing apostasy. He mentions that the great sages and rabbis Eliezer and Meir [BT ʿAvodah Zarah 16b–17a and 18b, respectively] themselves feigned apostasy under coercion.

The key to Maimonides's argument is the distinction between what is done willingly or for pleasure (*bi-retson nafsho*) and what is done under coercion (*be-ʾones*) or out of necessity (*be-hekhreaḥ*). Also important is the distinction he makes between transgressing in public with deeds and transgressing in private with mere words. While accepting martyrdom to glorify God's name fulfils the commandment, feigning conversion or transgressing in another way to escape death—unless it be by committing idol worship, incest, or bloodshed, which are always forbidden, even under coercion—is not a sin worthy of death or severe condemnation. As Maimonides pointedly asks, "How can one pass the [same] judgment against one who acts under coercion as against one who acts willingly?"

The following translation includes key selections from the beginning and ending sections of the letter. For reasons of conciseness, many of the detailed exegetical arguments are omitted.

TEXT

Moses the Spaniard, son of R. Maimon, of blessed memory, said: A man from among the men of our generation asked a question of a man who was, according to him, among the wise. It concerned something that happened not only to them [of our generation] but also to many communities of Israel, namely, forced conversion (*shemad*)—may God abolish it. He [who made the inquiry] was asked to confess that "that man" [i.e., Muḥammad] is, in his apostleship, a true prophet. Should he acknowledge him in order not to die, even though his sons and daughters be assimilated among the gentiles, or should he die and not testify, since he is [thus] obliged by the Torah of Moses, our teacher, peace be upon him, and [since] such testimony would lead to the giving up of all the commandments?

The man who was asked answered with a weak answer, lacking in discernment, deficient in expression and substance. . . . In this answer, he said that whoever acknowledges that "that man" is a messenger has already denied the Lord, God of Israel. He brought forth as evidence for this what they of blessed memory said: "All who profess idolatry are like those who deny the whole Torah" [BT Nedarim 25a, Qiddushin 40a, etc.]. In this analogy, there is no difference (*lo haya etsel zeh ha-heqesh hefresh*) between someone who professes idolatry without coercion but rather with pleasure in [his own] soul, like Jeroboam, son of Nebat, and his companions, and someone who, out of necessity (*be-hekhreaḥ*), calls someone a prophet out of fear of the sword. . . .

When we looked again at his words, we found that he said this: "Whoever says that [about Muḥammad], even if he fulfils all of the Torah alone in private, is indeed a gentile." . . . If this is so, this sharp-witted man does not differentiate in any way between a person who does not keep the Sabbath out of fear of the sword and a person who willingly fails to keep it. . . .

When I saw this thing that sickens the body and the eyes, I set out to gather remedies and the finest spices (*besamim rosh;* Exod. 30:23) from the books of the ancients, from which I will make useful medicines to cure this sickness and to heal it. I saw fit to divide this matter into five categories: (1) the division of the commandments in a time of coercion (*ha-ʾones*); (2) the definition of the profanation of the Name and its punishment; (3) the ranks of those who are killed in order to sanctify God's name and of those converted by force during persecution; (4) the question of this persecution among all persecutions, and what a person should do in it; and (5) an explanation of the means by which a person survives this persecution, may God separate us [from it].

First category: the division of the commandments in a time of coercion (*ha-ʾones*). There are three parts. The rule concerning the commandments about idol worship, incest, and bloodshed is that when a person is forced to do any of these, he is commanded, in all places and at all times and no matter his circumstances, to be killed rather than transgress (*yehareg ve-al yaʿavor*).

For all other commandments except these three, if he is coerced, let him consider (*yabit*). If [the coercion] is meant for [an oppressor's] own pleasure, [a Jew] may transgress and not be killed, whether it be in a time of persecution or not in a time of persecution, whether it be in private or in public. . . .

If [an oppressor] intends to make him transgress, let him consider it in this way: if the time is a time of persecution, he is to be killed and not transgress, whether [he is] in private or in public. But if it is not a time of persecution and it is in private, let him transgress and not be killed, and if it is in public, let him be killed and not transgress. . . .

Second category: the definition of the profanation of the Name and its punishment. . . .

Third category: the ranks of those who are killed in order to sanctify God's name and of those converted by force during persecution. Know that wherever they of blessed memory (*ḥazal*) say, "Be killed and do not transgress," [they mean that] if one is killed, he has already sanctified [God's] name. . . . If he transgresses under coercion and is not killed, he has not acted rightly, and under coercion has desecrated God's name. Yet surely he is not to be punished by any of the seven punishments [i.e., *malkot,* whipping; *ḥenek,* strangulation; *hereg,* slaughter/beheading; *serefah,* burning; *sekilah,* stoning; *karet,* extirpation; *mitah bi-yedei shamaim,* death by God's hands; cf. *Mishneh torah, Hilkhot sanhedrin,* 14]. We do not find anywhere in the Torah God imposing as sentence a punishment on someone who is forced, whether for light things or grave ones. Rather, [He punishes] someone who acts willingly . . . but not someone who is forced. Thus it is written throughout the Talmud: "The forced one is within the law [of the Torah]" (*ʾanus de-oraytah hu*). . . . In many places they said: "The Merciful One [i.e., God] exempts the forced one" (*ʾanus raḥmana petareh*). He is called neither a criminal nor a wicked person, nor is he disqualified to testify, unless he committed offenses for which he is disqualified from testifying. Although he has not fulfilled the commandment of sanctifying the Name and is called "one who profaned the name of heaven under coercion," by no account [can he be called] "a willing profaner of heaven's name." . . . He is commanded to [let himself] be killed [rather than transgress], but if he is not killed, he is not [for this reason] condemned to death, and even if he commits idol worship under coercion, he is not to be cut off (*eyno ḥayav karet*) and, even less, executed by a court of law. . . . These matters are clear in themselves and there is in no way any need to adduce proof for them. How can one pass the [same] judgment against one who acts under coercion as against one who acts willingly?

Fourth category: the question of this persecution among all persecutions, and what a person should do in it. . . .

Truly, nothing can be said about anyone who is killed for not recognizing the apostleship of "that man" except that he fulfilled the commandment with a great reward before God and will be lifted up in order to give his soul to the sanctification of the Name. But whoever comes to ask us whether he should be killed [rather than] acknowledge [the prophecy of Muḥammad], we tell him to acknowledge it and not be killed, but [at the same time] not to remain in the kingdom of that king. He should stay at home until he can leave that kingdom, and if he must do something with his hands, let him do it in secret. . . . When our rabbis of blessed memory said, "Be killed and do not transgress," they did not seem to speak of something that does not include action. One is to be killed [only] when he is compelled to do something or transgress something that he was warned of. . . .

Fifth category: an explanation of how a person should regard himself in these days of persecution. . . .

From the day we were exiled from our land, our persecution has not ceased, because "from our youth it grew up with us as [with] a father and from our mother's womb it has guided us" [cf. Job 31:18]. It says throughout the Talmud, "Religious persecution is likely to be abolished" (*shemada ʿavid ve-betil*). May God abolish it for us and bring about in our days what he said: "In those days and at that time, says the Lord, the iniquity of Israel shall be sought, and there shall be none; and the sins of Judah, and none shall be found; for I will pardon those whom I leave as a remnant" [Jer. 50:20]. May it thus be [God's] will. Amen.

FURTHER READING

Hartman, David. "Rabbenu Moshe ben Maimon's *Iggeret ha-Shemad*," *Jerusalem Studies in Jewish Thought* 2 (1988): 362–403.

Kramer, Joel. *Maimonides: The Life and World of One of Civilization's Greatest Minds* (New York: Doubleday, 2008), 104–15.

Lorberbaum, Yair, and Haim Shapira. "Maimonides' Epistle on Martyrdom in the Light of Legal Philosophy," *Dine Israel* 25 (2008): 123–69.

Soloveitchik, Haym. "Maimonides' *Iggeret Ha-Shemad:* Law and Rhetoric," in *Rabbi Joseph H. Lookstein Memorial Volume,* ed. Leo Landman (New York: Ktav, 1980), 281–319. Also in Haym Soloveitchik, *Collected Essays* (Oxford: Littman Library of Jewish Civilization, 2013–14), 2:288–330.

37

Apostasy in Jewish Responsa

The Geonim of Babylonia and Abraham Maimonides (second/ninth–early seventh/thirteenth centuries)

Oded Zinger

Title: *Teshuvot* (Responsa)
Genre: Legal writing (responsa)
Language: Hebrew, Judeo-Arabic

INTRODUCTION

Responsa (Heb. *she'elot u-teshuvot*) are answers provided by legal authorities to questions posed to them.

The Islamic conquests brought faraway Jewish communities into contact with the Jewish centers in Iraq at the heart of the ʿAbbasid Empire. The heads of the Babylonian academies (called Geonim) championed the Babylonian tradition as the correct version of Judaism and their academies as the custodians of its most authoritative text, the Babylonian Talmud.

Responsa were the primary channel through which Jewish communities received guidance from the Babylonian institutions and through which the latter projected their authority. The thousands of preserved responsa are our richest source for Jewish history in the three and a half centuries following the Islamic conquests.

When it comes to conversion, responsa naturally provide an internal perspective, focusing on what conversion meant to those who remained Jewish. This can be seen in the way they refer to converts as apostates (Heb. *meshumadim*)—that is, people who left the Jewish fold—without bothering to note the religion they converted to. Our assumption is that most conversions mentioned in Gaonic responsa were to Islam, but it is rarely possible to be certain of this in a specific case.

Conversion posed an interesting problem for the Geonim. Jewish law does not specify principles according to which a person ceases to be Jewish. On the one hand, the idea that the apostate is still Jewish facilitated an easy return to the fold and was generally in line with the established sources of Jewish law. On the other hand, if the apostate is still considered a Jew, a whole slew of social problems arises: Does he inherit from his father? Does his wife remain married to him? Is his child considered Jewish? How should Jews interact with him?

In their answers, the Geonim sought to regulate the boundaries of Jewish communal membership by offering diverse solutions that fell on the spectrum between assertion and rejection of the apostate's Jewishness. The questions themselves, however, often reveal diverse interactions between apostates and the Jewish communities. We hear of mixed couples in which an apostate has married a Jewish woman, circumcision of apostates' children according to Jewish practice, and apostates visiting Jewish homes. Some of the questions even allow us a glimpse into the wishes of converts, as seen below. Such interactions challenge a neat division between the religious communities.

The responsa translated below are arranged in chronological order. In the first four responsa, the answers were written by Geonim who resided in Baghdad. The questions usually came from outside of Iraq, most commonly from North Africa or Spain. The last two responsa are from two hundred years later and were written in Egypt. They allow us to see how the answers of Jewish jurists to similar questions changed with the passing of time. Responsa 1–3 were translated from Hebrew (often mixed with Aramaic), and responsa 4–6 were translated from Judeo-Arabic. I have consulted and used partial translations found in Blidstein's and Simonsohn's articles, cited below.

Responsum 1, "Is an apostate a Jew?," was addressed to Rav Sa'adya Gaon, the head of Sura Academy (in office 316–30/928–42). The questioner asks whether a child born to an apostate and a married Jewish woman is a *mamzer,* meaning a child born to a Jewish married woman from a Jew who is not her husband, thus making the child and all of his or her descendants henceforth forbidden from marrying an ordinary Jew. The status of the child depends on whether his apostate father is to be considered a Jew. In his answer, Sa'adya makes a distinction between commandments and matters of personal status, suggesting that the consideration of Jewishness depends on context.

Responsum 2, "Does an apostate inherit?," was addressed to Rav Natronai Gaon, an earlier head of Sura Academy (in office 243–51/857–65). The question, perhaps sent from Lucena in Spain, asks whether apostasy nullifies the right of inheritance. Natronai argues that only an offspring that traces his lineage to his father inherits. He then demonstrates through biblical quotations that for lineage it is not enough to be a biological son; a person also needs to share his father's belief in God. The first demonstration requires some explanation: Natronai bases his argument on the linguistic similarity of the two consecutive verses (Gen. 17:7–8). Since the apostate has removed himself from the adherence to God that pertains to the offspring ("to be God to you and your offspring to come"), he has also abandoned the inheritance of the Holy Land promised to the offspring ("I assign to you and your offspring to come the land"). Therefore, the apostate does not inherit.

Responsum 3, "Circumcising the apostate's son," is attributed to Rav Sherira Gaon, head of Pumbedita Academy (in office 357–94/968–1004, d. 396/1006). Here the petitioner inquires whether it is permitted to circumcise a boy born to an apostate and his Jewish wife on the day of the Sabbath. Jews circumcise their male children on the eighth day after their birth. If a boy is born on the Sabbath, the circumcision will take place on the following Sabbath (both the day of the birth and the circumcision are counted, thus making eight days). Here the question revolves around whether the boy is considered Jewish (in which case he should be circumcised on the Sabbath) or not Jewish (in which case the Sabbath should not be desecrated on his behalf). The question reflects an interesting situation in which a Jewish apostate remained married to his Jewish wife. The fact that the question was even raised suggests at the very least a passive agreement on the part of the apostate that his son be circumcised by Jews and after eight days according to Jewish law. Sherira's answer also suggests that the father may have wavered in his apostasy, perhaps reflecting a reality in which Jews converted to Islam and later returned to Judaism (or at least allowed their children to remain in the Jewish community). It is useful to compare Sherira's answer to Abraham Maimonides's answer to a similar situation (see responsum 5).

Responsum 4, "Marriage with an apostate," was addressed to the son of Rav Sherira Gaon, Rav Hayya Gaon (also spelled Hai), who was also head of Pumbedita Academy (in office 394–429/1004–38). He is commonly considered the last Babylonian Gaon of the Gaonic period. If in the previous questions it was unclear whether the apostate and his Jewish wife were living together, this question inquires directly whether they are permitted to continue dwelling together. From the way the second part of the question is phrased, we learn that someone from the community officiated a marriage between the apostate and a Jewish woman. It is very likely that the questioner knew the (clearly negative) answer to the question of whether such marriages are permissible, but he wanted to have the authoritative answer of the Gaon to bolster his position in the confrontation. The question reveals a situation in which a Jewish convert to Islam wanted to marry a Jewish woman and even married her with a Jewish marriage contract. Only the beginning of the answer was preserved (not provided here).

Responsum 5, "Circumcision of the apostate's son revisited," was addressed to Abraham Maimonides (lived 582–635/1186–1237). The last two questions take us beyond the Gaonic period. The respondent in both cases is Abraham Maimonides, who took over the leadership of Egyptian Jewry from his father, the great jurist and philosopher Moses Maimonides (lived 532–601/1138–1204). The first question presents a case similar to that in responsum 3. Here, however, both parents are apostates, which makes the question why they would want Jews to circumcise their son according to Jewish law more acute. Abraham's answer is quite different from Sherira's. One way to explain the difference is that in Abraham's case both parents are apostates. Another possible explanation is that in the two hundred years that have passed since the first case, the boundaries between the Jewish and Muslim communities have become more sharply drawn.

Responsum 6, "Interaction with an apostate," was likewise addressed to Abraham Maimonides. The question testifies to social interaction between a Jew and an apostate Jew in an intimate setting: the Jew's private home. The questioner asks whether it is permissible to serve an apostate nonkosher food. It is not clear why the Jew wants to do so. It is possible that such food was cheaper. However, the wording of the question may suggest that the apostate held a higher social status and the Jew needed to accommodate his newly acquired tastes. Notice that Abraham's answer deals only with the permissibility of serving such foods to an apostate and does not try to sever the social interaction.

TEXTS

Responsum 1: Is an apostate a Jew?

Question:

You inquired about a married woman whose husband traveled overseas and in the meantime an apostate Jew married her in a gentile custom. She gave birth to a boy, and later her [first] husband came back and gave her a bill of divorce. The apostate desecrates the Sabbath publicly. Now, is this boy a legitimate Jew because his father is considered a gentile, and any child of a gentile or a slave and a Jewish woman is a legitimate Jew? Or perhaps the child is a *mamzer* because if [the apostate father] repents he is a complete Jew?

Answer:

So it appears to us: the child is a *mamzer* not because if an apostate repents he is a Jew in every matter, but because the [apostate's] conception and birth were in holiness. In this matter, we do not follow the observance or desecration of Sabbath. It is necessary to know that the laws regarding an apostate are of two respects. The first respect: in commandments such as blessings, the invitation [for the grace after meals], and renouncing [one's share in a private or public] domain [for moving objects on the Sabbath], we look to see whether [the apostate] observes the Sabbath or violates it, as [the sage] said: "An apostate Jew who observes the Sabbath in public may renounce a domain, but one who does not observe the Sabbath in public is like a gentile and may not renounce his domain" [BT 'Eruvin 69b]. The second respect: in matters such as betrothal, divorce, release of levirate bonds, . . . *mamzer,* and other such commandments, we look to see whether [the apostate's] conception and birth were in holiness; if yes, his betrothal, divorce, and release of levirate bonds are all valid and the sons he sires from forbidden relations are *mamzer*s, as the sages said: "Regarding gentiles, if their conception and birth were in holiness they are like Jews in every matter" [Tosefta Yevamot 12:1, BT Yavamot 97b].

The simple rule is this: regarding commandments [you should] rule according to Sabbath observance, and regarding personal status [you should] rule according to conception and birth. In this matter, since [the apostate] was conceived and born in holiness and had sex with a married woman, the child is a complete *mamzer.* There is no doubt in this matter; this is the law and no deviation can be allowed.

Responsum 2: Does an apostate inherit?

Question:

You inquired whether an apostate inherits from his Jewish father or not.

Answer:

Thus we were shown by heaven: an apostate does not inherit from his Jewish father. Why? Because once he apostatized he abandoned the holiness of Israel and the holiness of his father. We find that inheritance is not given except to a Jew whose lineage is traced to his father, as it is written, "I assign to you and your offspring to come [the land you sojourn in, all the land of Canaan, as everlasting holding. I will be their God]" [Gen. 17:8], that is, a legitimate (*kasher*) offspring who traces his lineage to a Jew, as it is written, "[I will maintain My covenant between Me and you, and your offspring to come, as an everlasting covenant throughout the ages], to be God to you and your offspring to come" [Gen. 17:7], meaning he whose offspring is traced to his lineage. Therefore, an apostate is not traced to the lineage of his Jewish father.

We also find this in [relation to] Abraham who was promised by God: "Know well that your offspring shall be strangers in a land not theirs" [Gen. 15:13]. Even though he had both Ishmael and Isaac, this came true only for Isaac (when he was an exile in Gerar; see Gen. 26), as it was said: "For it is through Isaac that offspring shall be continued for you" [Gen. 21:12]. When it came to Isaac, even though he had Esau and Jacob, this came true only for Jacob, who went to Egypt. This is also the case of inheritance: only the offspring that is traced to his father's lineage and through whom his father's family is continued may inherit. But with an apostate an estate is transferred from one nation to another nation, and this should not be done. . . .

Responsum 3: Circumcising the apostate's son

Question:

You inquired about an apostate Jew with a Jewish wife who had a male son born by her on the Sabbath: Is it permissible to circumcise him on the Sabbath or not?

Answer:

Thus we were shown by heaven: it is permissible to circumcise him on the Sabbath. Why? Because he is the seed of Abraham and the worm of Jacob [Isa. 41:14]. [In this case,] the generations of converts have not become entrenched, but only one man has apostatized. It is possible that he is uncertain and will leave his son in the Jewish religion. Furthermore, his mother is Jewish and it is possible he will follow her. We do not presume that he will go astray [i.e., apostatize]. Therefore, we do not have the power to forbid his circumcision on the Sabbath and we are not allowed to diverge in this case [from the law pertaining to Jews]. If, when it comes to slaves, the sages said: "He whose mother is defiled through birth must be circumcised at eight [days]" [BT Shabbat 135a], how much more so with the progeny of a Jew!

Responsum 4: Marriage with an apostate

Question:

What do you say regarding a Jew who apostatized and left for the religion of the gentiles?

The wife who was with him while he was still a Jew has not apostatized or left the religion of the Torah. Is he permitted to dwell with her or not? And if a Jew apostatized but requested to marry a Jewish woman who observes the religion of the Torah, is he permitted or not? If it is not permitted, what is required regarding the person who writes them a marriage contract (*ketubba*)?

Responsum 5: Circumcision of the apostate's son revisited

Question:

May our rabbi teach us: a man and his wife who both apostatized had a baby boy born on the Sabbath. His parents want to perform the commandment of circumcision. Is it permitted for a Jew to circumcise the baby on Saturday even though his parents desecrate the Sabbath in public?

Answer:

A gentile ought to undertake this, and a Jew ought to avoid doing it. Written by Abraham ben Moses, may the memory of the righteous be blessed.

Responsum 6: Interaction with an apostate

Question:

May our rabbi teach us: an apostate behaving like a complete gentile in every matter honors a proper Jew [by visiting the latter's home]. Is it permissible [for the Jew] to feed him forbidden food, such as nonkosher meat, dairy, and leavened food on Passover, knowing that he does not avoid eating any of these things, or not? May our rabbi instruct us.

Answer:

A Jew absolutely cannot feed him such things. "Transgressors should not be encouraged" [e.g., Shevi'it 5:9]. Written by Abraham ben Moses, may the memory of the righteous be blessed.

FURTHER READING

Blidstein, Gerald J. "Who Is Not a Jew? The Medieval Discussion," *Israel Law Review* 11, no. 3 (1976): 369–90.

Irshai, Oded. "The Apostate as an Inheritor in Gaonic Responsa: Basics of Decision Making and Parallels in Gentile Law" [in Hebrew], *Shenaton ha-mishpat ha-'Ivri: Annual of the Institute for Research in Jewish Law* 11–12 (1984–86): 435–61.

Simonsohn, Uriel. "The Legal and Social Bonds of Jewish Apostates and Their Spouses according to Gaonic Responsa," *Jewish Quarterly Review* 105, no. 4 (2015): 417–39.

38

Several Documents from the Cairo Geniza Concerning Conversion to Islam

Anonymous (fifth/eleventh–seventh/thirteenth centuries)

Moshe Yagur

Genre: Documentary sources
Language: Judeo-Arabic

INTRODUCTION

The Cairo Geniza is the common name for a treasure of more than three hundred thousand manuscripts piled up in a special room in the old synagogue and several other sites in Fusṭāṭ, ancient Cairo. While most of the manuscripts are literary works of various genres and subjects, mostly in Judeo-Arabic, some are documentary in type, such as private and communal letters, court deeds, and bills of marriage and divorce. These documents give us an exceptionally nuanced, "bottom-up" view of daily lives in medieval Egypt.

The Geniza offers a rather less familiar angle on conversion to Islam, one that reflects the point of view of the convert's former coreligionists. Among the different reactions shown by the Jewish community to conversion to Islam, the extant documents reveal the recurrence of lasting contacts between Jews and converts to Islam on various levels. This does not necessarily mean that conversion to Islam bore no consequences for social relations, particularly given the nature of the documents at our disposal, which tend to speak more of those who "stayed around" rather than of those who burned all bridges. Yet the examples given here strongly suggest that ties between converts and their former coreligionists were not necessarily cut off.

Our documents say little about the new religion of the converts, though it stands to reason that in most cases it was Islam. The documents are also silent regarding the circumstances in which conversions took place or their motives. The convert was usually called "a criminal" (Heb. *poshe'a*) or, more traditionally, "apostate" (Heb. *meshūmad*, lit. "annihilated").

Together, the examples below reveal a complex picture of porous communal boundaries in which kinship ties between converts and Jews remained intact; apostates remained married to their Jewish spouses, or even married them after conversion; the possibility of reversion after conversion was a viable one; and conversion could at times occur unintentionally. It appears that converts and Jews could remain in close contact, close enough to demand their dowries or inheritances or to cooperate in business ventures. Most importantly, conversion, real or imagined, could be used as a weapon by all sides to an internal communal conflict, even by the most dignified rabbis and communal leaders.

Text 1 is an entry from a community register from Fusṭāṭ that was written in 617/1221. One leaf of the register contains several entries concerning marriages and real-estate property agreements. On the margins of the leaf is the first paragraph below, mentioning the birth of a *mamzeret* (lit. "a bastard girl," referring to a Jew whose lineage is tainted according to rabbinic law). A paragraph clarifying the reason for the newborn's legal state is given in perpendicular, noting the conversion of her mother. Thus the document serves as an example of some of the social and legal problems that could result from the marriage of a Jewish apostate. In addition, it suggests enduring ties between converts and their former community, given the prospect that the "bastard" daughter might choose to retain her place in the Jewish community.

Text 2 is a legal query that was probably addressed to a Muslim jurisconsult concerning a Jewish woman whose husband converted to Islam and later traveled to India, where he seems to have disappeared. The query lacks any details that would allow its dating. The text reveals the reality of enduring marital bonds between converts to Islam and their non-Muslim wives.

Text 3 is a private letter from a son in Alexandria to his father in Fusṭāṭ, describing an incident in the market around the early thirteenth century. It offers a rare glimpse into the legal aspects of a minor's conversion to Islam and brings to the fore questions pertaining to the sincerity and efficacy of conversion to Islam.

Text 4 is an account by a communal official from Fusṭāṭ that was written in 544/1150. The account records the inheritance of a deceased woman, which was spent to cover the expenses of her funeral and of the suits of her converted children. The deceased's sister, who was supposed to inherit what had remained, was left with nothing, since her converted nephews, and the various figures involved in the compromise settlement with them, took all that was left. The case relates to the different and contradicting opinions in both Jewish and Islamic legal traditions regarding inheritance of non-Muslims by their Muslim relatives.

Text 5 concerns a legal query that was addressed to Moses Maimonides (d. 600/1204) regarding the dowry of an apostate woman. It is a brief note, probably written by Maimonides himself, in which he orders his addressee to deny any acquaintance with the woman or the witnesses who signed her marriage bill, and thus to thwart the convert's attempt to win her dowry.

Texts 6a and 6b are excerpts from two letters containing mutual accusations of apostasy leveled in the course of a conflict over leadership of the Palestinian community of Fusṭāṭ in the mid-440s/1050s. In both letters the anonymous writers support the candidacy of Rav Yehudah ben Yosef. The first excerpt refers to the allegation that Rav Yehudah had apostatized; the second accuses one of Rav Yehudah's opponents and accusers of having apostatized himself. It is interesting to note that the second letter describes how the alleged convert married a Jewish woman although he was considered an apostate.

TEXTS

1

A daughter was born to the "son of the known one" (*ibn ya ʿalmū*) from Bint Tuwayr al-ʿAshā, and she is a "bastard" (*mamzeret*). [It happened] in the year 1432 [of the Seleucid era, corresponding to 616–17/1220–21]. And [she is a bastard] because her mother had apostatized while she was married to Ephraim al-Damīrī, and he did not write a bill of divorce for her, and she married Bu ʿAlī "son of the known one" in a Muslim court [lit. "by non-Jewish law"].

2

[. . .] Concerning a Jewish [man] who converted to Islam (*aslama*) and was attached to a Jewish woman, after he had converted, for a year. Then he wished to travel, and the aforementioned wife said to him, "You will not leave without giving me my bill of divorce," to which he replied, "I won't be gone but for a little while." And he left and has now been missing for ten years. And she requests to [re]marry, seeing her dire economic condition, for she lacks support due to the hardships of the hour and the difficulties of the time. Is it possible that she will marry after all this time, and no news were heard from him, since he is in India (*fī bilād al-Hind*)?

3

[. . .] As for what happened on the Day of ʿArava [last day of the Feast of Tabernacles]: Yaʿaqūb b. al-Muʿalim argued with his crossed-eyed son and beat him in the middle of the market with his shoe. And so the boy cried out [in the name of] Islam, and the Muslims gathered in his support (*wa-ʾinna al-muslimīn ta ʿaṣṣabū ma ʿahu*), and they took him [the father] and brought him before the governor. He [probably the boy] said to them, "The punishments of Islam (*ḥadd*) are not applicable, since I am not mature yet." The *qāḍī* Ibn Ghāriḍ deliberated [the matter] and ratified his conversion to Islam (*raja ʿa jaddada ʿalayhi al-islām*). And there were many debates concerning this, [which] will be too long to elaborate.

4

[. . .] for the testimony of the *qāḍī*—ten silver coins. Payment for Abū Muḥammad—1.5. This was on Sunday, in the middle ten days (*al- ʿashar al-awsaṭ*) of the month of Iyyar 1461 (mid-*Muḥarram* 545/mid-May 1150), in the presence of Barakāt al-Kohen, Khūlayf ben al-Ḥazan, and Fūrayj ben Mūnīn. Abū Muḥammad took it [the sum] in their presence when the apostate (*posh'im*) children of her [deceased] sister demanded their share. The next day they took forty silver coins by way of compromise (*ṣulḥ*). In addition—six dirhams to the representative. In addition—two dirhams to the messenger [. . .] in the presence of Khūlayf ben al-Ḥaza[n . . .] and for the document to the second *qāḍī*—five coins. In sum: sixty-four and a half, out of a total of one hundred and sixty-four. Taken from our pocket: four coins.

5

Shall his honor, my father and patron, al-Shaykh Thika al-Amīn, send for al-Shaykh al-Ḥaver, [may his] r[ock] p[reserve him], and inform him that he is not permitted, under any circumstances, to testify at the [court of] the Muslim *qāḍī* regarding the dowry (*ketubah*) of that apostate woman (*posha'at*). Instead, he should claim that this is a bill of dower (*ṣadāq*), and we do not know the witnesses. I do not allow, under any circumstances, deviation from this. Also, the witnesses are not allowed to testify regarding this bill. May your peace increase.

6a

[. . .] and Ḥunayn went and gathered some potters and quarrelsome people, and hired about fifty of them, and they wrote legal deeds about the Rav, [saying] that he had apostatized (*pasha'a*) in al-Shām and [later] arrived in Egypt to re-Judaize (*yatahawwada*).

6b

[. . .] and Surūr b. Sabra is slandering you, vilifying you with every kind of ridiculous slur . . . and this letter from him, which I came across, speaks of you and me and Rav Yehudah the rabbi . . . and we have already agreed unanimously, I and the congregation, that we will excommunicate him on the Sabbath [. . .] and please notify the "head," the judge, that the people of Jerusalem [. . .] that he, Surūr b. Sabra, this accursed one, had apostatized in the Maghrib and remained an apostate for several years. And his wife, Ibn Muhayyar [should be Ukht Muhayyar, as below] . . . was from the most despicable people. And when Ibn Sabra came nobody wanted him except Ukht Muhayyar, for the people considered him an apostate (*fāshī ʿ*).

FURTHER READING

Goitein, Shelomo D. *A Mediterranean Society: The Jewish Communities of the Arab World as Portrayed in the Documents of the Cairo Geniza* (Berkeley: University of California Press, 1967–93), 2:299–311.

Simonsohn, Uriel. "The Legal and Social Bonds of Jewish Apostates and Their Spouses according to Gaonic Responsa," *Jewish Quarterly Review* 105, no. 4 (2015): 417–39.

Stroumsa, Sarah. "Between Acculturation and Conversion in Islamic Spain: The Case of the Banū Ḥasday," *Mediterranea: International Journal on the Transfer of Knowledge* 1 (2016): 9–36.

39

Conversion to Islam in the Period of the Crusades

John of Ibelin (d. 664/1266), Odo of Deuil (d. 557/1162), Pope Alexander III (d. 576/1181), and Anonymous (ca. 596/1200)

Uri Shachar

Titles: (1) John of Ibelin, *Le Livre des Assises* (The book of laws); (2) Odo of Deuil, *De Profectione Ludovici VII in Orientem* (The journey of Louis VII to the East); (3) no official title; (4) *Le Livre au Roi* (The book of the king)
Genres: (1) legal writing; (2) historical writing (chronicle); (3) documentary sources (papal decretal); (4) legal writing
Languages: Old French, Latin

INTRODUCTION

The Latin Kingdom of Jerusalem was founded in 492/1099 following the successful conquests of Syria and Palestine during the First Crusade (489–92/1096–99). Over the course of the first decade of the twelfth century the kingdom consolidated and expanded its borders, stretching at its largest from the county of Edessa in the north to the Red Sea in the south. The population of the newly founded kingdom included Europeans who chose to stay in the East after the First Crusade, as well as those communities of Eastern Christians, Jews, and Muslims that survived the conquests and the subsequent period of instability. The Franks implemented a policy of strict segregation only in the Holy City, where Jews and Muslims were not allowed to dwell or even to enter. Elsewhere in the kingdom religious minorities could, in theory, reside, travel, work, and practice their religion freely. Although the big cities (such as Acre, Tyre, and Antioch) were more ethnically diverse, with various Christian denominations and Jewish communities cohabiting, there were also some mixed villages in rural areas. Still, the majority of the Franks were city dwellers, and most Muslims in the Latin Kingdom lived in small, socially secluded communities.

The long-lasting presence of the Franks in the eastern Mediterranean created multiple opportunities for economic, political, intellectual, and consequently social encounters between Christians and Muslims. In some, admittedly rare, cases the communities even came to share liturgical spaces, typically in shrines that were associated with saints and ancient sages. But as the texts below illustrate, this proximity also created tensions, resulting in various attempts to regulate and minimize interreligious contact.

TEXTS

(1) Apostates cannot give testimony in the High Court (from John of Ibelin, Le Livre des Assises)

[*Chapter 58 in John of Ibelin's* The Book of Laws *betrays anxiety with regard to the credibility of religious minorities and those who cross political borders, with or without renouncing their faith. John of Ibelin, count of Jaffa, was one of the most prominent aristocrats in the Latin Kingdom of Jerusalem during the thirteenth century. He completed his Old French treatise, the longest and most authoritative of those that survive from the Latin Kingdom, in 662/1264.*

This chapter regulates the involvement of non-Catholics in the High Court. Among the categories of people who are not allowed to testify are converts or those who have collaborated with Saracens against Christians. The chapter also states that Eastern Christians can testify only against individuals belonging to their own denominations. The author equates, for legal purposes, those who have renounced their faith and those who provide extended military service to enemies of the church. In other words, the author questions the credibility of those who have been shown to breach their vows and, significantly, places converts in the same category as mercenaries. The second half of the chapter betrays skepticism as to whether a non-Catholic Christian can testify against someone belonging to a different religious group. In the mind of the author, religious minorities are likely to choose communal allegiance over the truth, and there is thus no reason to trust cross-communal depositions. On the other hand, the testimony of renegades and those whose integrity is questionable is rejected wholesale, even if it pertains to individuals belonging to the same religious community.]

Chapter 58: Those who cannot give testimony in the High Court:

The following are those who cannot give testimony (*porter garantie*) in the High Court and who have neither a voice nor an answer in court: perjurers; oath breakers (*foy menties*); traitors; bastards; adulterers; those whose champion lost in a duel;

those who renounced [their faiths] or who served the Saracens for [more than] a year and a day against the Christians or the Greeks; and those who belong to groups (*nacion*) that do not obey Rome: Greeks, Syrians, Armenians, or Jacobins. People from groups that do not obey Rome cannot give testimony in the High Court, unless it is against members of the same group (*nacion*), and only to prove age and lineage.

Neither women nor men of religious orders, priests or monks, even if they belong to the law of Rome, can give testimony in the High Court except [to provide] proof of age and lineage. Children under fifteen years of age cannot give testimony in the High Court. No one can give testimony in the High Court concerning that about which he is partial (*parsonier*). A serf cannot give testimony in the High Court.

(2) French soldiers convert to Islam during the Second Crusade (from Odo of Deuil, De Profectione Ludovici VII in Orientem, trans. Virginia Berry)

[*The following passage shows that conversion to Islam was sometimes the result of tensions between the Catholic Franks and the various Eastern churches. Recurring political clashes with Constantinople and the struggle over control of the Jerusalem patriarchy resulted in intra-Christian relations that one modern commentator has described as "rough tolerance." The chronicler Odo of Deuil finds it lamentable yet perhaps unsurprising that in this context some found in Islam a desirable alternative. Odo was King Louis VII's chaplain and a participant in the Second Crusade during the years 541–43/1147–49. He kept a record of the expedition, which he offered to Suger, abbot of St. Denis, as a source for writing a biography of the king. Surviving in one medieval Latin manuscript, the work, which has an epistolary character, was not nearly as popular as some of the other contemporary Crusade narratives.*

The passage translated here appears to reinforce Odo's animosity toward the Christian Byzantines, a notion that recurs throughout the work. The author repeatedly presents the Byzantines as cunning and greedy, in contrast to the Muslims, who were persistent combatants but always courteous and honorable. In this episode the author bemoans the consequences of this difference, in that the defeated French crusaders had a clear preference for the Muslims, who did not even force anyone to convert, over their (previous) coreligionists, who proved to be far more cruel.]

By the blood of these soldiers the Turks' thirst was quenched and the Greeks' treachery was transformed into violence; for the Turks returned to see the survivors and then gave generous alms to the sick and the poor, but the Greeks forced the stronger Franks into their service and beat them by way of payment. Some Turks bought our coins from their allies and distributed them among the poor with a liberal hand; but the Greeks robbed those who had anything left. Therefore, avoiding the fellow believers who were so cruel to them, the Franks went safely among the unbelievers, who had compassion for them; and, we have heard that more than three thousand young men went with the Turks when they departed. O, pity more cruel than any betrayal, since in giving bread they took away faith (although it is certain that the Turks, content with the service they gained, did not force anyone to deny his faith)!

(3) What happens to the partners of those who convert to Islam? (from Pope Alexander III's decretal)

[*This papal bull shows that the conversion to Islam of married individuals was not uncommon. So much so that the pope was asked to address urgently a legal issue that arose from such situations. The pope wrote a letter in Latin to the archbishop of Tyre, agreeing to address this question, which had been brought to his attention. The pope had been told that it often happened that married individuals converted to Islam, leaving their former spouses wondering when, and if, they would be allowed to remarry. In his decretal, the pope rules that remarriage is not allowed in such cases so long as the renegade spouse is still alive. He justifies this stance by categorizing conversion as "spiritual fornication" and drawing on a scriptural proof text according to which even if a marriage is dissolved as a result of fornication, the wronged spouse must refrain from remarrying until the wrongful partner dies.*]

You mentioned to us that in your province it often happens that one of two spouses who are bound to each other by conjugal ties either passes over willingly to the enemies of the name and faith of Christianity or is drawn there unwillingly. There he [the spouse] renounces his faith and discards the Christian religion and, marrying another, does not return in an orderly fashion to the permanent companion [who awaits] in the previous dwelling house but instead neglects to return altogether.

Those who remain at home, wishing to observe the completeness of the faith, never admitting other company, fatigue you with their complaints after the long wait, and with much urgency they ask that you grant them authorization to transition [lit. "migrate"] into a second marriage.

In the same way, you suffer grave annoyances from those who either have been captured by the infidels or join the superstition of the enemy by negating the Christian faith, while in both cases the other [spouse] remains a pure adherent of the Trinity, until divine grace leads him [the first spouse] and he returns to the proper belief. But because you truly seek our response on these [matters], we shall respond to your request: since they are united in the flesh by the bond of matrimony, the marriage cannot be dissolved for any reason (ratione) without ecclesiastical judgment, nor can he [the abandoned spouse] be allowed to transition into a second marriage at any time, for the Holy Scriptures state that a man cannot dismiss a woman except by cause of fornication, and then he must either be reconciled or remain chaste while she is alive. We believe that the same should be observed in [the case of] spiritual fornication.

(4) When a knight leaves his fief and goes to the land of the Saracens (from Anonymous, Le Livre au Roi)

[*In contrast to the position found in the papal decretal above, in the following passage the marriage of a converted individual is dissolved after a year and a day. This, too, is evidence that conversion to Islam, even among married people, was a rather frequent affair—frequent enough for the jurists to adopt a more lenient position than the pope.*

Le Livre au Roi *is the first surviving legal treatise from the Latin Kingdom of Jerusalem. It was composed in Old French for King Aimery of Lusignan around 596/1200. It comprises fifty-two chapters, which deal mostly with reciprocal obligations between the king and his vassals.*

According to the author of the treatise, an apostate knight ceases to form part of the legal and feudal system of the Latin Kingdom. In renouncing his Christian faith, the knight loses his possessions for perpetuity, and they pass into the hands of his (former) lord and/or wife. This is an example of a mindset in which legal rights are inextricably tied to socioreligious identities. A complication arises for the jurist in determining the fate of the fief in case the knight was married before renouncing his Christian faith. The wife is entitled to her dowry levied on all their common possessions, and, as stated above, the marriage itself is eventually dissolved.]

Chapter 23: Here you will hear what one must do to a knight who leaves his fief and goes to the land of the Saracens, where he renounces the law of Jesus Christ for that of Muḥammad.

If it happens that a knight leaves his fief without taking leave of his lord and goes to the land of the Saracens and renounces the law of Jesus Christ, taking instead the law of the Saracens, reason rules that his fief and all that is in his possession must pass over to his lord forever.

But if that knight had a wife, reason dictates that she should have her dowry on the fief and on all the other possessions that belonged to her husband and her. But if she did not have an assigned dowry, because the fief was inherited by the wife, reason dictates that she should have as dowry the worth of half of the rents and of all the goods that he and she had possessed, minus the [cost of] service due for that fief, and no more. And after she takes her assigned dowry, as it was not specified otherwise, reason dictates that she can take another lord after a year and a day has passed since her husband renounced his faith, for that is the rule and reason behind the legislation of the Kingdom of Jerusalem.

FURTHER READING

Bishop, Adam. "The Treatment of Minorities in the Legal System of the Kingdom of Jerusalem," in *Religious Minorities in Christian, Jewish, and Muslim Law,* ed. Nora Berend, Youna Hameau-Masset, Capucine Nemo-Pekelman, and John Tolan (Turnhout: Brepols, 2017), 369–80.

Kedar, Benjamin. "Multidirectional Conversion in the Frankish Levant," in *Varieties of Religious Conversion in the Middle Ages,* ed. James Muldoon (Gainesville: University Press of Florida, 1997), 190–99.

———. "Muslim Conversion in Canon Law," in *Proceedings of the Sixth International Conference of Medieval Canon Law, Berkeley 1980,* ed. Stephan Kuttner and Kenneth Pennington (Vatican City: Biblioteca Apostolica Vaticana, 1985), 21–32.

———. "The Subjected Muslims of the Frankish Levant," in *Muslims under Latin Rule, 1100–1300,* ed. James M. Powell (Princeton, NJ: Princeton University Press, 1990), 135–74.

MacEvitt, Christopher. *The Crusades and the Christian World of the East: Rough Tolerance* (Philadelphia: University of Pennsylvania Press, 2009).

40

Conversion Tales in the Vita of Shaykh ʿAbd Allāh al-Yūnīnī, the Lion of Syria

Aḥmad b. Muḥammad b. Aḥmad ʿUthmān (d. ca. mid-twelfth/eighteenth century; written in 1157/1744)

Daphna Ephrat

Title: *Kitāb Manāqib al-Shaykh ʿAbd Allāh al-Yūnīnī* (The life and virtues of al-Shaykh ʿAbd Allāh al-Yūnīnī)
Genre: Religious instruction (hagiography)
Language: Arabic

INTRODUCTION

Shaykh ʿAbd Allāh al-Yūnīnī, known as the "Lion of Syria" (Asad al-Shām; d. 617/1221), was a Sufi shaykh celebrated as holy (*walī Allāh*, lit. "friend of God"). He lived in the village of Yūnīn in the vicinity of Baalbek in the Beqaa Valley (present-day Lebanon) during the counter-Crusader period and took part in the ongoing confrontation with Frankish troops by Saladin's side. Tales related by disciples and companions of ʿAbd Allāh al-Yūnīnī—some preserved in works by contemporary and later Damascene historians, others still circulating in oral tradition—were put together in a hagiographical treatise on his life and outstanding virtues and marvels.

Aḥmad b. Muḥammad b. Aḥmad ʿUthmān (d. ca. mid-twelfth/eighteenth century), the author of the saintly vita, was a Sufi legal scholar and native of Baalbek. According to his testimony, he was an associate of a biological descendant of Shaykh ʿAbd Allāh al-Yūnīnī. It may be surmised that his intent was twofold: to be linked to a lineage of celebrated shaykhs, spiritual ancestors, and models of virtue that extended back to ʿAbd Allāh al-Yūnīnī, and to perpetuate the glorious legacy of his city as a center of Islamic religious learning and spirituality and as a locus of Islamic revivalism in the counter-Crusader period.

ʿAbd Allāh al-Yūnīnī's saintly vita portrays him as a courageous warrior as well as a paragon of virtue, renowned for his reverence, asceticism, and upright behavior. Numerous accounts illustrate the enactment of his outstanding virtues and saintly marvels (*karāmāt*) and his bestowal of divine grace (*baraka*) in performing the role of a patron saint and benefiting members of the local community, among them indigenous Christians. We may assume that the Greek Orthodox, who, more than other Eastern Christians, suffered hardship during the time of the Crusades, found figures such as al-Yūnīnī appealing. The accounts given here indicate that their individual conversion to Islam entailed forsaking their old life and entering a life of servitude under the Sufi shaykh's guidance.

Drawing converts to Islam must have held significant meaning in a period marked by constant efforts to restore Islam's supremacy and revitalize the legacy of its prophet. This is probably why the conversion stories preserved in the vita of ʿAbd Allāh al-Yūnīnī are embellished with references to his awe-inspiring appearance (as, for example, in story 1) and make note of the central role he played in disseminating the true religion and uprooting improper practices such as drinking or selling wine (as in story 3). Seemingly even more important are the parts in the vita that praise the shaykh's generosity toward his Christian neighbors and his willingness to intercede with God on their behalf (stories 2 and 4). The tales depicting the encounters leading to their conversion attest to the shaykh's prominent stature, the breadth of his activity, and the fascination with his presence and marvels. Drawing converts to Islam is thus displayed in the vita as yet another manifestation of the virtues and powers of the Sufi shaykh.

Islamic hagiography is our richest source for observing the claims and acts of holy men in a given community. In the context of their role as agents of conversion, hagiographic narratives serve as a testimony to the importance of premodern Sufi saints as disseminators of the true religion and shed light on the methods they deployed. At the same time, conversion stories also echo the motivations and expectations of converts to Islam and speak of the shared as well as different features of conversion to Islam in diverse regional and historical settings. In addition to their belief in the existence and influence of saints, who were blessed with divine power and grace, non-Muslims must have been attracted to these figures, given the failure of their leadership and communal institutions to avert calamities and cater to their spiritual and material needs.

TEXTS

(1) The shaykh rescues his disciples and draws the Frankish assailants to Islam (fols. 9a–b)

Shaykh Muḥammad b. al-Faḍl related: "I encountered three shaykhs who expressed to me their desire to visit Shaykh ʿAbd Allāh al-Yūnīnī. My father had a small shop, and when I approached him and told him of my desire to join them, he gave me the key to the shop's safe and told me to take anything I desired. I took five hundred dinars and bought candles and sweets for provisions. I joined the company of the three shaykhs, and we proceeded on our way until we arrived at the shaykh's lodge (*zāwiya*) and stayed there as guests for four days. On the fifth day, the three shaykhs wanted to ascend Mount Lebanon. They consulted with the shaykh, but he forbade them to go lest they be assailed by Frankish thieves. But they did not heed him. The shaykh said to me, 'Stay here; do not join them.' But when they went out [of the shaykh's lodge], I joined them. When we stopped under a lemon tree near a pool at the foot of the mountain, we encountered five men with bows and weapons. One of them shot an arrow at me and hit my leg, leaving a mark; another arrow hit another man. I then beseeched the help of ʿAbd Allāh al-Yūnīnī. I cried out loud, 'O shaykh, if you are *walī Allāh* come to our aid at once!' And I swear in the name of God—at that moment the shaykh appeared. In his hand he held a bow, and he began to describe before those present the reward that God has prepared for his friends (*awliyāʾ*). Upon seeing the shaykh and hearing his words, the assailants prostrated themselves before him and accepted Islam. We took them with us and returned home."

(2) The story of Ibrāhīm the Christian (fols. 12b–13a)

Shaykh Muḥammad al-Sakākinī, one of the close adherents of Shaykh ʿAbd Allāh al-Yūnīnī, related: "One night I was staying in the town of Baalbek, after one of the men had invited me, insisting that I accept his invitation to spend the night in his home. In the middle of the night I said to myself, 'How can I sleep here when the shaykh [ʿAbd Allāh al-Yūnīnī] is on the mountain?' So I rose and walked out, until I arrived at the place of the pillar of the monk [?]. Then I descended, left the village, and went up to the shaykh's lodge. I found the shaykh, may God hallow his name, standing at the entrance to his lodge. The shaykh said, 'O my companion, are you sending to me people so that I provide for their needs? Who am I for you to send me people to provide for their needs? Ibrāhīm the Christian (*al-Naṣrānī*) from [the Beqaa village of] Jibbat Bushra came to me for assistance and asked me to pray for him and intercede with God on his behalf.'

"At night, I retired to go to sleep at the shaykh's lodge. At sunrise ʿAbd Allāh al-Yūnīnī came to me with a jug of water and awakened me for prayer. I spent the whole day with him, and on the second night, as I was sitting at the entrance to the lodge, I saw someone and wondered what this person was doing here, for there was nothing that he might be able to receive. I rose and gazed at him, and then discovered it was Ibrāhīm the Christian from Jibbat Bushra. I asked him, 'What do you seek in this place?' He asked for the shaykh's whereabouts, and I replied that he was in a cave immersed in contemplation and recollection of God (*dhikr*). I asked, 'What do you want from him?' He replied, 'Yesterday, in a dream, I saw the

Messenger of God, God pray for him and give him peace, and he said, "Go to Shaykh ʿAbd Allāh and convert to Islam by his hand, as he has already interceded with God on your behalf."'

"I then accompanied him on his way to the shaykh who at that time was sitting in the cave. When the shaykh saw him he inquired, 'Yes, companion, what is your need?' and then the man related what he had seen in his dream. When the shaykh heard the story his eyes filled with tears and he said, 'The Messenger of God has designated me to be a shaykh.' Ibrāhīm converted to Islam and was a good and righteous man to whom God will be merciful."

(3) The story of a Christian wine merchant (fols. 16a–b)

Jamāl al-Dīn al-Yaʿqūb, the judge of [the town of] Karak [east of the River Jordan and the Dead Sea, and known for its Crusader castle], related: "Once I saw Shaykh ʿAbd Allāh, God be pleased with him, performing ablution in the River Tora, close to the White Bridge in Damascus, when a Christian passed by him and with him was a mule carrying wine. All of a sudden, the animal stumbled on the bridge and the load fell down. I then saw the shaykh who had finished the ablution. This was a very hot day. No one besides me and the shaykh was on the bridge at that time. The shaykh approached me and said, 'Come here, O jurist, and help us place this load on the animal.' And so I did. The Christian mounted the mule and embarked on his way. I was overwhelmed by this deed of the shaykh, and followed the Christian and his mule as I was heading to the city. The Christian took the animal to [the Damascene neighborhood of] ʿUqayba, and went to a wine seller there. The seller started to inspect the load and to his great amazement found out that it contained vinegar, not wine. The Christian burst into tears and said, 'I swear to God this was wine. Now I know where this comes from.' He then tied his mule in a nearby rest house (*khān*) and set out on foot to the mosque. Upon entering the mosque, he observed the shaykh who had already performed the midday prayer and was engaged in praising the almighty God. The Christian approached him and said, 'O my master, I embrace Islam as my creed. I proclaim that there is no god but God and that Muḥammad is the Messenger of God.' And from that time on he became a pious ascetic and a virtuous believer."

(4) The story of a Christian from the village of al-Rās (fol. 39b)

Sharaf al-Dīn Abū al-Ḥasan transmitted an account according to which Shaykh ʿAbd Allāh al-Yūnīnī, God bless his soul, traveled to Aleppo one day. When he left Aleppo for Homs, numerous people escorted him to bid him farewell. When he left Homs in the direction of Baalbek, a Christian from [the Beqaa village of] al-Rās followed him. When they were on the way to the town, the Christian thought, "If only the shaykh had given me a small portion of his possessions, it would have been enough to meet my own needs and those of my entire family."

When the shaykh approached the olive trees of the village, he addressed his servant, saying, "Give to the Christian all our possessions." The servant obeyed the shaykh's order. The Christian was so amazed that he almost lost his mind. He then returned to his house and family and related to them all about his encounter with the shaykh. They were extremely happy, converted to Islam, and began to serve the shaykh until they became his close companions.

FURTHER READING

Levtzion, Nehemia. "Conversion to Islam in Syria and Palestine and the Survival of Christian Communities," in *Conversion and Continuity: Indigenous Christian Communities in Islamic Lands, Eighth to Eighteenth Centuries,* ed. Michael Gervers and Ramzi J. Bikhazi (Toronto: Pontifical Institute of Medieval Studies, 1990), 289–311.

Renard, John, ed. *Tales of God's Friends: Islamic Hagiography in Translation* (Berkeley: University of California Press, 2009), 1–11: "Introduction: Islamic Hagiography, Sources, and Contexts."

Rodriquez, Jarbel. *Muslim and Christian Contact in the Middle Ages: A Reader* (Toronto: Toronto University Press, 2015), chapters 12 and 13.

PART THREE

Sultans, Conquerors, and Travelers

(ca. thirteenth–sixteenth centuries)

Luke Yarbrough

BY 656/1258, THE YEAR IN WHICH Mongol mounts trampled to death the last reigning ʿAbbasid caliph of Baghdad, Islam was more than half a millennium old. Muslims had voyaged by camel, horse, and sailing ship to all but the most distant reaches of Africa, Asia, and Europe. Within the societies over which their political authorities presided, they had experimented with myriad configurations of social, political, and intellectual life. The situation of world Islam was thus altogether different from what it had been in the tenth century, when political fragmentation could still be seen as a disturbing aberration, let alone in the seventh, when Muslim identity of any sort was new and fragile. In short, by the thirteenth century, Islamic civilization—and with it the perennially important act of conversion—had become a highly complex, deep-rooted, and far-flung human phenomenon.

Yet much about Islam on the world stage was still a far cry from what it would become in the early modern era, and farther still from the globalized religion of the present day. Conversely, many facets of it, including aspects of conversion, had survived more or less intact from earlier centuries. These enduring practices would be transmitted and subtly shaped in the era that the historian Marshall G. S. Hodgson rather dryly called the "Later Middle Period" of Islamic history. In the final part of this book, a series of textual snapshots offers glimpses of conversion in different modes: pushing new frontiers of geography and practice, distantly prefiguring patterns yet to come, and creatively replicating forms familiar from Islam's early days. Within the perennial dance of old and new, one can discern the outlines of major features that made this intermediate age a distinctive part of the story of conversion to Islam. In the historical heartlands of the Islamic world, conversion followed certain familiar patterns and provoked responses akin to those of earlier centuries, even as it now affected wholly new groups of people, notably the descendants of those same Mongols who had sacked Baghdad. At the frontiers of the Islamic world, in West Africa, eastern Europe, and the Indo-Malay lands, Muslim communities expanded by military conquest and, far more importantly, by travel and trade. By the sixteenth century the borders of that territory very closely approximated those of the Muslim-majority world that exists today. And wherever conversion took place in this era, the Islamic mystical tradition of Sufism tended to have more to do with it than had been the case previously, or than one might expect based on the lower profile of Sufism in Islamic societies today. In sum, the conversions that occurred between the thirteenth and sixteenth centuries built up the foundations on which twenty-first-century global Islam rests, and the ways in which those conversions were represented mediated ideas about conversion in the subsequent imaginations of Muslims and non-Muslims alike. Owing to the vagaries of source availability, the last pair of selections venture beyond the sixteenth century into that subsequent age of world Islam.

OLD PATTERNS AND NEW CONVERTS IN THE HEARTLANDS

Regions of the world that had long had a strong Muslim presence—from the western Mediterranean to Central Asia and the Indus Valley—generally saw that presence marginally bolstered by conversion between the thirteenth and sixteenth centuries, though there were exceptions. Given such continuity, it is hardly surprising that the sources present some of these conversions in ways that are familiar from earlier ages. For instance, we read of a solemn and celebrated conversion of Jewish scholars in Damascus in 701/1302 (selection 45). This event had followed earnest conversations between the Jews and Muslim scholars, including the renowned Sunni firebrand Ibn Taymiyya. A more stereotypical intellectual conversion could hardly be wished for, though the incident is far from timeless; Ibn Taymiyya, a trenchant critic of Sufism, boasts of having succeeded where a certain Sufi rival of his had previously failed in persuading the Jewish shaykh to convert.

Similarly, a poetic Syriac *cri de coeur* from the region of Erbil in what is today northern Iraq (selection 47) bewails the conversion of a Christian deacon in terms that connect it thematically to the Syriac *Chronicle of Zuqnin* of at least five centuries earlier (see part 1, selection 13), even as its verse form lends the sentiments a novel texture. Still more resonant with much earlier conversion narrative is the account of a West African king's miraculous conversion that is given by the Ibāḍī scholar al-Darjīnī (selection 41). Although al-Darjīnī identifies the missionary-trader in the story as his own great-grandfather, close examination reveals that the same tale occurs almost verbatim in the work of a much older source. Authors in this later era evidently found earlier accounts of conversion to be valuable resources for making their own claims to distinguished lineage. Conversely, the conversion of elites through the agency of isolated travelers was clearly not limited to later periods, even if it resonated especially well with later authors (compare also the account of conversion among the Volga Bulgars in part 2, selection 24).

Even when the geographies and language of sources that deal with conversion in this later period closely track earlier precedents, their literary forms are sometimes so different as to lend them a strikingly novel quality. One such case is a set of accounts from sixteenth-century Damascus that depict conversions of individuals from many walks of life (selection 54). One gets the sense in reading these tales that they narrate incidents of a kind that could well have been taking place in earlier centuries, too, though the prominence of Franks and Jews in comparison to Syrian Christians is somewhat surprising. However, the emergence of a new narrative form—the Arabic ego-document or diary—sheds light on these conversions that earlier chronicles did not. The details that emerge are intriguing and compelling, but given the newness of the literary form it is not surprising that those details should possess a newly granular quality. Another example is the treatment of a well-known legal issue—the conversion of one spouse—in the work of the fourteenth-century Syrian scholar Ibn Qayyim al-Jawziyya, who was Ibn Taymiyya's principal student (selection 49; compare to part 1, selections 7 and 10). Ibn al-Qayyim's work *Aḥkām Ahl al-Dhimma* is a unique compendium of Muslim legal rulings concerning subordinate non-Muslims (*dhimmīs*). More comprehensive than its relatively disconnected forebears, it presents the legal discourse in a new light by the sheer range of views it includes.

It is also significant that this work was penned in an era when the region's non-Muslims had come under unprecedented negative pressure caused by foreign invasions and responses by insecure local governments, as well as popular and elite Muslim antagonism. In late thirteenth- and fourteenth-century Egypt and, to a lesser extent, Syria, Christians and Jews experienced considerable pressure to convert, to a degree that had not previously been sustained in those regions for such a long span of time. Urban rioting, coerced conversion of elites, and large-scale forcible transfer of property led to wave after wave of mass conversions, which may have been decisive in producing modern Egypt's Muslim demographic majority. This circumstance also highlights the fact that places where conversion to Islam had long been taking place could see conversions of new kinds and on different scales. These particular events were presented by the historian al-Maqrīzī as the Copts' long-overdue comeuppance for their haughtiness and undeserved prosperity in Muslim society (selection 46).

Indeed, even in the by-now old Islamic lands over which the first wave of the Muslim conquests had swept, distinctive kinds of conversion narratives were now being produced thanks to new macrohistorical developments. In the western Mediterranean, for example, newly enhanced European military and navigational power helped catalyze a heightened level of connection, exchange, and conflict between Muslim and Christian rulers and populations. In these settings a menagerie of renegades, turncoats, spies, and waverers—not to mention zealots, ascetics, and pious preachers—took up and modified Islamic and Christian ideologies with gusto. One prominent voice to emerge from this environment was that of Anselm Turmeda (who adopted the name ʿAbd Allāh al-Tarjumān). Turmeda was a Franciscan friar who converted to Islam, entered the service of the Ḥafṣid dynasty in North Africa, and wrote a number of polemical works against Christianity. In selection 50, we encounter an erstwhile Christian associate of Anselm urging him in writing to return to his original faith. The letter, which was read out publicly at the Ḥafṣid court, propounds the unmistakably Qurʾānic Christian doctrine that God is "the third of three" (Q. 5:73). This Qurʾānic echo raises questions about the letter's authorship—could a Christian priest possibly have written such a thing?—and more broadly about the range of rhetorical uses to which stories of conversion and opposition thereto could be put, notably by converts like Anselm themselves. The case of Anselm—and the pressure to revert that he experienced—also draws our attention to the significant trend of conversion away from Islam between the thirteenth and sixteenth centuries, particularly in Iberia and the western Mediterranean more generally.

Comparable questions arise regarding the conversion of the Mongol prince Ghāzān from Buddhism in the late thirteenth century (selection 44), which illustrates a broader transhistorical pattern of assimilation to mainstream Islam on the part of warlike conquerors from the margins. This very public event transpired in a land in which Islam had long been dominant but whose society had just been drastically reshaped by the violent invasions of Mongol warriors, who subsequently held power. The invaders adhered to a variety of non-Muslim religions, and Ghāzān's conversion was one of the most important milestones marking their assimilation to the Islamic milieu. This conversion was an extraordinarily complex event, however, in both its historical and its narrative aspects. It involved stiff factional conflict within the Mongol army as well as prophecies of glorious Muslim and Iranian kingship, to say nothing of the multiple interwoven and competing narrative representations from which we gather our knowledge of these things. Such narrative complexities were no less prominent in the sources on conversion in this era that emanated from more far-flung regions of the Islamic world.

CONVERSION AT THE EDGES

Two of the most commonly spoken languages among the world's Muslims today are Malay—including Indonesian and Malaysian dialects—and Mandarin. This fact owes a great deal to processes of conversion to Islam in the period from the thirteenth to the sixteenth century. While both militant conquest and peaceful diffusion contributed to conversion in this era, and were frequently inseparable, it was diffusion that would be more historically significant, especially in East and Southeast Asia and via the distinctive networks and idioms of Sufism. And as the geographical scope of Islam stretched even farther from its birthplace, the sources on conversion kept pace in their range and richness.

The accounts of conversion to Islam nearer the edges of the Islamic world in this section reflect these trends. To be sure, some of these geographic edges were on the western rather than the eastern fringes of the Islamic world. The expansion of Muslim power in eastern Europe, for instance, hovers in the background of the life of the thirteenth-century Turkic Sufi shaykh Sarı Saltuq, composed by Ibn al-Sarrāj, who was a Sufi opponent of Ibn Taymiyya (selection 43). The events described here, like many Sufi conversion accounts and indeed like some accounts of conversions effected by Christian saints, belong to the realm of the miraculous. The Bektashi Sarı Saltuq persuades a Christian to convert by turning himself into a falcon that kills the Christian's enemies. He also converts whole Turkic tribes to Islam on the western Eurasian steppes, founds new Muslim towns, and plays a leading role in the jihad against unbelievers, all of which later make for good stories to burnish his reputation and stir the enthusiasm of Sufi audiences for the same causes.

The agency of Sufi saints in conversion to Islam could also be very different from this model. Conversely, conversion and conquest went hand in hand on other frontiers even when the Sufi element was absent. A different Sufi case is that of Sayyid Aḥmad Bashīrī, active in the region of Samarqand in the fourteenth and fifteenth centuries (selection 51). Here the accounts of Sayyid Aḥmad's miraculous feats of conversion—which involve an Arab Christian theologian and a female refugee-turned-devotee, among others—serve the rhetorical purpose of defending him as an Uvaysī, a Sufi saint not belonging to a major Sufi order. Sufis are also prominent in the tale of Cheraman Perumal (Shakarwatī Farmāḍ) from the Malabar Coast of South Asia (selection 42). Sufis play a key role in authenticating the Indian king-hero's vision of the Prophet Muḥammad's miraculous splitting of the moon, and they eventually escort him to Arabia to meet the Prophet himself. The story makes implicit claims for, among many other things, the high standing of Sufis in later medieval Malabar. Still another Sufi model is found in an account of Niẓām al-Dīn Awliyā, a master of the Chishti order who was active in Delhi in the fourteenth century (selection 48). In the near-contemporary Persian account by his disciple Sijzī, Niẓām al-Dīn, adopting an unusually retiring stance, advises a would-be Hindu convert that sincere desire to cultivate his soul is more important than formal conversion. He cites both a failed forced conversion under an early Muslim caliph and the story of a Jewish neighbor of the ninth-century Persian Sufi saint Bisṭāmī. After the saint's death, this Jew explained that he had not converted to Islam for two reasons: because he despaired of practicing it as Bisṭāmī had done, and because he would be ashamed to practice it as most Muslims do.

Although large numbers of people in South Asia embraced Sufi Islam in this period, contemporary discourses around conversion there were clearly not always enthusiastic or triumphalist.

Elsewhere, too, the march of conversion sometimes moved laterally or even backward, as we perceive from the petulant diatribe of the late fifteenth-century North African al-Maghīlī (selection 53), which concerns sub-Saharan Africa. The obstreperous al-Maghīlī supplied the contemporary ruler of the Songhay Empire with pretexts for attacking his backsliding, lax, and altogether insufficiently converted neighbors. His arguments would be reprised by the nineteenth-century reformist warrior ʿUthmān b. Fūdī (Usman dan Fodio), and they give testimony to the variable fortunes of large-scale conversion in Africa over the *longue durée* and to the role of anxieties over its failure in justifying militant aggression.

We should remember, however, that conversion in newly Islamized lands need not have directly involved either conquest, missionary merchants, or Sufis. As Ottoman power waxed in the sixteenth century, conversion was a profoundly important gateway to Ottoman elite society, roughly as it had been for elites in earlier Islamic empires (though the Ottomans' forcible conscription of their own subjects, the *devshirme* among Balkan Christian boys, was a novel twist). Here, however, we glimpse only a sliver of this process in action, through the lens of Ottoman Turkish bureaucratic records (selection 55) in which the conversions of both elite bureaucrats and ordinary citizens are recorded. Most of these converts received tangible benefits as they entered Islam, and many hoisted members of their familial networks with them up the rungs of Ottoman society.

Finally, it is scarcely possible to conceive of conversion narratives that lie farther—either geographically or thematically—from the established patterns of the central Islamic lands than those emanating from the eastern Indo-Malay and Chinese worlds. Take, for example, the highly syncretic *Hikayat Raja Pasai,* which refers to conversion to Islam in northern Sumatra in the late thirteenth century (selection 52). In building up the sacred authority of the first Muslim ruler of the kingdom of Pasai, this tale draws elements from the indigenous traditions of Sumatra, from Japanese folktales, and from South Asian epic literature. Like the story of Cheraman Perumal from medieval Malabar, it also encloses a narrative effort to ascribe the agency in the conversion to the Prophet Muḥammad himself, thereby notionally eliding the gulf between thirteenth-century Sumatra and seventh-century Mecca. In much the same way, a token of Islam's deep past appears in *Matinya Raden Darmakusuma,* an account of the conversion of the Javanese prince Darmakusuma by the *wali sanga* (nine saints who, according to legend, converted Indonesia) in the late fifteenth or early sixteenth century (selection 56). Keyed to the *Mahabharata,* this tale makes a special place for an Islamic amulet containing the Arabic-script *kalima shahada* (Islamic profession of faith) that had protected the prince from death, unbeknownst to him, since long before his conversion. By pronouncing the Arabic phrase and thus converting, he is able to achieve the peaceful death he had long sought, thereby enacting a novel, culturally specific twist on traditional accounts of miraculous conversion.

Like these tales, our conversion narrative from Qing China is so deeply embedded in its own cultural milieu that the casual observer could almost miss the conversion entirely (selection 57). The protagonist, She Yunshan, is a precocious student who excels at the qualifying exams and earns a place as a Confucian mandarin. At first his only distinctly Muslim attribute is a certain distaste for statues of the Buddha. His conversion, and probably that of the women in his family, take place thanks to his adoption by a Muslim general of the Manchus, but beyond these details and a brief mention of his industry in Islamic scholarship, his life story as told by his Chinese Muslim disciple is dominated by the trappings of his native Han Chinese culture. Although many Muslims in Yuan, Ming, and Qing China were of Turkic or other "Western" background, this passage illustrates that Islam took hold among the Han Chinese as well. Islam was thus functionally integrated into Chinese culture and attracted less negative attention from China's rulers than did either Buddhism or Christianity.

All this is quite different both from the conversion-cum-conquest model that we sporadically encountered in Central Asia and West Africa and from the transformative, miraculous conversions reportedly effected by Sufi saints. By the eve of modernity, conversion had expanded the borders of the Islamic world considerably, and its themes reproduced distinct preexisting patterns, but it retained the capacity to surprise with its almost limitless variation in both representation and reality.

41

The Conversion of Medieval Ghāna as Narrated by a Later Ibāḍī Scholar

Abū al-ʿAbbās Aḥmad b. Saʿīd al-Darjīnī (d. ca. 670/1271, composed ca. 650/1252–53)

Luke Yarbrough

Title: *Kitāb Ṭabaqāt al-Mashāyikh bi-l-Maghrib* (The book of the generations of elders in the West)

Genre: Didactic and entertaining literature (biography)

Language: Arabic

INTRODUCTION

The following semilegendary account of conversion in West Africa comes from the pen of Abū al-ʿAbbās al-Darjīnī, an Ibāḍī Muslim scholar, jurist, and poet from a Berber family in what is now west-central Tunisia. The Ibāḍīs are the major surviving representative of Kharijite Islam, the smallest of the religion's three major early branches after Sunnism and Shiʿism. Today Ibāḍīs live mainly in Oman and Algeria.

The book that contains this account, *Kitāb Ṭabaqāt al-Mashāyikh*, is al-Darjīnī's principal work. It was written in response to a request from some Ibāḍī scholars of Oman for information concerning Ibāḍī history and learning in North Africa. The author includes not only excerpts from older works that relate the political history of Western Ibāḍism but also biographies of more recent local scholars. The present tale belongs to the latter category. In fact, it concerns al-Darjīnī's own great-grandfather, the pious scholar and Sahara trader ʿAlī b. Īkhlaf. However, even though it was repeated in modified form by later Ibāḍī authors, notably the well-known figure al-Shammākhī (d. 928/1522), it is not quite the family story that it would appear to be. Al-Shammākhī notes, as al-Darjīnī himself does not, that its core is derived from a passage found in the famous geographical work by the Andalusian Muslim scholar al-Bakrī (d. 487/1094), *Kitāb al-Masālik wa-l-Mamālik* (The book of routes and realms). It would be a mistake, however, to dismiss al-Darjīnī's account as wholly derivative and thus irrelevant to the history of conversion in Africa. It is not at all implausible that Ibāḍīs may have been agents of that conversion, or that ʿAlī b. Īkhlaf would in fact have encouraged the conversion of non-Muslims during his travels, though he lived far too late to have inspired al-Bakrī's story.

Regardless, this tale fits with the patterns of West African conversion, which began with rulers and their courts, spread unevenly to more remote areas, and produced forms of Islam that some Muslims criticized as unorthodox and superficial. On the last point, notice that ʿAlī teaches the king only a bare minimum of the Qurʾān and Islamic law after having him pronounce the double *shahāda* and imitate the motions of the ritual prayer. Nor does he impart Islamic learning to local scholars. This story also shows that it was a point of pride for a medieval Muslim to count as a forebear a man who had converted an African kingdom. Indeed, the distinction of having done so was contested by competing Muslim sects, a fact brought out in al-Shammākhī's later rendition. Finally, note that the geography here contains points of terminological obscurity that trace back to al-Bakrī's version. The "Nile," for instance, probably referred originally to the Upper Niger or Upper Senegal Rivers. "Ghāna" refers to a region far to the north of the modern country.

TEXT

It is related by many of our fellow Ibāḍīs (*jamāʿa min aṣḥābinā*) that ʿAlī b. Īkhlaf journeyed to Ghāna in the year 575 (1179–80 CE). He arrived at the city of Mālī, where the king honored him greatly. This king was a pagan who ruled over a great kingdom and many subjects, all of whom were pagans like him. He owned twelve mines, whence he obtained raw gold. Hardly ever did he hold court but that he seated ʿAlī with him, marveling at his appearance, his character, his frequent worship, and how closely he kept his religion. This went on until ʿAlī had finished his work and was preparing to depart.

Now this was a year of severe drought. The king's subjects complained to him of the affliction that had befallen them, and so he commanded them to make supplication for rain. They began supplicating and performing their customary sacrifices. They slaughtered various living things—cattle, sheep, donkeys, even human beings and house cats—but no rain fell. The king said to ʿAlī, "Will you not call upon your god whom you worship, that he might bring us rain?" ʿAlī said to him, "I am unable to do as you ask, for you disbelieve in Him, rebel against Him, and worship others. But if you believed in Him and obeyed Him, I would do it. It is my hope that He would then relieve your drought." "Then teach me Islam and its requirements," the king replied, "so that I might follow you in it, and that you might supplicate on our behalf." So he taught him how to make the double profession of faith (*al-shahādatayn*), and he learned it.

Then he said, "Come with me to the Nile River," and he did so. He taught him how to make purification, and he did so, and he put on clean clothes and climbed with him upon a hill overlooking the Nile. He taught him to perform the ritual prayer, and he prayed. Then he said, "When I pray, do what you see me do, and when I call upon God, say 'Amen.'" So they spent the night in their worship and in beseeching God, powerful and glorious. When the time of the morning prayer had passed, God, most highly praised, made a cloud. They had just begun their descent from the hill when the torrents cut them off from the city. A boat came to them upon the Nile, and they rode in it until they reached the city. The cloud remained for seven days without withdrawing, raining down night and day. Thus did it increase the believer in his belief and call the unbeliever to believe (*istadʿat īmān al-kāfir*).

When the king saw what God, most highly exalted, had done, he called upon all his household to embrace Islam, and they agreed. Then he called upon the people of the city, who said, "We are your servants," and agreed. Then he called upon those of his servants who were far from the city, and most of them agreed. Then he called upon those who were farthest away, and they said, "We are your servants who owe you obedience. Leave us in that to which our fathers accustomed us." He gave them permission, but issued a law that none should enter the city who disbelieved in God and His Messenger, and that if any unbeliever be seen in it he should be killed. Then he said, "Teach me the Qurʾān and the ways (*sharāʾiʿ*) of Islam," and so ʿAlī taught him until he learned enough to benefit him.

While he was there with him teaching him, a letter arrived from his father, calling him to come back and forbidding him to remain. He said to the king, "Know that I must travel soon." The king replied, "It is not right for you to abandon us to go back to blindness after having shown us the religion of guidance." But he said, "Know that among the requirements of this religion is to treat parents with kindness. My father has forbidden me to stay. This is his letter." When the king saw his seriousness of purpose, he soon came round, and ʿAlī departed. They remained in Islam, praise be to God, Lord of the Worlds.

FURTHER READING

Levtzion, Nehemiah. *Ancient Ghana and Mali* (London: Methuen, 1973), 183–99.

Levtzion, Nehemiah, and J. F. P. Hopkins, trans. *Corpus of Early Arabic Sources for West African History* (Princeton, NJ: Markus Wiener, 2000), 82–83, 368–69 [translations of the parallel accounts by al-Bakrī and al-Shammākhī].

Lewicki, Tadeusz. "Al-Dardjīnī," in *Encyclopaedia of Islam*, 2nd ed., 2:140–41.

42

Cheraman Perumal and Islam on the Malabar Coast

Anonymous (after ca. 545/1150)

Luke Yarbrough

Title: *Qiṣṣat Shakarwatī Farmāḍ* (The story of the world-ruler Farmāḍ [Perumal])
Genres: Religious instruction (hagiography); historical writing
Language: Arabic

INTRODUCTION

The practice of Islam on the Malabar Coast of southern India has roots deep in Islamic history. Because of maritime connections across the Arabian Sea, the peoples of the region regularly hosted Muslim traders and missionaries. On their own travels westward, they visited early Islamic societies. As a result, today the Muslims of Kerala—the largest group among whom are known as the Mappilas—can plausibly lay claim to an Islamic heritage of great antiquity. Some claims of this kind have historically been made through a set of stories according to which an ancient South Indian king, Cheraman Perumal, who figures in non-Muslim legends as well, was the region's first convert to Islam. Such stories were told in oral and written form in several languages, notably Arabic, Persian, Telugu, and Malayalam. They entered the colonial archive in Portuguese and English when agents of European empires made inroads in southern India. As we shall see, they allowed local Muslims to make a number of implicit arguments about Islam on the Malabar Coast, vis-à-vis the counterclaims both of Muslims from other regions (e.g., northern India, Arabia) and of local Muslim and non-Muslim neighbors and rivals.

Qiṣṣat Shakarwatī Farmāḍ—the account that is partially translated here—is increasingly regarded as the oldest and most complete version of the tale that exists in any language. Found in undated, anonymous manuscripts in the British Library, it tells a story set at the time of the Prophet Muḥammad. Scholars have recently given different dates for the story's composition, ranging from the mid-twelfth through the fourteenth century CE (Prange) to the mid-sixteenth (Kugle and Margariti) (see "Further Reading" below). The story centers on a sultan in Kerala named Shakarwatī Farmāḍ; Shakarwatī is the Sanskrit Chakravarti, or world-ruler, and Farmāḍ is an Arabic adaptation of the Malayalam title Perumal. The sultan sees the Prophet's miraculous splitting of the moon in a dream. This occurrence, duly verified, eventually leads him to accept Islam. He divides his realm among various lieutenants, travels to Arabia to meet Muḥammad, and some years later dies. The story was absorbed into many later texts, including Mappila folk songs and the *Tuḥfat al-mujāhidīn fī baʿḍ akhbār al-burtughāliyyīn* (The jihad-fighters' gift concerning accounts of the Portuguese), a sixteenth-century Arabic work by Zayn al-Dīn al-Maʿbarī (d. after 990/1583) that relates the (often hostile) dealings the region's native Muslims had with the first Portuguese to reach India. In these works the story took different forms. For example, the *Tuḥfat al-mujāhidīn* relocated its events chronologically from the seventh century CE—the time of the Prophet—to the early ninth. These and other variations are evident in prominent modern appropriations of the story in India that—despite the skepticism of many South Asian historians—trace the origins of Islam in Kerala to the time of the Prophet and the agency of Cheraman Perumal.

Where the excerpt below picks up, the scene has already been set by the narration of (otherwise unknown or scantily attested) events from the Prophet Muḥammad's career. In response to a challenge from his own tribe, the Quraysh, Muḥammad effects a miracle that is demanded by the tribe's putative leader, Ḥabīb b. Mālik. He causes the night to grow pitch dark and the moon itself to perform several feats: it rises; testifies eloquently that Muḥammad is a prophet; descends and passes through his sleeves; splits in two; and reunites in the middle of the sky. In the lead-up to this successful probative miracle—which in broader Muslim tradition is known, with different details, as "the splitting of the moon" (*inshiqāq al-qamar*; cf. Q. 54:1–9)—the angel Gabriel tells Muḥammad that a sultan of India will learn of the miracle and believe in his message. The scene then moves to India, where our excerpt begins.

Following our excerpt, after the converted Shakarwatī Farmāḍ has spent five years in Arabia with the Prophet, he sets out to return to India and propagate Islam there. He falls ill, however, in Shiḥr, in Hadhramaut, and gives Arab emissaries detailed instructions about how to accomplish the mission in India after his death. In the end they carry out his instructions, establishing a number of mosques and endowments and developing land on the Malabar Coast, while strengthening its ties to Hadhramaut. The significance of the present tale is thus manifold. Its principal implicit claims concerning Islam on the Malabar Coast are (1) its antiquity; (2) its deep historical connections to South Arabia, particularly Hadhramaut, and to distinguished local learned families of Arabian lineage; (3) its intrinsic importance, attested by the Prophet's personal attention to its original convert; (4) its superiority to other revealed religions (Hinduism hardly appears, but Scott Kugle and Roxani Eleni Margariti show that the story echoes Sanskritic traditions of a just ruler who disappears, widespread local communal origin stories like that of Saint Thomas establishing local Christianity, and broader Islamic Indian Ocean conversion and origin stories). The tale also underwrites the legitimacy of local Muslim customs and property rights in specific locales of Malabar, and the primacy of Sufism, whose adherents facilitate Shakarwatī Farmāḍ's conversion on their way to visit the well-known footprint of Adam in Ceylon, present-day Sri Lanka.

TEXT

On that very night, God most highly praised showed the sultan of India the splitting of the moon just as it happened. Astonished, he wrote down the date on which the splitting had occurred. Since his mind was greatly troubled at how such marvels had come to pass, he summoned to him priests and astrologers and asked them to explain this miracle. He gave them forty days to accomplish this and elucidate the miracle. When they failed to do so within the allotted time, they said, "We know nothing of this; it was not in our book." For a long time thereafter the king would ask those learned Muslims and [Ṣūfī] renunciants and foreigners who passed through from different regions, but none of them had any knowledge of the matter.

Then one night in his sleep he saw the Prophet—God bless and keep him—as though with his own two eyes. The Prophet said to him, "You have seen, have you not, my miracle: the splitting of the moon." "Yes," the king replied, and he told him the story of the splitting from beginning to end. Suddenly the sultan awoke with a feeling of great affection in his heart for Muḥammad, God bless and keep him. So badly did he desire to enter into his religion, and so much did he love the Prophet, God bless and keep him, that he neither ate nor drank nor found pleasure upon any bed. At that time his sultanate was in the town of Kodungallur.

For a long time thereafter, Sultan Shakarwatī remained in consternation out of his love for the Prophet, God bless and keep him. One day there arrived on a great ship a multitude of Jews and Christians with their wives and children. They had all come to serve the sultan. They requested that he provide them with lands, orchards, houses, and fields, and the sultan granted their request. Then he asked them, "From what land have you arrived, and what afflicted you there?" They all replied, "By God, we come from the noble, pleasant, and thriving city of Mecca. Recently a man has appeared there by the name of Muḥammad b. ʿAbdallāh. He claims to be a messenger and prophet, sent by the Lord of the Worlds to the Arabs and to all people. He contradicts our religion and subjugates our people. Many have believed in his religion because of his magic and his deception and his craft." The king asked, "What magic and deception and craft does he have?" In reply, they told him the whole story of the splitting. At this the sultan knew that these were his enemies and enviers, and so he kept hidden from them his love for the Prophet, God bless and keep him.

Years went by until one day many dervishes arrived. With them there was a righteous, sincere, observant, learned, and benevolent old man named Shaykh Ẓahīr al-Dīn, son of Shaykh Zakī al-Dīn al-Madanī. These men wished to pay a visit to the footprint of Adam, peace be upon him. The sultan heard about the arrival of the renunciant ascetics and summoned them. He showed them great hospitality and powerful support and lavished them with wealth. Then he took Shaykh Ẓahīr al-Dīn aside and asked him about the splitting of the moon. The old man told him the whole story. Then he asked him about the date on which the splitting had occurred, and it emerged that the dates coincided perfectly. At this the Indian sultan rejoiced, and Shaykh Ẓahīr al-Dīn marveled at his inner sincerity and at the low regard in which he held his own kingdom. The sultan said to Shaykh Ẓahīr al-Dīn, "Which is better, the Qurʾān, or the Torah and the Gospel?" The old man replied, "The Qurʾān is better than the Torah and the Gospel, because it is the uncreated speech of God." He then said, "All laws are abrogated except for that of Muḥammad." Then he summoned scholars from among the Jews and Christians and took from them the Torah and Gospel. He also took from the old man an account of what is in the Qurʾān. He removed a page from each scripture without their knowledge, then summoned the learned Jews and Christians and the Shaykh Ẓahīr al-Dīn al-Madanī and commanded them both to recite. The Jew who recited did so according to what he saw before him, but the old man recited up until the missing page. Realizing that a single page had been removed, he said to the sultan of India, "A single page has been removed." The Jew, however, was unaware of the missing page. Then the sultan knew that the Qurʾān truly was better than the Torah.

He said to the ascetics and renunciants who had arrived with the Shaykh Ẓahīr al-Dīn, "Where are you bound?" The old man replied, "I set out in order to pay a visit to the footprint of Adam, peace be upon him, that is on the island of Ceylon. I arrived here with great difficulty, and only a short journey now remains. Allow me to make the visit and return to your service." So he gave him permission, but instructed him to say nothing of the sultan's secret to anyone of Malabar. The old man and his companions left and traveled to the island of Ceylon, where they visited the footprint of Adam, peace be upon him. After this they returned to the town of Kodungallur, to the sultan's council. The sultan again took the old man aside and commanded him to make preparations for a journey. The old man found in the harbor of Kodungallur many ships that had arrived bearing foreigners from the ports of al-Shiḥr and al-Hurmūz. The old man said to the captain of one of the ships, "I and a group of ascetics intend to travel on your ship." The captain bade them welcome and they set about procuring rations and water.

Then the sultan commanded his whole household and his ministers, saying, "Let none of you come in to me for a period of seven days." He considered all the people of his realm and identified a person to appoint in every town and village. Then he wrote detailed documents specifying for each of them the boundaries of their territories over a distance of 140 Malabari parasangs [the parasang is an ancient Iranian unit of measurement generally denoting several miles], so that none of them would trespass against another in drawing their boundaries. This itself is a long story. Then the sultan took with him precious jewels, large pearls, and a great deal of gold and silver and coins, and boarded the ship with the old man and the dervishes on the night of Monday, the seventeenth of the month of Rajab.

Here is the story of his journey. They departed from the harbor and arrived at that of Pantalayini, where they remained for a day and a night. They proceeded thence to the harbor of Darmfatan, remaining there for three nights before setting sail for Shiḥr. As they were out in the open sea, they saw ships of pirates which circled their ship and pelted them with stones, oil, and arrows. But by the blessing of the Prophet, God bless and keep him, not one of these struck their bodies. All the ship's company said to one another, "Truly we saw a host of creatures drawn up in ranks around the ship. Their faces and their clothing were all white, and when they gestured with the sleeves of their garments toward the pirates, the latter were broken and routed and began fighting and striking one another."

When they had been delivered from the pirates they rejoiced that these had been repulsed. Continuing on, they arrived at their destination, the port of Shiḥr, where they disembarked and remained for ten days. There they heard that the Messenger of God was at the blessed site of Jedda, so they departed with a caravan of merchants. When they arrived in the vicinity of Jedda, the Messenger of God, God bless and keep him, heard of their arrival. The Messenger of God, God bless and keep him, went forth with his companions to receive them. And God, highly praised and exalted, determined that the face of the noble Prophet should meet the beloved sultan, who had long been burning with the fire of yearning, on the morning of Thursday the twenty-seventh of the month of Shawwāl. He fell at his blessed feet, which walk above the high heavens, and the Messenger of God, God bless and keep him, took his hand and embraced him, and they all returned together to the house of the Prophet, God bless and keep him. The Prophet, God bless and keep him, showed him fine hospitality, and instructed him to make the profession of faith (*al-kalima al-shahāda*), saying: "Say, 'I testify that there is no god but God alone, Who has no partner, and I testify that you are the Messenger of God.'" He said, "As you instruct, O Messenger of God: Islam and faith!"

Then Abū Bakr al-Ṣiddīq said, "O Messenger of God, who is this newly arrived man whom you have embraced and exalted and honored?" He replied, "He is a sultan in a land that produces pepper and ginger, which is called the land of India, in Malabar." Abū Bakr, God be pleased with him, said, "So he is a sultan in the land of India. How then has he left his realm and his sultanate?" The Prophet said, "He saw in his own place and his own abode the miracle of the splitting of the moon, as Ḥabīb b. Mālik requested of me. After that he saw me in such and such a manner in his sleep, and love entered his heart, love for me due to my prophethood, and he believed in my message." The sultan of India was amazed upon hearing what the Prophet, God bless and keep him, said concerning hidden things. The Prophet, God bless and keep him, asked, "What is your name?" He replied, "My name is Shakarwatī Farmāḍ." That very hour the Prophet, God bless and keep him, renamed him Sultan Tāj al-Dīn al-Hindī al-Malībārī. And he asked him, "What is the extent of your realm?" He replied, "Nearly 140 parasangs, according to the parasang of Malabar." He then made a request of the Prophet, saying, "In my kingdom there are many villages, and in each of them I have appointed a ruler, strong or weak. I seek your prayer concerning my sphere of authority, that the strong not take from the weak." So the Messenger of God prayed and God answered his prayer that very hour. He said, "Fear not, and do not mourn concerning your territory. It is preserved as you desire." At this he rejoiced and his heart was delivered from cares concerning his territory. The noble age of the Messenger of God at that time was fifty-seven years.

This news spread throughout Arabia, and all the tribe of Quraysh came to see the sultan of India. His hajj coincided with the great hajj of the Messenger of God, God bless and keep him, and his companions. Ḥabīb b. Mālik and his half-brother (through their mother) Mālik b. Dīnār heard the news, along with all the children and companions and troops, as they were of Quraysh and had come to visit the sultan of India. There arose a great love between the sultan of India and Ḥabīb b. Mālik, his brother Sharaf b. Mālik, his brother, and their children. They agreed together to travel with the sultan of India to the land of India. The sultan Tāj al-Dīn married the sister of Mālik b. Dīnār, whose name was Rajīna, and he remained in the company of the Messenger of God and his companions and of Ḥabīb b. Mālik for five years.

FURTHER READING

Friedmann, Yohanan. "*Qiṣṣat Shakarwatī Farmāḍ:* A Tradition Concerning the Introduction of Islām to Malabar," *Israel Oriental Studies* 5 (1975): 233–58.

Jacob, Wilson Chacko. *For God or Empire: Sayyid Fadl and the Indian Ocean World* (Stanford, CA: Stanford University Press, 2019), 55–59, 194–96.

Kugle, Scott, and Roxani Eleni Margariti. "Narrating Community: The *Qiṣṣat Shakarwatī Farmāḍ* and Accounts of Origin in Kerala and around the Indian Ocean," *Journal of the Economic and Social History of the Orient* 60 (2017): 337–80 [full translation].

Prange, Sebastian. *Monsoon Islam: Trade and Faith on the Medieval Malabar Coast* (Cambridge: Cambridge University Press, 2018), 92–157.

43

The Conversion Miracles and Life of the Dervish Sarı Saltuq

Muḥammad b. ʿAlī b. ʿAbd al-Raḥmān b. ʿUmar b. ʿAbd al-Wahhāb b. Muḥammad b. Ṭāhir b. al-Sarrāj al-Qurashī al-Dimashqī al-Shāfiʿī (d. unknown; composed in 715/1315)

A. C. S. Peacock

Title: *Tuffāḥ al-Arwāḥ wa-Miftāḥ al-Arbāḥ* (The apple of souls and the key of gain)

Genre: Religious instruction (hagiography)

Language: Arabic

INTRODUCTION

Little is known of the life of our author, Ibn al-Sarrāj, beyond the scant information that can be gleaned from his works. Originally from Damascus, he was in 700/1300 appointed *qāḍī* of the castle of Rawandan, near Kilis on the present-day Turkish-Syrian border (*Tuffāḥ al-Arwāḥ*, fol. 210b). He seems to have spent much of his life in this region, for the activities of its Kurdish holy men form a principal concern of his *Tuffāḥ al-Arwāḥ*, a collection of hagiographies dedicated to saints (*walī*, pl. *awliyāʾ*) affiliated with the Sufi Rifāʿī order to which he belonged. In addition to this work, one further book by Ibn al-Sarrāj survives in part, in a single and rather damaged manuscript, the *Tashwīq al-Arwāḥ* (MS Istanbul, Süleymaniye Library, Amcazade Hüseyin Paşa 272). From these works it is clear that Ibn al-Sarrāj was encouraged to compose these defenses of Sufism and Sufis by his rivalry with his better-known contemporary, the famous Ibn Taymiyya of Damascus, a noted opponent of Sufism. Ibn al-Sarrāj's aim in the collection is thus to demonstrate the power and efficacy of Sufi holy men, and this is done in part by highlighting the role of Sufis in converting unbelievers to Islam. Ibn al-Sarrāj's conversion narratives, which are present in many of his hagiographic notices of these holy men, thus emphasize the miraculous.

One of the most detailed accounts of a holy man in the *Tuffāḥ al-Arwāḥ* is devoted to Sarı Saltuq, a contemporary of Ibn al-Sarrāj. Sarı Saltuq is remembered by later oral tradition and literary texts as a leading figure in bringing Islam to eastern Europe, and several supposed shrines to the saint exist to this day. Ibn al-Sarrāj's account of Sarı Saltuq is the earliest to survive, and it illustrates many of the features of conversion narratives associated both with Sarı Saltuq and more generally with other Sufis in popular belief. In the first excerpt translated here, Sarı Saltuq effects the conversion of a Christian by turning himself into a falcon that kills the Christian's adversaries. The ability of holy men to work miracles by turning themselves into animal forms is commonly associated with the Bektashi Sufi order, which was widespread in Anatolia and the Balkans.

As well as converting individuals, holy men such as Sarı Saltuq were credited with the mass conversion of whole societies. In the second excerpt translated here, Sarı Saltuq is described as a wandering saint who is responsible for the conversion of whole tribes (*ṭawāʾif*) of infidels, which appears to refer above all to the Turkish-speaking non-Muslim population of the northern steppes of the Black Sea. This is explained in more detail in our third excerpt, which also emphasizes the role of the saint in expanding the borders of the *dār al-islām* by founding new towns; Sarı Saltuq miraculously makes a spring burst forth at the distant location of Sokji on the steppe, a place so remote that it is a month's journey from the outpost of Akkerman (in modern Moldova). Sarı Saltuq's creation of this spring makes the district fit for habitation and indeed fit to become a base for piety (*ʿibāda*) as well as types of holy war (*anwāʿ al-mujāhada*), doubtless referring both to the Sufi's inner jihad against the desires of the soul and more literally to the physical jihad against unbelievers. It was the latter aspect that was particularly remembered by later tradition, notably the sixteenth-century Turkish epic *Saltuk-name,* which deals with Sarı Saltuq's legendary wars on the steppe.

The text shows us that Sufis' involvement in conversion played an important role in defending the legitimacy of their claims to a special direct relationship with God. If the miraculous elements can be understood as part of this narrative strategy, there is also no doubt that holy men such as Sarı Saltuq did play a role in conversion and expansion on the peripheries of the Islamic world, joining piety with holy war, as this text suggests.

The numbers in angle brackets refer to folios of the Princeton manuscript, on which the present translation is based.

TEXT

<197b> One of the stories we have related: a Christian said, "Sir, the Franks have imprisoned my brother together with his merchandise. Although both are Christians, they belong to different sects." The shaykh said, "If I kill his captor, will you convert to Islam?" He said, "Yes." The shaykh at once cried out and produced from his cuff or from under his robe the captor's head, blood still running from it. After a few days, the captive came, bringing his merchandise and relating, "On such and such a day, while we were sitting, a white falcon swooped down on my captor and cut off his head, saying, 'I am Shaykh Saltuq.' When they saw this they let me and my companions go." The two brothers, their families, and many people converted to Islam because of this and on account of them. Praise be to God who guided them and protected them.

<198b> Shaykh Saltuq studied with [the Rifāʿī saint Shams al-Dīn Aḥmad al-Mustaʿjil] and took from him that with which God singled him out above other men of his time, and he traveled widely in the land of the infidels. Many tribes (*ṭawāʾif*) converted to Islam, and God guided men through him, so that his divine authority became clear and his divine proof became known. . . . He was fair in color, middle-sized in stature, and frequently looking into the skies. In appearance and service to knowledge, he was the closest of our brothers to the great Shaykh Taqī al-Dīn Abū al-ʿAbbās Aḥmad b. ʿAbd al-Ḥalīm b. ʿAbd al-Salām Ibn Taymiyya of Ḥarrān and Damascus, the Ḥanbalī. He did not differ from him in external appearance (*ẓāhiran*) except in his fairness, although in inner beliefs (*bāṭinan*) they were completely different.

<200a> As for Shaykh Saltuq, when smallpox struck, he was in a small town called Sokji in Qipchaq, meaning "the winnowing places" in Arabic, which contained about three hundred shops, a spring, and a mortar. The dervishes had asked Shaykh Saltuq to make a new [spring], and he struck a rock with his hand and the spring immediately burst forth and continued [to flow] in approval at their coming. This town is west of Akkerman, a great city, and its population consists of Oghuz [Turks]. It is nearly a month's journey from [Akkerman], of which twenty days are by sea and the rest by land. The tomb of the shaykh is nearly three hours' distance from the town of Sokji. Among the followers of the shaykh, who numbered in the thousands, were forty women. When he died they were living under his protection, and he had married one of them, who gave birth to daughters whom the [women] brought and put in their place to devote themselves to piety and types of holy war (*anwāʿ al-mujāhada*). The shaykh died at the age of around seventy in 697/1297, about eighteen years before the composition of this book.

FURTHER READING

Leiser, Gary. "Ṣari Ṣalṭūḳ Dede," in *Encyclopaedia of Islam,* 2nd ed., 9:61–62.
Norris, H.T. *Popular Sufism in Eastern Europe: Sufi Brotherhoods and the Dialogue with Christianity and "Heterodoxy"* (London: Routledge, 2006).
Öztürk, Eyüp. *Velilik ile Delilik Arasında (İbnu's-Serrâc'ın Gözünden Muvelleh Dervişler)* (Istanbul: Kitap Yayınevi, 2016).

44

The Providential Conversion of the Mongol King of Iran

Abū al-Qāsim ʿAbd Allāh b. ʿAlī b. Muḥammad al-Qāshānī (d. after 717/1317) and Rashīd al-Dīn Faḍl Allāh Abū al-Khayr (d. 718/1318)

Jonathan Brack

Title: *Tārīkh-i Mubārak-i Ghāzānī* (The blessed history of Ghāzān)
Genre: Historical writing
Language: Persian

INTRODUCTION

In 1295, the Mongol prince Ghāzān (r. 694–703/1295–1304), Chinggis Khan's (1162–1227) great-grandson, converted to Islam. Subsequently, with the support of the Muslim faction in the Mongol army and especially that of the Mongol commander and Muslim convert Nawrūz (d. 696/1297), Ghāzān defeated his cousin and rival and took over the throne of the Ilkhanate, the Mongol state in greater Iran, Iraq, and Azerbaijan (656–736/1258–1335). Ghāzān was not the first of the descendants of Hülegü (r. 1260–65), the Chinggisid founder of the Ilkhanate, to convert to Islam and implement Islamic policies; his conversion was preceded by that of his great-uncle, the Ilkhan (Mongol ruler) Aḥmad Tegüder (r. 681–83/1282–84). Still, Ghāzān's conversion and enthronement marked a new stage in Ilkhanid rule. Ghāzān's conversion was the culmination of a long and gradual process of Islamization (as distinct from conversion *sensu stricto*) that the Mongols—both the rank and file and the elite—had undergone since they arrived in the Middle East. Thereafter, the Ilkhanate presented itself as a Muslim empire, and the Mongol dynasty, the Ilkhans, identified as Muslims. Previously famous for their religious tolerance, the Mongols adopted a different attitude toward other religions after Ghāzān's conversion. Although members of the Mongol elite did continue to adhere to some of their Inner Asian religious traditions, such as ancestral veneration, the dynasty's treatment of other minority religions, especially Buddhism, which it had formerly supported, changed for the worse. Ghāzān's conversion, in fact, marked the end of nearly half a century's revival of Buddhism in Iran, centuries after Buddhism had entirely disappeared there following the spread of Islam. As the narrative below attests, Ghāzān himself had received training from renowned Buddhist masters as a child and later participated in their rituals and financed the construction of Buddhist shrines. The narrative, moreover, portrays Ghāzān's conversion as the Mongol ruler's departure from Buddhist worship, rather than from Inner Asian religious traditions.

The following is the earliest conversion narrative of Ghāzān, written in Persian at the Ilkhanid court. Composed only a few years after the event, it is found in an iteration of the *Tārīkh-i Mubārak-i Ghāzānī* (The blessed history of Ghāzān) by the Ilkhanid vizier and court historian Rashīd al-Dīn (d. 718/1318). However, this iteration of the work also seems to preserve, in part, another work on Ghāzān, penned by the court historian ʿAbd Allāh al-Qāshānī (d. after 717/1317). This later work by al-Qāshānī has not come down to us, but Rashīd al-Dīn has been shown to have copied from several of the other known works of al-Qāshānī, who was Rashīd al-Dīn's court protégé and, later, his adversary. Al-Qāshānī's account became the basis for the other, better-known, version of Ghāzān's conversion narrative, which appears in other iterations of Rashīd al-Dīn's history and has been included in Wheeler M. Thackston's English translation of *Tārīkh-i Mubārak-i Ghāzānī,* published in 1998.

The two narratives, which appear in different manuscripts of Rashīd al-Dīn's history, share several concerns. Both emphasize Ghāzān's gradually increasing internal conviction and his natural disposition toward monotheism and the Muslim faith, rather than toward Buddhism's idol worship. Both also posit a top-down model of group conversion, wherein Ghāzān's conversion initiated that of his Mongol officers and men. The latter claim, however, is refuted by the independent eyewitness account of Ghāzān's conversion by the shaykh Ṣadr al-Dīn Ibrāhīm b. Saʿd al-Dīn al-Ḥammūya, at whose hands the Mongol prince converted. The latter reported to a contemporaneous Syrian author a significant Muslim presence among the Mongol army in Ghāzān's camp prior to the prince's conversion. Ṣadr al-Dīn's observation has led some historians to suggest, compellingly, that Ghāzān converted in order to gain the Muslim faction's support in his succession struggle with his cousin.

Al-Qāshānī's narrative, however, also diverges significantly from Rashīd al-Dīn's version. First, al-Qāshānī's account attributes to the Mongol Nawrūz a far greater role behind the scenes. According to this version, it was Nawrūz who, taking advantage of Ghāzān's precarious position with his cousin, approached the prince and advised him to convert in return for his and the Muslim Mongols' support; he then secured Ghāzān's commitment to convert in due time. Nawrūz's central role and this "two-stage" conversion process are both confirmed by the independent account of Shaykh Ṣadr al-Dīn. The latter reports that Nawrūz beseeched him to delay his departure for the hajj and remain in Ghāzān's camp in the hope that it would prompt Ghāzān to follow through on his promise.

Al-Qāshānī's account offers a providential conversion narrative: Nawrūz, the former Mongol rebel, is not only Ghāzān's converter and enthroner but also the purveyor of a prophecy concerning the Chinggisid convert and the "revival" of Islam. The description of this prophesied king's utopian justice below registers both messianic Muslim resonances and Iranian ideals of just kingship. These ideals were epitomized in Persianate works of advice literature for princes and kings and in fables about pre-Islamic Iranian monarchs. Al-Qāshānī's conversion account thus matches the agenda of other Ilkhanid historians both before and after Ghāzān's watershed conversion, who justified Mongol rule by depicting the Ilkhans as another cycle of Iranian monarchy and aligning them with Persian-Islamic norms of government and justice.

As the account begins, Ghāzān has just consulted his commanders about how to overcome his adversary, Baidu, and it is Nawrūz's turn to speak. Note that the account goes on to report that after his conversion, Ghāzān promptly instituted patronage for Muslim scholars and Sufis, and fasted during Ramadan. In addition, al-Qāshānī remarks, it became obligatory for all Muslim rulers to submit to him, in accordance with Qur'ān 4:59, which enjoins obedience to God, His Messenger, and "those in authority among you."

TEXT

Inasmuch as Emir Nawrūz had earlier presented [his] advice (*bīlik*) [to convert], he kneeled and said . . . : "It is reported from the religious scholars of Islam, the astrologers and the composers of almanacs (*aṣḥāb-i nujūm va arbāb-i taqvīm*), that a great king (*pādshāh-i buzurg*) who would strengthen the religion of Islam was to appear around the year 690 [1291 CE] and that the Muslims, who have been weakened, were to be revived and renewed (*tāza va ṭarī shavad*) through his guidance. With this king's all-encompassing justice, the sheep would be protected from the wolf's harm and the gazelle from the hound's oppression; with his comprehensive equity, the feeble finch would be safe from the royal falcon's grip, and the partridge from its force and the dread thereof. The crown and the throne of kingship will be his for many years.

"Since the signs of his [the anticipated king's] qualities and the marks of his appearance are manifest and shining from the shape of the state and the face of the impressions on the shining forehead (*jabīn-i mubīn*) of the prince, time and again it has come to the mind of this slave [Nawrūz] that he [this king] might be Ghāzān Khan. If the prince were to convert to Islam and adhere to the [Muslim] faith's tenets and paths, he would certainly be the ruler of the age (*ūlī al-amr-i ʿahd*). He would enable the Muslims, who are enslaved in the lowest baseness and the lowest of places, to safely rise and thrive; and then, through the spread of religion and the cultivation of justice, the lords (*mavālī*) would be victorious and the enemies subdued. Thereafter, full, unsolicited obedience [to Ghāzān] would become a duty for each and every Muslim, and all the Muslims would become [his] supporters and friends. On account of the sincerity of [their] endeavors and heartfelt inclinations, God, glorious and exalted, would make [you] victorious. Thus, the religion of Islam would be revived through the prince's support after having been worn down by its subjugation to the infidel (*kuffār*) Tatars and the domination of tyrants and sinners (*ẓālimān va fāsiqān*) [probably the Ilkhans' enemies, the Mamluks in Syria and Egypt, 1250–1516]."

Since God, glorious and exalted, had adorned and enlightened the heart of the prince with the light of monotheism (*nūr-i tavḥīd*), and since his [Ghāzān's] noble existence became the treasury of the sacred secrets (*asrār-i quds*) and the bearer of gnosis (*ma ʿrifat*), the dawn of eternal felicity broke over him, and the veil of defect and doubt was lifted from his eye of discernment, and the wise speech of Nawrūz left its mark on his blessed heart . . . and [Ghāzān] answered [Nawrūz]: "The inclination to this purpose and the splendor of this motive have always been set before the eye of my mind. For how could it be in accordance with reason for an intelligent person (*khiradmand*) to put his head to the ground before a created inanimate object and not endeavor to reach proximity and access to the perfect soul, instead seeking assistance instead through the blessing of a personage (*shakhsī*) whose likeness is this idol? It is shameful to humble oneself before an idol and perform the acts of kissing and the rituals of osculation. Idol worship is the worst of errors and ignorance and the stuff of . . . derision. The religion of Islam is the best of religions and the quintessence of the divine laws (*khulāṣa-yi navāmīs-i ilāhī*), but the unceasing and continuous attachments and hindrances have blocked [me from] the guidance of the light of [the Muslim] faith (*nūr-i īmān*). [However,] where the water is close, there is no need for a long rope [meaning that Ghāzān did not need much incentive to convert]." Nawrūz's suggestion was heard and accepted. . . .

On the fourth day of Shaʿbān in the year 694 [June 19, 1295], in a palace (*kūshkī*) that had been the [summer] palace (*takhtgāh*) of [the Ilkhan] Arghun [r. 683–90/1284–91, Ghāzān's Buddhist father], in the meadow of Lār in Damāvand, they had a great feast and the prince washed and performed the ritual ablutions and dressed in clean garments. He ascended to the top of the elevated palace and stood like a candle at the foot of the throne as God's servant. Shaykh Ṣadr al-Dīn Ibrāhīm, the true successor of Saʿd al-Dīn al-Ḥammūya, mercy be upon him, instructed [Ghāzān] to make the profession of faith (*shahāda*). Prince Ghazan recited the words of sincerity [*ikhlāṣ*, in reference to the Qurʾānic *sūra* "al-Ikhlāṣ"] with full resolution from the true innermost part (*sirr*) of his heart and several times, with clear speech (*lisān-i faṣīḥ*) like the Messiah (*masīḥ*), repeated the profession of the unity of God (*tavḥīd*) and extolled God (*takbīr*).

The prince raised his finger, declaring God's unity. And all the emirs and soldiers, close to one hundred thousand disobedient polytheists, became believers (*mu'min va muvaḥḥid*). Although the Buddhist priests (*bakhshiyān*) had instructed him [Ghāzān] during the time of his youth and childhood in the worship of idols, and he had remained steadfast and constant in it, when he converted to the religion of Islam and listened with the ear of intellect and conceded to the prophetic community (*millat-i nabavī*) . . . he [Ghāzān] became more sincere [in his devotion] than Uways [al-Qaranī] and Salmān [al-Fārisī; two early converts, contemporaneous with the Prophet Muḥammad]. In this joy and happiness, they celebrated and feasted for some time, and out of sincerity and faith, all the peoples—Turks and Persians—were scattering dirhams and dinars, precious gems and desirable objects, over the blessed throne, and chanting:

> The wealth, health, years, portents, origins, descent, fortune and throne
> May they be yours (*bādat*) in kingship, stable and eternal:
> Abundant wealth, good health, fortunate portents, joyous years,
> Firm origins (*aṣl-i rāsī*), immortal descent, sublime fortune, and an obedient throne.
> [a poem by the Seljuq laureate Mu'izzī (d. ca. 542/1148)]

FURTHER READING

Amitai-Preiss, Reuven. "Ghazan, Islam, and the Mongol Tradition: A View from the Mamluk Sultanate," *Bulletin of the School of Oriental and African Studies* 59, no. 1 (1996): 1–10.

DeWeese, Devin. "Islamization in the Mongol Empire," in *The Cambridge History of Inner Asia: The Chinggisid Age,* ed. Nicola Di Cosmo, Allen J. Frank, and Peter B. Golden (Cambridge: Cambridge University Press, 2009), 120–34.

Jackson, Peter. *The Mongols and the Islamic World: From Conquest to Conversion* (New Haven, CT: Yale University Press, 2017).

Melville, Charles. "Pādshāh-i Islām: The Conversion of Sultan Maḥmūd Ghāzān Khān," in *Persian and Islamic Studies in Honour of P. W. Avery,* ed. Charles Melville (Cambridge: University of Cambridge, Centre of Middle Eastern Studies, 1990), 159–77.

45

The Conversion of ʿAbd al-Sayyid, a Damascene Jew

Quṭb al-Dīn Mūsā b. Muḥammad al-Yūnīnī (640–726/1242–1326)

Yehoshua Frenkel

Title: *Dhayl Mirʾāt al-Zamān* (Sequel to the mirror of the time)
Genres: Historical writing; didactic and entertaining literature (biography)
Language: Arabic

INTRODUCTION

The story translated below is narrated by several Mamluk historians in slightly different ways. Set in Damascus, it relates the conversion of the Jewish jurist and judge (*dayyān*) Yūsuf b. Isḥāq b. Yaḥyā al-Yahūdī to Islam on 4 Dhū al-ḥijja 701/July 31, 1302. The basic outline of the story is simple. A Jewish congregational leader and his sons come to the "palace of justice" (*dār al-ʿadl*), where the viceroy receives them. In the presence of a substantial number of scholars and jurists, the Jews publicly convert to Islam. Yūsuf is renamed Bahāʾ al-Dīn ʿAbd al-Sayyid b. al-Muhadhdhib al-Ḥakīm (the physician) al-Kaḥḥāl (the oculist) al-Isrāʾīlī. On the same occasion, other Jews, too, relinquish their faith and convert to Islam. A week later, during the great festival that commemorates the end of the hajj rituals in Mecca (*ʿīd al-qurbān* or *al-aḍḥā*), the new converts join the Muslims of Damascus on a parade to the prayer ground outside the city walls, invoking the slogan *Allāhu akbar* (God [is] the greatest). They are honored by many Muslims.

The Mamluk chroniclers offer a dramatic cycle of scenes, indoors and in open public space, official and popular, in the day and at night. Following their conversion to Islam, the male members of the Jewish judge's household are decorated with robes of honor and traverse Damascus in a ceremonial procession accompanied by bands of drummers and wind instruments. At night a festive ritual of Qurʾān reading takes place in the converts' house.

In an ego remark, the wordsmith Ibn al-Wardī claims that he happened to be in Damascus when ʿAbd al-Sayyid passed away, on 6 Jumādā II 715/Sunday, September 7, 1315. The deceased, he states, was a good Muslim. To commemorate him and his conversion he composed a short stanza:

> By converting to Islam he built his household, and by doing so he destroyed the mansions of his enemies.
> Their sorrow destroyed their warehouses, yet their conversion pleased Moses.

Mamluk religious savants emplotted an account that emphasizes the role of the *ʿulamāʾ* in the crossing of the religious line. They present Muslim scholars as playing the crucial role in spreading Islam.

Ibn Taymiyya, for example, employs the story as a tool in his campaign against (unruly) Sufi dervishes. He tells his readers that he met with ʿAbd al-Sayyid prior to his conversion and that at the time the latter served as the judge (*qāḍī*) of the Jews. ʿAbd al-Sayyid told him about a meeting he had had with a Sufi teacher named Sharaf al-Dīn al-Bālisī. To the dervish's call to convert, ʿAbd al-Sayyid had responded: "I will not give up the way of Moses and turn to the path of Pharaoh." Between the lines of Ibn Taymiyya's account we read that a true Muslim savant, such as himself, can convince even a devoted Jew to give up his imperfect religion and to convert to the true religion of Islam—an achievement that a Sufi dervish could not match.

In the passages translated below, the basic narrative is supplied by the Mamluk-era scholar al-Yūnīnī, with additional text in curly brackets by the later figures Ibn Kathīr (IK) and Ibn Ḥajar al-ʿAsqalānī (IḤ).

TEXT

In this year on Tuesday, 4 Dhū al-ḥijja [July 31, 1302] ʿAbd al-Sayyid b. al-Muhadhdhib, then the chief judge of the Jews of Damascus who inherited this post from his father and grandfather, came over to the *dār al-ʿadl* [palace of justice or court of grievances]. Together with him were his sons. They all converted to Islam. The viceroy [of Damascus] granted them robes of honor (*khilʿa*) and ordered that horses be prepared so they could ride in a parade in the city of Damascus and for drums (*dabādib*) to be beaten and horns (*abwāq/būqāt*) to be played at the tail of the procession. {The procession came to a halt at their house. There they celebrated at night. Jurists and judges participated with them in the reading of the Qurʾān.—IK} All this was for the purpose of publicizing their conversion to Islam. They regularly attended sessions (*majālis*) of Qurʾān studies and religious learning (*ʿilm*). {ʿAbd al-Sayyid converted a considerable number of Jews to Islam.—IK}

On the day of the holiday that commemorates the end of the hajj they all went out to the prayer ground on the outskirts of Damascus (*muṣallā*) to perform the ritual duties. {The converts and Muslims joined in,—IK} declaring that Allah is the greatest (*al-takbīr*). People treated them with high respect and warm admiration.

The viceroy appointed him [ʿAbd al-Sayyid] to head the hospital established by Nūr al-Dīn (*al-bīmāristān al-nūrī*) and made him one of its chief physicians. He took up the post and started to execute his duties. This ʿAbd al-Sayyid influenced a considerable number of Jews to convert to Islam, either with him or after him.

{He loved the Muslims and attended classes of *ḥadīth*. Jamāl al-Dīn Abū al-Hajjāj Yūsuf al-Mizzī [654–743/1256–1341] was among those who learned traditions with him.—IḤ}

FURTHER READING

Frenkel, Y. "Conversion Stories from the Mamlūk Period," in *Muslim-Jewish Relations in the Middle Islamic Period: Jews in the Ayyubid and Mamluk Sultanates (1171–1517)*, ed. Stephan Conermann, 75–94 (Göttingen: V&R UniPress and Bonn University Press, 2017).

Goldziher, Ignaz. "Mélanges Judéo-Arabes," *Revue des Études Juives* 43 (1901): 1–2; 60 (1910): 37–38.

46

An Account of the Conversion of Egypt's Copts under Duress at the End of the Thirteenth Century

Taqī al-Dīn Aḥmad b. ʿAlī al-Maqrīzī (d. 845/1442)

Frédéric Bauden

Title: *al-Mawāʿiẓ wa-l-Iʿtibār bi-Dhikr al-Khiṭaṭ wa-l-Āthār* (Exhortations and lessons in dealing with the quarters and historical remains)
Genres: Historical writing (topography)
Language: Arabic

INTRODUCTION

Al-Maqrīzī (766–845/1364–1442) is one of the major representatives of Islamic historical writing, particularly on his country of birth, Egypt. Born into a family of scholars working for the government, he followed the same path until he decided to retire from public life to devote himself to the writing of history. One of his first major works was the book he dedicated to the topographical history of Egypt and above all of its capital, Cairo, from which comes the following account regarding the beginning of the persecutions that the Copts (and, to a lesser extent, the Jews) had to endure from the end of the thirteenth until the mid-fourteenth century (the last of these campaigns of discrimination and intimidation took place in 755/1354). The account belongs to a section—one of the longest written by a Muslim author—whose subject is the history of the Copts and their beliefs and in which al-Maqrīzī narrates a succession of events that led to widespread conversions to Islam among Copts. Among the coercive measures adopted by the government, the harshest were the destruction of churches, the expropriation of endowments, and the prohibition to work as functionaries. The campaign started in 692/1293, under the sultanate of Qalāwūn's successor, al-Ashraf Khalīl

(r. 689–93/1290–93), who, two years earlier, had put an end to the Latin presence in Palestine by conquering Acre. In most cases, there were two sources of pressure for Coptic conversion: the government and the Muslim populace. Although members of the government often tried to limit the impact of measures taken by the sultan to satisfy the populace, as evidenced in the following account by the role played by the governor Baydarā, who pleaded in favor of the Coptic functionaries, they could not always avoid repression. Considered a turning point in Egyptian religious history, when the demographic transformation of Egyptian religion tipped decisively in favor of Islam, these events are analyzed by contemporary historians with a more critical eye. Al-Maqrīzī, born a decade after the last campaign of harassment, was not a direct witness of these events. Moreover, it has been demonstrated that even if these campaigns had a true impact on the level of conversion to Islam among Copts, it was more limited than has so far been contemplated; conversions were often limited to one generation and did not include the whole family.

TEXT

In the year 692 [1293 CE] the onslaught on the Christians took place. The emir Sanjar al-Shujāʿī [d. 693/1294] was held in wonderful honor in the days of al-Malik al-Manṣūr Qalāwūn [r. 678–89/1279–90] and the Christians rode on donkeys with girdles round their waists. No Christian ventured to address a Muslim on horseback, and if he were on foot, he was to make room for him with deference; neither could any Christian wear fine dress. But when al-Manṣūr [Qalāwūn] was dead and his son al-Malik al-Ashraf Khalīl [r. 689–93/1290–93] succeeded him, Christian secretaries were taken into service by the emirs who belonged to the sultan's retinue, and they subsequently showed themselves overbearing toward the Muslims and assumed superiority in their dress and demeanor.

One of them, who was secretary to an emir in the sultan's retinue known by the name of ʿAyn al-Ghazāl, one day met his master's granary agent [riding] in a street of Old Cairo (*Miṣr*). This man at once alighted and embraced the secretary's foot, upon which he [the Christian] began to abuse and threaten him about a sum of money still due from him of the price paid for the emir's produce. The agent implored and beseeched him, but this only served to aggravate his fault, until the secretary told his servant to get off his ass and to tie the agent's hands behind him and make him walk on. The people gathered round at this, so that by the time he came to the crossroads of the mosque of Aḥmad b. Ṭūlūn, a large crowd was following him, every man of which entreated him to let go of the agent, but he would not grant their request.

They then mustered in greater number, pulled him down from his donkey, and set the agent free. This happened near the house of his master, to whom he sent his servant to ask him to come and deliver him from his assailants. He came out with a batch of the emir's slaves and grooms, who rescued the secretary from the crowd and began to grab them with the aim of wounding them. But they shouted: "It is not lawful!" and ran hastily until they stopped under the citadel and cried, seeking aid: "God let the sultan triumph!" He [heard them and] sent to inquire about the matter. And they made known to him the overbearing way in which the Christian secretary had behaved toward the agent, and what had happened to them.

The sultan then sent for ʿAyn al-Ghazāl and addressed him thus: "How can you let your slaves behave as they have done toward Muslims for the sake of a Christian?" ʿAyn al-Ghazāl excused himself, saying that he had been busy in his office and had known nothing about it. Then the sultan sent to fetch all who were in ʿAyn al-Ghazāl's stable and ordered the people to bring to him all the Christians. He also sent for the emir Badr al-Dīn Baydarā [d. 693/1293], the governor (*nāʾib*), and the emir Sanjar al-Shujāʿī, and ordered them to bring before him all the Christians, to put them to death. Those two emirs, however, did not leave him until the matter was decided, and it was cried throughout Cairo (*al-Qāhira*) and Old Cairo (*Miṣr*) that no Christian or Jew should remain in service with an emir. And he ordered all the emirs to propose the faith of Islam to all the Christian secretaries they had, and to cut off the heads of all those who refused to embrace it, but to retain in their service all who did. He also gave orders to the governor to make the same offer to the stewards employed in the sultan's chancery, and to treat them in the same way.

An order was given to look for them, and they hid themselves; but the people forestalled them in their own houses, which they plundered, until the sack was general, both of the Jews' houses and of those of the Christians, one and all. They led away their women as captives and put to death a number of people with their own hands. Then the emir Baydarā, the governor, went to the sultan about the conduct of the people, and coaxed him until the prefect of police rode to Cairo and proclaimed that whosoever plundered the house of a Christian should be hanged. He also arrested a number of people and marched them about the city after having scourged them. They then stayed the plunder, after they had plundered the church of the Muʿallaqa in Old Cairo, and had put to death a number of people there.

Then the governor brought together a number of Christians who were secretaries of the sultan and of the emirs and placed them before the sultan, at a certain distance from him. The sultan ordered al-Shujāʿī and the emir of the armor bearers to take several of these men with them and to go down to the horse market under the citadel; and there to dig a large grave, to throw into it all the secretaries now present, and to light a fire of wood on top of them.

Then the emir Baydarā came forward and pleaded for them, but the sultan would not receive his plea, saying: "I will not have a Christian chancery in my government." Yet the emir did not quit the sultan until he had consented to this—that those secretaries who had embraced the faith of Islam should be retained in their offices, but that those who would not, should have their heads cut off.

He therefore brought them out to the house of the governor of the city and said to them: "O ye, all of you: I have not been able to prevail with the sultan on your behalf except on one condition, which is that anyone of you who prefers his religion is to be put to death, but that anyone who prefers Islam shall receive a robe of honor and keep his position."

Then al-Makīn Ibn al-Suqāʿī, one of the accountants, came forward and said to him: "O lord, which of us men high in office would choose death for this nasty religion? By God, a religion for which we should be killed and for which we would have to die would vanish. God would not have prescribed success to it. Tell us the religion you wish us to choose and to follow." Then Baydarā burst out laughing, and said to him: "Woe unto you! Do we choose another religion but Islam?" Then al-Makīn replied: "O lord, we don't know; do tell us, and we will follow you."

Then he [Baydarā] brought in professional witnesses, made them Muslims, and wrote deeds of witness thereof, wherewith he went to the sultan, who clothed them in robes of honor; and then they went in them to the council of the vizier al-Ṣāḥib Shams al-Dīn Muḥammad Ibn al-Salʿūs [d. 693/1294]. Then one of those present addressed al-Makīn Ibn al-Suqāʿī and handed him a sheet for him to write on, saying: "O judge, our master, write on this sheet." He answered: "O my son, it is not for us to decide." They did not leave the council of the vizier till the evening, when the chamberlain came to them and took them to the council of the governor, where the judges were already assembled; and there the secretaries renewed their conversion in their presence.

And thus, from men despised, they became honorable through their embracing Islam. But they also began to despise the Muslims, and to lord over them with a violence which Christianity would have forbidden them to use. So that it was, in fact, as someone wrote to the emir Baydarā, the governor, saying:

> The infidels have adopted Islam through the sword and by force,
> But no sooner were they alone than they sinned.
> They eluded a loss of gain and of life;
> And now they are free, but not Muslims.

FURTHER READING

el-Leithy, Tamer. "Coptic Culture and Conversion in Medieval Cairo, 1293–1524 A.D." (PhD diss., Princeton University, 2005).

Gervers, Michael, and Ramzi Jibran Bikhazi, eds. *Conversion and Continuity: Indigenous Christian Communities in Islamic Lands, Eighth to Eighteenth Centuries* (Toronto: Pontifical Institute of Mediaeval Studies, 1990).

Little, Donald P. "Coptic Conversion to Islam under the Baḥrī Mamlūks, 692–755/1293–1354," *Bulletin of the School of Oriental and African Studies* 39 (1976): 552–69.

O'Sullivan, Shaun. "Coptic Conversion and the Islamization of Egypt," *Mamlūk Studies Review* 10, no. 2 (2006): 65–79.

47

A Syriac Communal Lament over Apostasy

Anonymous

Thomas A. Carlson

Title: *ʿŌnīthā dh-ʿal mshamshānā ḥadh d-aḥnep āw kēyth shvaq tāwdīthā d-men qrīthā Meshkalg* (Poem on a deacon who became pagan, i.e., left the confession, who was from the village of Meshkalg)

Genre: Didactic literature (poetry, i.e., *ʿōnīthā,* a strophic poetic genre)

Language: Syriac

INTRODUCTION

This poem portrays the mourning of a Christian community over the apostasy of one of its deacons. The author is identified in some manuscripts as a member of the deacon's church, but no manuscript names the author. The work is poor in historical details; the rubric names the deacon's village (Meshkalg, identified as a village near Erbil), an acrostic indicates the apostate's name (Abraham), and verses give some details of his family structure (father, uncle, four brothers, unnumbered sisters and daughters). The lack of a date makes it difficult to describe a specific historical setting. Maroš Nicák (79–80) suggests a date in the second half of the thirteenth century, yet his reasoning presumes an unlikely degree of influence of Islamic *sharīʿa* on village songs in Syriac. We cannot date the text more precisely than between the thirteenth and fifteenth centuries. The purpose of the text, used in church services, was to remind the remaining Christians of the costs, both present and eternal, of conversion to Islam.

The poem references the various church celebrations and specifically the liturgical functions of deacons weeping over the apostasy. *Hpākhthā, sōgīthā,* and

ʿōnīthā are genres of liturgical hymns, as are *madhrāshē*. The stole and belt are a deacon's liturgical vestments. Annunciation (celebrated over the four weeks before Christmas), Nativity, Epiphany, Lent, Passover, Famous Friday (i.e., the Passion), the Resurrection, Ascension, and Pentecost are the major events of the church year, commemorating the life, death, and resurrection of Christ, while the Feast of the Cross was celebrated in September. Gazzē and Ḥudhrē are books of liturgical prayers, and *māwtbē* (sessions) are parts of church services. "Stay in peace" and "go in peace" are conventional words of parting.

Even in stylized poetic form, this text reveals the grief of the abandoned religious community at the act of conversion. It also reminds its audience that conversion was not just an individual preference, but a step with ramifications in terms both of community and of eternity. The communal impact of conversion appears in the missing liturgical functions and the suffering of the family. The references to "the death before death" (lines 52, 106) allude to spiritual death before physical death, while "death in death" (line 108) may refer to damnation as eternal death, the opposite of eternal life. The lack of a Christian burial (lines 109–20) reveals exclusion from the community, but also hints at the eternal suffering in store for apostates, made explicit by the end of the hymn. A metrical change at the end highlights the call to repentance and the final prayer.

The text translated here was collated from three early manuscripts and compared with Nicák's edition on the basis of later manuscripts, although his emendations have not been taken.

TEXT

Oh, how bitter is this news!
    Oh, how bitter is this tale!
  Bitter and provoking
    And troubling and grievous,
And painful and afflicting
    And disquieting and vexing,
  Which happened to this deacon,
    Which I am saying in an acrostic on his name [Abraham].
Awake, O sleeper, from your slumber,
    And from the burden of your drunkenness
  And see how harsh is your sin,
    And how great is your transgression.
Cry, and do not stop crying,
    And make others cry with you,
  For you took a pledge henceforth:
    The kindled fire that is not quenched.

Great was your name among your brothers,
And your reputation among your companions.
Why have you made sadness for those who love you,
And joy for your enemies?
Your noble *hpākhthās*,
And your many *sōgīthās*,
And your long *ʿōnīthās*,
To whom have you left them as an inheritance?
Who takes your [liturgical] stole?
And who puts on your belt?
Who plays on your lyre?
And who stands in your place after you?
Behold, in the church they are weeping for you!
Behold, in the monasteries they are mourning for you!
What's wrong with you, sunken one? What's wrong with you,
That you do not recognize what happened to you?
Woe to you! Woe to you! Woe to you!
And a thousand woes are too few for you,
That you departed from the great light,
You entered the great darkness.
The sea, if it should weep for you,
And make tears of suffering flow for you,
Is unable to purify and wash you,
And is not what bathes and absolves you.
The firstborn festival weeps for you,
That of the great Annunciation of the Son,
Since from that height of honor
You fell into the abyss of cut-off hope.
Nativity weeps for you with melodies,
And Epiphany makes mourning over you,
And the Fast of the Fifty [Lent] mourns over you,
And Passover implores and does not cease!
The famous Friday weeps,
And the great and known Saturday,
And the day of Sunday of the Resurrection [i.e., Easter],
For the dead one who died before death.
The shining festival weeps for you,
Of the Ascension of the Only-Begotten,
And the descent of the living Spirit [i.e., Pentecost]
Which came upon the twelvefold crowd [i.e., the apostles].
The Feast of the Cross weeps for you,

For a deacon, the son of Ṣlībā [a name meaning "cross"],
Who left the worship of the Cross
And loved those who deny the Cross.
The Church in her rites weeps for you,
And she mourns over you in all her ranks,
Since you left her mysteries [i.e., sacraments] with her types [i.e., symbols],
And her altars and her sanctuaries with her naves.
The chanting also weeps for you,
The mother of tones and melodies
With her sweet chants
And with her sad notes.
The evening and morning services weep for you,
And the memorials and Gazzē and Ḥudhrē,
And the *māwtbē*, with the songs of vigils
And the glorified and honored mysteries [i.e., sacraments].
The *madhrāshē* with their verses
Weep for you and mourn over you,
And the chants and their variations,
And the responsive hymns with their strophes.
"O Lord, I call upon you!" [i.e., Ps. 141] weeps over you,
And your hallelujahs and your litanies,
And your notes and your chants
And your relatives and your companions.
The feasts and the memorials weep
With their canon hymns and their harmonies,
Also the priests and the deacons,
And the readings with the candles.
Your elderly father weeps for you,
Since you have left him like a debtor,
And you became like an enemy to him,
And you became evil instead of good.
Your four brothers weep for you,
Since you bowed their head to the ground
And you made their heart sick,
And their sickness is worse than every sickness.
The sisters also weep for you,
The living with the dead,
And the little girls,
Your daughters that remained like orphans.
Jacob, your uncle, weeps for you,

If he perceives this action of yours,
And the teacher who taught you and trained you,
And subjected himself to you and subjected you.
Your houses and your courts weep;
Your vineyards and your fields mourn,
And your neighbors, men and women,
And the people of your church and your village.
They weep for you before death,
Since you have become dead before death,
And when the day of death arrived,
Your death became death in death.
Priests are not surrounding you,
Nor are deacons carrying you,
Nor are they bringing you into the church,
Nor are they placing you in front of the altar.
Nor are they saying, "Stay in peace,"
Nor are they answering, "Go in peace!"
"Church, you stay in peace,"
They are not saying over you on that day.
They are not making memorials for you,
Nor are they making offerings for you,
Nor are they acting as supplicants for you,
But shaven and bald-headed.
Where shall you go, poor man,
From before the judgment of the Judge?
Who will be a rescuer for you
From that fire of Gehenna?
When height and depth are trembling,
And humans and angels are quaking,
And mountains and hills are melting,
What will those who deny Jesus do?
Have you not heard the Lifegiver's mouth,
Who said to his friends thus:
"Whoever shall be a confessor of me,
Before the Father him I confess
And whoever denies me in the world,
This one which passes away like a dream,
I will deny him on that day
Before the angels that are on high" [cf. Matt. 10:32–33]?
The one whom the Son hates,
How can the Father love him?

And the one whom the Son throws down,
Who will support him as the lowest servant?
Wake up! Wake up, before you fall asleep!
And weep and repent about what has happened to you!
And become for yourself the judge!
Absolve, our Lord, the composer,
And the listeners of every region.
For your sheep who strayed, be the Finder,
And to you be praise in every time!

FURTHER READING

Carlson, Thomas A. *Christianity in Fifteenth-Century Iraq* (New York: Cambridge University Press, 2018).

Nicák, Maroš. *"Konversion" im Buch Wardā: Zur Bewältigung der Konversionsfrage in der Kirche des Ostens* (Wiesbaden: Harrassowitz, 2016).

48

Conversion to Islam in South Asia as Transformation of the Heart

Ḥażrat Khwāja Niẓām al-Dīn Awliyā and Amīr Ḥasan ʿAlā Sijzī (compiled 707–22/1308–22)

Raziuddin Aquil

Title: *Fawāʾid al-Fuʾād* (Moral teachings benefiting the heart)
Genre: Religious instruction (*malfūẓāt*, i.e., conversations/discourses/table talk)
Language: Persian

INTRODUCTION

Ḥażrat Khwāja Niẓām al-Dīn Awliyā (d. 1325) belonged to the first cycle of five great Sufi masters of the popular Chishti *silsila* (spiritual lineage) that flourished in the Delhi sultanate in the thirteenth and fourteenth centuries. He was a living legend, and the authorized collection of his conversations, *Fawāʾid al-Fuʾād,* compiled by a close disciple, Amīr Ḥasan Sijzī, over a period of fifteen years was something of a best seller in his own time, coinciding with the reign of Sultan ʿAlāʾ al-Dīn Khaljī (1296–1316), whom Niẓām al-Dīn did not consent to meet, though both Niẓām al-Dīn and Amīr Ḥasan resided in the sultanate's capital of Delhi. Significantly, both Amīr Ḥasan and the shaykh's closest disciple, Amīr Khusraw, were in the service of the sultan, but Niẓām al-Dīn wanted to maintain a critical distance between the political and spiritual domains.

Through his teachings, as shown in *Fawāʾid al-Fuʾād* and also in later hagiographies (*taẕkiras*), especially the well-known collection of biographies *Siyar al-Awliyā,* Niẓām al-Dīn tried to educate his followers in the Sufi way of the cultivation of the heart into the love of God, which was expressed through service to humanity, which in turn was considered the highest form of prayer. In doing so, he, like his Chishti predecessors, was presenting a tolerant and peaceful face of Islam, which sought to bring non-Muslims to the fold of Islam without using force or invoking political power. Thus, even if Sufis like him were not against the conversion of non-Muslims, for them reform within required urgent attention. In their understanding, the dichotomy in the moral integrity of people professing Islam was a more serious matter than was winning new converts.

Offering a face of Islam that was tolerant, accommodating, and peaceful, in addition to singing songs of love and pursuing charitable endeavors, Sufis were able to excel in an environment marked by spiritual competition with holy men of different hues. They attracted large numbers of followers all over the Indian subcontinent, with or without conversion to Islam. As historians have shown, a huge non-Muslim population did embrace Islam through the agency of Sufis over a long period of cultural introduction or accretion in many regions with substantial concentrations of Muslims, as in the Punjab, Deccan, and Bengal.

In the passage translated below, Niẓām al-Dīn is introduced to a Hindu visitor brought to him for the purpose of conversion. Instead of simply offering him the Islamic formula of faith in one God and in Muḥammad as His prophet, the Sufi gives an emotional lecture on the need for the cultivation of the heart to become a good Muslim rather than forcing non-Muslims to accept Islam as a mere formality. This point is illustrated with the story of the arrest of the king of Iraq after the Arab conquest under Caliph ʿUmar. The king refused to convert to Islam even on pain of death, but soon the company of a sincere practicing Muslim of the Sufi kind transformed his heart, so that he himself offered to embrace Islam. The concluding anecdote shows a Jewish neighbor of a prominent Sufi observing that the latter was creating a model of Islam that was difficult to achieve, and at the same time that the general conduct of Muslims appeared repulsive. Conversion to Islam of this kind was considered meaningless.

TEXT

Meanwhile, one of the disciples, a slave, arrived with a Hindu and said that he was [his] brother. When both were seated, the Khwāja (God remember him with His blessings) asked the slave whether his brother had any inclination toward Islam. He replied that it was precisely for this purpose that he had brought him to his service so that by the blessing of his glance he might become a Muslim (*musalmān shawad*). With tears in his eyes, the Khwāja (God remember him with His blessings) remarked that no matter what one says, one cannot change the hearts of these people (*qawm*), but one can hope that through the grace of the company of a pious person, they might become Muslim.

After this, he narrated the following anecdote. When ʿUmar Khaṭṭāb (God be pleased with him) acceded to the caliphate, there was a battle with the king of Iraq in which the king was captured and brought to the presence of ʿUmar. He was told that if he became a Muslim, the country of Iraq would be granted to him alone. The king said he would not embrace Islam (*man islām na khwāham āwarad*). ʿUmar commanded [him to choose] Islam or the sword (*imma al-islām wa-imma al-sayf*); if he did not accept Islam he would be killed. The king declared, "Kill; I will not accept Islam" (*be-kush man islām qabūl na mī-kunam*). ʿUmar ordered [his attendants] to bring the sword and call the executioner.

That king was very clever and wise. Observing the situation, he turned to ʿUmar and requested that he call for some water, as he was thirsty. ʿUmar asked that water be brought. It was brought in a glass vessel. The king said that he would not drink water from that vessel. ʿUmar commanded that since he had been a king, water be brought for him in gold and silver vessels, and this was done. Still not drinking, he asked for water to be brought in a vessel made of clay. A clay pot was filled with water and handed to him. Turning his face toward ʿUmar, he asked him to pledge that he would not be killed till he had drunk the water [from that pot]. ʿUmar committed and promised that he would not kill him till he had consumed the water. The king threw the pot on the ground; the pot was broken and the water spilled. Then he told ʿUmar that as he had not drunk the water, he should follow his promise not to kill him, and he should be pardoned immediately. Amazed at his sagacity, ʿUmar (God be pleased with him) agreed to offer amnesty to him. He was then entrusted to the company of a friend, who was an extremely capable and pious ascetic (*dar ghāyat-i ṣalāḥiyyat o zahādat būd*).

The king of Iraq was taken to the house of that friend. Soon the company of the virtuous man made such an impact on him that he sent a message to ʿUmar that he might be summoned to his presence to profess his faith in Islam. ʿUmar invited him and offered Islam (*ṭalabīd wa islām ʿarż kard*); he became a Muslim (*u musalmān shud*). When he had embraced Islam (*chūn islām āwarad*), ʿUmar (God be pleased with him) said he would now offer the governorship of Iraq to him. The king replied that the governorship was of no use to him [and requested that] instead he might be given a village in the country of Iraq, which should be adequate for his subsistence. When ʿUmar agreed, the king requested that he be granted a desolate village (*dihī kharāb*) so that he could cultivate it to make it habitable (*ābādān kunam*).

ʿUmar sent some people to the region of Iraq. They searched all over Iraq but could not find a single village that was in ruins. ʿUmar apprised the king of the fact that not a single village in Iraq was uninhabited. The king replied that his intention was to confirm that he had handed over a prosperous Iraq to him, and that he would be held answerable on the Day of Judgment (*qiyāmat*) tomorrow if a single village were deserted. Recounting this anecdote (*ḥikāyat*) with tears in his eyes, the Khwāja (God remember him with His blessings) was full of praise for the sagacity and ingeniousness of the king.

On this occasion, commenting on the integrity and honesty of Islam and Muslims (*ṣidq o diyānat*), he narrated the story of a Jew who lived in the neighborhood of Khwāja Bāyazīd Bisṭāmī (may his soul be hallowed). When Khwāja Bāyazīd passed away, [the Jew] was asked why he did not become a Muslim (*chirā musalmān na mī-shawī*). The Jew replied by asking what kind of Muslim they wanted him to become, [adding that] if Islam was what Bāyazīd practiced he would not be able to attain it, and if it were what they [the Muslims] have, he was ashamed of it (*mā rā az īn islām ʿār mī-āyad*).

FURTHER READING

Aquil, Raziuddin. *Lovers of God: Sufism and the Politics of Islam in Medieval India* (New Delhi: Manohar, 2017).

Faruqi, Ziya-ul-Hasan. *Fawa'id al-Fu'ad: Spiritual and Literary Discourses* (New Delhi: DK Printworld, 1996).

Lawrence, Bruce B. *Nizam ad-Din Awliya: Morals for the Heart* (New York: Paulist Press, 1992).

49

A Jurist's Responses to Questions Regarding the Conversion of One Spouse

Ibn Qayyim al-Jawziyya (d. 751/1350)

Antonia Bosanquet

Title: *Aḥkām Ahl al-Dhimma* (Rulings relating to the People of the Covenant of Protection)
Genre: Legal writing
Language: Arabic

INTRODUCTION

Ibn Qayyim al-Jawziyya was a Ḥanbalī theologian and jurist living in Mamluk Damascus. His work, *Aḥkām Ahl al-Dhimma,* is a predominantly legal text that focuses on the Jews and Christians living as permanent subjects under Muslim rule. Their status as *dhimmīs*, or *ahl al-dhimma,* entailed both rights and obligations, many of which are outlined in Ibn Qayyim al-Jawziyya's text. However, the author also discusses other questions relating to daily contact between Muslims and non-Muslims and to the social position of Jews and Christians in a Muslim society.

Damascus under the Mamluks was both culturally and religiously diverse, with a significant non-Muslim population. Although relations were largely harmonious, some texts written broadly around this period reveal Muslim anxieties that certain non-Muslims were acquiring too much political influence or a status higher than that of Muslims. This concern is also reflected in Ibn Qayyim al-Jawziyya's text.

Typically for his treatment of legal discussions in the book, Ibn al-Qayyim structures this passage by summarizing the teaching of earlier legal authorities who would have been well known to his readers. He comments on the teaching of each before moving on to the next view. One of the legal terms that he uses in this passage is the *ʿidda*, which refers to the waiting period that a woman must observe between becoming divorced and remarrying. Usually defined as the length of three menstrual periods, the *ʿidda* is portrayed in parts of this discussion as a period of contemplation for the non-Muslim husband, in which he may decide whether he, too, will convert to Islam or whether he will renounce his claim to his newly Muslim wife.

Ibn al-Qayyim does not mention how many cases of single-spouse conversion he has encountered in his own lifetime, and it is therefore not possible to draw conclusions regarding the prevalence of such conversions on the basis of this text. However, the question is clearly of relevance to its author. In addition to its practical import, discussion of the topic also serves as a springboard for emphasizing the hierarchy of the religions and of man and wife in a marriage. Islam's status as the superior religion makes it incongruent with the subordinate role which Ibn al-Qayyim assigns to the wife in domestic and sexual partnerships. At the same time, he is both sympathetic to the emotional and material difficulties that a separation would entail for the wife and concerned that too strict an interpretation will put both parties off conversion, rather than win new Muslims. His discussion gives an insight into the nexus of interests and concerns that surrounded the issue of conversion, both on the Muslim and on the non-Muslim side.

TEXT

Abū Ḥanīfa [d. 150/767] said, "If they are in the Realm of Islam and one spouse converts to Islam, the spouse who has not converted is given the chance to enter the religion. If they both become Muslims, their marriage continues. And if not, then they are separated with the spouse's conversion. And the *ʿidda* does not need to be observed in this instance."

[. . .] This is one teaching.

[. . .] And if both spouses live in the Realm of War and the woman leaves and comes to us [the Realm of Islam], as a Muslim or as a treaty partner (*muʿāhid*), the separation between them is effective from the moment of her arrival in the Realm of Islam and not before that. And if she does not leave the Realm of War, the separation is effective from the time when she completes three menstrual periods without her husband converting to Islam. Then she begins a waiting period of three menstrual periods, as an *ʿidda*. Does this separation constitute an annulment or a divorce? Abū Ḥanīfa has two teachings on the subject, and Abū Yūsuf [d. 192/798] regards it as an annulment. And if the husband converts before the woman has had three menstrual periods, they remain married. This is a second teaching.

Mālik [d. 179/795] said, "If the wife converts and the husband does not, and intercourse has not yet taken place, the couple is separated. If intercourse has already taken place, and if he converts during her *'idda,* the marriage continues. But if he does not convert before her *'idda* ends, she is separated from him. If the husband converts and the wife does not, she is given the choice of converting to Islam as well. If she becomes a Muslim, the marriage continues as before, and if she refuses, the marriage is annulled from the moment of her refusal, whether sexual intercourse has taken place or not."

And Ashhab [d. 204/819] said, "The separation can be completed more quickly if sexual intercourse has not yet taken place. But if sexual intercourse has already taken place, she must complete the *'idda.*"

[. . .]

There is another teaching from Ibn al-Qāsim [d. 191/806]: that this separation constitutes the second "single divorce statement" [*ṭalqa;* three such "single divorce statements" are required for a divorce to be final]. This is a third teaching.

And Ibn Shubruma [d. 144/761] gave a contradictory teaching: that if the wife converts before her husband, the separation is effective immediately. And if the husband converts before the wife and she converts during her *'idda,* their marriage continues. If not, the separation is effective when the *'idda* has been completed. This is a fourth teaching.

And al-Awzā'ī [d. 157/774] and al-Zuhrī [d. 124/741–42] and al-Layth [d. 175/791] and Imām Aḥmad [d. 241/855] and al-Shāfi'ī [d. 204/820] and Isḥāq [d. 238/853] said that if one partner converts to Islam before the other, and sexual intercourse has not yet taken place, the marriage is annulled. If sexual intercourse has already taken place, and the other spouse also converts during the *'idda,* the marriage continues. But if the husband has not converted by the time that the *'idda* has been completed, the marriage is annulled. This is a fifth teaching.

And Ḥammād b. Salama [d. 167/783] told—on the authority of Ayyūb al-Sakhtiyānī and Qatāda, both of whom recounted it from Muḥammad b. Sīrīn from 'Abd Allāh b. Yazīd al-Khaṭamī—of how a certain Christian's wife converted to Islam. And 'Umar b. al-Khaṭṭāb—God be pleased with him—gave her the choice: if she wished, she could leave him, and if she wished, she could stay with him. 'Abd Allāh b. Yazīd al-Khaṭamī was a companion of the Prophet. This does not mean that she remains subordinate to him while he is a Christian, but that she waits for him, anticipating his conversion. When he converts, she becomes his wife again, even if she has waited for years.

This is a sixth teaching. And it is the most correct of the positions held on this topic, and it is the teaching that is implied by the Sunna, as will be shown shortly. And it is the preference of the Shaykh of Islam, Ibn Taymiyya [d. 728/1328].

And Ḥammād b. Salama said on the authority of Qatāda, who said on the authority of Sa'īd b. al-Musayyab that 'Alī b. Abī Ṭālib—God be pleased with him—said about a married couple of which one spouse converted to Islam, "The husband has the prior claim on her as long as she remains in his home."

And Sufyān b. ʿUyayna [d. 196/811] said on the authority of Muṭarrif b. Ṭarīf on the authority of al-Shaʿbī on the authority of ʿAlī, "He has more right to her if she does not leave her country."

And this is a seventh teaching.

And Ibn Abī Shayba [d. 235/849] said, "Muʿtamar b. Sulaymān told us, on the authority of Muʿammar on the authority of al-Zuhrī, 'If the wife converts and her husband does not convert, they remain married so long as the ruler does not separate them.'" And this is an eighth teaching.

And Dāwūd b. ʿAlī [d. 270/884] said, "If the wife of the *dhimmī* converts but he does not, she may stay with him but he may not have sexual intercourse with her."

Shuʿba [d. 160/776–77] said, "Ḥammād b. Abī Sulaymān [d. 120/737–38] told us, on the authority of Ibrāhīm al-Nakhaʿī, about a *dhimmī* woman who converted while married to a *dhimmī* man. He said, 'She stays with him.' And this is the ruling of Ḥammād b. Abī Sulaymān."

I say, "What they mean is that the contractual obligations of marriage are upheld. The wife is owed her cost of living and the right to live under her husband's roof. But he is not permitted to engage in sexual intercourse with her. It is like the unanimous teaching regarding the slave woman who has a *dhimmī* child when they both convert to Islam." This is a ninth teaching.

Now we will summarize the objections to these teachings and the respective strengths and weaknesses thereof, and consider which teaching is the most correct.

[. . .]

[*Following an analysis of the different approaches to the question, Ibn al-Qayyim concludes that the ninth teaching is the best one. He gives the following explanation and justification:*]

[. . .] If the woman converts first, she has the right to wait for her husband. As soon as he converts, she becomes his wife again. But if the man converts to Islam, he is not permitted to confine his wife in his house and withhold the rights that her marriage contract awards her. He may not force her to convert to Islam, and he may not confine her in his house and he may not oppress her in respect to religion, or in respect to the marriage relation.

However, if the wife chooses to wait for her husband's conversion, she may do so, however long this takes. And if she chooses to marry another man, after her ʿ*idda* has ended, she has the right to do this. The purpose of the ʿ*idda* in this instance is to preserve the sperm of the first husband, and if either party converts to Islam during the ʿ*idda* or after it, the marriage continues. This is unless the man chooses divorce, in which case he may divorce her, as ʿUmar divorced two non-Muslim wives of his when God revealed the verse "Do not hold on to your marriages with unbelieving women" [Q. 60:10]. Or unless the wife chooses to remarry after ascertaining that she is not pregnant by her first husband. She has the right to do this.

Furthermore, this [ruling that the spouse's conversion necessitates immediate separation] discourages conversion to Islam. For if the wife or the husband knows that their marriage will end upon conversion and that they will have to leave their loved one, and that the husband cannot regain his wife except by renegotiating the marriage with her and with her guardian and by offering a new dowry, he or she will eschew conversion. By contrast, if they both know that when the husband converts the marriage can continue, and that they will not be separated unless one of them chooses so, this will draw them toward Islam and endear the religion to them, which makes it more likely that they will convert.

FURTHER READING

Friedmann, Yohanan. *Tolerance and Coercion in Islam: Interfaith Relations in the Muslim Tradition* (Cambridge: Cambridge University Press, 2003).

Simonsohn, Uriel. "Are Gaonic Responsa a Reliable Source for the Study of Jewish Conversion to Islam? A Comparative Analysis of Legal Sources," in *Jews, Christians, and Muslims in Medieval and Early Modern Times: A Festschrift in Honor of Mark R. Cohen*, ed. Arnold Franklin, Marina Rustow, and Roxana Margariti (Leiden: Brill, 2014), 119–38.

50

Anselm Turmeda/ʿAbd Allāh al-Tarjumān: A Former Mallorcan Franciscan in the Service of the Ḥafṣids in North Africa

Anselm Turmeda/ʿAbd Allāh al-Tarjumān (d. ca. 827–33/1424–30)

Clint Hackenburg

Title: *Tuḥfat al-Adīb fī al-Radd ʿalā Ahl al-Ṣalīb* (The cultured man's gift, in refutation of the people of the cross)
Genre: Religious instruction (conversion narrative, polemics)
Language: Arabic

INTRODUCTION

Anselm Turmeda was born around the year 1352 in Mallorca, where as early as the age of six he began his formal study of the Gospels. Over the course of the next three decades, Anselm's studies took him to Lleida, Paris, and Bologna. By 1375, Anselm had taken his Franciscan vows, and in 1379 he was ordained a deacon in the Palma Cathedral. According to his autobiography, while studying in Bologna he met Nicolau Martello (possibly Nicola da Moimacco, d. 1395), a mysterious priest who harbored hidden knowledge of the Gospels, Muḥammad, and God's true religion. He revealed the true identity of the Paraclete found in the Gospel of John (John 14:15, 25; 15:26; and 16:7–15) and encouraged Anselm to convert to Islam and journey to Muslim lands. Heeding the advice of his elderly mentor, Anselm left Bologna and traveled home to Mallorca; from there he set sail, first to Sicily and then to Tunis, arriving around 1387. It is worth noting that the archetype of the heterodox clergyman or monk, privy to secret information regarding Muḥammad's prophetic office, is found in the earliest Muslim literature in the figures of Waraqa

b. Nawfal and the monk Baḥīrā. Furthermore, given that this literary convention continued well into the Ottoman period, the narrative surrounding this Bolognese priest should be read with caution.

Once settled in Tunis, Anselm requested an audience with the Ḥafṣid ruler, Abū al-ʿAbbās Aḥmad (r. 1370–94), and, in the presence of both Christian and Muslim witnesses, recited the *shahāda* and adopted the name ʿAbd Allāh al-Tarjumān. Shortly after, Anselm/ʿAbd Allāh married, fathered several children, and began working as an official and translator for maritime customs under the Ḥafṣids. He also served intermittently as a personal translator and financier to the Ḥafṣid rulers, most notably during the 1390 Franco-Genoese siege of Mahdia.

During the course of his life, Anselm/ʿAbd Allāh authored several works in Catalan: *Libre de bons amonestaments* (Book of good advice), *Cobles de la divisió del regne de Mallorques* (Stanzas on the division of the kingdom of Mallorca), *Profecies* (Prophecies), and *Disputa de l'ase contra Frare Anselm Turmeda sobre la natura y noblesa dels animals* (Dispute of the donkey against Brother Anselm Turmeda about the nature and nobility of animals). However, the *Tuḥfat al-Adīb fī al-Radd ʿalā Ahl al-Ṣalīb* (The cultured man's gift, in refutation of the people of the cross), which details his religious metamorphosis, was his only Arabic work. The *Tuḥfa* is divided into three parts: (1) a concise autobiographical recollection of his conversion to Islam; (2) a slightly longer commendation of the Ḥafṣid rulers, Abū al-ʿAbbās Aḥmad and his son, Abū Fāris ʿAbd al-ʿAzīz (r. 1394–1434), in which Anselm emphasizes his dedication to the Ḥafṣids and Islam; and (3) a much lengthier polemic against Christianity, replete with scripture-based attacks on the doctrines of the Trinity and Incarnation as well as overt accusations challenging the transmission and integrity of the Gospels. An English translation of part 1 of the *Tuḥfa* can be found in Dwight F. Reynolds's *Interpreting the Self: Autobiography in the Arabic Literary Tradition.*

It must be noted that neither the life nor the works of this former Franciscan are without controversy, given that Anselm/ʿAbd Allāh allegedly penned his Catalan works after his conversion to Islam. In the Catalan works, in direct contrast to his Arabic autobiography, Anselm/ʿAbd Allāh defends the integrity of the Gospels and praises Christian doctrine and the Catholic Church. Moreover, the final, polemical portion of the *Tuḥfa* abounds with rather unconventional descriptions of certain Christian practices and frequent inaccurate citations of biblical verses. The second part of the *Tuḥfa* even contains a later Muslim interpolation in which a Sicilian priest describes God as "the third of three," a phrase found in the Qurʾān (5:73). These unmistakable inconsistencies have caused certain scholars to call into question the authenticity and authorship of significant portions of Anselm/ʿAbd Allāh's story of conversion to Islam and refutation of Christianity. A partial English translation of his account of his life under the Ḥafṣids, which not only sheds light on the interconnectedness of the medieval Mediterranean but also describes the efforts made by coreligionists to recover and reconvert lost souls, can be found below.

TEXT

Concerning that which happened to me in the days of our protector Abū al-ʿAbbās, and his son, our protector Abū Fāris ʿAbd al-ʿAzīz:

Five months after my conversion to Islam, the sultan placed me in charge of maritime affairs and customs. His intention in doing so was that I would learn the Arabic language, given the repeated opportunities for me to serve as a translator between the Christians and the Muslims. As a result, I learned the entirety of the Arabic language over the course of one year. Accordingly, when the Genoese and the French laid siege to the city of Mahdia, I translated their messages for the sultan. In due course God stifled them, and they subsequently dispersed, defeated. Later, I traveled with the sultan to the siege of Gabès, where I was assigned to oversee his treasury. I then traveled to the siege of Gafṣa, and it was there that his fatal sickness began. He died in the month of Shaʿbān in the year 796 [1394 CE].

After his death, the succession was entrusted to his son, our protector, Commander of the Faithful and Defender of Islam, Abū Fāris ʿAbd al-ʿAzīz. He renewed all of the duties bestowed upon me by his father, along with all of my customary payments and benefits. Additionally, he commissioned me to manage royal expenditures. It was during the days of his reign, while I was an official of maritime customs and translation, that a Muslim merchant vessel loaded with goods approached. When it anchored at al-Marsā, two vessels from Sicily attacked it, and once the Muslims had fled with their captain, the Christians commandeered their goods.

Subsequently our protector Abū Fāris ordered an official representative of customs to embark for Ḥalq al-Wādī [La Goulette] along with witnesses and negotiate with the Christians in order to ransom the goods belonging to the Muslims. When they arrived, they requested safe conduct for the translator who was with them. Once they granted him safe conduct, he climbed aboard their vessel and spoke with them regarding the ransoming of their goods, but although they conferred about the matter, nothing came of it.

On this vessel there was a priest of great esteem in Sicily with whom I had shared a great friendship and whom I had regarded as a brother while we were studying together. He had heard of my conversion to Islam, and it weighed heavy on him. He had journeyed with this vessel in order to encourage me to return to Christianity, relying on the friendship which had existed between us. When he met the translator who had come aboard the ship, he said, "What is your name?" The man said to him, "ʿAlī." He said, "ʿAlī, take this letter to ʿAbd Allāh, your official of maritime affairs and customs. Here is a dinar, and when you have brought me his response, I will give you another dinar."

Therefore, he took the dinar and the letter from him and went to Ḥalq al-Wādī, where he apprised the chief of customs of everything that the Christians had told him. He then reported what the priest had told him and presented the letter which he had given him and the dinar which he had paid him. Afterward, the chief of customs took the letter and had several Genoese merchants translate it for him. Next, he sent the original letter and the translated copy to our protector Abū Fāris, who read it.

He later called upon me, and when I was in his presence, he said to me, "ʿAbd Allāh, this letter has arrived by sea. Read it and tell us what is in it." Therefore I read it, and I laughed. He said to me, "What are you laughing at?" I said to him, "God grant you victory! This letter has been sent to me by a priest who was one of my friends. I will translate it for you now." I sat down beside him and translated it into Arabic; then I handed the translation to him, and he read it. He then told his brother Ismāʿīl, "By God, he has not omitted a letter." I said to him, "My lord, how could you know that?" He said, "From the other copy that the Genoese have translated for us." Then he said to me, "ʿAbd Allāh, what answer do you have for this priest?" I told him, "Lord, you know that I converted to Islam of my own free will and in search of the true faith. I will not comply with anything that he proposes."

He said to me, "We know the sincerity of your conversion to Islam, and we have no doubt about it, but war is treacherous; therefore, in your response, write that the captain of the ship should ransom the Muslim merchants' goods at an acceptable price. Next tell him, 'Once you [Christians] and the Muslims have agreed on a negotiated price, I [i.e., ʿAbd Allāh] will go out with the appraiser to determine the weight of the goods. Afterward, I will escape to you in the night.'" I did what he ordered me to do: I answered the priest with this reply. As a result, the priest rejoiced and they lowered the price of the ransom for the Muslims' merchandise. However, when the appraiser came out, I did not come out with him. Saddened by my actions, he readied his vessel and set sail.

Here is the text of his letter: "Peace be upon you from your brother Francis, the priest. I would like to inform you that I have come to this land on your behalf in order to bring you back with me to Sicily. I am currently in the service of the ruler of Sicily, with sufficient rank to dismiss and appoint, grant and forbid. All of the affairs of his kingdom are carried out by my hand. Listen to me and come with me toward the blessing of God. Do not fear losing wealth, status, or similar worldly things, for I have sufficient wealth and stature, and I will do whatever you want. Therefore, do not be deceived by any matters of this world, for they are ephemeral. Life is short, and God is on the watch. Fear God and repent to him, abandon the darkness of Islam and come to the light of Christianity. Acknowledge that God is the third of three in His sovereignty, and that there is no way to separate what God has united to Himself. Regarding all of these matters, I know that you know things that I do not. Nevertheless, I remind you of all this because the reminder benefits those who believe in the Trinity, who is God. Awake from the slumber of neglect. Send an answer to my letter and come join me. A man like you does not need a teacher. Peace."

FURTHER READING

Gugel, David. "Moor or Mallorquín? Anselm Turmeda's Ambiguous Identity in the *Cobles de la Divisió del Regne de Mallorca*," in *Self-Fashioning and Assumptions of Identity in Medieval and Early Modern Iberia*, ed. Laura Delbrugge (Leiden: Brill, 2015), 79–115.

Reynolds, Dwight F., ed. *Interpreting the Self: Autobiography in the Arabic Literary Tradition* (Berkeley: University of California Press, 2001).

Szpiech, Ryan. *Conversion and Narrative: Reading and Religious Authority in Medieval Polemic* (Philadelphia: University of Pennsylvania Press, 2013).

Thomas, David. "Conversion out of Personal Principle: ʿAli b. Rabban al-Tabari (d. c. 860) and ʿAbdallah al-Tarjuman (d. c. 1430), Two Converts from Christianity to Islam," in *Islamisation: Comparative Perspectives from History*, ed. A.C.S. Peacock (Edinburgh: Edinburgh University Press, 2017), 56–68.

51

Three Stories of Conversion from the Life of Sayyid Aḥmad Bashīrī, a Sufi of Timurid Central Asia

Anonymous, or Nāṣir b. Qāsim b. Ḥājjī Muḥammad Turkistānī Farghāna'ī (ninth/fifteenth century)

Devin DeWeese

Title: *Hasht Ḥadīqa* (Eight gardens) or *Ḥadā'iq al-Jinān* (Gardens of paradise)
Genre: Religious instruction (hagiography)
Language: Persian

INTRODUCTION

The three accounts of conversion presented here are all drawn from a single Persian hagiographical work written in the fifteenth century in Central Asia; the work survives in two manuscripts, representing slightly different recensions (one names the author, the other does not, and the titles given in the two copies differ). The subject of the work is a rural Sufi master called Sayyid Aḥmad Bashīrī, and one of his disciples was the compiler of the work. Sayyid Aḥmad Bashīrī is explicitly identified in the work as an Uvaysī, that is, a saint trained in spiritual fashion by the spirit of a deceased saint or prophet, not by a living teacher in a standard mode of Sufi initiatic and instructional transmission. The author is thus quite sensitive to criticism of his master for lacking direct training and initiation by a living master, and so he employs diverse strategies to legitimize him. Not unexpectedly, showing his master's prowess in bringing about conversion to Islam in the context of broad social groups—nomadic Turks, brought into Central Asia in the course of the Mongol conquest of the thirteenth century—that were still wholly or partly unassimilated to Muslim society is among these strategies.

In geographical terms, Sayyid Aḥmad Bashīrī's life and Sufi career unfolded in the region to the south and east of Samarqand (near the modern border between Uzbekistan and Tajikistan) in the later fourteenth century and the first half of the fifteenth; the author tells us that Sayyid Aḥmad Bashīrī's ancestors had come to that region from "Khiṭāy" (a term most likely referring, in this context, to Eastern Turkistan) in the time of the Chaghatayid ruler Qazān Sulṭān Khān (a son of Yasavur, known as a convert to Islam) in the mid-1340s. Sayyid Aḥmad Bashīrī is shown traveling to Samarqand, and once as far as Tashkent, but for the most part his sphere of activity was quite restricted; nevertheless, the work pays considerable attention to the many disciples who made up Sayyid Aḥmad's Sufi circle and who bear a wide range of Turkic and Persian names.

Of the three passages presented here, two (2 and 3) have been translated and discussed in a recent article; the other (1) has not been published or discussed elsewhere.

(1) The first passage involves Sayyid Aḥmad's intervention to convert, and thereby save the life of, a Christian Arab who is said to have come to the court of the Timurid ruler Ulugh Beg in Samarqand and to have disputed with the scholars there; neither the Muslim scholars at Ulugh Beg's court nor the more solicitous host of Sayyid Aḥmad in Shahrisabz could convince the Christian to adopt Islam, but Sayyid Aḥmad is able to induce the Prophet himself to appear to the man and thus win him over. Of interest is the author's insistence, at the end of the story, that no one present knew how or why the man's conversion had occurred; it is thus presented not as a "public" demonstration of Sayyid Aḥmad's power or effectiveness but as one confided to the author and, by extension, to the reader or hearer of this hagiographical tale. Sayyid Aḥmad's ability, in hidden, interior fashion, to accomplish what others could not further underscores the distinctive religious profile of Sayyid Aḥmad himself, whose spiritual training resembled the conversion of this Christian in having been effected by the direct intervention of the Prophet, without the involvement of other human beings. The account nevertheless hints at the mutability of religious boundaries and suggests that threats and coercion may be less effective in altering those boundaries than are compassion and "behind-the-scenes" influence.

(2) The second passage is remarkable for its handling of the status of the subject, Mawlānā Khiṭāyī: he is a Muslim from birth, despite his birth in an infidel community; he is educated and raised as a Muslim, by Muslims; and he is then rescued from death for being a Muslim by a female religious specialist who serves his idol-worshipping community but who is nevertheless envisioned as, in effect, an agent of the Prophet (and indeed, evidently, as in his company). Once again there is common ground between this "inner" story of Mawlānā Khiṭāyī and the ways in which he was recognized as a Muslim, on the one hand, and the story of his eventual master, Sayyid Aḥmad Bashīrī (who, the author of the work asserts,

was a *sayyid* without actually being a descendant of the Prophet, was trained by the spirit of the Prophet, and was the rightful successor to a host of Central Asian Sufi shaykhs despite never having met them in the flesh), on the other. Also of interest is the depiction of the idol-worshipping community: though the term used (*but-parast*) is most often applied in Central Asian sources to Buddhists, the rites ascribed to these infidels suggest that the term refers here to the indigenous pre-Islamic religion of the nomadic Turks.

(3) The story of the Moghūl woman, Bakht-Sulṭān, invokes the image of enslavement, in this case of an infidel—the Moghūls are assumed to be infidels in this work, and Moghūlistān is envisioned as lying outside the Dār al-Islām—taken captive by Muslim raiders. The account shows the experience, or imagination, of this woman—an outsider, marked by dress and speech as an infidel—of being snared and taken toward Samarqand and, presumably, its slave markets, and then her different reception at the dervish lodge, where the caretaker calls her his sister and offers her lodging. The account suggests the social disruptions experienced by nomadic communities in this era, and the opportunities that some in the Muslim community found, amid such social stress, to draw these groups closer to Muslim society. Though it, too, features dreams and visions, the common currency of Sufi hagiographies in this era, this story differs from the first two in not portraying the convert's attachment to the Muslim community as the result of a miraculous intervention.

TEXT

(1) It is related from his eminent holiness of good conduct (God hallow his soul) [i.e., Sayyid Aḥmad Bashīrī] that he said, "Once I had gone to meet with the notables of the district of Kesh. At the time when I was in the presence of Shāh Zāhid (mercy be upon him), a disturbance arose; a group of scholars and notables was also present, and the monitors of public morals (*muḥtasibs*) of Samarqand brought in a man who had been bound by the neck and dragged through the mud. Shāh Zāhid (mercy be upon him) said, 'Free his hands.' They did so. He asked what the story was. They replied, 'This man is a Christian who has come from Arabia (*ʿarabistān*), bringing with him the book of the Gospels (*injīl*); he engaged in disputation and argument with the learned men of Samarqand, in the presence of Mīrzā Ulugh Beg, but did not adopt the faith (*īmān nayāvarda*). The notables issued a *fatwā* [saying] that he should be killed. His highness the Mīrzā said, "It would be a shame to kill a scholar of this sort. Take him to the district of Kesh, to Shāh Zāhid, for he is a fair man; perhaps [the Christian] will accept his counsel and adopt the faith."'

"After a while his eminence Shāh Zāhid began to offer him advice; but the Christian adopted a disputatious stance and did not accept. In the end Shāh Zāhid (mercy be upon him) said, 'Christian, you are endangering your life. What you are speaking about is judgments based on the commands of the Gospel, namely that only the holy ʿĪsā [Jesus] (salutations and peace be upon him) is true; but nowadays the authority and mysteries of the Qurʾān are in effect. It would be better if you would adopt the faith.' The Christian said, 'As long as I do not see from your prophet (who is the holy Muḥammad Muṣṭafā, God bless him and keep him) what I have seen from my prophet, I will not adopt your faith.'"

His holiness, the eminent shaykh of good [conduct] (God hallow his soul), said, "When I heard these words from that Christian, compassion came over me, and I understood that his aim was the truth. So I appealed, in interior fashion, to the spirit of the holy Prophet (God bless him and keep him), and the Prophet came and stood above the head of that Christian, just as Shāh Zāhid and everyone else were left powerless and silent in the face of the Christian's words. All of a sudden, the Christian said, 'Now I will adopt the faith; I have understood that the religion of the holy Muḥammad Muṣṭafā (God bless him and keep him) is true.' At once he adopted the faith; Shāh Zāhid (mercy be upon him) and all the notables took him aside and put the rings [of servitude to God] on him (*ḥalqahā pūshānīda-and*). However, neither Shāh Zāhid nor that Christian nor the others present knew where this happy outcome (*tawfīq*) came from or what the reason for this good fortune (*dawlat*) was."

(2) It is related that the holy shaykh had a disciple named Mawlānā Khiṭāyī; he was by origin the son of the ruler and prince (*ḥākim va amīr-zāda*) of Qarā-khwāja, near the province (*vilāyat*) of Khiṭāy. They say that when he was born, he was afflicted with stomach pain; however much they tried to treat it and alleviate [the pain], it did no good. Finally they gave him into the care of a slave girl who was to look after him; she would constantly go about, carrying him. One day she took him to some merchants; that group was cooking food and gave him a bowl of it. The infant was inclined to eat it, and when he did eat some, his stomach pain disappeared and he regained his health. His father and mother were happy, and they cooked the same kind of food and gave it to him, but his stomach pain came back. Whenever he would eat the food of the merchants and Muslims, he would get better; from his parents' food he would get sick. In this situation, they saw no recourse other than to "rent" him as a son to one of the Muslim merchants. He taught [the child] the Qurʾān and instructed him in the ways of the faithful.

When he was seven years old, his father died. His paternal and maternal uncles told him, "Turn away from Islam and enter the religion of your own ancestors" (*az musulmānī bar-gard va bar dīn-i padarān-i khūd dar-āy*). He did not consent and did not turn away from Islam (*ū rāżī nashuda va az musulmānī bar-nagashta*). They took him before their idols and, acting in accordance with their customs and code, they cut pieces from the flesh of that faithful and trustworthy son, and placed them before their idols. Despite all this cruelty and torment, he did not turn away from the religion of Muḥammad, the Prophet of God, and they left him alone. He went [back] to his Muslim father; [but] after a few more years they took him again, [saying,] "Turn away from Islam and prostrate yourself to the idol (*but-rā sijda kun*)."

He uttered a hundred thousand curses upon the idol and the idol-worshippers, living and dead; after this, they sentenced him to be killed.

They bound his hands and his neck and led him to the side of a public road, intending to hang him from a tree. At that moment an old woman, who was the *shaykh* and guide (*pīshvā*) of the infidels, arrived and asked the reason for the killing of this young man. They laid out the whole story, from beginning to end, to her, and she said, "This young man was by origin born a Muslim; this sentence [of death] is for a person who has turned away from the idol and become a Muslim. Killing him is not proper." She took him from that group, brought him to her home, and sent him off with a caravan group to the lands of Islam.

It is related that Mawlānā Khiṭāyī (mercy be upon him) used to say, "When those infidels took me to the base of the tree and cast the rope around my neck, a wondrous state came over me. During it, I saw that a young man with a black beard, mounted on a white horse, wearing a shirt made of camel wool, and with a fur cap placed on his head, appeared and said, 'Son, do not fear, for behold, the holy Prophet has come to set you free!' Just then two other riders appeared, [one] with a *burqaʿ* in front of her face and [one with] a white turban atop his head; they were extremely majestic and awe-inspiring, and they stood above my head. I was busy staring at them when that woman freed me, and then those holy figures disappeared.

"Afterward I went with a caravan and came to Samarqand; wherever I would hear of a holy man, I would serve him, and I kept searching for that black-bearded young man who had said to me, 'Son,' crying and weeping just like a child who has lost his father. Though I entered the company of many shaykhs, such as Mawlānā Musāfir and Khwāja ʿUbayd Allāh and Shaykh Khādim and others, my mind nevertheless found no repose. One day I was at the public market center of Samarqand, and a horseman appeared whose head and beard and horse and shirt and cap were just of the kind that I had seen; as soon as I saw him, I recognized him, and I followed after him. He went inside a certain house, and I said to myself, 'I have found what I was searching for.' I waited at that same house, and the holy shaykh asked me about myself and my circumstances. I told him of my adventures, and he showed mercy to me and accepted me into his service."

They say that Mawlānā Khiṭāyī achieved exalted stations in the service and company of the holy shaykh; he had undertaken intense austerities, [but] he had the nature of one automatically "drawn" toward God, and was like God's "hidden saints" (*majdhūb-shiʿār va abdāl-vash*).

(3) It is related that there was a woman in Moghūlistān named Bakht-Sulṭān. She said, "Discord arose among the Moghūls, and so I came to Andijān; but there, too, events happened such that I [came to] the province (*vilāyat*) of Samarqand and stayed with a group of people (*jamāʿa*) in the steppe (*ṣaḥrāyī*) near Shīrāz. One day I left my home and was heading in a certain direction when suddenly [there appeared] a man on a white horse, and another man on foot, with a pale face and wearing a woolen

shirt, running by the stirrups of that other man. The mounted man had a wooden stick, with a cord made of greenish silk at its end, which they call *uqrūq* [i.e., lasso] in Turkic; he threw it around my neck and set off leading me toward Samarqand. I went for part of the way, and then collapsed and lost consciousness.

"When I came to myself, I saw that I had fallen with my head lying in the direction of Samarqand; when I came home, my condition changed, and I was constantly weeping, longing for that mounted man. In this condition I stayed for some time in Samarqand; a great agitation appeared in my heart and soul, and I was constantly restless (*bī-qarār*). One day, as if mad (*dīvāna-vār*), I went out of the city and started off in some direction; I did not know at all where I wanted to go. Taking the main road, and weeping and crying, I came to Miṣr by the time of the afternoon prayer (*namāz-i dīgar*). I asked if there was someone who would give a poor stranger a place to stay, and someone said, 'There is a square here, and a Sufi hostel (*khānqāh*) [nearby], and a dervish who serves travelers; go there.' When I went there, that dervish gave me a place to stay, and called me his sister. I stayed there for some time, and I told him my situation; I told him all about my longing for that handsome horseman, and about what I had experienced. One day I was in the courtyard of the hostel when a horseman and a man on foot, just as I had seen, came in; I recognized them, and I told the caretaker (*mujāvir*). When the caretaker looked, he said, 'The man that you saw is our great shaykh,' and he ran before him to offer service. Then when he found an opportunity, he presented my situation to the great shaykh, and [the shaykh] was merciful to me and showed me kindness; he sent me to the hostel, and from that time on I was engaged in service at the hostel."

There are many stories of this sort; were I to undertake writing about all of them, [the book] would become long and drawn out. In short, people were coming to [the shaykh], drawn from all parts of the world, and becoming his disciples (*murīd*), choosing servitude [to him] (God have mercy upon them).

FURTHER READING

Bashir, Shahzad. *Sufi Bodies: Religion and Society in Medieval Islam* (New York: Columbia University Press, 2011).

DeWeese, Devin. "Muslims and Infidel Nomads in Timurid Central Asia: Four Stories from the Religious Frontiers of Mawarannahr in the 14th and 15th Centuries," in *Central Eurasia in the Middle Ages: Studies in Honour of Peter B. Golden*, ed. István Zimonyi and Osman Karatay (Wiesbaden: Harrassowitz, 2016), 91–102 [texts 2 and 3; used with permission of the copyright holder, Devin DeWeese].

———. *An "Uvaysī" Sufi in Timurid Mawarannahr: Notes on Hagiography and the Taxonomy of Sanctity in the Religious History of Central Asia* (Bloomington: Indiana University, Research Institute for Inner Asian Studies, 1993). Reprinted in DeWeese, *Studies on Sufism in Central Asia* (Farnham: Ashgate, 2012), no. 4.

52

The Conversion of the Kingdom of Pasai, Indonesia

Anonymous

Alexander Wain

Title: *Hikayat Raja Pasai* (The chronicle of the Pasai kings)
Genre: Historical writing (court chronicle)
Language: Malay

INTRODUCTION

The Malay-language *Hikayat Raja Pasai* (*HRP*) is an anonymous, late fourteenth- to early fifteenth-century court chronicle produced in Pasai (or Samudera-Pasai), a premodern Islamic kingdom once located in the Acehnese region of northern Sumatra, modern-day Indonesia. Its conversion narrative is rooted in events of the late thirteenth century, when centuries-long commercial interaction between Southeast Asia's indigenous population and Muslims from the Middle East, India, and China culminated in the conversion of several regional entrepôts, for whom embracing Islam was a means of gaining material advantage via the facilitation of trade. Pasai was an early example of such a kingdom, although perhaps not, as the text claims, the first.

The author (or authors) of the *HRP* labels its conversion account *hikayat cerit-era,* a hybrid Arabic-Malay phrase meaning "legend" or "romance." This term guides our reading of the text: rather than straightforward history, it constitutes a heavily mythologized narrative created with the intention of legitimizing the authority of Pasai's ruling elite via an appropriation of sacred power. As elsewhere in the premodern world, in Pasai the rulers grounded their authority in traditional conceptions of the sacred; the purpose of the *HRP* conversion account is to establish that grounding, which it does in two ways. First, the account utilizes earlier Sumatran legends founded in the Hindu-Buddhist tradition to accord divine ancestry to Pasai's first Muslim ruler, Merah Silau. His parents are therefore identified as the semidivine Puteri Betung ("the Bamboo Princess," a figure derived from the tenth-century, Buddhist-tinged Japanese folktale *Taketori Monogatari,* "The tale of the bamboo cutter") and Merah Gajah ("the Elephant Chief," a Hindu figure from the eleventh-century Indian text *Karthasaritsagara,* "Ocean of the stream of stories"). Second, the text binds Pasai's rulers to the divine authority of Islam by tracing Merah Silau's conversion to direct intercession from the Prophet Muḥammad. This final section constitutes an excellent example of what Mimi Hanaoka terms "centering the periphery," when Muslims on the fringes of the Islamic world insert themselves into the heart of the Islamic tradition by claiming possession of divine relics, contact with the Prophet's companions, or (in this instance) visions of the Prophet Muḥammad.

While for many modern observers claims of divine ancestry rooted in Hindu-Buddhist mythology might seem incompatible with an Islamic worldview, for the rulers of Pasai, embracing Islam created a need to reestablish their divine authority by entrenching their new religion within preexisting and deeply rooted Southeast Asian conceptions of the sacred. The *HRP*'s version of the Merah Gajah story amply demonstrates this. In addition to the story's provision of Arabic names for its apparently non-Muslim protagonists, the old man whom Raja Ahmad encounters in the jungle resides in a *surau* (Muslim prayer hall), greets Raja Ahmad with *salam,* and finally disappears mysteriously, for which the Arabic-derived word *ghaib* is used, implying supernatural occultation. Islamic identity markers are therefore combined with an old Hindu tradition not merely to "Islamize" the latter but to co-opt the sacred power of both traditions simultaneously. This syncretic approach aptly characterizes the *HRP* conversion narrative as a whole.

TEXT

This is the legend (*hikayat ceritera*) of the first king to embrace Islam in Pasai. According to those who possess this story, of all the nations beneath the winds, Pasai was the first to have faith in God and His Messenger.

There were once two kings who were brothers, one named Raja Ahmad and the other named Raja Muhammad, of whom Raja Ahmad was the elder. Together these two brothers wanted to establish a country in Samarlanga.

Accordingly, Raja Muhammad traveled out, with all his people slashing through the jungle. When they reached the heart of the forest, they encountered a bamboo thicket too dense to cut through; slash though all the people might, it would not diminish. Only when the king himself began to hack at the bamboo did it begin to clear. In the midst of the bamboo, Raja Muhammad espied a stem larger than all the others; when he struck it, out came a girl of most pleasing countenance. Throwing away his sword, Raja Muhammad immediately picked the infant up and, cradling her in his arms, brought her back to his residence. . . . Then Raja Muhammad informed his brother from beginning to end of how he had found the child in a bamboo stem. Because of this, Raja Muhammad named her Puteri Betung [the Bamboo Princess]. From that point on, she became the adopted daughter of the king, with handmaidens and garments in full measure. . . .

After an interval, Raja Ahmad also established a country in Balik Rimba, several days' journey from the country of his brother. . . . When some time had gone by, Raja Ahmad went hunting in the wildest part of the jungle, but could find nothing to kill. Instead, in the midst of the wild, he came across a prayer hall (*surau*). Inside was an old man. Raja Ahmad greeted (*memberi salam*) this old man, who immediately returned his salutation (*disahutinya salam*). Then Raja Ahmad began to tell the old man of how his brother had found a princess in a bamboo stem. Said the old man, "Ah, my son, if you wish a child, then I will show him to you. Wait here a moment, sire." So Raja Ahmad waited. After a short while, there arrived a large elephant with a boy sitting on its head. The elephant washed the boy in the river. After it had finished, it carried the boy back to the riverbank, before descending again to wash itself. When it, too, had finished bathing, it placed the boy back on its head and carried him into the jungle. . . . Said the old man, "O my son, you must devise a stratagem so that we might obtain this boy." Said Raja Ahmad, "My father, if gold or jewels were shown to me, or if I were given them, I would desire nothing more than this child. . . . "

[After returning to his kingdom] Raja Ahmad, with all his soldiers, returned to the jungle, to where the elephant had bathed the child, only to find that the old man had mysteriously disappeared (*ghaiblah*) along with his prayer hall, no trace of either being apparent. Then, on the Thursday, all the people began digging a hiding place in the ground from which to capture the child. When Friday arrived, out came the elephant from the jungle carrying the child, to bathe him in the river, in the same spot as before. After it arrived at the river, the elephant bathed the child; when it had finished, it carried the child to the riverbank, before descending again to bathe itself. At that moment Raja Ahmad quickly snatched the child and carried him away. When the elephant saw this, it stormed after Raja Ahmad until the soldiers drove it away. . . .

Raja Ahmad then traveled back to his country with all his soldiers. When he arrived at his palace, his wife stood at the gate to welcome him. When she saw the child, she immediately took him from Raja Ahmad. Both Raja Ahmad and his wife were very pleased to see the goodly appearance of the child. They named him Merah Gajah [the Elephant Chief]. . . . After a long time had gone by, the two children [Merah Gajah and Puteri Betung] grew up. Then Merah Gajah married Puteri Betung. . . .

According to the legend of Puteri Betung and Merah Gajah, as told by those who possess it, after a period of time spent together as man and wife, by the will of God ([*subhanahu wa-*]*taala*), Puteri Betung became pregnant; when she completed her term, she gave birth to a boy. They called him Merah Silau. . . .

Later [when he reached maturity], Merah Silau traveled in search of a place to reside, eventually going upstream to Hulu Semenda. Arriving in a country called Buluh Telang, he met with Megat Sekandar, who entertained him with food and drink. Once the entertainment had ended, Megat Sekandar said to Merah Silau, "What would my lord ask of me?" Said Merah Silau, "As to why I have come to you, my lord, I wish to ask for a place to stay, as currently I have nowhere to live." Then said Megat Sekandar, "If that is so, surely you must stay here with me; if the paddy fields remain wide, and the buffalos good, there will be plenty to eat." Merah Silau said, "If you have mercy on me, I will treat you like my own father. . . . "

As for Megat Sekandar and [his brother] Megat Kedah, these two were brothers of Sultan Malikul Nasir of Rimba Jerana; and all [their] people loved Merah Silau [because of his largess]. . . . Then arrived a day of consultation between Megat Sekandar and all the nobles and all the elders and all the people of that country. Said Megat Sekandar, "O my lords, what shall we discuss concerning Merah Silau? I say that we make him our king. He is certainly ready to be so and, what is more, very wealthy; doing so will bind us to him." . . . So all the people agreed with Megat Sekandar to make Merah Silau king.

After he had become king, Merah Silau became the enemy of Sultan Malikul Nasir of Rimba Jerana, going to war with him. Finally [after several battles], Merah Silau triumphed, defeating Sultan Malikul Nasir. . . . After that, Megat Sekandar made Merah Silau king of Rimba Jerana.

It is said by those who possess this story that long ago the Prophet Muhammad, the Messenger of God (*salla Llahu ʿalayhi wa sallam*), when he still lived, said to his companions in Mecca, "After I have died, there will be a nation from beneath the winds, called Samudera. When you have news of this nation, dispatch a ship with the royal regalia and bring its people into Islam. Thereafter Allah (*subhanahu wa taala*) will cause many God-fearing Muslims to arise there. But first there shall be a *fakir* in the land called Mengiri [also read as Maʿabri]; take him with you to Samudera."

As has been said, Merah Silau was in Rimba Jerana. One day he went out hunting. Accompanying the hunt was a dog, named Si Pasai. When Merah Silau released this dog, it began barking atop some high ground; there Merah Silau espied an ant as big as a cat. Merah Silau captured this ant and ate it, later ordering his people to clear the high ground. There he built his palace; when it was completed, he resided in it, with all his warriors and people settling there. Merah Silau named this country Samudera, meaning "the giant ant," and he dwelled there as king.

A long time after the Prophet (*salla Llahu ʿalayhi wa sallam*) passed away, news reached the Syarif of Mecca of a nation from beneath the winds called Samudera; the Khalifah Syarif therefore ordered a ship to convey the royal regalia there. When the ship was duly prepared, [its captain] Syarif Syeikh Ismail was ordered to [first] visit the country of Mengiri. Once all was ready, Syeikh Ismail boarded the ship and set sail. After a long time traveling upon the sea, he arrived at the country of Mengiri, anchoring in its bay. The king of that country was called Sultan Muhammad. A man of Mengiri, chancing to see the anchored ship in the bay, immediately entered the presence of the said king, paid due reverence and said, "My lord, king of the world (*shah alam*), a ship has anchored in our harbor." Sultan Muhammad therefore said to his prime minister, "O prime minister, inspect this ship!" So the prime minster went out, ordering one of the boat people to inspect the vessel. When this man's boat reached the ship, he proceeded to ask, "From whence does this ship come and what is the name of your captain and to where do you want to go?" Replied a crewman, "This ship is from Mecca and the name of our captain is Syeikh Ismail, who was ordered by the Khalifah Syarif of Mecca to go to a nation called Samudera." When the boatman heard this news, he returned to land and went to the prime minister, repeating what the crewman had said. Then the prime minister entered the presence of the king, paid due reverence and said, "O my lord, king of the world, the ship is from Mecca, the name of its captain is Syeikh Ismail, and it wishes to travel to the country of Samudera."

Concerning Sultan Muhammad, he was a descendant of Abu Bakar al-Siddiq (*radia Llahu anhu*). He ordered the sending of supplies and other bountiful items to Syeikh Ismail. Once these had arrived, the sultan appointed his eldest son as regent over the nation of Mengiri. With the younger of his two sons, he then donned the mantle of an ascetic and left his kingdom, going down from his palace to board the ship. He said to those on board, "Bring me to Samudera." In their hearts, the ship's crew said, "This is surely the *fakir* spoken of by the Messenger (*salla Llahu ʿalaihi wa sallam*)." So the *fakir* [foretold by the Prophet] was brought aboard the ship, which then set sail. For a long time they were on the ocean.

At this time, Merah Silau had a dream. In that dream he saw a man holding his chin with all the fingers [of one hand] and closing his eyes with four fingers [of the other], saying, "O Merah Silau, utter with me the *syahadat*." Replied Merah Silau, "I do not know what to say to him." The man said, "Open your mouth!" So Merah Silau opened [his mouth]; the stranger spat into it, his saliva tasting rich and sweet. Then said the man to Merah Silau, "O Merah Silau, your name is Sultan Malikul Saleh; now you are a Muslim after reciting the *syahadat*, and every living animal is lawful (*halal*) for you to slaughter and eat; but if it is not slaughtered [correctly], do not eat it. In another forty days a ship will arrive from Mecca; everything the people of this ship say and everything they do is in accordance with the teachings of Islam; do not disobey [them], and [instead] desire the guidance of these teachers."

Then Merah Silau said, "Who are you, my lord?" Replied the voice in the dream, "I am the Prophet Muhammad, the Messenger of God (*salla Llahu ʿalayhi wa sallam*), who resides in Mecca." Then the Prophet took away his hand from Merah Silau's chin. Said the Messenger of God (*salla Llahu ʿalaihi wa sallam*) to Merah Silau, "Bow yourself down." So Merah Silau bowed down and, to guard him from sleep, he saw the Truth. Then he said, *Asyhadu an la ilaha illa Llah wahdahu, la syarika lahu, wa asyhadu anna Muhammadan ʿabduhu wa-rasuluhu.* After saying the testament [of faith], he read all thirty *juz* of the Qurʾān from memory, without having studied it with anyone. Many of the people and all the chieftains then said about Merah Silau, "Is that our king speaking? None of us know what he says."

According to those who possess this story, after a while the ship of Syeikh Ismail arrived at the Bay of Terli, where it anchored. The *fakir* [Sultan Muhammad] came ashore. Meeting with a fisherman, he asked, "What is the name of this country?" Replied the man, "The name of this country is Samudera." Then said the *fakir,* "What is the name of your chieftain?" Replied the fisherman, "The name of the king of this country is Merah Silau, who bears the title Sultan Malikul Saleh." After exchanging these words, the fisherman went back and the *fakir* returned to his ship.

The following day, Syeikh Ismail also came ashore, traveling into the country, to Sultan Malikul Saleh. When he arrived before the sultan, he said "O sultan, utter the *syahadat.*" So the sultan said the *syahadat,* thus: *Asyhadu an la ilaha illa Llah wahdahu, la syarika lahu, wa-asyhadu anna Muhammadan ʿabduhu wa-rasuluhu.* After that, Syeikh Ismail stroked his beard. The following day the *fakir* arrived, bearing a copy of the Qurʾān for Sultan Malikul Saleh, which he offered to him. Greeting the *fakir* with reverence, the sultan took the book, opened it, and began to read; without requesting any instruction, he knew how to read by himself. The *fakir* and Syeikh Ismail together said, *Al-hamdu li-Llahi Rabbi l-ʿalamin.*

After that, Syeikh Ismail ordered the gathering together of all the chiefs and people of the kingdom, large and small, old and young, men and women. When all were assembled, Syeikh Ismail taught them to say the *syahadat;* all of them willingly repeated the *syahadat* with utmost sincerity, from the heart. Because of that, Samudera became known as Negeri Darulsalam, since none of the people were compelled and none objected and none tired in their efforts to enter Islam.

FURTHER READING

Hall, Kenneth R. "The Coming of Islam to the Archipelago: A Reassessment," in *Economic Exchange and Social Interaction in Southeast Asia: Perspectives from Prehistory, History, and Ethnography,* ed. Karl L. Hutterer (Ann Arbor: University of Michigan, Center for South and Southeast Asian Studies, 1977), 213–32.

Hanaoka, Mimi. "Perspectives from the Peripheries: Strategies for 'Centering' Persian Histories from the 'Peripheries,'" *Journal of Persianate Studies* 8, no. 1 (2015): 1–22.

Marrison, G. E. "The Coming of Islam to the East Indies," *Journal of the Malayan Branch of the Royal Asiatic Society* 24, no. 1 (1951): 28–37.

Strathern, Alan. "Global Patterns of Ruler Conversion to Islam and the Logic of Empirical Religiosity," in *Islamisation: Comparative Perspectives from History,* ed. A. C. S. Peacock (Edinburgh: Edinburgh University Press, 2017), 21–55.

53

A Tract against "Unbelieving Believers" in West Africa

Muḥammad b. ʿAbd al-Karīm al-Maghīlī (d. ca. 910/1505)

Ulrich Rebstock

Title: *Ajwibat al-Maghīlī ʿan Asʾilat al-Amīn al-Ḥājj Askiyā* (The replies of al-Maghīlī to the questions of al-Amīn al-Ḥājj Askiyā)
Genre: Legal writing (responsa)
Language: Arabic

INTRODUCTION

A "reformist *faqīh* [jurist] of Tlemcen"—this is how J.O. Hunwick described al-Maghīlī, the author of *Ajwibat al-Maghīlī ʿan Asʾilat al-Amīn al-Ḥājj Askiyā* (The replies of al-Maghīlī to the questions of al-Amīn al-Ḥājj Askiyā), in the second edition of the *Encyclopaedia of Islam*. That this scholar from the northern fringes of the Algerian Sahara was more than a reformer is clear from his writings—twenty-nine titles are reported—and, more importantly, from his network of scholarly connections. In particular, his role as the reputed link between the Egyptian "renewer [of Islam]" (*mujaddid*) Jalāl al-Dīn al-Suyūṭī (d. 911/1505) and the West African branch of the Qādiriyya Sufi brotherhood heavily colors his image in the later sources. He certainly had a lifelong mission: the call (*daʿwa*) to "command the right and prohibit the wrong" (*al-amr bi-l-maʿrūf wa-l-nahy ʿan al-munkar*) in Africa of his day. This mission did not always go well; expelled from his home oasis of Tuwāt for anti-Jewish campaigns, he turned south and spread his reformist teaching across the Sudanic countries (*bilād al-sūdān*). By around 1498, when he made the acquaintance of King Askiyā Muḥammad, the addressee of our text and, after the mysterious death of his predecessor, Sunnī ʿAlī, the "new" ruler of the Songhay Empire on the Niger, his reputation had reached courts and villages alike and had become an integral part of the Islamic reform project in the western Sudan. More than three centuries later and five hundred miles to the southeast, the founder of the Sokoto Caliphate in northern Nigeria, ʿUthmān b. Fūdī (d. 1232/1817), himself called "renewer of the century" because of his successful jihad movement, not only made extensive use of the same arguments against backsliding and lukewarm believers that al-Maghīlī had given his royal Songhay host but also composed his own epistle, *Sirāj al-Ikhwān* (The lamp of the brethren), almost entirely by copying and pasting the Askiyā's questions and al-Maghīlī's replies, though not without conscientiously adapting the text to his own milieu. (As an example, compare *Ajwibat al-Maghīlī*, Ar. p. 36, line 8f, with *Sirāj al-Ikhwān*, Ar. p. 18, line 1.)

The axis connecting *Ajwibat al-Maghīlī* and *Sirāj al-Ikhwān* testifies to the continuous fight for rightly guided belief and leadership in a situation of political and religious insecurity during the entire period of Islamization and conversion to Islam in the Sudan. When Askiyā Muḥammad returned from his Meccan pilgrimage in 1498, he turned his pious zeal into action. Motivated by well-known supporters such as al-Maghīlī and al-Suyūṭī, and by basing his propaganda on the distinction between the rightly guided scholars and the "scholars of evil" (*ʿulamāʾ al-sūʾ*), the new Askiyā launched his jihad against the idolatrous and unbelieving rulers in his region and the inhabitants of their kingdoms. While the former neglected their responsibility for the morals and religion of their subjects, the latter constantly fell prey to unlawful and sinful actions. The force of this project of re-Islamization was directed against the unbeliever "who was a Muslim and openly apostatized from Islam" and "who claims to be a Muslim and whom we judge to be an unbeliever." That the project took place at all demonstrates the gradual and uncertain progress of conversion to Islam in late medieval and early modern Sudanic Africa. The Askiyā's campaign successfully swept away pagan rulers and customs; the Islamic Songhay Empire expanded into the neighboring Tuareg, Fulani, Soninke, and Malinke realms, much as the Sokoto Caliphate of ʿUthmān b. Fūdī was to expand into the Hausa and Bornu kingdoms three centuries later.

TEXT

[The question:] Ever since God favored us with Islam, an affliction has beset us in this land on account of [our] lack of faith in those scholars of our land who are reputed to be learned. One of their characteristics is that they are non-Arabs, understanding nothing of the Arabic language save a little of the speech of the Arabs of their land, in so distorted, corrupted, and barbarous a fashion that they do not understand the arguments of the scholars nor yet are they aware of the distortion and corruption. Despite this they possess books which they study and have tales and histories [which they relate]. Among them are judges and exegetes who make pronouncements concerning God's religion and claim that they are among the scholars who are the heirs of the prophets and that it is our duty to emulate them. . . . I ask that you give me a legal opinion . . . concerning these scholars.

Now Sunnī ʿAlī from childhood to manhood used to frequent them a great deal, to the extent that he grew up among them and became stamped with their pattern of polytheism and with their customs. . . . However . . . it was his habit to make superficial profession of the two *shahādas* and other similar words of the Muslims without knowing their significance. . . . He used to fast in Ramadan and make abundant alms of slaughtered beasts and other things at the mosques. . . . In spite of that he used to worship idols, believe in the soothsayers, seek help from magicians, and venerate certain trees. . . . Another practice of his was that where women were concerned he did not confine himself to marriage or observe any of the other Islamic conditions. . . . Another practice of his was making lawful the [shedding of the] blood [and seizure of the] property of the Muslims. He put to death scholars, jurists, pious people, [women, infants, and others, mutilating some by ablation of the phallus and testes or by cutting off the nose and the hands]. . . . He continued thus throughout his life. Then after his death the *amīr* Askiyā . . . ruled and possessed the land and brought people back from polytheism and evil. . . . What, then, is the judgment concerning Sunnī ʿAlī and those oppressors who were his supporters . . . are they unbelievers or not? And are their offspring to be enslaved after their death . . .?

If it is said to him, "What you are doing is forbidden (*ḥarām*)," he says, "God preserve me from the *ḥarām;* everything we do is lawful (*ḥalāl*); I know better than you do."

Also, some of the Muslims to our east and west, having heard of me, asked if they could enter into allegiance to me. Should I grant them this or should I confine myself to ruling [only] the land which God caused us to inherit from Sunnī ʿAlī?

[The reply:] . . . It is not lawful for a group of Muslims to be without ruler (*muhmalūn*). God Most High has said: "And hold fast all of you to the rope of God and do not disperse yourselves" [Q. 3:103]. And in the *Ṣaḥīḥ* of Muslim [there is the statement] . . . : "I heard the Messenger of God . . . say: 'Whoever withholds his hand from [the bond of] obedience shall meet God on the Day of Judgment having no argument in his defense; and whoever dies with no oath of homage (*bayʿa*) upon his neck dies a non-Islamic (*jāhilī*) death.'" So, strive against them with the sword until they all enter into [the bond of] obedience to you in obedience to God and His Messenger. That is one of the worthiest and most important jihads . . . a land whose people have an emir who looks after their worldly and religious interests so far as it is possible in his age. It is not lawful for any one of these people to abandon their allegiance to him, nor may any man lay claim to such an emir's subjects, for he has a better right to them than anyone else. . . . And in the *Ṣaḥīḥ* of

Muslim . . . on the authority of Abū Saʿīd al-Khudrī, [the Prophet] said: "If two caliphs have homage paid to them, kill the second of them."

As for what you asked concerning declaring people unbelievers, an explanation of the grounds on which a man may be declared an unbeliever has already been given. Whoever can be proved to have declared unlawful taxes to be lawful or [who has pursued] any other like method of falsely devouring people's wealth must be judged to be an unbeliever; likewise anyone who denies the manifest truth and confounds it with falsehood.

Such people must be forced to recant on pain of death. . . . Such a person's body should not be washed or shrouded nor should he be buried in a Muslim graveyard.

FURTHER READING

Fisher, Humphrey J. "The Juggernaut's Apologia: Conversion to Islam in Black Africa," *Africa* 55, no. 2 (1985): 153–73.

———. "Many Deep Baptisms: Reflections on Religious, Chiefly Muslim, Conversion in Black Africa," *Bulletin of the School of Oriental and African Studies* 57, no. 1 (1994): 68–81.

Levtzion, Nehemia, and Randall Pouwels. *The History of Islam in Africa* (Athens: Ohio University Press, 2000).

54

Conversions to Islam in a Late Medieval Chronicle from Damascus

Shihāb al-Dīn Aḥmad b. Ṭawq (d. 905/1509) and Shams al-Dīn Muḥammad b. Ṭūlūn (d. 953/1546)

Tamer el-Leithy

Titles: Ibn Ṭawq, *al-Taʿlīq* (The commentary); Ibn Ṭūlūn, *Mufākahat al-Khillān fī Ḥawādith al-Zamān* (Banter with friends concerning events of the present era)

Genre: Historical writing (chronicle-diary)

Language: Arabic

INTRODUCTION

The following are selected excerpts of individual conversions to Islam in late fifteenth-century Damascus as described by Shihāb al-Dīn Aḥmad b. Ṭawq (d. 1509) in his chronicle/diary *al-Taʿlīq*. The author was a modest notary and professional legal witness; his daily life consisted of witnessing legal transactions and drafting documents for litigants. Unlike most medieval Arabic chronicles, which primarily focus on public and political events (i.e., on kings, courts, and battles), Ibn Ṭawq's text is an intimate daily journal. In it the author recorded details of his work as well as many local and personal events, including many he heard about from others. In daily entries covering more than two decades (885–908/1480–1502), Ibn Ṭawq describes, with curious relish and abundant commentary, everything he experienced and witnessed around him, including topics as varied as a quarrel with his wife that led him to sleep on the couch; his own dreams; his son's progress in elementary school; skirmishes between urban gangs; and the prices and availability of foodstuffs. The result is a distinctly author-centered text, with local horizons and much colloquial Arabic, especially in quoted direct speech. In these respects, Ibn Ṭawq's diary foreshadows later memoirs by eighteenth-century Damascene commoners, including a barber, a soldier, and a Christian priest (on these, see the work of Dana Sajdi cited below). The text covers the last decades of Mamluk rule in Damascus—the Mamluk Empire's second-largest urban center after the imperial capital, Cairo—shortly before the Ottoman conquests of the region in 1516–17. Greater Syria was then administered by the Mamluk governor, who resided in the citadel of Damascus. Scholars estimate that the population of greater Damascus in the late fifteenth century was about sixty thousand to one hundred thousand.

The accounts provide a range of different cases of conversion to Islam, including converts of different religious backgrounds, status, and occupations (peasants, merchants, bureaucrats, etc.) and a variety of settings (individual vs. family; rural vs. urban). Also included are two additional notices of conversion (cases 1 and 15) included by another Damascene scholar, Ibn Ṭūlūn (d. 1546), in his own chronicle. This selection is not exhaustive; still other cases appear in the two chronicles.

Ibn Ṭawq's brief notices provide a window onto different conversion practices in late medieval Damascus, as well as a modest Muslim notary's reception and representation of these various conversions. In most entries, the authors describe the specific motives and immediate context of the conversions. Naturally, the motives of individual converts varied, but it is worth noting certain patterns among them. Ibn Ṭawq describes the ways in which different converts came to "see the light," which merit careful comparison with the stock picture of conversion as a flash of sudden divine inspiration, an image derived largely from the Christian tradition. Converts' agency and volition are also important issues for Ibn Ṭawq in several of the accounts (e.g., cases 2 and 8: "[converted] *of his own accord*"; 7: "[converted] *from the heart*"). Such details indicate the author's concern to highlight the converts' uncoerced choice of Islam, but they also raise questions about the other, more numerous accounts that lack such explicit reference to agency and/or choice. They also draw scrutiny to the combination in case 2 of such unmolested choice alongside the reference to the unmistakable economic burden of the poll tax.

It is important to note patterns among the religious backgrounds, occupations, ages, and settings of the conversions described. Consider, for example, whether members of one community appear more in cases of poor rural converts, while another community's converts appear to be drawn from urban, higher-placed bureaucrats or rich merchants. Or observe whether certain age groups appear more often than others. Ibn Ṭawq's attention to such details was not only related to his occupation as a legal professional; his accounts also quietly reference Islamic legal categories and doctrines about normative conversion. In some cases, the account demonstrates that part of the legal ritual of conversion to Islam involved appearing before a judge, who confirmed the validity of the conversion *and* issued a document, a conversion certificate, confirming the convert's new Muslim identity (e.g., case 5). It is worth noting that while a few models of such documents appear in Islamic formularies (as document "templates" for use by notaries; see selection 25 in the present volume), hardly any actual specimens have survived.

Finally, it is striking that in a city of ca. eighty thousand inhabitants, more than twenty separate cases of conversion (several involving multiple converts, such as cases 9 and 12) are recorded here—yielding a rate of more than thirty newly minted Muslims over the course of only two decades, in a period that is not normally seen as one of marked or increased conversion to Islam (unlike, e.g., early fourteenth-century Egypt).

TEXTS

(1) A druggist in the marketplace (Monday, 18 Shaʿbān 885/October 23, 1480)

[*The marketplace mentioned here was near al-Qaṣab Mosque, in Damascus's northern extramural suburb and the neighborhood where Ibn Ṭawq lived. The conversion took place during the first year covered by Ibn Ṭawq in his chronicle, but it does not appear there; instead, it is described by Ibn Ṭūlūn (although Ibn Ṭūlūn was clearly reproducing an earlier historian's account, since he was only five years old at the time).*]

A Jewish druggist named ʿAbd al-Ḥaqq converted to Islam; his shop is by the entrance to the Old Dār al-Ṭaʿm marketplace.

(2) Why the Christian peasant boy decided to convert (Wednesday, 18 Dhū al-ḥijja 886/February 7, 1482)

[*The village of Bukhʿā lies about thirty-five miles northeast of Damascus. The Hijri date given in the original Arabic corresponds to a Thursday in the Gregorian calendar. Both the day of the week and the Gregorian date have been maintained despite the contradiction, in this case and in cases 4, 6, 8, 9, and 13–15 below.*]

Yesterday, ʿĪsā the Christian [peasant] from [the village of] Bukhʿā, a youth with no beard, converted to Islam on account of the poll tax, so he converted of his own accord.

(3) A rejected gallows conversion (Sunday, 3 Rabīʿ I 890/March 20, 1485)

[*Sbīna is located southwest of Damascus. Baalbek, now in eastern Lebanon, lies thirty-five miles north of Damascus, whence it was then administered as part of the province of Greater Syria.*]

That day, the governor hanged Ibn Kishwān, his associate, and Ibn Kurbāj—[all] from [the town of] Sbīna—along with a thief whom Sībāy, the chamberlain [of Damascus], had brought from Baalbek during the absence of the governor, and [yet] another person—making a total of five. He also executed [lit. "cut"] seven people, among them the slave of Ibn al-Sukkarī al-Ḥarīrī and a Christian man. The latter reportedly converted to Islam when he beheld the torture [of the others]. But the governor said, "Execute [lit. 'cut'] him—even if he converts!" We ask of God His forgiveness and good health!

(4) Dangerous liaison, risky operation (Monday, 14 Jumādā II 890/June 28, 1485)

[*Note that Ibn Ṭawq consistently uses the phrase "my lord the shaykh" to refer to his patron, the notable judge Taqī al-Dīn b. Qāḍī ʿAjlūn.*]

Last Saturday night, a Frank was found in one of the new apartments owned by my lord the shaykh. He was caught while visiting a woman who lived there with her husband, and he was getting drunk at her place. He was arrested by Ibn Nāṣir and his entourage and taken over to Shaykh Faraj; there, the Frank converted to Islam. Meanwhile, the woman and her husband fled. The next morning, the Frank was taken before Shaykh Shams al-Dīn al-Khaṭīb, where he was circumcised.

(5) Lapsus linguae? A local Frankish-looking Jewish boy converts (Friday, 9 Rabīʿ II 891/April 14, 1486)

[*Here, Ibn Ṭawq's explicit reference to the hand of the scribe, al-Yāsūfī, likely refers to the physical conversion certificate issued to new Muslims upon legally confirming their conversion to Islam. Here and wherever Ibn Ṭawq uses the term* murāhiq, *I have used the term "pubescent" rather than the now-common "adolescent," in order to avoid an anachronistic age category.*]

On the eve of Friday [i.e., on Thursday], [a group of] Muslims brought a pubescent Jewish boy, claiming that he had uttered the *shahāda* [credal profession that ritually effects conversion to Islam]. Along with the boy came his father, his mother, and another Jew—all of them [dressed] in the manner of the Franks. He converted to Islam before my lord the shaykh at the Dawlaʿiyya School. Then my lord the shaykh sent for the chief Ḥanafī judge's brother, Muḥyī al-Dīn, also known as "Sheep of the Persians," who duly issued his verdict confirming the [legal] validity of the conversion. In attendance [for this event] were my lord the shaykh and our lord, his paternal cousin, the shaykh and judge Muḥibb al-Dīn. The ruling was written by Badr al-Dīn al-Yāsūfī.

(6) A Frankish merchant sees the light . . . and dodges debts? (Saturday, 7 Rabīʿ II 895/February 28, 1490)

Yesterday, a Frankish merchant converted to Islam. So the head chamberlain bestowed on him a sleeveless tunic and a Turkish turban and mounted him on a [ceremonial] horse. The convert rode around until he reached a notable, [who gifted him] one hundred silver [dirhams]. Now the Frank had reportedly owed debts of some five thousand [gold] dinars—but possessed on [i.e., had wrapped around] his waist only about two thousand dinars. It may well be that his conversion to Islam was on account of the[se] debts that he owed the Franks. All of this was related to me. God, the Exalted, is the [best] custodian of secrets!

(7) Heartfelt conversion of an orphaned Jewish boy (Saturday, 27 Rabīʿ I 897/January 28, 1492)

Today, a pubescent Jewish youth, an orphan bereft of both mother and father, converted to Islam from the heart, as was related [to me].

(8) A Frankish boy-servant converts of his own accord (Friday, 7 Ramaḍān 898/June 22, 1493)

A Frankish boy—who was a servant to the Franks—converted to Islam. It was related that he converted of his own accord.

(9) All together but in order: A rural Christian family converts (Saturday, 12 Shawwāl 898/July 28, 1493)

[*The trio of villages mentioned here lie in close proximity to one another in the Qalamūn Mountains, roughly twenty-five miles northeast of Damascus.*]

A group of men from the village of al-Tawānī came before my lord the shaykh bringing with them a Christian man, who originally hailed from the village of Jabb ʿĀdīn and was [now] one of their neighbors in [the village of] Jubbat ʿAssāl. In the last days of Ramadan [i.e., about two weeks earlier], the man had converted to Islam along with his wife and their children, [the latter comprising] one girl and five boys; of these [children], the girl and one of the boys had reached puberty. The wife had preceded them in converting to Islam. . . . May God almighty guide them! And may He guide us to all that pleases Him of our words and deeds!

(10) A beardless boy from Jawbar (Friday, 5 Rajab 899/April 11, 1494)

[*The small town of Jawbar—which boasted a significant Jewish community as well as a two-thousand-year-old synagogue and shrine of the prophet Elijah, which attracted Jewish pilgrims throughout the Middle Ages—lies about two miles northeast of Damascus's old city walls.*]

[Today] a beardless Jewish boy from [the village of] Jawbar converted to Islam.

(11) The unconverted entourage of a young Christian convert (Friday, 14 Rajab 900/April 10, 1495)

On Wednesday, a pubescent Christian boy converted to Islam. His father, who works as a woodcutter for my lord Muḥammad al-Ḥiṣnī, sent the boy to my lord the shaykh in the company of his relative, al-Sayyid al-Ṭawīl, and [other?] Christians. Then they all went over to the chief Ḥanbalī judge: [the boy] converted before the judge, and [the latter] issued his verdict confirming the [legal] validity of the boy's [conversion to] Islam.

(12) Where the young converts go (Sunday, 11 Jumādā I 902/January 15, 1497)

On that day, two Jewish boys converted to Islam. It was related that the judge's nephew took the elder [boy into his household].

(13) A costly revision: A convert reverts to Christianity, fifteen years later (Friday, 26 Rajab 902/March 30, 1497)

After the [Friday communal] prayers, the governor [of the Syrian provinces] struck the neck of a former Christian, who had converted to Islam but now apostatized [i.e., returned to Christianity]—this after having lived as a Muslim for a good while now, perhaps fifteen years.

(14) Another Christian peasant (Wednesday, 23 Shawwāl 903/June 14, 1498)

[Today] a Christian from [the village of] Maʿrūniyya converted to Islam.

(15) A convert's progress: From torture to honor (Tuesday, 25 Rabīʿ II 922/May 28, 1516)

Today, Yaʿqūb, the governor's money changer, converted to Islam—this [right] after being subjected to punishment and monetary extraction [i.e., official confiscation]. Upon converting, he received a ceremonial parade and [several] robes of honor. The next day, he was appointed [to two senior jobs:] overseer of the treasury and superintendent of the bureau and received [yet more] robes of honor for these [appointments].

FURTHER READING

el-Leithy, Tamer. "Coptic Culture and Conversion in Medieval Cairo, 1293–1524 A.D." (PhD diss., Princeton University, 2005), esp. part 2, "Suspicious Muslims: Biographical Representations of Converts."

Sajdi, Dana. *The Barber of Damascus: Nouveau Literacy in the Eighteenth-Century Ottoman Levant* (Stanford, CA: Stanford University Press, 2013), esp. chapter 4.

Wollina, Torsten. "A View from Within: Ibn Ṭawq's Personal Topography of 15th-Century Damascus," *Bulletin d'Études Orientales* 61 (2012): 271–95.

55

Documentary Records of Conversions among Ottoman Palace Personnel

Ottoman Officials and Elite Servants of the Sultan (ca. 963–67/1556–60)

Sanja Kadrić

Title: Excerpts from *mühimme defterleri* (Ottoman registers of important affairs)

Genre: Documentary sources (imperial records)

Language: Ottoman Turkish

INTRODUCTION

This is a collection of excerpts from the "registers of important affairs" (*mühimme defterleri*) kept by the Ottoman state. The registers presented here are held in Istanbul in the Ottoman Archives of the Prime Minister's Office (Başbakanlık Osmanlı Arşivi, BOA). These particular excerpts attest to conversion among the familial networks of *kapı kulları* (lit. "servants of the gate"), elite bureaucratic and military servants of the Ottoman sultan, as well as among regular subjects. Most of the excerpts feature the term *agha,* a title given to certain senior Ottoman officials, most notably high-ranking attendants within the imperial palace and commanders of the Janissary corps, the elite infantry of the Ottoman Empire. Conversion is indicated by the term *Islama gelip,* literally meaning "coming to Islam," as well as the acceptance of a new Muslim name. In some cases, these excerpts upend the idea, widespread among observers of the Ottoman Empire, that elite servants of the sultan were completely removed from their relatives and native networks. Instead, the former seem to have benefited the latter greatly by bringing them into Ottoman service. Conversion sometimes worked in tandem with connections to the Ottoman elite. Both could result in such lucrative benefits as grants of state land, known as *timar*s, which were usually bestowed in compensation for service and loyalty to the sultan. Other benefits included appointments to salaried positions within the imperial palace of Istanbul, such as service in the imperial gardens (*hass bahçeleri*) as part of the Gardeners' Corps (*bostancıları*). These appointments gave one access to the sultan, as well as political connections with the remainder of his retinue, opening the door to the highest military and bureaucratic positions within the Ottoman Empire. In other cases, beneficiaries received salaried positions outside of the imperial palace, such as in Ottoman forts. These records speak to Islamization in the mid-sixteenth-century Ottoman Empire, with conversion as its central act, but also to Ottomanization, in the limited sense that serving the Ottoman state and converting to Islam made one an Ottoman.

TEXTS

(1) An agha's converted nephew (13 Rebiyülevvel 963/January 26, 1556)

The nephew (*karındaşı oğlu*) of Ali Agha, a eunuch of the Old Palace of Istanbul (*eski saray ağası*), has converted to Islam and taken the name Mehmed. He has been appointed as an usher (*bevvab*) at the upper gate and given a salary of two *akçe*s.

(2) An agha's converted relative (25 Cemaziyülevvel 963/April 6, 1556)

He, who converted to Islam in the Imperial Council and who has taken the name Ali, . . . he, who is a relative (*akrabasından olup*) of Sinan Agha, the chief of the imperial halberdier corps, the imperial messengers, and the sultan's bodyguard (*çavuşbaşı*), . . . he is awarded a land grant (*timar*).

(3) Converts going to the imperial gardens (29 Cemaziyülahir 963/May 9, 1556)

This is a notice to Ali Agha, the chief of the imperial porters (*kapıcılar kethüdası*) . . . : Mehmed and Iskender, being new Muslims (*yeni Müslüman olan*), have been ordered to join the recruits going into imperial garden service (*hass bahçe oğlanları*).

(4) An agha's converted relatives (Zilhicce 963/October 1556)

This is a notice to the governor-general (*beylerbeyi*) of Rumelia: In the administrative district of Aştıp [present-day Štip, Macedonia] and the village of Tartarus [likely present-day Tarintsi, Macedonia] . . . the children of a relative of Yakup Agha, the white eunuch who served as chief of the outer palace treasury (*hazinedarbaşı*), have been awarded a land grant (*timar*) on the occasion of their conversions to Islam (*Islama gelip*).

(5) A recruit's converted brother (13 Zilhicce 963/October 18, 1556)

The brother (*karındaş*) of one of the recruits for palace service (*kapı oğlanı*) has been awarded a land grant (*timar*) on the occasion of his conversion to Islam.

(6) An agha's converted relative (Rebiyülevvel 964/January 1557)

A relative of Mahmud Agha, a palace eunuch, has converted to Islam and taken the name Mustafa. He is appointed to guard a fort (*hısar gedik*).

(7) A converted subject (1 Rebiyülahir 967/December 30, 1559)

This is a notice to Mehmed Agha, the superintendent of the ushers (*kapıcılar kethüdası*) . . . : A non-Muslim subject (*zimmi*) named Gin from Çatalça [present-day Prača, Bosnia and Hercegovina] who has converted to Islam and taken the name Mehmed has been appointed to serve in the imperial gardens.

(8) Another converted subject (1 Rebiyülahir 967/December 30, 1559)

A non-Muslim subject (*zimmi*) named Yorgi has converted to Islam and taken the name of Kurt ["wolf" in Old Turkic]. He has been appointed to serve in the imperial gardens.

(9) An agha's brother (19 Şevval 967/July 13, 1560)

The brother (*karındaşı*) of Ahmed Agha, the current chief of the imperial falconers (*şahincibaşı*), has converted to Islam and taken the name Mahmud. He is awarded a land grant (*timar*) valued at six thousand *akçes*.

FURTHER READING

Kadrić, Sanja. "The Islamisation of Ottoman Bosnia: Myths and Matters," in *Islamisation: Comparative Perspectives from History*, ed. A. C. S. Peacock (Edinburgh: Edinburgh University Press, 2017), 277–95.

Krstić, Tijana. *Contested Conversion to Islam: Narratives of Religious Change in the Early Modern Ottoman Empire* (Stanford, CA: Stanford University Press, 2011).

Minkov, Anton. *Conversion to Islam in the Balkans: Kisve Bahası Petitions and Ottoman Social Life, 1670–1730* (Leiden: Brill, 2004).

56

A Conversion Tale from Java, Indonesia

Anonymous

Ronit Ricci

Title: *Matinya Raden Darmakusuma* (Prince Darmakusuma's death)
Genre: Didactic and entertaining literature (oral tale)
Language: Indonesian

INTRODUCTION

This anonymous and undated tale forms part of a corpus of stories narrating the conversion efforts and successes of the *wali sanga*, the nine "saints" to whom tradition attributes the spread of Islam on Java. The conversion of the Indonesian archipelago was a gradual process, and there is little unambiguous evidence of its earliest stages. The *walis* are said to have lived in the fifteenth and sixteenth centuries and to have converted local people by way of their special powers, miracle working, and willingness to accommodate local culture. This tale was written down by A. M. Noertjahajo, who heard it from elders at the Demak Mosque in the 1970s.

The key to understanding this story lies in realizing that it is in dialogue with the *Mahabharata*, one of the two great Indian epics that were transmitted to Java and, in their localized forms, had a lasting and profound impact on its literature, performing and plastic arts, language, and social and political ideals. To this day, many of the shadow puppet performances in Java (*wayang kulit* or *wayang purwa*) are based on scenes from the *Mahabharata*, with the Great War (*Bratayuda*) constituting a popular favorite. Readers should pay special attention to the interface between the epic and the conversion tale.

Prince Darmakusuma is one of the names by which Yudhishtira, the eldest of the Pandawa brothers in the *Mahabharata*, is known. In the tale he meets Sunan

Kalijaga, the leader of the nine *wali*s. Prince Darmakusuma asks for directions to Bintara ("place of the sweet-smelling grass called *bintara*"), the site where Demak, the first Muslim sultanate on Java's north coast, was built in the early sixteenth century and ruled by Raden Patah. Darmakusuma, who has lost everything in the war, wishes to die. The magical charm that protects him from death is that of a previous era, now bygone, which turns out to be the *kalima shahada*, that is, the Islamic profession of faith. Thus, unknowingly, Darmakusuma was protected by an Islamic power. However, only once he is able to acknowledge Islam and convert by reciting the Arabic words is he free to attain his death.

Java's Hindu-Buddhist past and Muslim present are inextricably intertwined in this story, as well as in the *walis*' ethos of conversion more broadly, like the amulet entangled in Darmakusuma's hair. The past is not erased or annihilated but is brought into the fold and given new meaning.

TEXT

Once, in the days when the *wali*s were busy spreading Islam in Java, Sunan Kalijaga was walking southward when he met a tall, large man who addressed him politely. "Brother," he said, "may I ask that you direct me to Bintara?" In a manner that was no less cordial, Sunan Kalijaga pointed the way, and added, "What is your purpose in going to Bintara? And who might you be?"

"My name is Darmakusuma," said the foreigner. "I am from the Kingdom of Ngamarta, where in the past I ruled as king, but following the Bratayuda War everyone is dead and I am alone. I therefore wish to die. I've already attempted death in various ways, but it has all been in vain."

"What is your purpose in going to Bintara now?" asked Sunan Kalijaga again.

"To meet a man called Sunan Kalijaga, as I have received a sign from god [*dewa*, usually referring to a Hindu deity] to come to this world [*marcapada;* Darmakusuma was coming from heaven] to meet him. According to god it is only Sunan Kalijaga who can show me how to die. Therefore, brother, I will be very pleased if you can tell me the way to Sunan Kalijaga's house and how I might arrange to meet him."

"Your Majesty," replied Sunan Kalijaga, "it is fitting that you first accept my respect and deference [*sembah sujud; sembah* is to pay obeisance to rulers with folded hands raised to the forehead; *sujud,* from Arabic, is to prostrate oneself in prayer] as a resident of this world. And I am also very pleased to inform you that I am the one known as Sunan Kalijaga. By God's grace I may be able to show you the path toward death, but you should know that there are conditions you must fulfill."

"Thank you very much, Sunan Kalijaga. I, too, feel very pleased to meet you face-to-face after searching for so long. Tell me what the conditions are to attain death. I hope I will be able to fulfill them."

"Your Majesty, let us go to Bintara. There you will meet the other *wali*s, and they will assist me in directing you. Please go ahead and I will follow from behind."

And so Prince Darmakusuma, king of Ngamarta, walked toward Bintara, followed by Sunan Kalijaga.

The people of Bintara were amazed to see such a tall, large man, and so were the *wali*s who were immediately assembled by Sunan Kalijaga. After they all sat down on the mosque's veranda Prince Darmakusuma told them of his journey from Ngamarta to this earth as well as many details of the kingdom he once ruled: about its subjects, their language, dispositions, and habits, culture and arts, and all the rest. The *wali*s listened intently to all of his stories, which were written down by the mosque's scribe [*ketib*, from Arabic] Kyai Bicak.

Sunan Kalijaga inquired of Prince Darmakusuma, "May I ask if you by chance possess an amulet [*azimat*, from Arabic] that makes you immortal?"

"I have absolutely no amulet, Sunan Kalijaga," replied Prince Darmakusuma, "besides the amulet of Ngamarta which is always in my hair [*sanggul*, hair tied in a bun]."

"Would it be possible for you to show us the amulet?" asked Sunan Kalijaga further.

"I'm sorry, brothers," said Prince Darmakusuma, "but that amulet is entwined in my hair, and it is unlikely that I would be able to release it."

"In that case," said Sunan Kalijaga, "allow us to try." Prince Darmakusuma nodded his head as he spoke: "Please, brothers, go ahead."

Then all the *wali*s, led by Sunan Kalijaga, meditated [*semedi*, from Sanskrit], and they all requested that God, who is all-powerful, allow the Ngamarta amulet to emerge from Prince Darmakusuma's hair. The *wali*s' plea was accepted and the amulet appeared from within Prince Darmakusuma's hair in the form of a torn bit of paper inscribed with the Arabic words "Kalimah Syahadat."

"Your Majesty," said Sunan Kalijaga, "according to a sign from God you will die only once you've read the writing on this Ngamarta amulet."

"Oh, Sunan Kalijaga, how can I possibly read this writing? I do not recognize the script. Might it be possible for you, the *wali*s, to teach me how to read these letters?"

And so the king of Ngamarta was taught to read the Arabic script, and in the end he was indeed able to read the writing on the amulet. And after reading those two words Prince Darmakusuma, king of Ngamarta, passed away. The *wali*s handled his body and buried it according to Islamic tradition near the Demak Mosque.

Visitors to the Demak Sultanate's cemetery can see Prince Darmakusuma's tomb not far from that of Raden Patah, whose tomb is the longest of all.

Now, having heard Prince Darmakusuma's stories about "the people of old," the *wali*s were not yet satisfied and wanted to know more. Therefore they meditated again so that God would reveal to them those earlier people's forms and voices. By

God's will, the *walis* saw a black shadow (*wayang*) that represented "the people of old," whose voices could be heard as well. And so that they will not be forgotten by the residents of the earth the shadow puppet theater (*wayang purwa*) and all of its repertoire of stories were created.

Now the amulet of Ngamarta that was shaped as a bit of paper bearing the words Kalimah Syahadat was given the name Kalima Sada, and it goes like this: *ashhadu an lā ilāha illā Allāh, wa-ashhadu anna Muḥammadan rasūl Allāh* . . . , which means "I bear witness that there is no god but God and I bear witness that Muḥammad is God's Messenger."

FURTHER READING

Ricci, Ronit. "Islamic Literary Networks in South and Southeast Asia," *Journal of Islamic Studies* 21, no. 1 (2010): 1–28.

Rinkes, D. A. *Nine Saints of Java*, trans. H. M. Froger (Kuala Lumpur: Malaysian Sociological Research Institute, 1996). Originally published as an article series titled "De Heiligen van Java," in *Tijdschrift voor Indische Taal-, Land- en Volkenkunde*, 1910–13.

Sears, Laurie Jo. *Shadows of Empire: Colonial Discourse and Javanese Tales* (Durham, NC: Duke University Press, 1996).

Supomo, S. "From Sakti to Shahada: The Quest for New Meanings in a Changing World Order," in *Islam: Essays on Scripture, Thought, and Society; A Festschrift in Honour of Anthony H. Johns*, ed. Peter G. Riddell and Tony Street (Leiden: Brill, 1997), 219–36.

57

The Story of Master She Yunshan's Conversion in Changzhou, China

Zhao Can (ca. 1080s–1140s/1670s–1730s; composed ca. 1126/1714)

Suofei Liu and Zvi Ben-Dor Benite

Title: *Jingxue Xizhuanpu* (Biographies and lineage of scholars of Islamic scripture)
Genre: Didactic and entertaining literature (biography)
Language: Chinese

INTRODUCTION

When Matteo Ricci (1552–1610), the great Jesuit missionary to China, discusses Chinese Islam in his *Prolegomeni,* he presents it as a species of idolatry. It entered China from the west, he explains, spread through the country, and in his own day was practiced in nearly every province. At the same time, he admits that Chinese Muslims were not known for proselytizing. They lived in general harmony with Chinese laws and customs, and despite their lowly status they sometimes earned admission to the ranks of the bureaucracy and were assimilated to the high culture of the literati.

Apart from the imputation of idolatry, Ricci's account is remarkably accurate. In its relative unconcern to win converts, Islam differed sharply from the two other foreign religions in Ricci's day, namely, Buddhism and (Catholic) Christianity. Tellingly, both Buddhism and Catholicism were subjected to state restriction at certain junctures, Buddhism in the eighth century and the Jesuits in the early eighteenth. Chinese Muslims were spared such treatment for a variety of reasons, not the least of which was that they did not try to make converts on a scale sufficient to draw attention from state authorities. The low intensity of conversion to Islam in China makes it a far more difficult process for historians to trace than conversion to Buddhism, Christianity, or even Manicheism. The historian, therefore, must rely on sporadic anecdotal evidence.

One such anecdotal case, from a slightly later era, is the conversion of the bureaucrat She Yunshan, as related by his student Zhao Can and translated below. She lived under the Qing Dynasty (1644–1912). Under the previous dynasty, the Ming (1368–1644), the most noteworthy trend in Chinese conversion to Islam had been the marriage of Chinese women into Muslim families, a process that helped bring about the "sinification" of hitherto diverse Muslim groups and was significant enough to elicit a short-lived government ban on intermarriage with Muslims. Because women were central to this process, however, it left only scant traces in the sources. We are on stronger footing when it comes to another mechanism of conversion in premodern China: the adoption and conversion of male Chinese orphans, especially those who, like She Yunshan, later rose to prominence.

Born as Yuandu in 1635 to a family of low-ranking Chinese officials—the Weis of Changzhou in east-central China—She Yunshan would become one of Chinese Islam's most prominent teachers. During the war following the Manchu conquest of China (1644), Yuandu's village was occupied by a Muslim general fighting for the Manchus, one She Yinju. The general's wife met Yuandu's grandmother by chance, and when the boy's father died, Yinju adopted the son, who took his name (She) and converted to Islam. In the following account, the boy's conversion is described as bringing him joy, peace, and clarity. Of course, not everyone remembered their conversion this way, if they remembered it at all.

The account here, which was written by one of She's students, gives details of the arrangement between the Wei family and the adopting Muslim family. General She, who had no sons, would adopt the young boy, whose mother and grandmother would join his household. We do not know whether the two women converted to Islam, but it seems probable that they did. The writer did not consider the matter of their conversion important enough to discuss.

This rather reverential conversion tale is striking for several reasons, among which is that the convert is a thoroughgoing Han Chinese. While Islam in China was and is often thought of as a foreign, Western religion, and many of its practitioners had non-Chinese family backgrounds, it is clear from this account that She Yunshan was fully immersed in Chinese culture and learning. Other than his conversion itself, the only aspect of the narrative that marks him as a Muslim is his precocious aversion to Buddhist images and statues. Note that "Lord Ma" probably refers to a Muslim, Ma being a Muslim surname that is usually short for "Muḥammad."

TEXT

Wuxi had a son, Yuandu [1638–1703], which is my master's original name. Yuandu was an extraordinarily intelligent youth; taciturn in his infancy, he acquired a strong build and a resounding voice as he grew up. After brushing his clothes and sitting on his stool, he would sit straight without taking rest all day. [Yuandu] was sent to school when he was about five. The school was located on Tiger Valley Mountain. One day when the teacher took all the students out, Yuandu leaned on the balustrade over the brook and sighed, "Human beings cannot grasp the meaning of life!"

[Although just a child,] the master was constantly absorbed in the recitation of old books, as he was already dedicated to studying the wisdom of the ancients. By the age of eight, Yuandu would every day commit to memory a thousand new characters, practice the *Classic of Poetry*, and learn literature and art, while [already] composing several remarkable verses.

Wencheng [Yuandu's great-uncle] once mentioned that Taiyi [Yuandu's great-grandfather], while reciting a couplet from the poem *Yellow Crane Terrace* [by Cui Hao, 704–54 CE], forgot the second line. Yuandu asked, "What does the first verse mean?" The great-uncle replied, "The pavilion leans against the open sky; standing by the balustrade, I see waves of vapors above the Seven Lakes, and screens of clouds above the Nine Rivers. I listen to the iron flute of the immortals, and the wind blowing the plum blossoms to the ground in the Fifth Month." Yuandu thought it over for a short while and then replied [with this parallel verse]: "History books spread all over the short desk; while discussing, we discovered the beautiful landscapes of a thousand autumns, the grandiose sights of a hundred generations. We asked about important news from the Golden City, and when the yellow cranes will arrive." The great-uncle was amazed by him.

When Yuandu would enter a Buddhist temple, he would not pay respects to the sacred images. Other temple-goers found his behavior unusual. "You are not a Muslim," they said, "so why don't you revere the [sacred images]?" Yuandu answered, "These images are just stone and wood, and have no benefit for me. Why should I show them devotion?"

[Once] he was singing about his time on Tiger Mountain, and one of his poetic couplets went like this: "Walking in the woods, I enjoy the wonderful variety of scenes; chanting languidly by the stream, I pluck the autumn glow." Those who heard him uttered these words in admiration: "Serene and powerful, pure and fresh—just like Tang poetry!" Such extraordinary stories about the master are too many; there is not enough time to report all of them.

When Yuandu was about nine, roaming gangs of reckless bandits started to ravage all areas in Chu [the South]. Hence, our Qing emperor set out to pacify Chu according to the Mandate of Heaven. The person who eventually restored order in Chu, Lord Ma, appointed Bannerman Vice General She [a Muslim, named Yinju, and styled Fengshan], as acting assistant brigade commander of Chenzhou. Vice General She promptly reached the city and, after stationing the troops and completing the repairs, summoned his wife, Lady Li, to reside with him there. During a banquet organized for local relatives . . . Lady Li was introduced to Yuandu's grandmother Wu, with whom she had a pleasant conversation. The following morning, as Lady Li was driven up to the main hall to salute the personnel, Yuandu rushed toward her platform and bowed before her. Although this was their first meeting, Lady Li became so fond of Yuandu's dignified and elegant demeanor that she started to consider adopting him into her family as an heir.

When Yuandu was eleven, in the winter, members of the Imperial College arrived to select candidates for office. It was the first time Yuandu took the annual examination at the prefecture level, but since his essay was judged refined and elegantly austere, the evaluators assumed the author must be an experienced scholar and thus recommended him as the best candidate. However, Yuandu had not achieved the official status of degree holder of the first level because his father Wuxi unexpectedly fell ill and died right after the first month of the year. Yuandu, out of dejection, destroyed all supplies that had been prepared for his imminent trip to the provincial school and buried his father in the ancestral grave.

When bandits began to approach from Qian and Dian, the people in Chenzhou started to panic. Vice General She ordered everyone to stay inside the city walls. Yuandu's grandmother was at home crying. Lady Li was informed about it and sent [people] to check on her. Wu lamented, "My poor family is so unfortunate. My youngest son has just passed away, and I am afraid that we will not have a place to stay after the bandits break into the city." Lady Li replied, "You need not worry. My place is the Old Residence of the Great Lady (formerly part of the government quarters) and there are empty buildings in which you could reside." Wu agreed and moved to live within the city. Shortly after, the bandits arrived and started their violent plundering. Vice General She waited for the bandits to lose their momentum, then he deployed his troops and easily defeated them.

The bandits had fled, but the people were still afraid of leaving their houses. [In those circumstances] Lady Li confided to Grandmother Wu, "I have no child who could become the family's heir. I highly admire the nature of your grandson's talent and virtue. May I ask for him to take the responsibility of filial duty to me as I become older? I will do my best to help and support him in all his life endeavors. And should he have sons, they could inherit both families' fortunes and achievements. I sincerely hope that you can agree." Wu replied, "I am deeply indebted for your help, and only if I were stupid and stubborn would I dare to decline your request. However, as for arranging a good marriage for Yuandu, my poor family still has some resources. Therefore, why do we not all look for a suitable spouse, and once children are born they will adopt both families' surnames?" Li was delighted with the answer and thanked Wu. Thereupon they invited Vice General She, and Yuandu, prompted by his grandmother, bowed before him. Then the She couple in turn thanked and paid homage to Wu. When Yuandu entered Islam the next day, his heart suddenly became open and clear, as if he had acquired pure light. He was overjoyed [as though] his life had found the source of long-lasting happiness. Subsequently, he changed his name to Qiling ["rising spirit"] and adopted the courtesy name of Yunshan ["containing goodness"].

When the bandits had retired far away from the city, Wu took all her family back home. Yunshan began to travel between the two places. One day, during a conversation with Vice General She, he said, "[I am] doing nothing every day. How could I waste all my time indulging in idleness? Studying the classics and other texts would be a better option." "You can do whatever you want," replied She, "and [I will] support you so that you can succeed." [Yunshan] said, "Learning all year for the examinations, which is also a duty, and constantly fretting about them might feel like being a silverfish, which, although always between the pages of a book, is unaware of its contents. However, nothing is better than studying the classics when it comes to investigating the right path and penetrating the arcane doctrines of the ancestors. Surely this is a most rewarding endeavor." [She] said, "I approve."

[Yunshan] was sent to study under Teacher Yang at the military camp. In less than a month, Yunshan read several volumes of the classics, absorbed their extraordinary lessons, and was able to cite the words of the sages to persuade the people. At this point [Yunshan] asked his teacher, "Are we going to interrupt my study of the classics here?" [Yang] answered, "The study of the classics is like the ocean; once you go through it and become familiar with its different areas, you can explore in other directions. [In other words,] it is not possible to achieve greater goals unless you travel and study somewhere else." Thus [Yunshan] asked, "Where are the best places for learning nowadays?" [Yang] answered, "Qin, Chu, Wu, and Liang all have schools with masters who teach in systematic ways. Talented people gather there. However, the best of all are Master Chang and Li [from the area of the] Ji River." Yunshan listened and quietly set it as a goal.

Grandmother Wu died not very long after. Around the same time, Vice General She was appointed to pacify Wuling. Yunshan talked with his mother, Hu, and decided to join the army in the hope of recording important achievements. Hu approved. Yunshan entrusted the family affairs to the care of the servants, then followed Vice General She. [In the army] Lord Ma (named Jiaolin) had the opportunity of praising Yunshan whenever he saw him in action. However, during his traveling, Yunshan always missed studying the classics.

Vice General She, because of his numerous successes, was appointed governor of Wuling, with orders to garrison the area. He was followed there by his wife, Lady Li. Shortly after, She dispatched the troops to Hengzhou. [At the same time,] because of the scarcity of administrative personnel, Li summoned Yunshan's mother, Hu, from Ruanling. They would spend long hours in conversation, and [Hu] began to feel at home there.

The following year, Master Yong'an was expected to leave Chu and return to Qin. [At the same time,] Vice General She was preparing a campaign to retake Jingzhou.

Upon his departure, Yunshan addressed him: "I would like to go to Qin and engage in serious study of the classics. Luckily, Master Yong'an is planning to return there. Could I follow him?" She said, "This is a great time for gaining fame. How could you miss such an opportunity?" [Yunshan] replied, "I am not old yet, and I could still gain fame after completing my studies." She [thus] gave him his permission.

Thereupon Yunshan went back to the vice general's hometown, the village of Linkou in South Wei. Since She's prestige had not yet faded, the locals warmly welcomed [his adoptive son, Yunshan,] and held him in high respect. Yunshan had spent only a couple of months there when the village administrators invited Master Fengsi, who is the brother of the man who raised me, to organize a school, in which Yunshan enrolled. [Yunshan] could understand every text the first time he read it. When the teacher asked [him] to declaim, [Yunshan] uttered every single word without mistakes. In the following days, [Yunshan] requested to be allowed to study ten more pages, and the master obliged reluctantly. Not very long after, [they] started focusing on the *Anmote*. They had spent only five days studying it when, at around the tenth page, [Yunshan] could already anticipate the last half of the book. At this point, the teacher felt ashamed and left. [Yunshan] spent several months relaxing. When his relatives started to plan for his marriage, there were more than ten families who agreed to accept him as groom.

FURTHER READING

Benite, Zvi Ben-Dor. *The Dao of Muhammad: A Cultural History of Muslims in Late Imperial China* (Cambridge, MA: Harvard University Asia Center, 2005).

———. "Follow the White Camel: Islam in China to 1800," in *New Cambridge History of Islam*, vol. 3, *The Eastern Islamic World, Eleventh to Eighteenth Centuries*, ed. David O. Morgan and Anthony Reid (Cambridge: Cambridge University Press, 2010), 409–26.

Lipman, Jonathan Neaman. *Familiar Strangers: A History of Muslims in Northwest China* (Seattle: University of Washington Press, 1997).

APPENDIX

Sources

PART I. THE PROPHET AND THE EMPIRES OF THE CALIPHS (CA. SEVENTH–TENTH CENTURIES)

1 (Saeed)
Translated by contributor.

2 (Anthony)
Ibn ʿAsākir, *Tārīkh Madīnat Dimashq*, ed. ʿUmar b. Gharāma al-ʿAmrawī (Beirut: Dār al-Fikr, 1995–2000), 63:12–14 (translated by contributor).
Yūnus b. Bukayr al-Shaybānī, *Kitāb al-Siyar wa-l-Maghāzī*, ed. Suhayl Zakkār (Beirut: Dār al-Fikr, 1978), 124, 132–34 (translated by contributor).

3 (Lecker)
Ibn Hishām, *al-Sīra al-Nabawiyya*, ed. Muṣṭafā al-Saqqā, Ibrāhīm al-Ibyārī, and ʿAbd al-Ḥafīẓ Shalabī (Cairo: Muṣṭafā al-Bābī al-Ḥalabī, 1355/1936; repr., Beirut: Iḥyāʾ al-Turāth al-ʿArabī, 1391/1971), 1:226–28 (translated by contributor).

4 (Abbou Hershkovits)
Abū ʿAbd Allāh Muḥammad b. Saʿd, *Kitāb al-Ṭabaqāt al-Kabīr*, ed. ʿAlī Muḥammad ʿUmar (Cairo: Maktabat al-Khānjī, 2001), 3:248; 10:219 (translated by contributor).

5 (Landau-Tasseron)
Abū ʿAbd Allāh Muḥammad b. Saʿd, *Kitāb al-Ṭabaqāt al-Kabīr*, ed. ʿAlī Muḥammad ʿUmar (Cairo: Maktabat al-Khānjī, 2001), 1:257, 264, 280–82 (translated by contributor).

6 (Webb)

Hishām b. Muḥammad b. al-Kalbī, *Kitāb al-Aṣnām,* ed. Aḥmad Zakī Bāshā (Cairo: Dār al-Kutub, 1924), 39–40 (translated by contributor).

Abū ʿAbd Allāh Muḥammad b. Saʿd, *al-Ṭabaqāt al-Kubrā,* ed. Muḥammad ʿAbd al-Qādir ʿAṭā (Beirut: Dār al-Kutub al-ʿIlmiyya, 1997), 1:252 (translated by contributor).

Abū ʿUbayd Allāh Muḥammad b. ʿImrān al-Marzubānī, *Muʿjam al-Shuʿarāʾ*, ed. ʿAbbās Hānī al-Jarrākh (Beirut: Dār al-Kutub al-ʿIlmiyya, 2010), 1:128 (translated by contributor).

Abū Muḥammad ʿAbd al-Malik b. Hishām, *al-Sīra al-Nabawiyya,* ed. Muṣṭafā al-Saqqā, Ibrāhīm al-Abyārī, and ʿAbd al-Ḥafīẓ Shalabī (Beirut: Dār al-Maʿrifa, n.d.), 4:503–13 (translated by contributor).

Abū ʿAbd Allāh Muḥammad b. Sallām al-Jumaḥī, *Ṭabaqāt Fuḥūl al-Shuʿarāʾ*, ed. Maḥmūd Muḥammad Shākir (Cairo: al-Maʿārif, 1974), 1:150 (translated by contributor).

7 (Melchert)

Ibn Abī Shayba, *al-Muṣannaf,* ed. Ḥamad ʿAbd Allāh al-Jumʿa and Ibrāhīm al-Luḥaydān (Riyadh: Maktabat al-Rushd, 2004), 6:46–47, 312–13, 462–66 (translated by contributor).

8 (Friedmann)

ʿAbd al-Razzāq b. Humām al-Ṣanʿānī, *al-Muṣannaf,* ed. Ḥabīb al-Raḥmān al-Aʿẓamī (Beirut: al-Maktab al-Islāmī, 1972), 10:173–74 (no. 18720), 312 (no. 19220) (translated by contributor).

Abū Bakr Aḥmad b. Muḥammad al-Khallāl, *Aḥkām Ahl al-Milal min al-Jāmiʿ li-Masāʾil Aḥmad b. Ḥanbal* (Beirut: Dār al-Kutub al-ʿIlmiyya, 1994), 10, 39–40 (translated by contributor).

9 (Papadogiannakis)

André Binggeli, ed., "Anastase le Sinaïte: *Récits sur le Sinaï* et *Récits utiles à l'âme;* Édition, traduction, commentaire" (PhD diss., Université Paris IV, 2001), 233–34, 251, 252 (translated by contributor).

10 (Tannous)

Carl Kayser, ed., *Die Canones Jacob's von Edessa übersetzt und erläutert* (Leipzig: J.C. Heinrichs, 1886), 8, 13, 28 (translated by contributor).

Thomas J. Lamy, ed., *Dissertatio de Syrorum fide et disciplina in re eucharistica* (Louvain: Excudebant Vanlinthout et socii, 1859), 98–171 (translated by contributor).

Mardin Church of the Forty Martyrs 310, 387–429 (= fols. 195a–216b) (translated by contributor).

Karl-Erik Rignell, ed., *A Letter from Jacob of Edessa to John the Stylite of Litarab* (Lund: CWK Gleerup, 1979), 52 (translated by contributor).

Arthur Vööbus, ed., *The Synodicon in the West Syrian Tradition I* (Louvain: Secrétariat du CorpusSCO, 1975), 233–72 (Syriac, with page numbers referring to the Syriac), 215–47 (English) (translated by contributor).

11 (Azad)

Extract from Azad, Arezou and Edmund Herzig with Ali Mir-Ansari, eds. and trs., *Faḍā'il-i Balkh or "Merits of Balkh" written by Shaykh al-Islām Abū Bakr 'Abd Allāh al-Wā'iẓal-Balkhī and translated into Persian by 'Abd Allāh al-Ḥusaynī*, Cambridge: Gibb Memorial Trust, 2021.

12 (Hawting)

Abū Muḥammad 'Abd Allāh b. 'Abd al-Ḥakam, *Sīrat 'Umar b. 'Abd al-'Azīz*, ed. Aḥmad 'Ubayd (Cairo: al-Maktaba al-'Arabiyya, 1346/1927; 6th repr., Beirut: 'Ālam al-Kutub, 1404/1984), 82–84 (abridged) (translated by contributor) [cf. translation, commentary, and analysis of this text by H. A. R. Gibb, "The Fiscal Rescript of 'Umar II," *Arabica* 2 (1955): 1–16].

Aḥmad b. Yaḥyā b. Jābir al-Balādhurī, *Futūḥ al-Buldān*, ed. M. J. de Goeje as *Liber expugnationis regionum* (Leiden: Brill, 1863–66), 368 (translated by contributor) [cf. English translation by Philip K. Hitti and Francis C. Murgotten, *The Origins of the Islamic State* (New York: Columbia University Press, 1916 and 1924)].

Aḥmad b. Yaḥyā b. Jābir al-Balādhurī, *Ansāb al-Ashrāf*, ed. Suhayl Zakkār and Riyāḍ al-Ziriklī (Beirut: Dār al-Fikr, 1417/1996), 8:152–53, 163 (translated by contributor).

Muḥammad b. Jarīr al-Ṭabarī, *Ta'rīkh al-Rusul wa-l-Mulūk*, ed. M. J. de Goeje et al. as *Annales quos scripsit Abu Djafar Mohammad ibn Djarir al-Tabari* (Leiden: Brill, 1879–1901), part 2, 1122–23 [cf. English translation by Martin Hinds, *The History of al-Ṭabarī*, vol. 23, *The Zenith of the Marwānid House* (Albany: State University of New York Press, 1990), 67], and part 2, 1353–54 [cf. English translation by David Stephan Powers, *The History of al-Ṭabarī*, vol. 24, *The Empire in Transition* (Albany: State University of New York Press, 1989), 83] (translated by contributor).

13 (Sahner)

J.-B. Chabot, ed., *Chronicon anonymum Pseudo-Dionysianum vulgo dicto* (Louvain: L. Durbecq, 1949–89), 2:381–91 (translated by contributor) [cf. English translation by Amir Harrak, *The Chronicle of Zuqnīn Parts III and IV, A.D. 488–775* (Toronto: Pontifical Institute of Mediaeval Studies, 1999)].

14 (Pahlitzsch)

A. Papadopoulos-Kerameus, ed., *Sbornik palestinskoj i sirijskoj agiologii/Syllogē Palaistinēs kai Syriakēs hagiologias* (St. Petersburg: Tipografiia Kirshbaum, 1907–13; repr., Thessaloniki: Pournara, 2001), 1:42–59, here 45–48 (translated by contributor).

15 (Cooperson)

Muḥammad b. 'Abdūs al-Jahshiyārī, *Kitāb al-Wuzarā' wa-l-Kuttāb*, ed. Muṣṭafā al-Saqqā, Ibrāhīm al-Ibyārī, and 'Abd al-Ḥafīẓ Shalabī (Cairo: Muṣṭafā al-Bābī al-Ḥalabī, 1938), 229–31 (translated by contributor).

'Alī b. Yūsuf al-Qifṭī, *Ibn al-Qifṭī's Ta'rīḫ al-Ḥukamā': Auf Grund der Vorarbeiten Aug. Müller's*, ed. Julius Lippert (Leipzig: Dieterich'sche Verlagsbuchhandlung, 1903), 140 (translated by contributor).

Abū al-Faraj al-Iṣfahānī, *Kitāb al-Aghānī*, ed. Iḥsān 'Abbās, Ibrāhīm al-Sa''āfīn, and Bakr 'Abbās, 3rd ed. (Beirut: Dār Ṣādir, 2008), 5:102–4 (translated by contributor).

16 (Greenwood)

Patmut'iwn tann Artsruneats', ed. Gēorg Tēr-Vardanean (Antilias: Armenian Catholicosate of Cilicia Press, 2010), 178, 180–82, 186, 227–28 (translated by contributor).

17 (Wolf)

Juan Gil, ed., *Corpus Scriptorum Muzarabicorum* (Madrid: Instituto Antonio de Nebrija, 1973), 2:366–459 (*Memoriale sanctorum*), 2:475–95 (*Liber apologeticus martyrum*) (translated by contributor) [cf. complete English translation by Kenneth Baxter Wolf, *The Eulogius Corpus* (Liverpool: Liverpool University Press, 2019)].

18 (Roggema)

Mu'taman b. al-'Assāl, *Majmū' Uṣūl al-Dīn wa-Masmū' Maḥṣūl al-Yaqīn*, ed. Wadī' Abullīf Malik 'Awaḍ (Cairo: al-Markaz al-Fransīskānī li-l-Dirāsāt al-Sharqiyya al-Masīḥiyya wa-Maṭba'at al-Ābā' al-Fransīsiyyīn, 1998–99), 1:278–83 (translated by contributor).

Samir Khalil Samir and Paul Nwyia, trans., "Une correspondance islamo-chrétienne entre Ibn al-Munağğim, Ḥunayn ibn Isḥāq et Qusṭā ibn Lūqā," *Patrologia Orientalis* 40 (1981): 524–723, here 686–701 (a longer and more personal version of Ḥunayn's treatise) (translated by contributor).

19 (Gordon)

Muḥammad b. Jarīr al-Ṭabarī, *Ta'rīkh al-Rusul wa-l-Mulūk*, ed. Muḥammad Abū al-Faḍl Ibrāhīm (Cairo: Dār al-Ma'ārif, 1960–69), 9:262 (translated by contributor).

'Alī b. Mūsā b. Sa'īd al-Andalusī, *al-Mughrib fī Ḥulā al-Maghrib*, ed. Zakī Muḥammad Ḥasan et al. (Cairo: Jāmi'at Fu'ād al-Awwal, Kulliyyat al-Ādāb, 1953), 74 (translated by contributor).

20 (Sahner)

The Rivāyats *of Ādurfarnbag ī Farroxzādān*, Eng. trans. Prods Oktor Skjærvø and Yishai Kiel (unpublished, 2018), 2:48, 70–71 (translation adapted by contributor, used here with the kind permission of the translators); ed. and transcr. Behramgore T. Anklesaria as *The Pahlavi Rivāyat of Āturfarnbag and Farnbag-Srōš* (Bombay: M. F. Cama Athornan Institute, 1969), 1:2–3, 27–28 (text), 1:101, 115–16 (transcription).

The Rivāyats *of Ēmēd ī Ašawahištān*, Eng. trans. Christian C. Sahner; ed. and transcr. Behramgore T. Anklesaria, *Rivâyat-î Hêmît-î Asavahistân*, vol. 1, *Pahlavi Text* (Bombay: K. R. Cama Oriental Institute Publication, 1962), 9–12 (translated by contributor) [cf. English translation by Nezhat Safa-Isfehani, ed., *Rivāyat-i Hēmīt-i Ašawahistān: Edition, Transcription, and Translation; A Study in Zoroastrian Law* (Cambridge, MA: Harvard University Printing Office, 1980), 19–24 (transcription and translation)].

21 (Yarbrough)

Abū 'Umar Yūsuf b. 'Abd al-Barr al-Namarī al-Qurṭubī, *Bahjat al-Majālis wa-Uns al-Mujālis wa-Shaḥdh al-Dhāhin wa-l-Hājis*, ed. Muḥammad Mursī al-Khūlī (Cairo: al-Dār al-Miṣriyya li-l-Ta'līf wa-l-Tarjama, 1967–70), 2:756 (translated by contributor).

PART II. THE ISLAMIC COMMONWEALTH (CA. TENTH–THIRTEENTH CENTURIES)

22 (Hackenburg)

Ibn Taymiyya, *al-Jawāb al-Ṣaḥīḥ li-Man Baddala Dīn al-Masīḥ*, ed. ʿAlī b. Ḥasan b. Nāṣir, ʿAbd al-ʿAzīz b. Ibrāhīm al-ʿAskar, and Ḥamdān b. Muḥammad al-Ḥamdān (Riyadh: Dār al-ʿĀṣima, 1993–99), iv, 88–145, 158–82 (translated by contributor).

23 (Cook)

Abū al-Faraj al-Iṣfahānī, *Kitāb al-Diyārāt*, ed. Jalīl al-ʿAṭiyya (London: Riyāḍ al-Raʾīs, 1991), 48–52; partial version in Sibṭ b. al-ʿAjamī al-Ḥalabī, *Kunūz al-Dhahab fī Taʾrīkh Ḥalab*, ed. Shawqī Shaʿth and Falīḥ al-Bukūr (Aleppo: Dār al-Qalam al-ʿArabī, 1996), 1:66–67 (translated by contributor).

24 (Mako)

Aḥmad b. Faḍlān b. al-ʿAbbās b. Rāshid b. Ḥammād, *Risālat Ibn Faḍlān*, ed. Sāmī al-Dahhān (Damascus: al-Jāmiʿ al-ʿIlmī al-ʿArabī, 1959), 67–68, 115–16, 124–25, 135 (translated by contributor).

25 (Jones)

Ibn al-ʿAṭṭār (Muḥammad b. Aḥmad al-Umawī), *Kitāb al-Wathāʾiq wa-l-Sijillāt*, ed. Pedro Chalmeta and Francisco Corriente (Madrid: Instituto Hispano-Arabe de Cultura, Academia Matritense del Notariado, 1983), 405–12 (translated by contributor).

26 (Papaconstantinou)

Jean Ziadeh, "L'Apocalypse de Samuel, supérieur de Deir-el-Qalamoun," *Revue de l'Orient Chrétien* 20 (1915–17): 374–404 (edition of Arabic text and French translation based on Paris. Ar. 150) (translated by contributor).

Samir Khalil Samir, "L'Apocalypse de Samuel de Qalamūn et la domination des Hagaréens," in *"Guerra santa" e conquiste islamiche nel Mediterraneo (VII–XI secolo)*, ed. Marco Di Branco and Kordula Wolf, 17–63 (Rome: Viella, 2014) (list of twenty-two manuscripts and some textual amendments) (consulted by contributor).

27 (Yavari)

Maḥmūd b. ʿUthmān, *Firdaws al-Murshidiyya fī Asrār al-Ṣamadiyya*, ed. Īraj Afshār (repr., Tehran: Anjuman-i Āsār-i Millī, 1979), 26–29 (translated by contributor).

28 (Swanson)

Aziz Suryal Atiya, Yassā ʿAbd al-Masīḥ, and O. H. E. Khs.-Burmester, eds., *History of the Patriarchs of the Egyptian Church, Known as the History of the Holy Church, by Sawīrus ibn al-Mukaffaʿ, Bishop of al-Ašmūnīn*, vol. 2, part 2: *Khaël III–Šenouti II (A.D. 880–1066)* (Cairo: Publications de la Société d'Archéologie Copte, 1948) (translated by contributor).

29 (Tor)

Ibn al-Jawzī (Sibṭ), *Mir'āt al-Zamān fī Ta'rīkh al-A'yān*, ed. Kāmil Salmān al-Jubūrī and Mūsā b. Muḥammad Yūnīnī (Beirut: Dār al-Kutub al-'Ilmiyya, 2013), 13:200 (translated by contributor).

30 (Fierro)

Ibn Rushd, *Kitāb al-Bayān wa-l-Taḥṣīl wa-l-Sharḥ wa-l-Tawjīh wa-Ta'līl li-Masā'il al-'Utbiyya*, ed. Muḥammad Ḥajjī et al. (Beirut: Dār al-Gharb al-Islāmī, 1984–87; 2nd rev. ed. 1988), 16:432–35 (translated by contributor).

'Abd al-Fattāḥ Muḥammad al-Ḥulw, *Fahāris al-Bayān wa-l-Taḥṣīl li-Abī al-Walīd b. Rushd* (Beirut: Dār al-Gharb al-Islāmī, 1991) (translated by contributor).

31 (Conterno)

Jean-Baptiste Chabot, trans., *Chronique de Michel le Syrien, patriarche jacobite d'Antioche (1166–1199)* (Paris: Ernest Leroux, 1899–1910), 3:156–57; ed. George Kiraz, *Texts and Translations of the Chronicle of Michael the Great: The Edessa-Aleppo Syriac Codex* (Piscataway, NJ: Gorgias Press, 2009), 573–74 (translated by contributor).

32 (Conterno)

Jean-Baptiste Abbeloos and Thomas J. Lamy, ed. and trans., *Gregorii Barhebræi Chronicon ecclesiasticum* (Leuven: Peeters, 1872–77), 3:347–51 (translated by contributor).

33 (Schwarb)

Ghāyat al-Maqṣūd fī al-Radd 'alā al-Naṣārā wa-l-Yahūd, ed. Imām Ḥanafī Sayyid 'Abd Allāh (Cairo: Dār al-Āfāq al-'Arabiyya, 2006); *Badhl al-Majhūd fī Ifḥām al-Yahūd*, ed. Aḥmad Ḥijāzī and Aḥmad al-Saqqā (Giza: Maktabat al-Nāfidha, 2005); *Ifḥām al-Yahūd wa-Qiṣṣat Islām al-Samaw'al*, ed. Muḥammad 'Abd Allāh al-Sharqāwī (Cairo: Dār al-Hidāya, 1986); Ibrahim Marazka, Reza Pourjavady, and Sabine Schmidtke, eds., *Samaw'al al-Maghribī's (d. 570/1175) "Ifḥām al-Yahūd": The Early Recension* (Wiesbaden: Harrassowitz, 2006).

Moshe Perlmann, ed. and trans., *Ifḥām al-Yahūd: Silencing the Jews* (New York: American Academy for Jewish Research, 1964). Reprinted with permission of the publisher (translation adapted by contributor).

34 (Talmon-Heller)

Shams al-Dīn al-Dhahabī, *Siyar A'lām al-Nubalā'*, ed. Bashār 'Awwād Ma'rūf and Muḥyī al-Dīn Hilāl Sirḥān (Beirut: Mu'assasat al-Risāla, 1985), 20:553 (translated by contributor).

Ibn Rajab, *Dhayl Ṭabaqāt al-Ḥanābila*, ed. Muḥammad Ḥamīd al-Fiqī (Cairo: Maṭba'at al-Sunna al-Muḥammadiyya, 1952–53), 2:44–45 (translated by contributor).

Ḍiyā' al-Dīn al-Maqdisī, *al-Ḥikāyāt al-Muqtabasa fī Karāmāt Mashāyikh al-Arḍ al-Muqaddasa*, trans. and intr. Daniella Talmon-Heller, "*The Cited Tales of the Wondrous Doings of the Shaykhs of the Holy Land* by Ḍiyā' al-Dīn Abū 'Abd Allāh Muḥammad ibn 'Abd al-Wāḥid al-Maqdisī (569/1173–643/1245): Text, Translation, and Commentary,"

Crusades 1 (2002): 111–54, at 137. Reprinted with permission of the publisher (translation adapted by contributor).

35 (La Porta and Pogossian)
Yakob Manandean and Hrach'ea Achaṙean, eds., *Hayots' Nor Vkanerě (1155–1843)* (Vagharshapat: Mother See of Holy Ejmiatsin, 1903) (translated by contributor).

36 (Szpiech)
Translation A
Yitsḥak Shailat, ed., *Iggerot ha-Rambam* (Ma'aleh Adumim: Ma'aliyot, 1988–89), 1:25–59 (including variants from other manuscripts and material from translation B; this and all other witnesses below translated by contributor).
Abraham Geiger, ed., *Iggeret ha-shemad le-ha-Rambam*. In *Moses ben Maimon: Studien* (Breslau: L. J. Weigert, 1850), I:2a-7b (Heb).
Zvi Hirsch Edelman, ed., *Ḥemdah genuzah* (Koeningsberg: Gruber & Euphrat, 1856), 5b–12a.
Abraham Lichtenberg, ed., *Qovets teshuvot ha-Rambam ve-iggrotav* (Leipzig: H. L. Shnoys, 1859), II:12a-15d.
Mordechai D. Rabinowitz, ed., *Iggrot ha-Rambam* (Tel Aviv: Rishonim, 1951), I:29–68.
Yosef Qafiḥ, ed., *Iggerot ha-Rambam* (Jerusalem: Mossad ha-Rav Kook, 1972), 107–20.

Modern English Translations (based on Hebrew translation A)
Leon D. Stiskin, ed. and trans., *Letters of Maimonides* (New York: Yeshiva University Press, 1977), 34–69.
Abraham Halkin, trans., with discussions by David Hartman, *Epistles of Maimonides: Crisis and Leadership* (Philadelphia: Jewish Publication Society, 1985), 13–90 (consulted by contributor).
Abraham Ya'akov Finkel, trans., *The Essential Maimonides: Translations of the Rambam* (London: Jason Aronson, 1993), 51–78 (consulted by contributor).

37 (Zinger)
Benjamin M. Lewin, ed., *Otsar ha-Geonim*, vol. 7, *Yebamoth* (Jerusalem: n.p., 1936), 196–97, no. 474 (responsum 1) (this and all excerpts below translated by contributor).
Robert Brody, ed., *Teshuvot Rav Natronai bar Hilai Gaon* (Jerusalem: Ofeq Institute, 1994), 2:544–47, no. 369 (responsum 2).
Benjamin M. Lewin, *Otsar ha-Geonim*, vol. 2, *Shabbath* (Haifa: Warhaftig Press, 1930), 130, no. 398 (responsum 3).
Mordechai A. Friedman, "Responsa of Hai Gaon—New Fragments from the Geniza" [in Hebrew], *Te'uda* 3 (1983): 75–81 (responsum 4).
Avraham H. Freimann, ed., and Shelomo D. Goitein, trans., *Teshuvot Rabenu Avraham ben ha-Rambam* (Jerusalem: Mekitse Nirdamim, 1937), 54–55, no. 53 (responsum 5); 55, no. 54 (responsum 6).

38 (Yagur)
Text 1: JTSA: ENA 2560.6v; unpublished (this and all excerpts below translated by contributor).

Text 2: CUL: T-S Ar. 40.96; unpublished.
Text 3: CUL: T-S 12.305; unpublished.
Text 4: CUL: T-S K 15.95; unpublished.
Text 5: Mosseri VII 178.1; transcription and Hebrew translation published in Shmuel Glick, *Seride Teshuvot: A Descriptive Catalogue of Responsa Fragments from the Jacques Mosseri Collection, Cambridge University Library* (Leiden: Brill, 2012), 275–77.
Text 6a: CUL: T-S K 25.244; transcription and Hebrew translation published in Moshe Gil, *Palestine during the First Muslim Period (634–1099)* [in Hebrew] (Tel Aviv: Tel Aviv University and the Ministry of Defense, 1983), vol. 2, no. 399.
Text 6b: CUL: T-S NS J 360; transcription and Hebrew translation published in Moshe Gil, "Palestine during the First Muslim Period (634–1099): Additions, Notes, Corrections" [in Hebrew], *Te'uda* 7 (1991): no. 449a.

39 (Shachar)

John of Ibelin, *Le Livre des Assises*, ed. Peter Edbury (Leiden: Brill, 2013), 167–68 (translated by contributor).

De Profectione Ludovici VII in Orientem, trans. Virginia Berry (New York: W. W. Norton, 1948 [Copyright © Columbia University Press]). Reprinted with permission of the publisher (translation adapted by contributor).

Decretales ineditae saeculi XII, ed. Stanley Chodorow (Vatican: Biblioteca Apostolica Vaticana, 1982), 166–67 (translated by contributor).

Le Livre au Roi, ed. Myriam Greilsammer (Paris: Académie des inscriptions et belles-lettres, 1995), 203–4 (translated by contributor).

40 (Ephrat)

Aḥmad b. Muḥammad b. Aḥmad ʿUthmān, *Kitāb Manāqib al-Shaykh ʿAbd Allāh al-Yūnīnī*, MS Princeton University Library, Department of Rare Books and Special Collections, Manuscripts Division, Islamic Manuscripts Collection, 259H (translated by contributor).

PART III. SULTANS, CONQUERORS, AND TRAVELERS (CA. THIRTEENTH–SIXTEENTH CENTURIES)

41 (Yarbrough)

Abū al-ʿAbbās Aḥmad b. Saʿīd al-Darjīnī, *Kitāb Ṭabaqāt al-Mashāʾikh bi-l-Maghrib*, ed. Ibrāhīm Tallāy (Constantine: Maṭbaʿat al-Baʿth, 1974), 2:517–18 (translated by contributor).

42 (Yarbrough)

Yohanan Friedmann, "*Qiṣṣat Shakarwatī Farmāḍ*: A Tradition Concerning the Introduction of Islām to Malabar," *Israel Oriental Studies* 5 (1975): 233–58 (translated by contributor).

43 (Peacock)

MS Princeton University Library, Department of Rare Books and Special Collections, Manuscripts Division, Garrett Collection, 97, fols. 197b–200a (copied in the sixteenth

century from an original dated 895/1489) (this and all excerpts below translated by contributor).
MS Staatsbibliothek zu Berlin, Ahlwardt, 8794, fols. 107a–111a.
Nejdet Gürkan, Mehmet Necmettin Bardakçı, and Mehmet Saffet Sarıkaya, trans., *Tuffâhu'l-Ervâh ve Miftâhu'l-Irbâh: Ruhların Meyvesi ve Kazancın Anahtarı* (Istanbul: Kitap Yayınevi, 2015).

44 (Brack)
Rashīd al-Dīn, *Jāmiʿ al-Tawārīkh*, ed. ʿAbd al-Karīm ʿAlī Zāda (Baku: Farhangistān-i ʿUlūm-i Jumhūr-i Shuravī-yi Sūsīyālistī-yi Ādharbāyjān, 1957), 3:604–7 (translated by contributor).

45 (Frenkel)
Li Guo, *Early Mamluk Syrian Historiography: Al-Yunini's Dhayl mir'at al zaman* [the years 697–701/1297–1302] (Leiden: Brill, 1998) [vol. 1 (English translation); vol. 2 (Arabic text): 255]; ed. Ḥamza ʿAbbās (Abu Dhabi: al-Majmaʿ al-Thaqāfī, 2007), 1:656 (translation adapted by contributor and used with the permission of the publisher).
Abū l-Fidā Ismāʿīl Ibn Kathīr (701–774/1301–1373), *al-Bidāya wa-l-nihāya*, ed. ʿAbd Allāh b. ʿAbd al-Muḥsin al-Turkī (Cairo: Hajar, 1998), 18:10–11 (translated by contributor).
Shihāb al-Dīn Aḥmad b. ʿAlī Ibn Ḥajar al-ʿAsqalānī (773–852/1372–1449), *al-Durar al-kāmina fī aʿyān al-miʾa al-thāmina* (Beirut, n.d.), 2:366–67 (bio. no. 2419) (translated by contributor).

46 (Bauden)
Taqī al-Dīn Aḥmad b. ʿAlī al-Maqrīzī, *al-Mawāʿiẓ wa-l-Iʿtibār fī Dhikr al-Khiṭaṭ wa-l-Āthār*, ed. Ayman Fuʾād Sayyid (London: Al-Furqān Islamic Heritage Foundation, 2013), 4b:1014–16.
Solomon Caesar Malan, *A Short History of the Copts and of Their Church* (London: D. Nutt, 1873), 99–102 (translation adapted by contributor with slight revisions).

47 (Carlson)
MS Bibliothèque nationale de France, Syr. 181, fols. 75a–78b (this and all witnesses below translated by contributor).
Chaldean Cathedral of Mardin [HMML CCM] 396, fols. 210a–b.
Chaldean Cathedral of Mardin [HMML CCM] 414, fols. 66b–68b.

48 (Aquil)
Ḥażrat Khwāja Niẓām al-Dīn Awliyā, *Fawāʾid al-Fuʾād*, comp. Amīr Ḥasan ʿAlā Sijzī, Persian text with Urdu trans. by Khwaja Hasan Sani Nizami (Delhi: Urdu Academy, 1990; repr., 2001), 4:305–8, *majlis* (session) 40 (translated by contributor).

49 (Bosanquet)
Ibn Qayyim al-Jawziyya, *Aḥkām Ahl al-Dhimma*, ed. Ṣubḥī al-Ṣāliḥ (Beirut: Dār al-ʿIlm li-l-Malāyīn, 1981), 2:318–22, 344 (translated by contributor).

50 (Hackenburg)

Míkel de Epalza, ed., *Fray Anselm Turmeda ('Abdallāh al-Tarǧumān) y su polémica islamo-cristiana: Edición, traducción y estudio de la Tuḥfa* (Madrid: Libros Hiperión, 1994), 231, 233, 235, 237, 239, 241, 243 (translated by contributor).

51 (DeWeese)

MS Tashkent, Institute of Oriental Studies of the Academy of Sciences of Uzbekistan, inv. no. 1477, briefly described in A.A. Semenov, ed., *Sobranie vostochnykh rukopisei Akademii nauk Uzbekskoi SSR*, vol. 3 (Tashkent: Izdatel'stvo Akademii nauk UzSSR, 1955), 271, no. 2441 (fols. 4b–5a [1]; 40a–41a [2]; 41a–b [3]) (translated by contributor).

MS Islamabad, Iran-Pakistan Institute of Persian Studies, Ganjbakhsh Collection, inv. no. 4031, described in Aḥmad Munzavī, ed., *Fihrist-i Nuskhahā-yi Khaṭṭī-yi Kitābkhāna-yi Ganjbakhsh*, vol. 4 (Islamabad: Markaz-i Taḥqīqāt-i Fārsī-yi Īrān va Pākistān, 1982), 2109–10, cat. nos. 2501 (title), 5835 (manuscript; pp. 120–23 [2]; 123–25 [3]) (translated by contributor).

52 (Wain)

Russell Jones, ed., *Hikayat Raja Pasai* (Kuala Lumpur: Yayasan Karyawan dan Penerbit Fajar Bakti, 1999) (a Romanized version of MS Raffles Malay no. 67, kept at the Royal Asiatic Society in London) (translated by contributor).

53 (Rebstock)

Edition of *Ajwibat al-Maghīlī* in J.O. Hunwick, ed. and trans., *Sharī'a in Songhay: The Replies of al-Maghīlī to the Questions of Askia al-Ḥājj Muḥammad* (Cambridge: Cambridge University Press, 1985), 60–61, 71–72, 79, 80–83, 91 (Arabic pp. 2, 14–16, 20, 26–28, 30, 42, 92) (translated by contributor).

Edition of *Sirāj al-Ikhwān fī Ahamm Mā Yuḥtāj ilayhi fī Hādhā al-Zamān* in Ulrich Rebstock, *Die Lampe der Brüder ("Sirāǧ al-iḫwān") von 'Uṯmān b. Fūdī: Reform und Ǧihād im Sūdān* (Walldorf-Hessen: Verlag für Orientkunde, 1985), 71, 83–85, 90–93 (Arabic pp. 5, 12–13, 15–17, 26–28) (translated by contributor).

54 (el-Leithy)

Shihāb al-Dīn Aḥmad b. Ṭawq, *al-Ta'līq. Yawmiyyāt Shihāb al-Dīn Aḥmad b. Ṭawq. Mudhakkirāt Kutibat bi-Dimashq fī Ākhir al-'Ahd al-Mamlūkī*, ed. Ja'far al-Muhājir (Damascus: al-Ma'had al-Faransī li-l-Dirāsāt al-'Arabiyya, 2000–2007), 117 (#2), 453–54 (#3), 487 (#4), 611 (#5), 933 (#6), 1103 (#7), 1202 (#8), 1208 (#9), 1274 (#10), 1339 (#11), 1462 (#12), 1479 (#13), 1622 (#14) (continuous pagination) (translated by contributor).

Shams al-Dīn Muḥammad b. Ṭūlūn, *Mufākahat al-Khillān fī Ḥawādith al-Zamān*, ed. Muḥammad Muṣṭafā (Cairo: al-Mu'assasa al-Miṣriyya al-'Āmma, 1962), 24 (#1), 323 (#15) (translated by contributor).

55 (Kadrić)

Başbakanlık Osmanlı Arşivi (BOA), Mühimme Defteri 2, no. 108 (13 Rebiyülevvel 963/January 26, 1556) (this and all excerpts below translated by contributor).

BOA, Mühimme Defteri 2, no. 464 (25 Cemaziyülevvel 963/April 6, 1556).
BOA, Mühimme Defteri 2, no. 670 (29 Cemaziyülahir 963/May 9, 1556).
BOA, Mühimme Defteri 2, no. 1505 (Zilhicce 963/October 1556).
BOA, Mühimme Defteri 2, no. 1573 (13 Zilhicce 963/October 18, 1556).
BOA, Mühimme Defteri 2, no. 2009 (Rebiyülevvel 964/January 1557).
BOA, Mühimme Defteri 4, no. 34 (1 Rebiyülahir 967/December 30, 1559).
BOA, Mühimme Defteri 4, no. 35 (1 Rebiyülahir 967/December 30, 1559).
BOA, Mühimme Defteri 4, no. 1036 (19 Şevval 967/July 13, 1560).

56 (Ricci)

A. M. Noertjahajo, *Cerita Rakyat Sekitar Wali Sanga* (Jakarta: Pradnya Paramita, 1974), 32–35 (translated by contributor).

57 (Liu and Benite)

Zhao Can, *Jingxue Xizhuanpu* (Xining: Qinghai People's Publishing House, 1989) (translated by contributor [Liu]).

CONTRIBUTORS

KEREN ABBOU HERSHKOVITS, The Open University of Israel

SEAN W. ANTHONY, The Ohio State University

RAZIUDDIN AQUIL, University of Delhi

AREZOU AZAD, University of Oxford

FRÉDÉRIC BAUDEN, University of Liège

ZVI BEN-DOR BENITE, New York University

ANTONIA BOSANQUET, University of Hamburg

JONATHAN BRACK, Ben-Gurion University of the Negev

THOMAS A. CARLSON, Oklahoma State University

MARIA CONTERNO, Independent scholar

DAVID COOK, Rice University

MICHAEL COOPERSON, University of California, Los Angeles

DEVIN DEWEESE, Indiana University Bloomington

TAMER EL-LEITHY, Johns Hopkins University

DAPHNA EPHRAT, The Open University of Israel

MARIBEL FIERRO, Spanish National Research Council (CSIC)

YEHOSHUA FRENKEL, University of Haifa

YOHANAN FRIEDMANN, Hebrew University of Jerusalem and Shalem College, Jerusalem

MATTHEW GORDON, Miami University of Ohio

TIM GREENWOOD, University of St. Andrews

CLINT HACKENBURG, Heidelberg University
GERALD HAWTING, School of Oriental and African Studies, University of London
LINDA G. JONES, University of Pompeu Fabra
SANJA KADRIĆ, Texas A & M University-Commerce
ELLA LANDAU-TASSERON, Hebrew University of Jerusalem
SERGIO LA PORTA, California State University, Fresno
MICHAEL LECKER, Hebrew University of Jerusalem
SUOFEI LIU, Saint Louis University
GERALD MAKO, University of Cambridge
CHRISTOPHER MELCHERT, University of Oxford
JOHANNES PAHLITZSCH, Johannes Gutenberg University of Mainz
ARIETTA PAPACONSTANTINOU, University of Reading
YANNIS PAPADOGIANNAKIS, King's College, University of London
A. C. S. PEACOCK, University of St. Andrews
ZAROUI POGOSSIAN, Ruhr University Bochum
ULRICH REBSTOCK, Albert Ludwig University of Freiburg
RONIT RICCI, Hebrew University of Jerusalem and Australian National University
BARBARA ROGGEMA, Ruhr University Bochum
ABDULLAH SAEED, University of Melbourne
CHRISTIAN C. SAHNER, University of Oxford
GREGOR SCHWARB, School of Oriental and African Studies, University of London
URI SHACHAR, Ben-Gurion University of the Negev
URIEL SIMONSOHN, University of Haifa
MARK SWANSON, Lutheran School of Theology at Chicago
RYAN SZPIECH, University of Michigan
DANIELLA TALMON-HELLER, Ben-Gurion University of the Negev
JACK TANNOUS, Princeton University
D. G. TOR, University of Notre Dame
ALEXANDER WAIN, International Institute of Advanced Islamic Studies (IAIS), Malaysia
PETER WEBB, University of Leiden
KENNETH BAXTER WOLF, Pomona College
MOSHE YAGUR, Ben-Gurion University of the Negev
LUKE YARBROUGH, University of California, Los Angeles
NEGUIN YAVARI, University of Leipzig
ODED ZINGER, Hebrew University of Jerusalem

INDEX

Abbreviation conventions
GI = General introduction
I1 = Introduction to part 1
S1 = Selection 1

'Abbasids, GI, I1, S3, S14, S15, S18, S19, S21, I2
'Abd al-Sayyid b. al-Muhadhdhib (Yūsuf b. Isḥāq al-Yahūdī), S45
'Abd 'Amr b. Jabala al-Kalbī, S6
abrogation, S25, S33, S42
Abū Bakr al-Ṣiddīq, I1, S42
Abū Bakr Muḥammad b. 'Abd al-Karīm, S27
Abū Ḥanīfa, S49
Abū Jahl, S4
Abū Lahab, I1, S4
Abū Najāḥ *al-kabīr,* S28
Abū Yūsuf, S49
Ādurfarnbag son of Farroxzād, S20
Africa, Islam in, GI, I1, I3, S41, S50, S53
  agents of conversion
    merchants, GI, I2, S24, I3, S41, S51
    saints, GI, I2, S40, I3, S43, S51, S56
    scholars, I2, S34, S45
    Sufis, GI, I2, S27, S40, I3, S42, S43, S48, S51
    warriors, GI, S11
Aḥmad b. Muḥammad b. Aḥmad 'Uthmān, S40
alcohol, S6, S40
'Alī b. Abī Ṭālib, S49
'Alī b. Īkhlaf, S41
'Alī b. Yaḥyā b. al-Munajjim, S18
Anastasius of Sinai, S9
Anselm Turmeda ('Abd Allāh al-Tarjumān), I3, S50
apocalypses, S26
apostasy
  from Christianity, I1, S9, S10, S13, S14, S16, S17, S22, S39, S47, S50
  from Islam, GI, I1, S8, S9, S11, S17, I2, S28, S30, S35, S53, S54
  from Judaism, I2, S36, S37, S38
  from Zoroastrianism, S20
A'raj, 'Adī b. 'Amr b. Suwayd al-, S6
Armenians, S16, I2, S35
Arqam, al-, house of, S4
Artsruni family, S16
Arwā bt. 'Abd al-Muṭṭalib, I1, S4
Aṣbagh b. al-Faraj, S30
Ashhab, S30, S49
Ashraf Khalīl, al-, S46
Asīd b. Sa'ya, S3
Askiyā Muḥammad, S53
'Ayn al-Ghazāl, S46

Bagratuni, Bagarat, S16
Balādhurī, Aḥmad b. Yaḥyā al-, S12
Balkh, conversion of, S11
Balkhī, Abū Bakr ʿAbd Allāh al-Wāʿiẓ al-, S11
Bar Hebraeus, S32
baraka, S27, S40
barbarians, S26
Barmakī, Faḍl b. Yaḥyā al-, S11
Barmakī, Jaʿfar al-, S15
Barmakī, Yaḥyā b. Khālid al-, S15
Baydarā (governor), S46
Bible
  Hebrew, S29, S33, S36, S42
  New Testament, S22, S42, S50
biographies, as sources on conversion, G1, S2, S3, S4, S5, S6, S12, S15, S19, S28, S32, S34, S41, S57
Buddhism
  conversion to, S57
  conversion to Islam from, S11, I3, S44, S56, S57
Bulgars, S24, I3
Buyids, I2

Cheraman Perumal, S42
children
  conversion of, G1, S8, S9, S10, S15, S26, S34, S37, S38, S51, S54, S57
  status of, S8, S10, I2, S25, S32, S37, S38
China, Islam in, I3, S57
Christianity
  conversion to, S21, S34, S35
  conversion to Islam from, GI, I1, S7, S9, S10, S12, S13, S14, S16, S17, S18, S21, I2, S22, S25, S26, S28, S29, S32, S34, S39, S40, I3, S46, S47, S49, S50, S51, S54
  conversion to paganism from, S10
  conversion to Zoroastrianism from, S16
  creed of, S22
  as "Islam," S8
  as rival to Islam, S42
churches, destruction/plunder of, S28, S46
circumcision
  as marker of Islam, GI, S12, S20, S31
  as marker of Judaism, S37
clientage, GI, S7, S12, S15
clothing, as religious marker, S5, S13, S14, S20, S28, S29
coercion in conversion, GI, I1, S1, S5, S9, S14, S16, I2, S28, S32, S35, S36, I3, S46, S48, S54
conversion
  experience of, GI, I1, S6, S13, S15, S21, S22, S33
  feigned, GI, S16, S17, I2, S28, S36
  group, GI, I1, S5, S6, S10, S11, S13, S24, S31, S41, S43, S44, S52
  involuntary, S14, S17, S18
  legal aspects of, GI, I1, S7, S8, S10, S12, S20, S25, S30, S32, S36, S37, S38, S39, S49, S54
  role of sponsor/patron in, GI, I1, S12, S15, S25, S42
  sources on premodern, GI, I1
  See also under individual religions
Copts, S26, S28, I3, S46
Crusades, S39, S40

Darjīnī, Abū al-ʿAbbās al-, I3, S41
Darmakusuma (prince), I3, S56
Dāwūd b. ʿAlī, S49
declaration of faith (*shahāda*), GI, S8, S30, S33, I3, S41, S42, S44, S50, S52, S53, S54, S56
delegations, I1, S5, S6
Dhahabī, Shams al-Dīn al-, S34
dhimmīs, *ahl al-dhimma*, GI, S8, S12, S28, S29, S30, S34, I3, S49, S55
divorce, S7, S37, S38, S49
dreams, S2, S27, S33, S34, S40, S42, S47, S51, S52

East Asia, Islam in, I3, S57
Elkesites, S16
Ēmēd son of Ašawahišt, S20
Eulogius of Córdoba, S17

Faḍl b. Sahl b. Zādhānfarrūkh, al-, I1, S15
families, mixed. *See* children; marriage
Fāṭima bt. al-Khaṭṭāb, I1, S4
fire worship, S27
fiṭra (natural disposition), S1, S8, S30
food, as religious marker, S1, S5, S8, S10, S37

Gabriel, S2, S42
gabrs, S11, S27
gender. *See* women
Geniza, I2, S38
genres. *See* biographies; *ḥadīth;* hagiographies; historical writing; poetry; responsa
Geonim, S37
Ghāzān, I3, S44
ghiyār, S28
group conversion. *See* conversion: group

Ḥabīb b. Mālik, S42
Hadhramaut, S42
ḥadīth, S7, S8

Ḥafṣids, S50
hagiographies, as sources on conversion, S9, S12, S14, S17, S27, S28, S35, S40, S42, S43, S51
Ḥajjāj b. Yūsuf, al-, S12
Ḥākim bi-Amr Allāh, al-, S28
Ḥammād b. Abī Sulaymān, S49
Ḥammād b. Salama, S49
Ḥanbalīs, S8, S29, S34, S49
Ḥasan b. Ayyūb, al-, S22
Hayya Gaon, S37
Hinduism, S42, S48, S52, S56
historical writing, as source on conversion, S4, S5, S6, S11, S12, S13, S15, S16, S19, S28, S29, S31, S32, S34, S39, I3, S41, S42, S44, S45, S46. *See also* biographies; hagiographies
Ḥunayn b. Isḥāq al-ʿIbādī, S18

Ibāḍīs, S41
Ibn ʿAbd al-Ḥakam, ʿAbd Allāh, S12
Ibn Abī Shayba, S7, S49
Ibn al-ʿAṭṭār, S25
Ibn al-Dāya, S19
Ibn al-Hayyabān, S3
Ibn al-Jawzī, Sibṭ, S29
Ibn al-Kalbī, S6
Ibn al-Qāsim, S30, S49
Ibn al-Sarrāj, I3, S43
Ibn Baṭṭūṭa, GI
Ibn Faḍlān, Aḥmad, S24
Ibn Ḥanbal, Aḥmad, S8, S49
Ibn Hishām, S2, S3
Ibn Isḥāq, S2, S3
Ibn Muqbil, Tamīm b. Ubayy, S6
Ibn Mūṣilāyā, S29
Ibn Qayyim al-Jawziyya, I3, S49
Ibn Rajab, S34
Ibn Rushd al-Jadd, S30
Ibn Saʿd, S4, S5, S6
Ibn Sallām al-Jumaḥī, S6
Ibn Shubruma, S49
Ibn Ṭawq, Shihāb al-Dīn Aḥmad, S54
Ibn Taymiyya, I3, S43, S45, S49
Ibn Ṭūlūn, Aḥmad, S19
Ibn Ṭūlūn, Shams al-Dīn Muḥammad, S54
Ibn Wahb, S30
Ibrāhīm al-Mawṣilī, S15
Ilkhanids, S44
incentives to convert
  material, GI, I1, S5, S8, S12, S13, S15, S16, S18, S30, S31, S35, I3, S52, S54, S55
  romantic/familial, GI, S3, S4, S23, S35, S49
  political, GI, S15, S17, I2, S28, S29, S31, S46, S55
  See also coercion in conversion
India. *See* South Asia
inheritance, by/of converts, S20, S25, S29, S30, S37, S38
Iṣfahānī, Abū al-Faraj al-, S23
Isḥāq b. Nuṣayr al-ʿIbādī, S21
Islam
  conversion to/from. *See under other religions*
  definition of, GI, S1, S6, S8, S30

Jacob of Edessa, S10
jāhilī ancestors, S5, S6
Jerusalem, Latin Kingdom of, S39
Jesus, nature of, S12, S13, S22, S25, S33
Jibraʾīl b. Bukhtīshūʿ, S15
jihad, I3, S19, S42, S43, S53
jinn, S1, S2
jizya, GI, I1, S1, S12, S13, S27, S30, S54
John of Ibelin, S39
Judaism, conversion to Islam from, GI, I1, S3, S7, S8, S12, S25, S33, S36, S37, S38, I3, S45, S54

Kaʿb b. Zuhayr b. Abī Sulmā al-Muzanī, S6
Kāzarūnī, Abū Isḥāq al-, S27
Khadīja bt. Khuwaylid, I1, S2
Khallāl, Abū Bakr al-, S8
kharāj, S12, S30
Khosrov of Gandzak, S35
Khuzāʿī b. ʿAbd Nuhm al-Muzanī, S6
Kodungallur, S42
kustīg, S20

language, religious significance of, S11, S20, I2, S26
Livre au Roi, Le, S39
Livre des Assises, Le, S39

Maghīlī, Muḥammad b. ʿAbd al-Karīm al-, I3, S53
Maḥmūd b. ʿUthmān, S27
Maimonides, Abraham, S37
Maimonides, Moses, I2, S33, S36, S38
Malabar Coast, S42
Malay, I3, S52
Malayalam, S42
Mālik b. Anas, S30, S49
Mālik b. Dīnār, S42
Maʾmūn, al-, I1, S15
Manṣūr, al-, I1
Maqdisī, ʿAbd al-Ghanī al-, S34
Maqdisī, Ḍiyāʾ al-Dīn al-, S34
Maqrīzī, Taqī al-Dīn Aḥmad, I3, S46

marriage
effect of conversion on, I1, S3, S7, S10, S17, S20, S25, S38, S39, I3, S49
interreligious, S7, S10, S32, S35, S37, S38
outside one's tribe, S3
without guardian, S20
martyrs, S9, S14, S17, S23, S28, S35, S36
masāʾil. *See* responsa
mass conversion. *See* conversion: group
mawālī. *See* clientage
Merah Gajah, S52
Merah Silau, S52
Michael of Damrū, S28
Michael the Syrian, S31
miracles, GI, S22, S27, S33, S40, I3, S42, S43, S51
Mongols, GI, I3, S44
monks, S9, S13, S23, S26, S30, S39, S50
Moses, S2, S13, S22, S25, S33
Muḥammad, the Prophet
conversion of relatives of, S2, S3, S4
mission of, GI, I1, S1, S2, S3, S6, S12, S42
role in later conversions of, GI, I3, S42, S51, S52
status of mother of, S5
Muqtadī, al-, S29
Muqtadir, al-, S24
Mutawakkil, al-, S16, S18, I2

names, as religious marker, GI, S5, S13, S15, S24, S25, S26, S42, S52, S55
Natronai Gaon, S37
Naw Bahār, S11
Nawrūz (Mongol commander), S44
Nīzak Ṭarkhān, S11
Niẓām al-Dīn Awliyā, I3, S48

Odo of Deuil, S39
Ottomans, GI, I3, S55

paganism
conversion to, from Christianity, S10
conversion to Islam from, S5, S6, S8, S31, S34, S41, S53
Pasai, Kingdom of, I3, S52
People of the Book (*ahl al-kitāb*), S12. See also *dhimmīs*
Persian, role in Islamization of, S11
poetry, conversion in, S6, S21, S47
polemics, S22, S33, S50
poll tax. See *jizya;* taxes
polytheism, S1
conversion to Islam from, S6, S8
Pope Alexander III, S39
prayer, as criterion of conversion, S12, S25, S30
Puteri Betung, S52

Qalamūn, monastery of, S26
Qāshānī, Abū al-Qāsim ʿAbd Allāh al-, S44
Qāsim b. Yaḥyā al-Maryamī, al-, S21
Qurʾān
conversion in, GI, I1, S1
in conversion, GI, S24, S34
Quraysh, tribe of, S2, S3, S4, S5, S6, S42
Qurayẓa, tribe of, I1, S3
Qutayba b. Muslim, S11

Rashīd al-Dīn Faḍl Allāh Abū al-Khayr, S44
repentance, S1, S10, S13, S16, S20, S30
responsa, S8, S10, S20, S30, S36, S37, S53
rivāyats, S20

Saʿadya Gaon, S37
Sabbath observance, as criterion, S36, S37
saints, S14, S28, S35, S40, S43, S51, S56
blessings of (Christian), S10, S17, S26
Samawʾal b. Yaḥyā al-Maghribī, S33
Samuel of Qalamūn, S26
Ṣanʿānī, ʿAbd al-Razzāq al-, S8
Sarı Saltuq, I3, S43
Sayyid Aḥmad Bashīrī, I3, S51
scripture, falsification of, S33, S50
Seljuqs, GI
shahāda, S8, S30, S33, S41, S42, S44, S50, S52, S53, S54, S56
Shakarwatī Farmāḍ. *See* Cheraman Perumal
Shammākhī, al-, S41
Sherira Gaon, S37
She Yunshan, I3, S57
Shiḥr, S42
Shujāʿī, Sanjar al-, S46
Sijzī, Amīr Ḥasan ʿAlā, I3, S48
slaves
conversion of, I1, S9, S19, I2, S34, S51. *See also* clientage
sex with, S7, S25
Sokoto Caliphate, S53
Songhay Empire, I3, S53
South Asia, Islam in, GI, S42, S48
Southeast Asia, Islam in, GI, I3, S52, S56
Sufis, GI, I2, S27, S40, I3, S42, S43, S45, S48, S51, S53
Sufyān b. ʿUyayna, S49
Sunan Kalijaga, S56

Ṭabarī, Muḥammad b. Jarīr al-, S12, S19
taxes
  impact of conversions on, I1, S12
  as incentive to convert, GI, I1, S12, S13, S30, S54
  See also *jizya*
ṭayyaye, S13, S31, S32
Telugu, S42
testimony, S25, S30, S36, S38, S39
Thaʿlaba b. Saʿya, S3
Torah, S22, S33, S36, S42
T'ovma Artsruni, S16
triumphalism, Muslim, GI, I1
Ṭulayb b. ʿUmayr, S4
Turks, GI, I1, S19, I2, S31

ʿUmar b. ʿAbd al-ʿAzīz (ʿUmar II), I1, S7, S12
ʿUmar b. al-Khaṭṭāb, I1, S4, S49
Umayyads, GI, I1, S12
Umm Kulthūm bt. ʿUqba b. Abī Muʿyat, S4
ʿUtbī, Abū ʿAbd Allāh Muḥammad al-, S30
ʿUthmān b. Fūdī, I3, S53

violence. *See* coercion in conversion

Waraqa b. Nawfal, S2, S50
women
  as agents of conversion, GI, I1, S3, S4, S49, S57
  conversion of, S2, S4, S7, S8, S9, S10, S23, S25, S38, S49, S51, S54, S57

Yovsēp' of Duin, S35
Yūnīnī, ʿAbd Allāh al-, S40
Yūnīnī, Quṭb al-Dīn Mūsā al-, S45

Zacharias (patriarch), S28
Ẓahīr al-Dīn b. Zakī al-Dīn al-Madanī, S42
Zhao Can, S57
Zoroastrianism
  coexistence with Islam of, I1, S11, S20
  conversion to, S16
  conversion to Islam from, GI, I1, S11, S12, S15, S20, S27
zunnār, S13, S14, S28
Zuqnīn, Chronicle of, S13, I3

www.ingramcontent.com/pod-product-compliance
Lightning Source LLC
Chambersburg PA
CBHW031419230426
43668CB00007B/358
9780520296732